Transatlantic Vistas

Transatlantic Vistas
American Journalists in Europe, 1900–1940

Morrell Heald

THE KENT STATE UNIVERSITY PRESS
Kent, Ohio, and London, England

Library of Congress Catalog Card Number 87-35901
ISBN 0-87338-365-6
Manufactured in the United States of America

Library of Congress Cataloging-in-Publication Data
Heald, Morrell.
    Transatlantic Vistas: American journalists in Europe, 1900–1940 /
Morrell Heald.
      p. cm.
    Bibliography: p.
    Includes index.
    ISBN 0-87338-365-6 (alk. paper) ∞
    1. Foreign correspondents—United States—Biography.   2. Foreign
correspondents—Europe—Biography.   3. Journalism—United
States—History—20th century.   4. Journalism—Europe—History—20th
century.   I. Title.
    PN4871.H36 1988
    070.4′33′0922—dc19
    [B]   87-35901
                                                                              CIP

British Library Cataloging-in-Publication data are available.

For Leland Stowe
and the members of a gallant generation,
and for two members of a new generation,
Diana and Julia

Contents

Preface

■ The first third of the present century witnessed the development and testing of an elaborate system of international news gathering, reporting, and interpretation by American newspapers and press associations. Foreign correspondence at the turn of the century was quite different from today's highly technical, intricate, and responsive system, although the sources and beginnings of change were already in sight. Journalism as a whole, in fact, was changing rapidly in response to many of the economic and technical influences that were helping to recast the structure of American industry and society. The telegraph and the transatlantic cable had greatly expanded the range, subject matter, and audience for news; shortly, the telephone and the radio would further intensify the process. Costlier, more versatile printing equipment lowered production costs of newspapers and magazines, encouraging expansion and diversification while increasing capital outlays. Organization, systematization, consolidation, and the drive to increase advertising and sales were already the order of the day.[1] Although it lagged behind domestic news, international reporting also was responding to the forces of change.

As early as 1870 the *New York Tribune* had taken advantage of the newly laid transoceanic cable to organize an integrated European news service based in London under the direction of veteran reporter George W. Smalley. With greater difficulty, a number of leading American newspapers attempted to establish a cooperative international news system of regular correspondents supplemented by a larger number of occasional "stringers" in most of the major countries of the world. Shortly after 1900 this effort would result in the creation of the foreign news service of the Associated Press.

The new system expanded and regularized the earlier, more haphazard, and decentralized international reporting provided by a few individual newspapers along lines pioneered before the Civil War by James Gordon Bennett's *New York Herald*. The scope and quality of such foreign correspondence had varied widely, depending on the interests of individual publishers and reporters. The latter had often been hired on the basis of literary reputation, personal connections, or other grounds not necessarily conducive to the production of useful, reliable, and widely interesting information to add to business and economic news usually gathered from other sources. The fact that most correspondents and many of their readers were members of a well-educated elite of intellectuals and professionals had limited the appeal of much overseas correspondence, while the political or social prejudices of editors and reporters in an age of highly personal journalism often strongly colored news content. Moreover, heavy dependence upon items clipped from the foreign press meant that American readers often received news originally prepared for others.[2]

By the turn of the century American editors were recognizing that the growth of a more diverse urban middle class called for news with broad appeal, while competitive pressures for increased readership placed a premium on speedy reporting and lively writing. Americans' higher levels of education and more frequent travel combined with the nation's growing involvement in international economic and political affairs to arouse interest in a wider range of foreign social and cultural subjects. Some such an assessment of needs and opportunities, at any rate, must have moved publishers and editors if we are to account for the considerable expansion of international coverage they undertook.

Another element essential to the expansion of international journalism at this time was the appearance of a group of young writers and would-be writers ready to launch themselves in new, unfamiliar but challenging directions—to venture overseas in pursuit of ideas and experiences they felt lacking at home. This group of alert young Americans, born for the most part in the closing decades of the nineteenth century or the early years of the twentieth, provides the central subject of this book. Sensitive, curious, and ambitious, they soon found ways of getting to Europe. Seizing virtually any opportunity for travel, they also discovered that they could pay expenses by supplying the foreign news which American papers now were seeking more actively than ever before.

The men and women who constituted the first two generations of professionally oriented foreign correspondents have not received the attention they merit both for the importance and the interest of their work. As reporters for major newspapers and press associations between 1900 and the Second World War, they felt compelled to convey their own deepening awareness of international events and trends to American readers. With their help, by the mid-1930s the basic structure and patterns of modern international news gathering had been established. The decades surrounding the Second World War—the 1930s, 1940s, and 1950s—have sometimes been termed the "Golden Age" of American foreign correspondence; but its foundations had been laid earlier. It was in the teens and twenties that the young and largely inexperienced corps of foreign correspondents considered here became caught up, in ways none had anticipated, in events that awakened them to a more ambitious conception of their role. At a time when America's new international status was far from fully understood, and with the structure of journalism itself presenting formidable obstacles to their efforts, they enlarged their view of the service they could provide to others—including leaders of government and business as well as the general public. With the State Department's Foreign Service still not fully professionalized and the academic study of international relations still in its infancy, these jounalists established a claim to consideration as among the nation's leading foreign affairs experts.

The history of American foreign correspondence in the twentieth century is too complex to be treated in a single volume. By the twenties at least three major press associations had developed and maintained sizable overseas staffs, while a number of smaller, specialized press services also employed correspondents abroad. A dozen or more major metropolitan papers created and maintained, with greater or less success, their own overseas offices and staffs. Special interest journals—business, labor, and others—supplied international news to their own constituencies, while various general interest publications offered their readers periodic reports and interpretations of international events sometimes supplied by free-lance reporters on roving assignments and sometimes by regular foreign correspondents of other publications supplementing their salaries or seeking wider audiences. Several hundred American journalists served either as regular or occasional correspondents for one or more of these publishers in the first four decades of the century.

To consider in one study the full range and variety of institutional arrangements and personal experiences included in such a mushroom growth is impossible; yet, just as clearly, the emergence, performance, significance, and success of the new overseas journalism calls for recognition and evaluation. Few histories of individual newspapers or press associations have given detailed consideration to their foreign correspondence.[3] My approach to this tangled but vital subject has been through the writings and reminiscences of a small group of reporters widely recognized as among the ablest and most respected that foreign correspondence has produced then or since. I have limited myself to reporters in western Europe, and have excluded Russia and most of the non-European world since at that time Europe still provided the bulk of foreign news for American readers.

The invasion of Europe by this corps of American journalists occurred, roughly speaking, in two waves. The first reached their overseas assignments between 1900 and 1920. They devoted themselves to extending and strengthening the reporting systems already in place. As Europe slid toward war, some began to envision a new kind of interpretive reporting which reflected their growing awareness that Europe's problems posed issues for America as well. The challenges of wartime reporting put their work to the test, demonstrating their effectiveness while posing new obstacles to their purpose. When peace returned, they were the tested veterans of America's overseas news service. Among the leaders of this group were three influential correspondents of the *Chicago Daily News*, Edward Price Bell, Paul Scott Mowrer, and Raymond Swing.

The second wave of correspondents came as part of the broader postwar exodus of young American writers, artists, and intellectuals to Europe. They included Dorothy Thompson, John Gunther, Vincent Sheean, William L. Shirer, Leland Stowe, H. R. Knickerbocker, Negley Farson, Herbert L. Matthews, Edgar Ansel Mowrer, and Louis Lochner, many of whose names became well known in the 1930s. With the veteran correspondents as guides and models, their own energy and ambitions for motive power, and the tumultuous stage of postwar Europe for their subject, they combined the elements that would bring American foreign correspondence to the top of its form.

Of course, listings of names and classifications of generations must be to some extent an oversimplification. Some of the correspondents of the twenties had actually experienced Europe earlier but in other capacities. And the leading names can never fully represent the diversity of a still larger community of American reporters. Those others whom I shall consider less fully, among them George Seldes, Carroll Binder, David Darrah, Floyd Gibbons, Albion Ross, Sigrid Schultz, Clarence Streit, and John T. Whitaker, indicate even more clearly the variety of talents and accomplishments of this extraordinary group. They joined the leaders as among the most active and outspoken American journalists in Europe at the time.

Yet the institutional framework within which the foreign correspondents operated also shaped their behavior in important ways. To explore the implications and limitations inherent in this crucial relationship I have examined in some depth transactions between the overseas staff and the editorial and business offices of one newspaper, the *Chicago Daily News*. Scattered evidence from other papers indicates both parallels and divergences from the *Daily News*'s patterns. For most of the years in question, that paper's foreign service was highly respected and served as a model for others, so that its experience illuminates common issues and problems.

Further study of the operations of other papers and the lives of other reporters no doubt will expand our understanding of the subject. But the cross section examined here shows clearly that foreign correspondence had matured and that its practitioners had evolved more effective techniques of interpreting world events and America's relationship to them during the very years when the nation's need for such resources was irrevocably growing.

These journalists found themselves at the vanguard of those who were beginning to recognize that closer ties between the United States and the rest of the world were an inevitable consequence of broad social, economic, and technological developments. Many Americans still, of course, rejected or resisted the implications of such changes. But a growing number understood that the dream of American separateness or isolation—which, in fact, had never accurately described the nation's posture—was becoming increasingly irrelevant and even dangerous. Although the present work claims no extraordinary wisdom or foresight for the correspondents, it still demonstrates that their circumstances enabled them to serve as antennae, as interpreters and expositors of a more realistic assessment of what America's international status and role actually had become. It took, of course, a second world war before anything like full recognition of the new realities became widespread. Even before that cataclysm occurred, however, the correspondents had helped to create an elaborate and sensitive system of international communications upon which, whatever its imperfections, the nation would depend heavily.

Acknowledgments

■ It is a pleasant duty to acknowledge the assistance of the many people without whose help the preparation of this book would have been more difficult, less pleasant, or less successful. Librarians and archivists, as always, head the list of those whose skills and sympathetic assistance have been invaluable. The reference staff of the Case Western Reserve University libraries, especially Elmer Newman and Elsie Finley, were thoughtful, imaginative collaborators. Diane Haskell and her assistants at the Newberry Library were extraordinarily efficient and considerate. The staff members of the Wisconsin State Historical Society Archives Division also deserve special thanks.

Most of all, the former correspondents and members of their families who generously shared their time, memories, ideas, and papers with me gave my work a perspective and an immediacy it could not otherwise have achieved. I am grateful to Mrs. John Gunther, the late Sigrid Schultz, William L. Shirer, the late Clarence Streit, and Sally Swing Shelley. Leland Stowe and his charming wife, Dollika, became warm friends in the course of this project. Without their unfaltering help, enthusiasm, and occasional prodding, its completion would more than once have been in doubt. I intend the book's dedication as a small symbol of unlimited appreciation.

Students and colleagues with whom I have discussed the work over the years have offered support and encouragement. Several generations of students in my course, The American International Experience, have served as sounding boards and helped me clarify my ideas about foreign correspondence. Bob Petrulis contributed a special bit of research. My colleague, Barry Levy, read an early version of the first chapter and encouraged me to consider the shaping influence of family experience on the correspondents' outlook.

Patricia Dussaux undertook much of the early typing, when my writing and thinking were even less clear than they later became, with great skill and understanding. Betty Suber was an instant source of encouragement and help at every turn. Members of the editorial staff of the Kent State University Press have rescued me from errors of omission and commission too numerous to brood upon.

For the sake of younger scholars, it may be worth noting that this work at no time had the benefit of foundation or other research funding, except for the continuing support provided by Case Western Reserve, notably through the Armington Research Professorship in 1984–85. For better or worse, I had to "do it my way" and in the end I do not regret the experience although there were discouraging moments along the way. Of course, the responsibility for all shortcomings, as well as credit for whatever value this study may have, would ultimately have been mine in any event.

Finally, my wife, Barbara, and the other members of my family have played an essential role. Despite occasional bemusement at the amount of time the work absorbed and at its failure to justify lengthy research trips to Europe, they provided steady support and kept my concerns in proper perspective with the variety of their own undertakings.

1

Beginnings

■ Americans in the 1890s were much preoccupied with a number of seemingly intractable domestic problems. The Panic of 1893, coming after nearly twenty years of unparalleled economic expansion and instability, posed troubling questions concerning the nation's ability to convert its newfound industrial capacity into healthier, happier living conditions for its people. At times, newspaper headlines seemed to be dominated almost entirely by bad news. Falling prices, closing factories, unemployment, strikes, rural unrest and protest, and the consolidation of many family-sized and middle-range businesses into ever-larger, more impersonal combinations occasioned deep concerns for the future. In the cities, poverty, deteriorating housing, inadequate municipal services, political corruption, and the presence of a large, ill-assimilated immigrant population offered added causes for alarm. On the political scene, a new, vaguely socialistic Populist movement threatened to unseat the dominant, if ineffectual, major political parties. Meanwhile, in Washington such perennial issues as the tariff, railroad rates, the currency, and the trusts were debated endlessly and inconclusively. Faced with such discouragements at home, some Americans had begun to look overseas for new opportunities and challenges, economic, religious, or political.

Whether because of the prospect of new markets for the nation's economic surpluses, the millions of Chinese and other "heathen" souls awaiting conversion to Christianity, the backward races needing to be awakened to the virtues of Anglo-Saxon democracy, or the cultural riches of Europe available to be absorbed or garnered to enhance the lives of

America's newly wealthy middle classes, the nation was reaching outside itself as never before in its history. The brief and at least superficially glorious little war with Spain that marked the century's closing years thus seemed both to proclaim and to popularize an expansion of America's horizons that was, in fact, already well under way. Shortly, however, the hero of San Juan Hill, Theodore Roosevelt, would be leading equally dramatic charges against trusts from the vantage point of the White House, and the Progressives' struggle to reorder America's political and economic landscape would, to some extent, refocus public attention on developments at home. Nonetheless, the nation had become too deeply involved, in too many ways, with the outside world to be able any longer to ignore it more than intermittently.

Conveniently for those persons greatly interested in overseas affairs for whatever reasons, new technologies of travel and communications—notably the railroad, the steamship, and the transoceanic cable—had greatly reduced the costs of travel and information exchange. As early as 1869, Mark Twain's *Innocents Abroad* had publicized and ridiculed the first organized package tour. In 1870 some twenty-two thousand Americans had left the country; ten years later the number had doubled, and by 1900 the annual exodus had multiplied tenfold. The growth of American communities in foreign capitals and commercial centers was marked by the formation of American chambers of commerce and of a variety of American social and religious agencies there. Expatriation, no longer the prerogative of artists and intellectuals alone, also was becoming fashionably middle class. Americans residing overseas numbered approximately ninety-one thousand in 1900. Europeans already bewailed the "American invasion," while the aping of European manners and the search for European spouses for the daughters of status-seeking Americans had attracted the wry and pointed attention of observers as diverse as Henry James and Thorstein Veblen. In the greatest exodus of all, the American expeditionary force of 1917–18 would carry overseas hundreds of thousands of Americans, many of whom would not have travelled there under any other circumstances.[1] Yet until the war, America's interest in European politics remained limited and intermittent.

Journalistic responses to broadening American international involvement ranged from such individual adaptations as the career of the first "matinee idol" foreign correspondent, Richard Harding Davis, to the systematic formation of worldwide networks by the Associated Press,

United Press International, and similar agencies. The career of Davis, a dashing figure whose travel and war reporting captured the public imagination in the 1890s, was one measure of changing tastes. His reports from far-off regions and crisis points were filed in breathtaking, colorful prose, and he was frequently interviewed at dockside on his return to the United States where he sparkled in the café society of the day. A popular novelist as well as a world traveller, Davis offered a model for young men of the succeeding generation who sought new outlets for their urge to write and travel. Whatever his limitations as a reporter, Davis sold copy; this was a language not lost on the most conservative and inflexible publishers.[2]

The new American press associations provided international reporting networks for many newspapers serving major urban centers which found materials provided by European news services unsatisfactory in style and point of view for American readers. In 1901 Melville E. Stone, president of the Associated Press, began a series of transcontinental negotiations with European governments for access to official sources and publicly controlled telegraph facilities. In 1910 the United Press, reorganized by E. W. Scripps in 1907, began the development of a second foreign service; and in 1911 the establishment by William Randolph Hearst of the International News Service (INS) rounded out the triumvirate of American news agencies overseas. In addition to supplying relatively regular and reliable news, these agencies cut costs for subscribing papers by providing common personnel and facilities.[3]

The work of these agencies was supplemented by that of several publishers who created their own foreign services, hoping to market them to others as well. Notable among these was Victor Lawson of the *Chicago Daily News* and *Record* who had been a leader in reorganizing the Associated Press. Of Scandinavian background, Lawson sensed a growing readership for international news tailored to an American audience. In 1899 he began to build what would be by the 1920s the ablest corps of European correspondents then available to any American newspaper. Edward Price Bell, already one of his crack domestic reporters, was sent to London to oversee the establishment of Lawson's international service. As the center of world cable facilities, London was the logical starting place for Lawson and Bell as it had been for Smalley and the *New York Tribune* thirty years before. Lawson expected wealthy Chicagoans to appreciate reports of their own and their friends' foreign travels and to repay such recognition in their capacity as advertisers and subscribers. Overseas news might be informative and colorful, but Lawson clearly wanted it to be profitable as well.[4]

Lawson was not alone in sensing a market for expanded international news coverage. William Randolph Hearst and Joseph Pulitzer had discovered the news value of international crises, real or manufactured, at the time of the Spanish-American War. From his residence in Paris, James Gordon Bennett, Jr., owner of the *New York Herald*, continued that paper's tradition of foreign correspondence. In 1887 Bennett had initiated a European edition of the *Herald*, largely for the American community in Paris of which he was a leading member. Meanwhile, Adolph S. Ochs was beginning a reorganization of the *New York Times* that within a few years would transform it from a waning journal to one of the nation's leaders. Ochs initially focussed his attention on domestic news, but could not long avoid responding to New York's international interests by strengthening his overseas staff as well. Other newspaper editors and publishers followed these leaders, more slowly but in the same direction.[5]

Editors and publishers were not alone in appreciating the new opportunities offered by international reporting. Journalism was already attracting the sons (and a few daughters) of the expanding middle class with visions of interesting, exciting careers as writers. Rising levels of material well-being, education, and leisure, together with the rapid growth of commercial and industrial centers along the Atlantic coast and deep into the maturing Middle West, opened new doors for curious and ambitious young Americans. Larzer Ziff's study of the 1890s points to the outlet journalism provided for aspiring writers of the new generation, both as a haven from the constrictions of rural and small-town life and as a school in the realities and styles of urbanization.[6] A job with a city daily promised excitement and diversity, even if it did not always deliver them. It confirmed the young writer's sense that society was diverging swiftly from old patterns, and it offered a ringside seat where the forces, both sordid and stimulating, that were shaping modern life could be observed closely. It provided a recognized, if still not entirely respectable, trade, a salary—steady, if meager—and a regular opportunity to write. Thus, men such as Stephen Crane, Frank Norris, Theodore Dreiser, and Sherwood Anderson, along with many others, found in journalism an observation post and a training ground.

In large metropolitan centers, communities of wealth, leisure, and intellect were forming where the latest London or Paris trends in arts and letters, fashion, politics, or society were discussed. At a more popular level, immigration had massed and juxtaposed ethnic communities in the cities' midst, and their strange or colorful ways bespoke a diversity of customs and cultures that could scarcely help but pique the curiosity of young journalists. Smaller cities had their own literary clubs, artists' guilds, and often their immigrant minorities as well. Cub reporters assigned to cover almost any American city scarcely could avoid contact with a cultural mosaic unfamiliar to most earlier Americans. Urban journalism thus attracted and contributed to the cosmopolitanization of a generation of young American writers.

Nowhere were the forces undermining, reshaping, and expanding the nation's social and cultural horizons more dramatically apparent than in the Middle West. Here, the old and the new, the provincial and the cosmopolitan most starkly and dramatically confronted each other. In two generations the region had been transformed from America's frontier to its industrial core. From the vantage point of Chicago's 1893 Columbian Exposition, Frederick Jackson Turner nostalgically pondered the passing of the older ways; within the decade, the Pullman strike and the Chicago Renaissance demonstrated how rapidly and far those ways already had receded. The industrialization of the prairies rapidly created urban metropolises in Cleveland, Detroit, Chicago, and St. Louis, and transformed smaller cities as well. It eroded the self-sufficiency of rural and small-town life, opening avenues of escape and opportunity while intensifying the sense of isolation among those it left behind. In the longer-established immigrant communities, growing security and self-confidence relaxed some of the constraints of ethnic separatism. The tensions and contrasts of middle western life were reflected in the region's extraordinary creativity in political and economic affairs, as well as in the arts and letters. The presence of a large number of active and outspoken middle westerners among the new foreign correspondents, as well as among the literary and artistic expatriates and the growing overseas missionary communities, lent an international dimension to the region's development.[7]

What is unmistakably clear from the lives and recollections of the men and women, whether from the Midwest or elsewhere, who played leading roles in the new foreign correspondence is that their interests in international matters were stimulated by exposure to ideas and people that diverged from traditionally accepted or understood standards. At many levels, these children of the growing middle class faced images and experiences that stirred their discontent with the old patterns of American life and their readiness to strike out in search of alternatives.

The eagerness many displayed to leave the country seems particularly striking in the light of the many changes and opportunities characterizing American political, economic, and social life. The Progressive decade, the war years, and the twenties encompassed much of the transition of the United States to a mature industrial society. The early twentieth century was a time not only of protest, discontent, and intransigent conservatism, but also of constructive achievements in economics, government, the arts, and many other fields. It was, in short, an interesting time in which to live in the United States. The fact that so many lively, imaginative, and ambitious members of the rising generation sought careers elsewhere, not only as journalists but as artists, missionaries, businessmen, or in other capacities, raises interesting questions about their drives and perceptions.

Among the future foreign correspondents two motives in particular seem to have predominated. For those with primarily literary ambitions, Europe was an irresistible attraction, as it had been for others with like interests in the past. Not only was it the home and source of the tradition they aspired to join, but also it offered the opportunity to relax, experiment, and savor intellectual and esthetic experiences still little appreciated in business-minded America. This need to escape the censorious, Puritanical American scene was one they shared with the other journalists who accepted overseas assignments with less elevated purposes in view. Overseas assignments also offered an escape from the increasingly confined and routine operations of an urban newspaper. Freedom from close editorial supervision was hard to come by in the highly competitive, pressured, and bureaucratized organizations that were setting the pace of modern journalism. For young writers with such ambitions and interests, the future in the United States may well have seemed less intriguing than the risks and uncertainties of life in distant, colorful lands.

Early in the century, the first group of institutional foreign correspondents ventured uncertainly into territory still largely unexplored, with little sense of their new roles and opportunities. By the time of the second wave of correspondents, it was evident that overseas journalism combined an intriguing mix of literary work, adventure, and gainful employment. Both groups had been prepared for their new work by their early experiences at home, whether enlightening or confining. Their family lives and community and educational associations had awakened wider interests than could be satisfied at home.

GROWING UP

In the early lives of these restless and ambitious young Americans we can observe at close range the events and exposures that helped to permanently structure their careers. Their experiences also reveal some of the forces at work on both individual and institutional levels of American life exposing it more broadly than before to world developments.

Among the earliest and most influential of the new generation of newspapermen to find the locus of their careers in Europe was Edward Price Bell, born in 1869 at Raccoon Creek, Parke County, Indiana. The son of an energetic, enterprising farmer, Bell attended rural schools but was encouraged by his parents to expand his horizons. The "big round" world of which young Bell dreamed was made flesh in the brother of a schoolmate who returned home for a visit: "...world traveller, man of the sea, survivor of shipwrecks, and wanderer who had been on all continents and islands and in a thousand ports." The sailor's yarns added fuel to the boy's dreams and ambitions, while the sailor added a rose tattoo to the young Hoosier's arm. Although Bell's father steered his sons toward pharmacy or medicine, Edward, perhaps influenced by his reading of Dickens, was intrigued by the idea of a writing career.[8]

After working in a Terre Haute drugstore, Edward apprenticed with a local newspaper. Jobs with a succession of small Indiana journals enhanced his reporting skills without satisfying his literary ambitions. He tried writing poetry on the side, but in 1894 he entered Wabash College for the academic training his poverty had denied him until then. While at Wabash, Bell seized the opportunity to visit London with a friend going to observe activities at Toynbee Hall, the renowned social settlement. To help defray expenses, Bell, who had already taken occasional local assignments as a stringer for the *Chicago Daily News*, arranged to send the paper reports of his trip.

For Bell, England was a revelation. It "shook us to the depths right off the bat," he wrote; he felt the world and its problems "roaring" at him. He returned, already a "modest cosmopolite," to graduate from Wabash. Shortly thereafter, he found himself at the city desk of the *Chicago Daily News*; but when Victor Lawson singled him out to open the paper's London office and initiate its new European service, Bell was ready to go.[9] In many respects Bell's path from Indiana fields to Trafalgar Square and London drawing rooms prefigured the motives, experiences, pressures, and opportunities touching the lives of other young journalists and attracting some of the ablest and most ambitious to foreign correspondence.

Frederic Wile, soon to join Bell in London to assist with the *Daily News*'s coverage of the Boer War, was a fellow Indianan. Born in 1873 in LaPorte, Wile enjoyed somewhat wider opportunities than had been available to Bell. His family had participated in the 1848 exodus from Germany, among a group of immigrants noted for its intellectual qualities. Frederic's father was well educated, a banker, a leader in LaPorte's Jewish community, and active in Democratic party politics. The Wiles were in touch with most of the intellectual and cosmopolitan elements stirring in their small city. Recalling his childhood, Frederic later found it unremarkable that he should have drifted into journalism since "every second Hoosier child" seemed in those days to have been born "clutching an inkpot, a sheaf of copy paper or a publisher's directory." At fourteen, Wile was already producing a family newspaper; and he felt himself very much at home in a society that had produced such figures as Lew Wallace, Theodore Dreiser, George Ade, and Albert Beveridge—newsmen who were already in the public eye.[10]

Far more isolated was the childhood of Webb Miller, born on a farm near Dowagiac, Michigan in 1892. His tenant farmer father worked part-time in a sawmill to supplement a meager income. The elder Miller had visited Chicago just once and Webb had seen Lake Michigan, a scant twenty miles away, only one time before he left home; yet the Millers' intellectual horizons were somewhat less confined. Webb's father transmitted his love of literature to the family. Books were borrowed from friends, neighbors, and nearby libraries. Later, Webb recalled how reading about Nineveh, China, and other faraway places had made him yearn to travel. After a short stint as a country school teacher, Miller fled his barren farm world for Chicago in 1912.[11]

Two future correspondents, Paul Scott Mowrer and his younger brother, Edgar Ansel Mowrer, spent their early years in Bloomington, Illinois. Their father was a travelling salesman, but this kind of travel entailed few "broadening" influences and Paul remembered the elder Mowrer as looking with contempt on all foreigners. Yet two uncles scandalized the family and flouted its religious biases by marrying Irish Catholic girls from Chicago. Paul himself was introduced to foreign ways by a succession of German or Scandinavian servants. One Swedish girl, to whom he felt particularly close, took him to visit her family; her homesickness for her native land impressed the boy. In 1893 the Columbian Exposition drew the Mowrers, like many other families, to Chicago. By then Paul was already reading and dreaming of travel and adventure. One can only guess how many visits to the "Streets of Cairo" or other exotic sights at the World's Fair were inspired, as Paul's were, by a hunger for the variety, color, and excitement these showplaces offered. For the Mowrers, the visit was soon coincidentally followed by permanent removal from Bloomington to Chicago. Paul's literary talents and intellectual enthusiasm blossomed at the Hyde Park High School where he showed himself a dedicated "amateur musician, actor, author, journalist," editor of the school's monthly journal, and active in athletics, dramatics, the English and Science clubs, the Mandolin Club, and the Double Quartet.[12]

Meanwhile Raymond Swing, born in Cortland, New York in 1887, was growing up in Oberlin, Ohio, where his father was a member of the college faculty. The Swings, like the Wiles, were of German descent. Both parents were Oberlin graduates and the father had studied theology at Yale. The family had spent three years in Germany and young Raymond had returned to the United States speaking only German. The Swings' home was a center of culture, deadened perhaps for Raymond by his father's stern, Puritanical outlook. His mother, a brilliant woman in her own right, was the sister of psychologist George Herbert Mead. Raymond often visited the Meads at the University of Chicago; at thirteen he spent a winter there, attending John Dewey's experimental university school. Perhaps by comparison with Chicago, he found Oberlin College repressive and dull, despite its liberal reputation. He had already formed a love of learning and a passion for life that drove him to defy college discipline and to seek an outlet for his energies in journalism.[13]

If the youthful correspondents who reached Europe before the First World War found their share of opportunities for intellectual and cross-cultural stimulation, the group whose overseas service coincided with or followed the war years found no less. Their backgrounds, too, reveal a mixture of parochial and cosmopolitan elements, although as Malcolm Cowley and others have argued the paths of this postwar generation to Europe seem in some ways to have been easier and more direct.[14]

Edgar Ansel Mowrer's childhood resembled that of his brother Paul, whom he remembered as a dominant influence. With their father often away on business and their mother chronically ill, Edgar, too, read and dreamed of "travel and high adventure." At eight he requested an atlas for Christmas and wore out its pages with repeated use. Paul's growing interest in literature may also have inspired him. Encouraged by a high school French teacher, Edgar's translation of a French poem won faculty plaudits. Such recognition, added to his experience on the school's yearbook staff, led him to consider a literary career.[15]

Louis Lochner, born in Springfield, Illinois in 1886, came from still another German-American family; his father, a Lutheran clergyman, had emigrated to the United States. The Lochners moved to Milwaukee when Louis was eight. Loving music, art, and literature, they revelled in the city's cultural life. Louis's stepmother, a church organist and choir director, conducted German and Norwegian singing groups. After graduating from the Wisconsin Conservatory of Music, Louis was sent on a European tour to visit relatives before going on to college. Few future foreign correspondents were so well equipped for their careers by family background and experience. The Lochners exemplified the deep infusion of cultural diversity and intellectual stimulation immigrants could bring to the life of many American communities.[16]

A desire to escape the safe, dull confines of small-town life is evident in the experience of William Stoneman, the son of a Congregationalist minister in St. Joseph, Michigan. Stoneman thought of his parents, both graduates of the University of Michigan, as "intellectuals," but their resources were limited and their pretensions few. Such religious or ethnic diversity as St. Joseph afforded produced "blotches of bigotry" more often than openmindedness, Stoneman later recalled; the town's Anglo-Saxon Protestant elite looked down on its German, Catholic, and Jewish neighbors. Stoneman made no claim of intellectuality or superiority for himself, but he nonetheless longed to escape. He began his career in journalism as a newsboy with visions of life in the big city, Chicago or beyond. Although he considered becoming "an engineer, a medical missionary or just anything that paid well enough to live on," he drifted into journalism and foreign correspondence in part because they required no special training or discipline. Their "only natural qualification," he wrote, "was a gregarious nature, plus a lust for travel and adventure which any normal kid might have."[17]

Like Stoneman, Albion Ross, later Berlin correspondent for the *New York Post* and the *New York Times*, was a product of small-town life and its discontents. His boyhood was spent in Marion, Cincinnati, Gallipolis, and other Ohio towns in which his father served as an Episcopal clergyman. Ross recalled Marion as a pleasant, comfortable community and his "last real home" before his family's moves began; but it was hardly the best preparation for the dynamic, confusing world into which his chosen profession projected him. His ambivalence toward both his origins and his destiny was underscored in his recollections of being always "haunted by the wailing cry of a night express, a summons of the faraway, a sense of exile from he knew not what."[18]

In Chicago, meanwhile, young John Gunther—destined to become the most widely recognized of any of the future correspondents—was reading and absorbing whatever information came to hand. His father was a businessman of uncertain means; his mother, a public school teacher who loved literature, history, and travel, provided the intellectual stimulus upon which Gunther drew. At age seven he had memorized long passages of *The Iliad* in translation; at ten he compiled a two-hundred-page encyclopedia organized around the topics that appealed to his obviously catholic interests: Greek and Roman historical characters, animals, world statistics, events in American history, and battleships. The energy and enthusiasm that would characterize Gunther's later career were already manifest. "I was interested in the world around me, in who ran it and how," he later recalled; "but the main thing I wanted to do was write literature, stories, novels. And I was hungry for travel."[19]

Another native Chicagoan, early transported to Cedar Rapids, Iowa, found that small city, the home of Coe College, a provocative combination of conformity and diversity. William L. Shirer was intrigued by the immigrant groups whose customs and beliefs enlivened the community. The Bohemians in particular were "so different from the rest of us... proud to remain apart, devoted to the Slavic way of life, which we thought strange and certainly inferior to ours, but which seemed best to them." Their love of beer flouted the dominant morality, but their thriftiness and hard work commanded respect and their dedication to music enriched the town. In addition, the nearby Amana experiment in religious and economic communalism—with its charming gabled houses, winding streets, and a system of production that turned out wares capable of competing with the best that capitalistic America produced—challenged orthodox assumptions.[20]

Outside St. Louis, Missouri, Edmond Taylor grew up in a family of "staunch Wilsonian internationalists." The Taylors were Catholics with ties to the French community that had earlier dominated the region. The family had seen better times, and they lived surrounded by mementos of a more glamorous, colorful past. Edmond's grandfather had fought with the Confederate army and had fled to Mexico for a time at the end of the Civil War. His grandmother, with a keen interest in public affairs, stimulated the child's imagination with myths, legends, the lore of Arthurian Britain, and similar fare. Edmond's reading reenforced these interests; he was appalled to learn that the frontier was closed and feared that America offered no more new worlds to conquer.[21]

However pervasive and powerful the influences noted here, it was only when they pervaded the conscious—and even the unconscious—minds of individuals that the foundation of a cosmopolitan outlook could begin to take shape. What was remarkable about turn-of-the-century America in this respect was that such broadening exposures, long the preserve of few but members of a privileged elite, had begun to spread to a wider constituency. Access to education, books, communications, and travel was opening new doors for members of the middle and lower middle classes. The democratization of the nation's social and intellectual life created new possibilities, practical as well as imaginative. For the sons and daughters of America's new majority, ideas of adventure and of the "far away" were not to be related merely to the world of dreams and of the "long ago," but pointed to real options and opportunities which they were eager to explore.

Like the midwesterners, Dorothy Thompson, an upstate New York clergyman's daughter, found in books and dreams of adventure the refuge from dreary surroundings in the small towns in which her clergyman father's family lived. In Connecticut, Leland Stowe's father encouraged him toward a career in the ministry but the boy's ambitions already pointed him toward a literary career and a world beyond the small-town life he knew. Negley Farson's family, wealthier and more self-consciously aristocratic than most, encouraged him to relish the cosmopolitan culture of New York City and the Atlantic seaboard. And in Alliance, New Jersey, George Seldes was reared in a utopian community founded by his father and heavily populated by refugees from the crime and corruption of urban life. The elder Seldes, an idealist and libertarian, had worked on behalf of Henry George in the 1886 New York mayoralty campaign; he corresponded with Tolstoy and Kropotkin and entertained Maxim Gorki in his Philadelphia drugstore on the latter's visit to the United States in 1906. Ideas, nonconformity, and a need to confront the world in its complexity and inequity were valued highly in the Seldes family circle.[22]

12

Thus in home, family, or community, in reading and in "real life," young Americans were finding that poverty, geographical isolation, or lack of formal education were no longer barriers to the stimulation that rapid change and new ideas were providing. Equally important, by the end of the nineteenth century access to a college education was becoming a reality for larger numbers than ever before. This meant that tastes and interests arising from accidental or casual associations could now be cultivated and pursued more seriously and fully than had been possible for more than a handful of the previous generation. College confirmed and extended the motives and influences that were pointing many young Americans toward journalism and internationalism.

COLLEGE LIFE

The interests and opportunities for personal growth offered on many campuses were strikingly exemplified in the college career of Louis Lochner. He had entered the University of Wisconsin in 1905 with one purpose already in mind, to win a Rhodes Scholarship. The idea had been planted by a Milwaukee friend, the first Wisconsin Rhodes Scholar, whose three years of study and travel abroad sparked Lochner's imagination. Joining the International Club, Louis studied industriously and even took coaching in extracurricular activities to prepare for the Rhodes competition. Although he failed to achieve his immediate goal, its pursuit inspired Lochner to grasp every opportunity for exposure to international affairs and culture. He found campus life, as he later recalled, "liberal and cosmopolitan," from his classics and political science professors to a course on journalism (one of the first offered at Wisconsin) and to the debating society where he first met and collaborated with a Negro law student.

But it was the International Club, of which he later became an officer, that engaged Lochner's energies most completely. The club brought together students from many lands for ethnic dances, international art programs, and similar social occasions. It welcomed and assisted new foreign students. Under its auspices, Lochner travelled to other colleges and universities for meetings with similar groups. There he encountered American and foreign students with similar interests. Such activities shaped what Lochner was later to call "the international mind" among college students. "We sought and found," he wrote, "men of good will everywhere, irrespective of race, color, and religion." Meanwhile, Louis was also developing his writing skills with a summer job on the *Milwaukee*

Free Press and, during his senior year, as managing editor of a newly formed student journal of opinion.[23]

Upon graduation, Lochner was selected editor of the *Wisconsin Alumnus*, which enabled him to remain active in campus life. In an article on "Internationalism Among Universities," he emphasized the role of campus groups in organizing support for such activities as an intercollegiate peace association, an international student federation, faculty-student international exchanges, and fellowships. He also pointed to the international character of scholarship, noting a wide range of course offerings on such topics as colonialism and imperialism, Asia, Africa, diplomatic history, and international law. He felt that these helped "to make our student body ripe, as it undoubtedly is, for the doctrine that international disputes must and can be settled by pacific rather than violent means."[24]

Lochner's campus involvement with international cultural and literary affairs was not an isolated example. Neither Paul nor Edgar Mowrer found the University of Michigan as stimulating as Lochner had found Wisconsin, but each took ample advantage of opportunities that further developed his literary inclinations and international interests. Reaching Ann Arbor after an interlude as apprentice reporter for the *Chicago Daily News*, Paul went to work for the campus newspaper and eventually became its managing editor. The money earned in that capacity he invested in a postgraduation bicycle trip through Great Britain and France, where he visited the sites to which his reading had already introduced him, and confirmed his commitment to a literary career. Only his inability to support himself as a writer and poet in Chicago drew him back at last to the *Daily News*.[25]

Edgar Mowrer, less patient than his brother, found most of his Ann Arbor classes boring, with the exception of biblical studies. He switched to the University of Chicago but was even less satisfied. On a trip in 1911 to Paris, where Paul then represented the *Daily News*, Edgar enrolled at the Sorbonne. Here was education more to his liking; it encouraged him to return to Michigan to complete his studies in literature and philosophy. Once again Mowrer, never easy to please, found most of the faculty dull, with a few "superb" exceptions. Yet he joined a faculty-student club, made friends among the foreign students, and undertook the "most exciting adventure of [his]...university life," the publication of a journal. *The Painted Window* was the vehicle for a self-conscious set of campus intellectuals and esthetes anxious to distinguish themselves as far as possible from the masses. A prize for poetry won Mowrer the funds which, along with his father's help, enabled him to return to Europe upon graduation.[26]

College experiences proved influential in shaping the writing abilities and intellectual curiosity of many future foreign correspondents. Edward Price Bell, after the Indiana fields and composing rooms, found college at Wabash an eye-opening experience. He discovered the Greek, Latin, and English classics, while his trip to England carried the exposure beyond the classroom and library. After London, Wabash proved a distinct disappointment, yet college had clearly helped to prepare him for the opportunities ahead. A generation later, John Gunther found the University of Chicago a challenge even to his extraordinary energy. He threw himself into campus literary life with zest. When a faculty committee rejected a prize essay on James Branch Cabell, Gunther managed to have it published in *Bookman*, a Chicago journal. The fifty-one-dollar publication fee, exceeding by just one dollar the prize he had missed, made him something of a campus hero. As literary editor of the university *Maroon* Gunther solicited publishers for review copies of books, thus building his personal library while exercising his critical talents. Since the *Maroon* circulated in the city as well as on campus, Gunther's reviews introduced him to Chicago literary circles which included older journalists and writers, Carl Sandburg among them. At about the same time, John T. Whitaker was encountering the works of Pushkin and Marx as a major in labor economics at Sewanee University in Tennessee. College gave Whitaker, as he later recalled, "an itch to know the truth of things" and kept him from becoming "a bond salesman—no small thing to get from college in the days of predepression wealth and synthetic values."[27]

Campuses that were intellectual meccas to some proved wastelands to others. Vincent Sheean, a classmate of Gunther's, found the Chicago campus "partly inhabited by a couple of thousand young nincompoops," whom he promptly joined. Their ambition was to get into "the right fraternity or club, to go to the right parties, and get elected to something or other." Sheean later acknowledged his own fault in neglecting the resources at his disposal, yet, even inadvertently, he found campus life broadening. For example, he naively pledged to a largely Jewish fraternity and was threatened with social ostracism on that account. Born to an Irish-American family in the small town of Plano, Illinois, Sheean had read about Jews but claimed never to have met one before reaching Chicago. Fortunately, he had received solid instruction in foreign languages from a German Lutheran teacher and an Irish priest in Plano. At the university, his linguistic facility placed him in advanced literary courses despite his professed effort to concentrate on easy ones. Literature led him, in turn, to philosophy and history for an understanding of social and intellectual backgrounds. Meanwhile, as he cavorted with the crass undergraduate majority Sheean began to respect the "bookworms" and the earnest summer school students who flocked to Chicago from many small midwestern colleges. His initial scorn for their drab appearance and social backwardness was shamed by recognition of their serious approach to learning. Sheean's description of the vying temptations to snobbery and superficiality, on the one hand, and to lively and cosmopolitan intellectuality, on the other, remains a classic picture of Midwest university life and of the influences on the maturing minds of lively students such as he.[28]

As the experiences of Bell, Lochner, the Mowrers, and Gunther show, college provided opportunities to write as well as to study; and many future journalists learned or polished their skills on campus publications. Frederic Wile had been a campus reporter for the Notre Dame *Scholastic* before moving to Chicago in the early 1890s. William Stoneman became a reporter and sports editor for the University of Michigan paper. Stoneman relished the seeming sophistication of 1920s campus life, with its fraternities, drinking parties, and associations with veterans recently returned from the European front. He studied French and Spanish and took some journalism courses, without taking them very seriously. Upon graduation in 1925, Stoneman followed the trail of other Michigan alumni to Chicago and to the *Daily News*.[29]

By the twenties, journalism courses and schools were growing in reputation and number, a response to the influences already steering young people toward the field. The University of Missouri, which had founded the first independent school of journalism in 1908, had developed particularly strong ties with American interests and newspapers in the Far East. Among its alumni was Edgar Snow, a correspondent noted for his efforts to explain developments in China to an unprepared American public before and during the Second World War. Columbia University, home of the nation's second journalism school, was the destination of Albion Ross, who worked as a dishwasher and movie doorman while taking a graduate journalism course there. Ross's journalistic education had a practical dimension as well. He shared a rooming house with a number of New York newspapermen, which seems to have dampened his initial enthusiasm for the profession.[30]

Clarence Streit, like Snow a Missourian by birth, had moved with his family to Montana where he majored in journalism at the state university, worked as a reporter on the campus paper, and eventually won a Rhodes Scholarship to Oxford. Streit's journalistic bent had manifested itself in high school, where he founded and edited the school paper. An encounter with Victor Hugo's *Les Miserables*, from which he read for an elocution class, aroused his desire to read the original French. At Montana State, he pursued his cultural interests by enrolling in French courses and by studying biology with a British faculty member. Meanwhile, working with immigrant laborers—Greeks, Italians, and Scandinavians—on summer railroad crews in the western states and Alaska exposed him to a variety of class and ethnic backgrounds. Although he actively opposed American involvement in World War I at first, Streit volunteered for overseas service when war was declared and reached France in August 1917.[31]

William L. Shirer, at Coe College after the war, had been sensitive to reverberations from the outside world. Before matriculating, he had followed intently the war news through the Chicago newspapers and press association reports. By this time the *Daily News*'s foreign service, in particular, was respected highly and syndicated widely in the Midwest. The *News* promoted it by sending such star reporters as Edward Price Bell on the lecture circuit to towns and campuses throughout its hinterland.[32]

Coe provided a natural focus for the cultural and intellectual life of Cedar Rapids. Symphony orchestras from New York and Minneapolis visited the campus, as did the Oxford University debating team and such famous performers as the soprano, Amelita Galli-Curci, and Sarah Bernhardt, whose advanced years and wooden leg failed to dampen Shirer's enthusiasm for her stirring delivery of the French language. The Shirer family shared and encouraged William's interests. As early as 1893 his father had won an oratory prize at Iowa College (later, Grinnell) for a speech titled "The World Citizen" which argued for world peace and world government in the light of growing international interdependence. By the time he entered Coe, Shirer had already settled on a career in journalism; he worked both for the *Cedar Rapids Republican* and the campus paper. As editor of the latter, he was criticized for too much attention to national and international, rather than college, news. Meanwhile, reading Dreiser, Twain, Howells, Mencken, and Sinclair Lewis sharpened Shirer's discontent with the provincialism and homogeneities of small-town life.[33]

When Shirer graduated in 1925, he borrowed one hundred dollars from the college president and worked his way across the Atlantic on a cattle boat. Ostensibly, his plan was to return home in two months and find a newspaper job. But he had already read an anthology of World War I correspondence and seemed sufficiently interested in remaining in Europe to be warned of its moral pitfalls by family members. Indeed, by this time—more than a quarter of a century after Edward Price Bell's assignment to London—the pathways to journalism and to overseas reporting opportunities were virtually wide open. The war had made more obvious than ever the fact of America's engagement with international affairs, although many Americans preferred to close their eyes to its implications. Now Shirer, Stowe, Thompson, Gunther, Sheean, and their peers became the second generation of American reporters to find a place in the newly regularized international news system.

Their college years had confirmed and strengthened in these fledgling journalists an awareness that a rich social and intellectual life lay beyond the limits of their immediate surroundings and associations, and that Europe held attractions for them that America seemed unable to offer. The local scene, rather than inviting, had already begun to appear confining and provincial. A beckoning wider world held out hope for richer, more varied experiences.

For these latecomers as well as for the early arrivals in Europe the purposes, limitations, challenges, and techniques of foreign correspondence would have to be learned by pursuing them on the job. Journalism courses or newspaper experience might help, but overseas work presented opportunities and problems different from those encountered at home. Family, community, and educational influences had readied them for new adventures and undertakings; apprenticeship as foreign correspondents would bring a still broader range of frustrations and fulfillments.

2

Apprenticeship

■ Despite their widening intellectual horizons at home, journalists who became foreign correspondents before 1914 did so more by accident than design. The duties and status of the position, still in the process of definition and elaboration, were too vague to attract them directly. The development of systematic foreign correspondence was chiefly the work of a few New York and Chicago publishers, intent on expanding and regularizing their overseas services, and of the new press associations. These together quickly established a steady flow of news reports from the major capitals and centers of population or trade. To supply the news, publishers continued to draw upon European sources even as they sought American reporters, with or without experience, who could produce the kind of stories that would appeal to their readership.

Victor Lawson's enthusiasm for expansion led him to hire an almost entirely American staff, including several quite inexperienced young writers. Yet even Lawson continued for a period to use materials purchased from foreign news services and casual correspondents. Adolph Ochs's *New York Times*, relying heavily on European news services and correspondents for its foreign coverage, probably hoped to obtain the best qualified and highly informed reporting. But this approach discouraged able young Americans from seeking overseas positions with the *Times*. Other editors and publishers pursued policies somewhere between those represented by Lawson and Ochs. Lawson's gamble on the young Americans, in fact, paid off handsomely. It attracted to the *Chicago Daily News* a disproportionate number of talented correspondents. By the 1920s the

News's foreign service had become a model for other papers, while Ochs's more cautious policy probably delayed the *Times*'s achievement of acknowledged leadership in the foreign news field by nearly a decade.[1]

A corps of inexperienced young reporters thus found themselves exploring and defining the nature of systematic foreign correspondence even as they inaugurated it. They might look to the careers of earlier journalists for models, but neither the adventurous Richard Harding Davis nor the more solid but elitist George W. Smalley had faced the demands and opportunities that would be theirs. The combination of early peacetime experiences with the pressures, constraints, and opportunities that the First World War was soon to supply set the framework within which the foreign news systems evolved their characteristic patterns. Meanwhile, trial and error, imagination and experiment, were inherent in the undertaking.

ON THE JOB TRAINING

At his new post in London, Edward Price Bell represented, as well as any single individual could, the changing character of overseas journalism. From an apprenticeship with the *Terre Haute Gazette* beginning in 1883, he had moved at age 15 to a position as a courthouse reporter with an Indianapolis paper. Soon Bell took an assignment covering a miners' strike in southern Indiana for the *St. Louis Globe Democrat* and managed as well to sell his stories to the *Chicago Daily News*. An encounter with Eugene V. Debs, then editing the *Locomotive Firemen's Magazine* in Terre Haute, aroused his interest in editing. A brief, family-financed stint as editor and one-man staff of his own paper, *The Raccoon Valley Independent*, was evidently discouraging, for soon Bell resumed the role of reporter, this time for the *Terre Haute Daily Times*. Restless, he again moved on quickly to the *Evansville Standard*, where an interview with Robert Ingersoll encouraged him to pursue his literary bent with a college education.

Upon graduation from Wabash in 1897, Bell was married and returned briefly to Terre Haute as a reporter; but he soon took a position with the *Chicago Record*, Victor Lawson's morning paper. Almost immediately, Bell's abilities won him recognition as a "star" reporter as he covered such varied assignments as race riots in North Carolina and the machinations of Charles T. Yerkes, the Chicago traction magnate. His stories attracted the attention of Lawson who was seeking a likely candidate to head his newly established foreign service. Bell later wrote that a "human interest" story he had done on a local Chinese laundryman and "the Chinese situation" at the time of the Boxer Rebellion struck Lawson as exactly the kind of reporting he wanted from overseas, "the emotional and intellectual side of the news." With the Associated Press providing "the facts," Lawson's staff was to contribute "side-lights": personal interviews, interpretations, and vignettes of human experience attractive to Chicago readers. Bell left for London in 1899 to cover the Boer War and also to oversee the work of Lawson's rapidly expanding staff of European and American reporters. He would remain there for nearly a quarter of a century.[2]

To assist Bell, Lawson and Charles H. Dennis, his editor, soon sent out another promising young staff member, Frederic Wile. A Hoosier like Bell, Wile had reached Chicago in 1892, directly from Notre Dame University. From his position with a bank, he became involved in the formation of the Bankers Athletic Association and was elected its secretary and editor. In 1898 he accepted a position with Lawson's morning paper, the *Chicago Record*. He had been impressed with Lawson's seriousness and commitment and by the quality of the *Record*'s staff, which included such men as Henry Justin Smith, Ray Stannard Baker, and Bell, and which, incidentally, was one of the first in the city to employ women reporters.[3] Wile's initial assignment, reflecting his business experience, was as a specialist on trusts. When he was shifted to the London bureau to assist the hard-pressed Bell, it was presumably his ability rather than any particular experience or interest that commended Wile for the foreign assignment. Despite his German-American background, he spoke no foreign language, had not previously travelled abroad, nor shown any special interest in a position overseas.

For all Lawson's advanced views on the importance of reliable and interesting international news, the Chicago publisher had an imaginative promotional streak as well. His London bureau offices were located on Trafalgar Square, convenient to the business, tourist, and theatrical centers. They were, at Lawson's insistence, comfortably if not lavishly furnished and well stocked with American newspapers. Reporters for the *Chicago Daily News*, to which Lawson transferred his foreign service in 1901, were expected to provide travel information and to arrange social, political, or business contacts for visiting Chicagoans. Although they had been longer established in London and had larger staffs, none of the New York newspapers maintained such imposing facilities. Lawson intended the office both to symbolize "his expansive idea about the news" and to enhance his paper's reputation, "especially when that fame might affect the minds of lavish advertisers." Lawson's tireless attention to these matters is reflected in the fact that most of his early correspondence with Bell dealt with the location, furnishing, and refurbishing of the London office rather than with news matters.[4]

Chicagoans who stopped by to sign Bell's guest book could be confident that their names would appear in the hometown paper for their friends to see. There was a substantial American business community in London, as well as a steady stream of tourists, artists, theater people, and others constantly passing through the city. Reporting on their activities constituted a major responsibility of Lawson's correspondents. Wile adjusted happily to these surroundings; his business background served him well in settling into his new job. When he was promoted in 1901 to head the *Daily News*'s Berlin bureau he found it operating on a similar basis, located in the same building as the American consulate and with facilities comparable to those in London.[5]

In addition to overseeing the Trafalgar Square office and establishing connections with potential news sources among members of London's American community and British press and government personnel, Bell was responsible for editing and transmitting copy sent by correspondents in Europe, Asia, and Africa to be forwarded by mail or cable to Chicago. This duty placed him strategically in the communications network. It also located him in the uncomfortable position of middleman between the home office's not always clear instructions and expectations and a remote, diverse staff of correspondents. For more than a decade Bell struggled valiantly and, on the whole, successfully to build the *Daily News* foreign service into a coherent and effective one. To explain Lawson's goals and desires to his fellow correspondents, Bell used every means at his disposal: letters of advice; critiques of work performed or not performed; conferences to settle misunderstandings or disputes; requests to Chicago for clarification; invitations to Lawson or Dennis to meet with correspondents in person; and sometimes—as a last resort—recommendations for the replacement of incapable or recalcitrant reporters.

Bell's position was complicated by the fact that on various occasions the Chicago office sent out very mixed signals indeed. Despite orders that his men not duplicate the straight factual reporting that was the province of the Associated Press, Lawson was not above complaining when correspondents failed to beat out a headline story by the AP or a rival paper. At other times he reprimanded Bell and his associates for sending trivial, wordy, or abstract material, and he emphasized especially the need for holding down the cost of expensive cable transmissions.[6]

The truth seems to have been that Lawson's original plan had outrun its economic base. After failing to interest various New York papers in a joint foreign service, he had decided to strike out on his own. He had expanded his overseas staff so that by 1899 he was paying more than ten thousand dollars per month for his foreign service and was publishing dispatches from more than fifty cities in twenty-nine countries. He had expected to finance his service by syndicating and selling its product to other papers. But its growth had outstripped the demand. Overextended, he was forced to cut back and contain his costs. Bell's own assignment to London indeed may have been an early step in this direction since one of his responsibilities was to supervise and edit the work of outlying correspondents. But if this was Lawson's motive, he never explained it clearly to Bell.[7]

Under such circumstances, it was not surprising that from time to time Bell protested strongly what he could only see as an inconsistency on Lawson's part. Thus, answering complaints from Dennis in mid-1901 that their stories were wandering "too far away from the news," Bell unloaded some of this own confusion and frustration:

[W]e must not handle anything that the London papers see fit to print or that the Associated Press can get hold of with its superb news connections in and out of London? Is it any wonder that we are driven into holes and corners, driven to hobknob [*sic*] with freaks and to strain to make the weird and the academic worth cabling? However, I cannot help thinking that if our stuff had not been pretty good, or if it had not, for all its faults, possessed a great amount of novelty, color and true worth, the *New York Herald* would not have opened its columns to so much of it.

Or again, in 1905:

To date, our instructions come to this: SEND NO SMALL STUFF. SEND STUFF EVERY DAY.

Theoretically, these do not necessarily cancel each other; practically they very nearly do so. They mean: SEND BIG STUFF EVERY DAY.

Sometimes, specially [*sic*] from the general point of view, Europe is newsless.

Just now the big things are chestnuts. We have examined them from every possible angle and pumped everybody dry about them.[8]

As if these trials and duties were not enough, Bell was also expected to act as tour guide and travel agent for Mr. and Mrs. Lawson on their visits to Europe. When Lawson experienced a nervous breakdown while touring the Continent he insisted that Bell accompany him for several months and leave the affairs of the London office in the hands of subordinates. At other times, Bell was called upon to provide Mrs. Lawson with advice on purchases of British goods for her Chicago home, the styles of women's clothes and jewelry at London parties, and vignettes of the coronation ceremonies for King George V in 1912. In between times, and with evident impatience, he supervised the enlargement and provisioning of the increasingly luxurious *Daily News* office and assisted visiting Chicagoans. The lavish hand Lawson wielded in this regard contrasted strikingly with his repeated emphasis upon holding news costs to a minimum. By 1907 Bell was complaining to Dennis that this was "the most arduous and least attractive part of our work"; and two years later he suggested to Mrs. Lawson that the offices seemed in danger of becoming "a resort for peers and peeresses."[9]

As he gained experience Bell was developing an ambitious idea of his role as a foreign correspondent. From the outset he tried to encourage his colleagues to interpret Lawson's guidelines as incentives to imaginative reporting rather than as merely restrictive. In 1901 he urged a Berlin correspondent to consider his mission more important than that of a "routine fellow worker" at the Associated Press. The latter's concern was with "bare facts," Bell wrote: "It is your business to gather matter that explains, that illuminates, the bare facts.... You should turn your faculties for large things and large things alone." As he warmed to his idea, his enthusiasm waxed rapidly. "I think," he wrote Frederic Wile a few months later, "it unfolds a distinct departure in journalism on a new and higher plane. All we have to do...is to graduate a staff of men worthy of the idea and we shall be the most picturesque and the most substantial news service in the world."[10]

Bell was caught between Lawson's uncertain leadership and a diverse group of colleagues scattered across Europe, most of whom were even more baffled than he as to their employer's intentions. It is difficult to be sure how consciously he was striving to redefine the correspondents' roles as he set about advising them. What is abundantly clear from his letters is that he articulated a concept of international journalism that, considering Lawson's strictures, was expansive enough to suit both his growing confidence in his own powers and his sense that the "news" of the world held as yet untapped potential for reporters.

"Can you not," Bell wrote a correspondent in Gothenburg in 1901, "give us an exclusive, vital, picturesque story once a week or once a fortnight.... There ought to be some movements of thought in Sweden that would be interesting to Americans. Do you not know of something...in the literary, art, scientific, educational or commercial world embodying the elements likely to appeal to everybody who thinks?...We have large numbers of Swedish readers in Chicago who would appreciate hearing regularly from Sweden." Earlier, Bell had written to the *Daily News*'s obviously disgruntled Berlin correspondent suggesting a different, but parallel, perspective for a major news center: "We do not think you ought to feel that you are 'subordinated to the Associated Press'...your mission is a more important and a pleasanter one than...to report current happenings with fidelity to the bare facts involved.... Try to do things that the Associated Press never thinks of doing. Keep a book in which you write down coming events and endeavor to get sidelights making these events thoroughly intelligible. Work quietly, secretly, do a lot of thinking; be a strategist."[11] Bell's leadership and example were clearly vital to Lawson's success in building an able, imaginative foreign service.

The *New York World*'s Wythe Williams, meanwhile, found his introduction to a foreign correspondent's career much more casual than Bell's. Born in Meadville, Pennsylvania, in 1881, Williams had attended Ohio Wesleyan University before becoming a reporter for a succession of middle western newspapers. In 1909 he found a position at the *World* city desk, covering strikes, crimes, and similar news stories. Williams later stated that at this stage of his career he had little interest in Europe except for a holiday visit. Approaching his editor for a leave of absence to survey the European scene, he found unexpected agreement that travel might broaden his outlook. Coincidentally or otherwise, Williams reached London just in time to assist the *World* staff there with one of the biggest stories of the decade, the death of Edward VII and the coronation of George V. Such events were of great interest to American editors and readers, matched only in William's later experience by the demand for news of the 1912 Olympic games and particularly of the American athletes who participated. These stories, and reports of the arrivals and departures of prominent Americans, were considered sufficiently important to warrant immediate cable transmission for inclusion in the next day's paper. Less exciting material was ordinarily written up on Fridays and mailed or cabled at cheaper weekend rates for publication in later Sunday editions.

Williams found that the pace of the correspondent's life in London mirrored the nonchalant outlook of his editors on most European matters. It was slower and more pleasant, if more formal, than at home. He and the *World*'s other London reporters met each noon at the Savoy Hotel bar, where they plied the barmaids for news of recently arrived American travellers. After a leisurely lunch, they proceeded to the West End hotels in search of more American visitors. Occasionally they dropped by the American Express or the U.S. embassy, although official news was usually sent over by the embassy staff or could be secured by telephone. In the evening, they reconvened to compare notes at some point in their round of social activities. Until the First World War, they customarily wore morning coats, silk hats, spats, and gloves and carried canes, the better to impress the hotel receptionists from whom they got their daily ration of news. Williams found the situation similar in Paris when he moved there in 1913 to head the *New York Times* bureau and encountered the American journalists congregating convivially at the Café Napolitain. Their home offices expected very much the same kind of news from France as from England, except that here fashion news was a matter of high priority.[12]

The arrival of Paul Scott Mowrer in Paris in 1910 symbolized the changes Victor Lawson was making in his *Daily News* overseas staff. Mowrer personified Lawson and Bell's conviction that an alert, young American reporter could provide better service than more knowledgeable but less aggressive Europeans. Mowrer's journalistic experience before reaching Paris had been limited, but his literary interests made him at home in the French capital. A year's apprenticeship as a reporter in Chicago had done little to arouse his interest in foreign affairs, and literary, rather than journalistic, concerns originally had led him to travel in Europe. Mowrer returned to Chicago eager for a writing career and questioning ingrained assumptions of America's cultural superiority, but still with little concern for foreign news. To support himself, he returned to the *Daily News* where, aside from Victor Lawson and Charles Dennis, he found little international awareness on the part of the staff. He daydreamed of Europe and took every opportunity to cultivate foreign visitors to Chicago. He applied for an opening in the Paris office in 1910 and soon found himself, at twenty-two years of age, in charge of one of Lawson's chief European posts.[13]

The attitudes toward foreign correspondence even on a relatively forward-looking paper such as the *Daily News* resembled those Wythe Williams had described. Mowrer's Chicago superior, the highly regarded Henry Justin Smith, had urged him to shun the Paris assignment: "A fellow goes to Europe to stay a few months and he stays years. He may be a pretty fair newspaperman when he leaves. He comes back at last, wearing spats and carrying a cane, too good for reporting, no good as an executive, no place for him anywhere, his career wrecked. What do you want to go to Europe for? What's the matter with Chicago?" And Mowrer soon found evidence in Paris of Lawson's approach to his foreign service. The *Daily News* office was located in the heart of the tourist district, across from the Café de la Paix and the Place de l'Opéra. It looked like an expensive club, "with palms, oriental rugs and leather armchairs," reading tables with the latest American papers, and desks amply supplied with stationery. There was the customary guest register for those who wished to have their names cabled home. Mowrer's orders were not to spend too much time on European politics, but to concentrate on human interest angles and make himself available to visitors as a guide. True to type, he adopted the requisite spats, mustache, and cane—although he justified these as necessary to distinguish himself from the tourists, and he soon abandoned the spats.[14]

From London, Bell wrote to welcome his new colleague with advice and assistance. He told Mowrer that Lawson saw the *Daily News* as "the foreign organ of the travelling and investigating Chicago public," and he warned against duplicating the AP's factual reports, noting his "distinct impression that Mr. Lawson has a decided liking for stories of dignity and strength." Yet Bell further suggested the appropriateness of "expository and comparatively abstract cables.... I cannot help believing that since they get so much light and picturesque and dramatic matter in America, they might well like for the foreign service to aspire to rather a higher level of real importance and of dignity."[15]

Bell's suggestions heralded the more serious journalistic approach which Mowrer himself would soon be espousing, but the young man initially resisted the veteran's patronage and supervision. Mowrer responded appreciatively, but held that he knew better what Chicago expected. Serious news might be appropriate for Bell; but "it must be remembered that *this* is Paris," he wrote. Americans regarded the city as "the most bizarre congeries of hare-brained individuals in the world."

> [T]he Daily News loves features. I have worked in the home office long enough to know this. They want stories that folks will talk about at the dinner table—stories that a man will tell his wife about, or a wife will mention to her husband .... Colorful sidelights on momentous events are also welcomed.... Let the dignified, enlightening, really worthwhile cables come from London and let Paris effervesce the freakish, the far-fetched, and the fantastic. No doubt an individual point of view can be found for every city.... At any rate I am convinced there can't be...any one rule to guide the entire foreign service.[16]

Mowrer's view of his function changed rapidly, however, as he gained familiarity with the European scene and began to sense serious problems behind the continent's superficially serene facade. By 1912 he found growing indications of war in the making and began to express impatience with Chicago's continued insistence upon light news. By 1913 he was agreeing with Bell on the need for closer coordination and centralized supervision of the foreign service, "in order to keep our men alive." But he continued to argue for a degree of local independence so correspondents could feel "that their problems are their own and that they are expected to solve them on their own responsibility."[17]

With Bell in London and Mowrer in Paris, Victor Lawson had set strong foundations for his European service. Soon he added another able young reporter with the appointment of Raymond Swing to the key Berlin post. A man of intense emotions and keen sensitivity, Swing also added an intellectual bent to the *Daily News*'s analytical resources. He had begun his academic career ingloriously—discharged from Oberlin College for high-spirited, irreverent behavior—but a flair for writing and ideas led him readily into journalism. After brief reporting jobs in Cleveland, he became editor of a small Orrville, Ohio paper, a position that left him time to serve also as a choirmaster and manager of the local basketball team. A year of this was enough for Swing, who moved on to Richmond, Indiana, and then to Indianapolis as statehouse reporter for the *Star*. Still restless, he shortly became managing editor of a new Indianapolis paper, the *News*. Here Swing found himself, at twenty-three, the youngest member of the staff, and the pressures of the position led to a collapse. For a respite, he undertook an assignment for his uncle, University of Chicago psychologist George Herbert Mead, gathering data on truancy, among the young poor of Chicago's West Side. He had returned to journalism with the *Cincinnati Times Star* when the Meads, in 1910, invited him to join them for a year of travel and study in Europe; he readily accepted.[18]

In Paris, where the Meads and Swing met Mowrer, the two journalists struck up a friendship. Moving on to Berlin, Swing encountered the *Daily News* representative there, Albert C. Wilkie, to whom he had an introduction from Mowrer. Swing found Wilkie a person "of charm and culture," highly regarded by his fellow correspondents in the German capital. However, Wilkie was already on unfavorable terms with his *Daily News* superiors, who thought him unreliable and suspected him of indulging too frequently and carelessly in the pleasures of the Hotel Adlon bar. When Wilkie was relieved of his post, Swing, on the recommendation of Mowrer and Bell, replaced him first as a temporary and then as a regular correspondent. A confrontation ensued when the rest of the Berlin correspondents' community, suspecting Swing of scheming for Wilkie's position, denied him admission to their circle. Only Mowrer's intervention with a full explanation of the circumstances cleared the way for Swing's acceptance by his fellow journalists. Among the latter was Frederic Wile, who had left the *Daily News* in 1906 to serve as Berlin correspondent for the *London Daily Mail.*[19]

The Berlin incident can be seen as one of a number marking the transition of the relaxed, casual foreign correspondence of the past toward a more serious, professional conception of the role. If the bars of the Savoy and Adlon and the cabarets and elite salons of Europe had provided the chief news sources for Wilkie, Wythe Williams, and their colleagues, the *Daily News* was fortunate to have such men as Swing and Mowrer established in Berlin and Paris as the continent plunged toward war in 1914. They brought to their duties an intellectual breadth and curiosity, as well as an interest in serious, analytical reporting that journalism would soon need.

Characteristically impatient, Swing was even more critical of Victor Lawson than was Mowrer. Years later Swing still bristled recalling Lawson's idea of an overseas news bureau as a combination of gossip mart and travel agency with the correspondent as chief "greeter." He felt that this "somewhat naive creation" could only have sprung from the "Midwestern mind" of Lawson, a man who was bent on impressing the wealthy tourists with his paper's "opulence and solicitude" and who "did not care a hoot about foreign news...the state of the world...the rising perils that darkened the political horizon...or the prestige that pioneer foreign correspondence might bring to him as a publisher." Swing resented cabling home the names of wealthy Chicagoans while his interviews with such people as Albert Einstein, Arnold Schoenberg, and the family of Richard Wagner—not to mention his increasingly urgent reports of German military preparations—had to be mailed for delayed publication and were often drastically edited and buried inside the paper, when not completely ignored. Mowrer also was increasingly restive at his orders to restrict political coverage in favor of "feature stories, quaint episodes illustrating French life, human interest stories," and the like. Even Frederic Wile, in many ways closer to the older generation of journalists, acknowledged that his work for the *Daily News* had been "journalistically tame" and undemanding compared with what the *London Daily Mail* expected of him.[20]

Yet despite its peculiarities and inadequacies, Lawson's concept of his foreign service, at this stage in its development, can be justified. More than his eager, young correspondents, Lawson probably had the surer sense of what interested American readers. Swing may have been correct in holding that good fortune rather than good planning had led Lawson to tap an extraordinary pool of journalistic talent for his overseas staff; but he also might have reflected that, had Lawson proceeded faster than the public was ready to follow, the entire enterprise could have collapsed prematurely—as it very nearly did. And Swing himself was not above matching Lawson's public relations emphasis with an offer of assistance to Americans seeking rental housing in the German capital.[21]

In London, Bell steered a middle course between young Turks of the Mowrer-Swing stripe and the relaxed, sociable patterns of the veterans. Bell was in many ways the ideal man to fill the role at this stage in the development of foreign correspondence. His reporting exemplified some of the attitudes and methods characteristic of each camp. His supervisory duties and the need to cultivate influential figures within the British establishment may have encouraged him in the traditional reliance upon interviews at the expense of broader, more intensive field investigations for his own stories. Yet he took a serious view of foreign correspondence, and he earned the admiration of members of London's social, political, and journalistic establishment as well as of his fellow American reporters for whom he served both as model and mentor.[22]

Bell welcomed the enthusiasm and drive of men such as Mowrer and Swing. He held that although their positions were new, ill-defined, and hardly prestigious they could win their spurs by conscientious, imaginative work. Reminiscing years later on the prewar situation, he recalled, "Journalists in those days were not held in very high esteem...doubtless did not deserve to be." But Bell had a vision of a different future: "We dreamed of workers in our profession (and profession we purposed it should be) worthy of and demanding respect." He repeatedly stressed a broader version of Lawson's reporting guidelines than Raymond Swing remembered: "Political, Social, Economic, Religious, Moral, Intellectual, these were my key words. What fresh things were going on in the correspondent's country in politics, in education, temperance, housing, philanthropy; in manufacturing, trade, finance; in religion and morality; in art, literature, science, philosophy, fashion?...'Dig deep for your stuff' was one of our battle cries."[23]

Although they could not discern clearly what the future held for their careers, Bell, Wile, Mowrer, Swing, and their counterparts serving other American newspapers were beginning to sense an opportunity for more serious journalism. Whatever the motives or accidents that had carried them across the Atlantic, their new familiarity with the Old World combined with their knowledge of the New to convince them that they could perform a service that would benefit their fellow Americans at home. Tested, committed, and ambitious, they were ready for the challenge.

THE WAR YEARS

War put the fledgling American news services to their first major test. At the outset, editors showed only limited interest in the events, and especially in the background, leading to the hostilities. Swing, Wile, and others who had tried to alert Americans to German war preparations were discouraged by editorial treatment of their reports. Swing later recalled that one of his stories which he considered a "major effort" to call attention to the military build-up was delayed for eight weeks and then only published with its central message deleted. And Paul Mowrer recounted the experience of the United Press's Rome correspondent who, in September 1914, received instructions from his preoccupied home office: "War interest diminishing. Hold down. World Series begins Monday."[24] As the war stretched on, however, and the United States became more involved, the hunger of readers for news from the scenes of activity increased. Openings appeared for American journalists who had not previously found European assignments. Some began actively to seek out what their more fortunate colleagues had earlier had thrust upon them: the variety, adventure, or chance to make their mark that overseas service might offer.

Webb Miller, who reached the London bureau of the United Press early in the war, was among the new arrivals. Miller had fled the isolation of rural Michigan in 1912 to work for the *Chicago American*. For a time he found in the city an answer to his intellectual yearnings. With his first wages he purchased the Harvard Five Foot Shelf of classics of Western literature from which he read hungrily on foreign literature and religions. He enjoyed Chicago's ethnic and cultural diversity, haunted the Opera House and the Art Institute. But the violence and crime to which he was exposed on the city desk disgusted Miller, while the search for adventure called him further afield. Severing his Chicago ties, he staked his future on free-lance assignments covering the pursuit of Pancho Villa along the Mexican border. Miller later conceded that he had no understanding of Villa's significance except as a colorful, newsworthy character; but he fell in with a group of newsmen covering the story and learned the political and economic ramifications of Mexican-American relations in the field. His gamble was rewarded when he attracted the attention of a United Press representative in the region. He was offered a regular job and, with the outbreak of war in Europe, assigned to Washington, D.C. London was the next stop in Miller's UP career, then Paris, and ultimately the management of the agency's entire European service.[25]

Among the American reporters Miller encountered along the Mexican border was Floyd Gibbons, a fellow midwesterner on assignment from the *Chicago Tribune*. Gibbons, born in 1887 in the national capital, had grown up in Iowa and Minnesota. After a not-very-serious fling at law school, he drifted into newspaper work in Minneapolis and discovered his calling. Work as a police reporter suited Gibbons's bent for human interest stories and his instinct for a "scoop," not always of the most respectable kind. He moved to the *Milwaukee Free Press* in 1909, then on to Chicago. In 1914 he covered the Illinois National Guard in action along the Mexican border where he, too, encountered Pancho Villa. Gibbons returned to Mexico in 1916 with the American expeditionary force under General Pershing.

Gibbons's assignment the following year as a war correspondent in the *Tribune*'s London office was his great opportunity, and he responded with a "natural" journalist's ingenuity and daring. Hoping for a story to spotlight the German submarine blockade, Gibbons booked passage across the Atlantic on a ship he considered a likely target. His instincts proved correct and his fortunes skyrocketed when the S.S. *Laconia* was, indeed, sunk off the coast of Ireland. Gibbons was rescued in time to file a dramatic story, one of the extraordinary feats that earned him a reputation as a daredevil, if not particularly weighty, journalist. In 1917 Gibbons was transferred to Paris where the *Tribune*'s publisher, Colonel Robert R. McCormick, was establishing a newspaper to provide the troops with wholesome, pro-American news. From this vantage point, Gibbons covered Pershing's arrival in France and the landing of the first American troops at Saint-Nazaire. Later, he covered the first American action at the front. He claimed to have recorded the names of the soldiers who fired the first shell and even to have retrieved the shell itself. Gibbons's daring in pursuit of a story cost him an eye at Belleau Wood in 1918. This episode and the eye-patch he sported thereafter fixed his image as a dashing reporter. The French and American authorities acknowledged his bravery and value to the war effort. He was sent back to the United States on a speaking tour to arouse enthusiasm for the war, carrying commendations from Generals Pershing and Foch and wearing the Croix de Guerre.[26]

Another experienced reporter for whom the war opened new opportunities was George Seldes, who had entered newspaper work as a court reporter in Pittsburgh in 1909 at the age of nineteen. Despite the *Pittsburgh Leader*'s liberal reputation, Seldes was disillusioned to find the paper mired in the sordid realities of corrupt urban politics and business manipulations. After failing to organize a press union, Seldes left for New York City in 1916. Short exposure to the life of a metropolis readied him for London, where he found a place with the United Press cable service. Here he encountered Miller and Gibbons, and when the latter moved to Paris for the *Chicago Tribune*, Seldes followed. Like Gibbons, he secured assignment to the Press Section of the American army. Already dubious of press and government motives, Seldes found much to confirm his suspicions. With few exceptions, among which he noted Wythe Williams's defiance of officialdom in publishing unapproved material, Seldes found little inclination toward independent, critical journalism among his Press Section colleagues. "So far as I know," he recalled later, "no one cared a damn about anything at all except about getting the news, preferably getting it first, and not necessarily getting it too objectively or truthfully."[27]

The war "drafted" still another young journalist, Edgar Ansel Mowrer, who was continuing his studies in literature and philosophy in Paris in

1913 after graduating from the University of Michigan. Immersed in a circle of artists and writers, Mowrer wrote on literary topics for journals on both continents. When war broke out he tried to isolate himself, but circumstances overtook him. While visiting his English fiancée, Mowrer was enticed by Bell to submit a story to the *Daily News* contrasting Paris and London in wartime. Next, Bell and Paul Mowrer induced Edgar to help out at the Paris office so that Paul could go to the front. Without previous newspaper experience, Edgar began by extracting the Paris papers for the rest of the staff. Soon he was scouring the London papers as well, and pumping his own friends and Paul's for news of preparations to meet the advancing Germans.

When Paul returned, Edgar went first to cover the war in Belgium and later to report from behind the German lines on Herbert Hoover's inspection of Belgian relief needs. Spirited and mercurial, Edgar had an unlimited capacity for enthusiasm and hostility. Later he admitted having suppressed news of German relief efforts in order to heighten the appeal for American aid. Expelled by the Germans, Mowrer continued in his dispatches from London to misrepresent Germany's position on Belgian relief. In 1915 he was offered an assignment either in Vienna or Rome for the *Daily News*. Since he was about to marry an English citizen who could not go to Vienna, he chose Rome. In Italy, Mowrer covered military news and worked for the United States Committee on Public Information, attempting to strengthen Italian morale and commitment to the Allied cause. This brought him into contact with a militant young Socialist editor, Benito Mussolini. He also prepared a report on the state of the Italian army for the American government. After a postwar visit home, Mowrer succeeded the *Daily News*'s regular Rome correspondent with whom he earlier had been on uneasy terms.[28]

Unlike the new arrivals, veteran correspondents on the European scene when war came had the advantage of connections and relationships, official or unofficial, already established. Mowrer and Swing, who had long chafed under restrictions imposed by their editors, found an increasingly welcome reception for almost any news they could gather. On the other hand, military secrecy and censorship soon made it clear that the older, genteel news gathering methods were no longer adequate; more subtle, aggressive techniques were needed. For example, when German authorities restricted his freedom of movement, censored his dispatches, and finally expelled him from Belgium, Richard Harding Davis retired from the journalistic ranks discouraged and tired. Paul Mowrer, however, met the new challenge by reorganizing the Paris bureau to free himself for more active field work. When official French displeasure with his reporting led to his banishment from the front, he sent Edgar in his place and returned to Paris to gather information from a wider variety of sources. He even pressed some of his French literary acquaintances into service, since they could go where Americans were not permitted.

As the war dragged on and the French government continued to withhold information, Mowrer's problems multiplied. He protested that, in its eagerness to satisfy readers' curiosity, the *Daily News* in Chicago was buying inaccurate news from other sources and ignoring the sound work he and his staff were submitting. Coordinating the Paris office became increasingly difficult, especially after additional correspondents and military "experts" were added to cover such specialized subjects as the war in the air. Their reluctance to accept Mowrer's supervision provoked his frequent complaints and transformed him into an ardent advocate of centralized authority. He wrote to Bell, "I am surrounded by an atmosphere of hate and heroism, madness and fervor, mobility and insanity, and I myself am reduced to a nothing. I have to fight just to keep my own head clear enough to do my day's work, and give what inspiration I can to those who are working here in the interests of the paper." The extent to which his complaints were justified, rather than were expressions of resentment at his associate's lack of deference, is difficult to determine, but he charged some of his colleagues not only with lack of cooperation and insubordination, but also with laziness, drunkenness, and generally boorish behavior earning the contempt of French and American authorities and reflecting unfavorably on the *Daily News*. Mowrer acknowledged the need for special reporters, but felt that the morale of his regular staff was undermined by their irresponsibility.[29]

Not only did Mowrer bombard Bell and Charles Dennis with complaints, but also he found other means of fortifying his control over the Paris bureau. When Raymond Swing was sent home from Germany early in 1917, Mowrer met with him in Switzerland and presented his arguments for direct relay to Victor Lawson. He seems also to have used his influence with Frederick Palmer, a former journalist in charge of the American army's Press Section, to consolidate his position as chief *Daily News* correspondent. With the assistance of American Ambassador Myron T. Herrick, Mowrer overcame the French government's suspicions to win official recognition as the responsible head of the *Daily News* service, accredited to the Anglo-American Press Mission at the French military headquarters. His problems with his recalcitrant colleagues continued, however, until they left at the war's end.[30]

Wythe Williams of the *New York Times* was also an Anglo-American Press Mission correspondent. Like Mowrer, Williams found the serious but exciting business of war reporting a welcome change from chronicling "the silly ways of fashion and the crazy ways of society." Setting aside his top hat and cane, he redoubled his efforts to score "beats" on his rivals. But this kind of old-style journalism, although more welcome than ever in the home offices, proved increasingly difficult as military controls were instated and journalists were barred from combat zones. After the Battle of the Marne, Williams and others secured government permission to visit the front, but he was arrested by military authorities and only gained his release with the help of Ambassador Myron T. Herrick. Also like Mowrer, Williams hired extra help and enlisted volunteers to augment his staff. Getting news out of France was difficult; telephone service to London was cut off before he could arrange a code for important stories. When he tried to bury military reports among his regular transmissions to New York, the home office did not grasp their significance. Desperate for news from the front, Williams enlisted as a Red Cross ambulance orderly, but this ruse also failed.[31]

Wartime conditions forced reporters like Williams and Mowrer to find ways of evading official controls while they cultivated closer ties with American and foreign government personnel. Without exploiting both approaches, they would have had few news resources but official communiqués and the rumor market, neither of which could be relied upon for accuracy. Despite his admiration for the French, Mowrer soon learned not to depend too greatly on government sources. For additional data, Williams and Mowrer both drew heavily on the American embassy where Herrick and his staff had access to information not otherwise available. Herrick recognized the value of getting accurate news to the American public whenever possible. He presented background information on a regular basis to correspondents he trusted.

The development of such informal working relationships between journalists and government officials served the purposes of both. Reporters tapped new sources, while officials opened informal communication channels both to the public and to other governments. As the war continued, the Allied governments developed formal procedures for expanding the flow of carefully supervised news. The character and limitations of this approach can be seen in the operations of the Anglo-American Press

Mission, to which Williams, Mowrer, and others were accredited. Membership in the mission was limited to those the French considered sympathetic and responsible. They were supplied with uniforms, billeted and fed by the military, driven by army personnel, and accompanied by French officers on their visits to the front. Their reports were carefully scrutinized, although their familiarity with censorship regulations and their dependence upon the military for information doubtless minimized the likelihood of their challenging the rules.

A considerable price was paid, perhaps more than they recognized at the time, for the privileges these newsmen enjoyed. Not only did they accept the perhaps inevitable restrictions the system imposed on their freedom, but by assuming a cooperative rather than an independent or adversarial stance, they voluntarily limited their critical functions. Evidence of possibly collusive relations between correspondents and officialdom can be seen in Williams's account of his experiences with the Anglo-American Press Mission. His book, titled *Passed by the Censor: The Experience of an American Newspaperman in France*, appeared in 1916 with an "endorsement by French Premier Clemenceau and an introduction by Ambassador Herrick" commenting on the close ties war had brought between press and embassy. Herrick remarked that the journalists had "recognized special responsibilities and assisted the Embassy and, therefore, the nation." Williams noted, in turn, that the embassy had considered its favored friends as "journalistic attaches," while the French had established the press mission in part to offset Germany's propaganda efforts.[32]

Williams's book offered no criticism of the system. The glowing tone of its treatment of the French army reflects the emotions naturally engendered by war as well as the possibility that his special privileges had colored his outlook. Yet Williams was later dismissed from the Press Mission for sending articles to *Collier's Weekly* without submitting them to censorship. His journalistic instincts may in this instance have outweighed the pressures to cooperate in return for favored treatment, but the temptations to do so were strong nonetheless, and such pressures on the press would become even stronger in the years ahead.

In Germany, meanwhile, Raymond Swing initially experienced less obvious government interference than did his colleagues in France. Although he had tried to report the military buildup, Swing was not unsympathetic to the German position at the outset; and he felt it his duty to give the German side of the story to *Daily News* readers. In an effort to counter Allied stories of German atrocities, Swing and other foreign correspondents were permitted a trip to Liège to observe the occupation of Belgium. But official favors did not imply complete freedom, for when Swing wrote of secret German siege guns along the route he took the precaution of giving his report to an American student headed for London to make sure the story got through. Despite this action, which the government may not have traced to Swing, he managed to remain in its good graces. Clearly, his hosts were as anxious to exploit him as he was to outwit their censors, for in interviewing Prime Minister Bethmann-Hollweg, Swing received a confidential peace feeler for relay to Sir Edward Grey, the British foreign minister; also, he was permitted a second visit to Belgium in the company of a group of German officers.

In 1915 the *Daily News* sent Swing to report on hostilities in Turkey. Here he encountered a familiar problem, one which further convinced him of the incompetence of his Chicago editors. He visited the front at Gallipoli, observed the British attack on the Dardanelles, and had an interview with the sultan; but only the latter, "worthless" story received front-page attention at home. As the war dragged on, anti-American sentiment grew in Germany and Swing, now returned from Turkey, angered the authorities by evading censorship, notably with a story concerning German designs on the French iron mines. With the breakdown of relations between Germany and the United States, Swing and other American journalists were sent home early in 1917.[33]

In London, Bell, although distant from the combat lines, was engaged in a complex series of relationships with British authorities concerning the release of war-related information. He had planned to return home in 1914, but war made him too valuable to be spared by the *Daily News*. He continued to strengthen his ties in British official and social circles. As a result, Bell himself became an extraordinarily well-informed news source. Bell tried to keep his reporting fair and factual, but a strong attachment to the British people and culture heightened his sympathy for their cause. On occasion he was warned by Lawson that some readers found him pro-British, while Bell himself criticized what he felt were Swing's pro-German sympathies. Swing, he wrote Dennis, had "forfeited the very birthright of the journalist—the reputation for impartiality."[34]

As the war progressed, Bell defended the United States against British charges that her neutrality policy was aiding democracy's enemies and urged relaxing censorship to create a better-informed American public. Gradually, the British government recognized the value of friendly public opinion and cautiously relaxed restrictions by cultivating the press, supplying information it wanted circulated, and permitting visits to the front. Bell and other American journalists were no doubt pleased by this new policy and happy to cooperate with it. Such blandishments reenforced Bell's already strong British sympathies, and his conviction that fundamental moral issues were at stake led him toward increasingly open advocacy of American entry into the conflict.[35]

The wartime experience of both neophyte and veteran correspondents demonstrated the difficulty of achieving balanced, reliable reporting at times of extraordinary stress and emotional pressure. Circumstances compelled even greater emphasis than previously on news of immediate, but transient, value—"scoops," human interest, or morale-building material—at the expense of more thoughtful work. If journalists resisted governmental or military controls, they risked access to important information; but when they cooperated with authorities, they incurred other dangers. Past experience had not prepared them for such pressures. It is hardly surprising, therefore, that there were enough errors in judgment, motive, and performance to provoke Phillip Knightley's later claim that truth was "the first casualty."[36]

Yet, there were some countervailing gains for journalism which improved the quality of foreign correspondence once the war ended. War and the issues it generated converted international journalism from a casual, amateur affair to a serious business. Thoughtful correspondents learned the value of their work as a source of public information and understanding. The enterprising found ways of eluding the censors or penetrating official propaganda, of searching out news in unlikely and unorthodox places, of cultivating well-placed individuals for the sake of unauthorized or secret data. Recognition and rewards for active, ingenious news gathering provided incentives such as had not existed before. And, if the perils of too-close involvement with officialdom were not apparent at the time, the heavy-handed efforts of governments to obstruct news gathering alerted them to the need to challenge official sources and to the desirability of establishing alternate information channels.

Finally, the war brought to Europe still another group of young men, these in uniform, whose interest and curiosity were so aroused that they readily seized the opportunity later to join the ranks of foreign correspondents. Thus, David Darrah and Lee Wood, who had worked for the *Cleveland Leader* before the war, visited Paris in 1919 while awaiting demobilization from the army. They hoped to find reporting jobs there that would enable them to enjoy the comforts and pleasures military service had lacked. Both signed on with the *Chicago Tribune*'s army edition on a temporary basis and were assigned to the forthcoming treaty negotiations. They lingered on in Europe, Darrah eventually taking over the *Tribune*'s Rome office in 1927.[37]

Clarence Streit, the Montana State University journalism major, had reached France with the Army Engineers in August 1917. He was soon transferred to the Intelligence Service, where his knowledge of French enabled him to mingle easily among the people. In December 1918 he was assigned to archives security for the State Department at Versailles. His night duties left him free to explore Paris by day, to absorb its art and theater, and to attend lectures at the Sorbonne by economist Charles Gide. When his Versailles assignment ended, Streit returned to Montana to complete his education, but within two years he was back.[38]

The paths taken by Louis Lochner and Negley Farson were more circuitous, but both led toward foreign correspondence. Lochner's experience at Wisconsin had involved him with the international peace movement both before and during the war. He attended student conferences at The Hague in 1909 and Rome in 1910, and later became secretary of the Chicago Peace Society and director of the American Peace Society's Central West District. In this capacity, Lochner became closely associated with Jane Addams and other leaders of the national and international peace movements. He accompanied Addams to The Hague Peace Conference in 1915, then went on to Germany to arrange a meeting with the Chancellor Bethmann-Hollweg. He joined Henry Ford's Conference for Continuous Mediation, accompanying Ford and Addams on the Peace Ship to Stockholm. From Stockholm, Lochner went with his family to Holland; but he returned to the United States in 1917 at Addams's request, to work for the Emergency Peace Federation. His German-American background, as well as his open advocacy of peace and wartime civil liberties, subjected Lochner to recriminations and pressure. When peace came, he moved to the Rand School for Social Sciences and edited an international labor news service. After his wife died in the influenza epidemic of 1919, Lochner was ready for a complete change; overseas journalism offered him a new location and a new career.[39]

Negley Farson, one of the most colorful correspondents of the 1920s, was already working as an engineer in England when the war broke out. He had studied at the University of Pennsylvania and worked as an oil salesman in New York City, where the vitality and ethnic diversity appealed to his love of variety and adventure. In 1914 he had taken a position in England with an American steel and pipe company owned by the father of a college friend. Farson fell in love with the dignity and solidity of the English way of life, but his inherent wanderlust soon broke through. He undertook a sales mission to Petrograd, where he met liberal American journalist John Reed. Russia fascinated Farson, although its corrupt bureaucracy blocked his business venture while it provided him with stories for Reed to incorporate into his reports of the czarist regime's incapacity.

Despite his business experiences, Farson acquired a romantic attraction to Russia, which he found "unspoilt" and full of promise for change. Having fallen in with a group of Western journalists, Farson tried his hand at submitting stories for publication. He returned to the United States but left again for the Soviet Union after the revolution, still hoping to develop business connections he had established earlier. Farson quickly soured on revolutionary Russia, however. When the United States declared war, he tried to volunteer but was disappointed when the American government would not pay his return passage. Instead, he joined the British army's Flying Corps, which fed his passion for travel further by sending him to Egypt. Once again, Farson fell in love with a new land; Egypt seemed "on the edge of the perfect life I had dreamed of as a boy," he wrote later. Its proximity to India, the East, and the rest of Africa stirred his adventuresome spirit. He returned home at the war's end; but neither marriage, business, nor two years in the forests of British Columbia settled him. As a salesman for the Mack Truck Company in Chicago, he met Victor Lawson, still on the lookout for reporters with a lively, human touch. Farson proposed to hire a boat and sail across the canals and rivers of Europe from the Rhine to the Black Sea sending back stories of life and people along the way. Lawson accepted readily and hired Farson as a special reporter in 1924. By 1926 he had become a regular and a star of the *Daily News* staff.[40]

The record of American foreign correspondence before and during the war is richer and more complex both in accomplishments and in failures than can be indicated here. For the small company of newsmen who emerged as leaders of the American journalistic community in postwar Europe, it was a demanding, often frustrating apprenticeship. Transferring skills and attitudes developed at home to unfamiliar surroundings offered challenges and opportunities that not all met with equal success. Resistance or lack of understanding on the part of editors and publishers often was matched by the snobbery or hostility of Europe's officialdom and social elite. Under such circumstances, it was not difficult for the correspondents to think of themselves as a select community and to evolve their own patterns of social and convivial—professional, if still highly competitive—cooperation.

With the return of peace many correspondents, of course, returned home; but for others the comforts, amenities, status, and opportunities for independent work that Europe offered proved highly seductive. The experience of David Darrah was not atypical. Restless and unsure of his future in 1921, he applied for a leave of absence from the *Chicago Tribune*'s Paris bureau. After three months with his family, visiting Akron, Cleveland, and Chicago, Darrah returned to Paris. "Somehow or other," he later wrote, "the center of things no longer seemed to be in America then but in that life I had left behind. . . . My values had been upset by the last four years."[41]

3

Comrades and Rivals

■ The postwar trek of Americans to Europe, which included artists, writers, impoverished students, wealthy expatriates, those who had missed the excitements and adventures of wartime, and those whose overseas military service encouraged an early return, has been chronicled many times and in many versions. It remains a revealing episode in the gradual, uneven, and continuing development of American international awareness. Even those who stayed home in the twenties to enjoy the pleasures and preoccupations of Jazz Age America could not wholly escape the international turmoil and change that challenged their comfortable hopes or assumptions. Indeed, continuing public interest in international affairs encouraged American newspapers to persist in carrying stories and feature articles from abroad, if not on the scale that the war had sustained, still with a depth and variety unknown to prewar journalism. Reporters and aspiring authors thus remained able to find positions on established overseas press services as well as with several new foreign services.

The place of these foreign correspondents in the story of the "lost generation" of the twenties seldom has been acknowledged, and their contributions to the cosmopolitanizing of a presumably "isolationist" era have been largely overlooked. This neglect may result in part from their deference to the small group of literary and artistic masters whose work has dominated our images of the period. Many journalists began with the same aspirations and goals as their literary compatriots. A number of correspondents did, in fact, publish novels or poetry, while others attempted to. At the same time, it was common for those whose mark was to be made in literature to support themselves for varying periods of time by writing for one or another of the press services; Ernest Hemingway offers only the most familiar example. Journalism and letters mixed readily during these years, which may have encouraged correspondents to deprecate their own efforts in comparison with the accomplishments of their literary friends.

Newspaper people may have suffered further in their own and others' esteem because, whatever the propriety of the term "lost generation" as applied to the artistic community, they were only on the fringes of that legendary group.[1] On the contrary and despite disappointed literary ambitions, these journalists quite literally "found" themselves in their new careers. They developed a sense of the importance of their work quite different from that of the earlier amateur correspondents. The change came slowly and unevenly, which may have lessened general recognition of its significance. It occurred, nonetheless, in the course of a decade of collegial, if not always genteel, rivalry and cooperation in defining and performing their duties. When recognition did come in the 1930s, it was shared by readers, government officials, and others eager for the insights and information about Europe's crisis that few but experienced journalists could offer.

THE POSTWAR GENERATION

Early entrants into the postwar community of American correspondents included some for whom overseas journalism offered a way to pursue the tastes they had only begun to sample in wartime Europe. These recruits were soon joined by a younger contingent for whom Europe seemed to hold the prospect of compensation for having missed the great adventure of their generation. There would be departures and still later arrivals, of course, but the circle of reporters who covered two decades of Europe's tribulations as it struggled to recover from one war, then spiralled dishearteningly downward to another, was assembled by this time.

Having devoted the war years to futile efforts to end hostilities and later to defend civil liberties at home in the face of militant superpatriotism, Louis Lochner was working for the International Labor News Service in New York City when peace came. In 1921 he returned to Europe as a free-lance labor reporter, counting on connections with the Federated Press Service, which he had helped to found, and on his ability to sell feature stories elsewhere to pay his way. His German background and labor interests made it seem natural for Lochner to settle in Berlin, where a new republic with a strong Socialist component was in the making. He reported on inflation, unemployment, and distress in the Weimar Republic while recruiting stringers to supply the Federated Press with labor news. In 1922 he covered an economic conference in Genoa and a Rome meeting of the International Federation of Trade Unions. Meanwhile, Lochner had remarried, to a German divorcée whose family was well-connected in social and governmental circles. Living with his wife's parents because of the housing shortage, the Lochners were soon very much at home in Berlin society. In 1924 Lochner took a position with the Associated Press; four years later, he became head of its Berlin office, a position he held until 1941.[2]

Clarence Streit, meanwhile, wrote a column on international affairs for the Montana State University newspaper until he was named a Rhodes Scholar for 1920–21. Without waiting for the Oxford term to begin, Streit hastened to Paris where he spent the intervening months working for a new international news service organized by Cyrus H. K. Curtis, publisher of the *Philadelphia Public Ledger*. Wythe Williams, having left the *New York Times* to head the *Public Ledger*'s Paris staff, was Streit's superior. Streit's Oxford year was abbreviated when he married a French girl with whom he had fallen in love. He returned to the *Public Ledger* and was assigned to cover the Greek-Turkish war over the Greek settlements on the Turkish coast. Streit had already published one small book, *Where Iron Is, There Is the Fatherland* (1920), based on postwar revelations of efforts by French and German iron and steel companies to defend their mutual interests despite the conflict between their countries. Constantinople in 1922 offered Streit an opportunity to observe Kemal Atatürk's overthrow of the sultanate and his establishment of a dictatorial regime dedicated to the modernization of Turkey. After Paris and Vienna assignments Streit covered the League of Nations in Geneva for the *New York Times* from 1929 to 1939.[3] Like Lochner, Streit was an early observer of the continent's postwar political and economic structures.

Negley Farson took somewhat longer to find his way back to Europe but returned nonetheless with a characteristic flair. In May 1924 he and his wife began the three-thousand-mile junket from Rotterdam up the Rhine and down the Danube that after eight months brought them to the Black Sea. The stories Farson sent back to the *Chicago Daily News* suited Victor Lawson admirably. Lively, down-to-earth, and eminently readable, they were soon published in book form with the title *Sailing Across Europe* (1926). Farson's easy-going style led many to assess him as the best writer among the journalists of his generation, and his instinct for excitement and local color made him something of a latter-day Richard Harding Davis. Serious political analysis and routine news were hardly Farson's forte; but his vignettes of everyday life may have given readers as clear an insight into conditions in remote, unfamiliar places as did more orthodox political reporting. His place with the *Daily News* was secure after his Balkan stories, and his ability to win choice assignments was soon the envy of his more workaday colleagues.[4]

By 1924 the relatively experienced Europeanists among the Americans were being supplemented by a group of youngsters, fresh from college and avid to enjoy the life, liberties, and happy pursuits which to their minds contrasted so sharply with the tiresome materialism and Puritanism of home. The promise of foreign correspondence as a means of justifying and supporting an overseas adventure was by then almost as widely recognized as was the extraordinary purchasing power of the American dollar. William Shirer may have been somewhat more brash than most when he borrowed his passage money from the president of Coe College, but others showed equal determination and ingenuity in seeking the new promised land and in besieging the American press offices for jobs upon their arrival.

John Gunther and Vincent Sheean left the University of Chicago and moved directly into journalism with the *Chicago Daily News*. Gunther's eyes were already on an overseas assignment; when none materialized he resigned in 1925 and went to London on his own. He applied directly to the *Daily News* bureau there and was given a few assignments. He found a position with the United Press but quit in 1926 to go to southern France, where he proposed to settle down and write a novel. Although Gunther continued to write novels for many years, literary poverty and discipline were not for him. Foreign correspondence at least offered regular pay and stimulating work. By the end of the year, he was again on the *Daily News* payroll; after a variety of short assignments he became bureau chief in Vienna in 1930.[5]

Sheean left college for the *Chicago Daily News* before he could graduate; but he lasted at the paper only a few weeks. Moving to New York he found a reporting job, becoming overnight, in his words, "the familiar friend of murderesses, the apologist of divorcées, a professional observer at the peepshow of misery." In addition to the scandals in which the *New*

York Daily News revelled, Sheean was exposed to crime, culture, and Bohemianism. He consorted with journalists and others who had travelled widely and spoke knowingly of revolution in Russia or treaty-making at Versailles. Within a year Sheean was ready to go to Europe to try his hand at writing a novel while living sparely in rural Normandy. Dwindling funds and discouraging progress soon ended this experiment. After a short trip to Italy, Sheean returned to the *Chicago Tribune* in Paris; by 1923 he was a full-fledged correspondent, assigned to the Lausanne Conference.[6]

Not all foreign correspondents either before or after the war were men, although that life-style attracted few, and welcomed even fewer, women. Nineteenth-century women travellers and expatriates, such as Margaret Fuller in Italy, had occasionally written for American papers and magazines in the genteel, literary style of the day. The institutionalizing of international journalism had not progressed sufficiently before 1914 to offer women many opportunities, and wartime conditions added further discouragement. But the affluence and new freedom of the twenties enabled women seeking travel or employment abroad to aspire to other roles than the traditional ones of missionary, nursemaid, or companion. Higher education led many women to think of writing careers, while publishers were simultaneously becoming more receptive to writing by or for women. Women participated heavily in the overseas exodus of the decade and a number won recognition, or notoriety, as journalists. Among the better known, Louise Bryant, Anna Louise Strong, and Agnes Smedley were drawn to the revolutionary movements in Russia and China.

In western Europe, Sigrid Schultz—born in Chicago of Scandinavian parentage and educated in Europe—assisted George Seldes in the Berlin office of the *Chicago Tribune* before herself becoming bureau chief in 1925, a position she held until 1941. And Anne O'Hare McCormick, wife of an American businessman in Europe, became a roving correspondent for the *New York Times* after submitting some articles in 1921. In 1936 she was named to the *Times*'s editorial board and contributed a regular column on European affairs. In 1937 she was awarded a Pulitzer Prize for her years of commentary.[7]

But it was Dorothy Thompson, a clergyman's daughter from western New York, whose energy and intelligence won her the widest audience. Thompson had been born in Lancaster, New York, in 1893; but her English-born Methodist father moved his family from one pulpit to another in the Buffalo region. Dorothy must have absorbed both the enthusiasm and mobility these circumstances offered, although she rebelled nonetheless at their limitations. Her restless imagination carried her in fantasies of travel and romance far from home. At fourteen, she went to Chicago to live with relatives. As a student she earned high marks in literature and history at the Lewis Institute, while developing self-confidence as a debater. On a visit to her family she demonstrated her talents and upheld her growing feminist sensibility by substituting for her ill father in the pulpit one Sunday. In 1912 Thompson matriculated at Syracuse University—a Methodist institution whose expenses her father could afford—although she had aspired to the more prestigious eastern colleges.

At Syracuse, Thompson enlisted in the feminist movement while working to support herself. She acquired a reputation as an independent and activist, but upon graduation her future direction remained undecided. She began as a suffrage campaigner in the Buffalo region, but this suited neither her abilities nor her ambitions. In 1917 she moved to New York City, hoping for a career in journalism. She found work with a Bible publishing society, but soon began to sell articles to newspaper Sunday supplements. Through feminist and social work ties, she secured a public relations job with an experimental community-organizing group in Cincinnati, where she spent the war years speaking and working for and among the poor. In 1919 she joined New York feminist writers, radicals, free thinkers, and society women while writing for a number of newspapers and journals, including *Outlook, Leslie's Weekly* and *The New Republic.*[8]

To escape an unhappy love affair, Thompson sailed with a friend to Europe in 1920. She had arranged to submit articles to several papers and she hoped to find public relations work with the American Red Cross in Paris. From London she went to Ireland to visit relatives. She sold several stories to the International News Service, which was eager for reports from the new Irish Republic. As unsalaried stringers for the INS, Dorothy and her companion crossed the English Channel hoping eventually to reach the Soviet Union. From Paris they travelled to Italy in search of labor and political news. Her Italian trip produced a few articles as well as a sketch for the obligatory novel before Thompson returned to London and Paris, paying her way with additional stories for the INS. Her public relations job for the Paris Red Cross, together with feature stories she sold to the *New York Post* and the *Christian Science Monitor,* kept her afloat but failed to satisfy her drive to become a full-fledged journalist.

Impressed with Thompson's work, Paul Mowrer suggested that she move to one of the less crowded capitals; and she persuaded Wythe Williams to appoint her an unsalaried correspondent for the *Public Ledger* in Vienna. With a Red Cross assignment in Budapest as well, she hoped to eke out expenses. She quickly made herself at home in the poor but richly cultured capital of the old Austro-Hungarian Empire. Under the guidance of Marcel Fodor, Hungarian-born correspondent of the *Manchester Guardian*, Thompson blossomed as a capable, hardworking reporter. Her reports on cultural and political affairs soon won her a position as a regular correspondent, with all the Balkan countries and Turkey as her beat. Thus, she entered the circle of professional reporters.[9]

Leland Stowe reached Paris in 1926 as an assistant in the bureau of the *New York Herald Tribune*. A native of Connecticut from an old New England family, Stowe long had been eager to travel and interested in writing. Upon graduating from Wesleyan University in 1921, he found work with the *Worcester* [Massachusetts] *Telegram*. Twenty months of this convinced him that "life," rather than fiction, was his métier and that he was ready for a larger stage. With unbounded enthusiasm and energy, Stowe was among the many who felt cheated that youth had denied them participation in the Great War. He headed for New York and became a reporter for the *Herald*. But exciting as big city life and reporting proved to be, they failed to satisfy his ambitions. He covered steamship arrivals and departures and sat at Battery Park during lunch hours, following the departing liners in his imagination.

The *Herald* offered its readers a steady diet of human interest stories which took Stowe into the city's diverse ethnic communities, its theaters, lecture and concert halls, to testimonial dinners and celebrity interviews. He honed his skills working with some of the city's ablest journalists while whetting his appetite for still further adventure. Transcribing a long dispatch in "cablese" (filling in the omitted articles and expanding the abbreviations) from the *Herald*'s Soviet Union correspondent gave Stowe a powerful sense of contact with history in the making. When the *Herald* and the *New York Tribune* merged in 1924, he left for a better-paying position writing film newsreel titles for Pathe News. Here he gained forced training in brevity and lively expression while editing incoming foreign film. Reviewing clips on international conferences, athletic events, natural catastrophes, and travel all further sparked his desire to get overseas. When a position opened in Paris with the *Herald Tribune*, he was rehired by the paper in time to be named a replacement; in July 1926 he left for Europe. Shortly, he was filing stories on topics ranging from the serious to the frivolous, from political leaders and the problems of Alsace, to American tourists, French divorce mills, and the inevitable Paris fashion market. As "A Man Among the Mannequins, A Mere Male [Who] Attends His First Paris Fashion Opening and Almost Swallows His Notebook," Stowe reported on "a bewildering tempest of silks, satins, crepe de chines, beiges, orchids, crepellas and hand-painted Turkish towels."[10]

Throughout the 1920s the transatlantic parade of those who wished to become correspondents continued. Eager to learn from their elders, but impatient, aggressive, and determined to make their own mark, they included a number of fine reporters who would join the veterans in describing a dramatic, eventful era for American readers. Among the new crop of correspondents were a few who entered the field almost inadvertently or reluctantly. One, a redheaded Texan named Hubert Renfro Knickerbocker, was an outstanding newsman who abbreviated his first two names to their initials to achieve byline status. For Alexander Woollcott, a colorful journalist himself, "Red" Knickerbocker matched the image of a dashing, daring, foreign correspondent more closely than anyone since Richard Harding Davis.

After college in Texas, Knickerbocker headed for New York in 1917 to study psychiatry at Columbia University. Unable to pay full tuition, he settled for a single journalism course, perhaps with an eye to supporting himself through his studies. After a year at Columbia, Knickerbocker worked for a number of New York papers before returning to Texas in 1922 to teach and head the journalism department at Southern Methodist University. His original purpose remained, however, and he resumed studies in psychiatry at the University of Munich. Once again, a need for funds forced Knickerbocker to take local assignments for the United Press. When he switched to the University of Berlin in 1924 he found a position as correspondent for the *New York Post* and the *Philadelphia Public Ledger*. In 1925 Knickerbocker accepted a two-year assignment to Moscow for the International News Service. He returned in 1927 to Berlin, where for a decade he held posts for the INS and the *Public Ledger,* and won recognition as "a quick moving, self-reliant, self-confident correspondent" with a "long-range view of political trends," a mentor and model for others.[11]

More typical in their pursuit of foreign correspondents' careers were William Stoneman and Edmond Taylor, although few men differed more widely from each other in their styles and interests. Stoneman had followed the well-beaten path from Ann Arbor to the *Chicago Daily News* in 1925. Hardly a serious student, he had apprenticed as sports editor for the campus journal, but he had a facility with foreign languages that would serve him well. After three years of the "romantic if futile life [of] a police reporter," Stoneman was "red hot anxious to get to Europe." Hal O'Flaherty, then returning from the London bureau to become foreign editor of the *Daily News*, advised Stoneman to learn Swedish in anticipation of an opening in Scandinavia. The job materialized quickly and in 1928 Stoneman established himself in Stockholm, where his work was not demanding but still called for the traditional spats and walking stick. Occasionally filling in for correspondents on leave from the major capitals, Stoneman's clear, hard-hitting reports won approval at home; and he was promoted to Rome in 1931.[12]

Meanwhile, Edmond Taylor had reached Paris in 1928 after several years as a reporter for the *St. Louis Globe Democrat*. Eager for cultural and intellectual engagement with Europe, Taylor joined the *Chicago Tribune*'s Paris edition. He readily made himself at home in France although the quickening pace of events required periodic assignments elsewhere even after he had become the *Tribune*'s regular Paris correspondent in 1930.[13]

Herbert L. Matthews, in the *New York Times*'s Paris office by 1931, had—like Knickerbocker and Edgar Mowrer—initially aimed at a different career. Bookish and withdrawn, Matthews had served in the U.S. army in France during the war; but, although he read French easily, he hated army life and made little effort to mingle with the French people. By his own admission ignorant of international affairs, he returned to America "knowing nothing about the French and caring less." He studied medieval culture at Columbia University, worked for the *Times* to help support himself, and spent a research year in Italy and France in 1925–26. Although he could hardly have escaped some awareness of fascism, Matthews claimed to have been so indifferent that he did not bother to read the newspapers. Returning to New York, he applied for a position with the *Times*'s book review section and was disappointed to find himself assigned to reporting. Soon, however, his knowledge of foreign languages brought a transfer to the cable desk. In 1929 he was sent on a press tour of Asia sponsored by the Carnegie Endowment for International Peace.

Married to an English woman and stimulated by his earlier European studies, he was now ready to return again. His Paris assignment from 1931–35 offered an opportunity to concentrate on economic affairs—about which most correspondents were blissfully ignorant—while enjoying the still substantial, although by now less dynamic, artistic life of the French capital.[14]

Two others who reached Europe at about this time would in time earn outstanding reputations. John T. Whitaker began with the *Chattanooga News* early in the twenties, covering police, city hall, and state legislative matters before becoming book editor. He moved to New York to report city and national news for the *Herald Tribune*. Jaded with routine newswork and disillusioned by the Hoover administration's attempt to wrestle with the economic crisis, he refused at first when offered an overseas assignment reporting on the League of Nations. However, the challenge finally shook Whitaker, who later conceded that he had "gone to seed intellectually" from his doldrums, and he accepted the position. In Geneva in 1931 he met other correspondents, including Streit, Paul Mowrer, Gunther, and Knickerbocker. The league's shortcomings stirred Whitaker's cynicism, but he found Geneva a good spot for an international perspective through contacts with officials and journalists from many nations.[15]

William L. Shirer exhausted all his funds in 1925 writing poems and short stories and haunting the city's concert halls and coffee shops, rubbing shoulders with recognized or unrecognized artists and intellectuals, before applying to the *Chicago Tribune*'s Paris edition. Shirer termed the Paris *Tribune*, which had strayed far from the original intent of its publisher, Colonel McCormick, "the world's zaniest newspaper, a crazy journal without a peer...the voice of America's voluntary exiles who had fled their homeland, who doubted whether it was worth saving, and who believed Europe was the only place in which they could work in freedom and decency." He worked next to James Thurber; other staff members included Elliot Paul, Eugene Jolas, and Vincent Sheean, whose reports of his visit to the Rifs of Morocco had first attracted Shirer to the *Tribune*. Like the others, Shirer cringed at encounters with "barbarian" American tourists who reminded him all too forcefully of the bourgeois society he had fled. Frustration with his literary efforts and the attractions of a correspondent's life sealed Shirer's career plans. He transferred from Paris in 1929 to represent the *Tribune* in Vienna, where he fell in with the circle that had already welcomed Dorothy Thompson and would soon include John Gunther.[16]

THE VETERANS

The arrival of the younger journalists infused the ranks of American correspondents with new energy and imagination. The end of hostilities had brought the recall of many correspondents who had been only on temporary wartime service, while some of the senior journalists were preparing to retire from the ranks. A small number whom the war had disciplined for serious reporting remained to guide and inspire their younger colleagues. The distinction between casual and professional journalism, already beginning to win recognition before the war, had been emphasized by wartime military and propaganda pressures. With heightened confidence in their own competence and knowledge, the veterans were ready to challenge the motives and directives of their editors and publishers at home as well. Like their younger colleagues, they enjoyed the comforts and contacts foreign correspondent status had afforded them. They had learned how easily the public could be misled by careless or venal journalism. Some had become, in the process, inveterate cynics; but others concluded that Americans lacked a clear understanding of international affairs and their importance for the United States. In this light their duties and opportunities took on new meaning, and they were anxious to make the most of them. Inexperienced reporters, if observant and ambitious, could not help but be impressed by the knowledge and work of the best of their elders.

Edward Price Bell lingered on in London until 1922. His reputation had not been damaged by his wartime identification with government policies and leadership. Indeed, he had received invitations from British publishers to join their staffs, usually at considerable increases over the relatively modest salary Victor Lawson paid him. After visiting America in 1919, Bell returned to London to bask in almost universal acclaim until his retirement. But, in fact, his journalistic grasp had begun to slip, and his desire to use his prestige and influence for the admirable purpose of promoting international peace and understanding was diverting his energies. Close ties to the British establishment colored Bell's approach to the Irish question, while his heavy reliance upon interviews with the elite distorted his approach to many issues. After more than twenty years in the field, Bell was no longer inclined to dominate and direct the work of the capable *Chicago Daily News* European staff he had helped to build.[17]

Bell's retirement left the leadership of Lawson's European service in the capable hands of Paul Mowrer. Tested by the war, Mowrer had gained confidence in himself, in his knowledge of European politics, and in the duties and opportunities of foreign correspondence. On a second tour of the Balkans and eastern Europe in 1920 to examine conditions in the new nations created out of the defeated Central Powers, he demonstrated his capacity for observation and analysis. He developed a system for quick, comprehensive information gathering based on statistical data and talks with technicians and political specialists whom he considered more informative than top officials.

Mowrer recognized early the conditions that would ultimately bring a resurgence of German and a decline of French influence in eastern Europe. His *Daily News* reports were subsequently published as a book under the title *Balkanized Europe* in 1922. This was the first book-length analytical study of postwar Europe by an American correspondent, a model for Mowrer's colleagues of what serious journalism could achieve. Mowrer also undertook a daring excursion through Spanish lines in Morocco to interview the rebellious Rif leader, Abd el-Krim, whom he saw as one of the first postwar rebels against European imperialism. This venture won him the respect of members of the old, Richard Harding Davis school of reporters while indicating his awareness of shifting world power relations.[18]

After resisting Bell's efforts to oversee his work in 1910, Mowrer had come to appreciate the need for closer coordination and control of a diverse, far-flung foreign press service staff. He had learned to value Bell's experience and ability to enhance his own understanding of French affairs. Mowrer's view of the correspondent's role had enlarged substantially. As he later wrote, "It was plain that no man who hadn't a high sense of honor and couldn't discipline himself was fit to be trusted with the responsibilities of a foreign correspondent, operating unobserved at thousands of miles from the central organization."[19]

With the war ended, Mowrer envisioned a more sophisticated approach to reporting with himself as a special roving diplomatic correspondent. When his ambitious concept was vetoed by Victor Lawson, Mowrer contented himself with assuming Bell's mantle as chief of the European service. New demands were being made upon the overseas staff: new nations to be covered; thorny political and economic issues to be interpreted; dynamic new ideologies and movements flourishing amid postwar confusion and distress. These demands, together with recurrent pressures from Chicago to reduce expenses and his own ambitious view of the correspondents' responsibilities, all enhanced Mowrer's role as counsellor, coordinator, and mediator. He maintained active contacts in French political and intellectual circles while offering encouragement and advice to younger reporters as well. It was no wonder that Mowrer was highly regarded by them. John Gunther, who reported that Mowrer's nickname was "Whispering Jesus," considered him a "strange duck... an amazing man. Solemn, extremely shy, dreamy, a little frail fellow with a beard," whose feat in securing the Abd el-Krim interview was all the more remarkable. Dorothy Thompson and Leland Stowe, among others, attested to the helping hand he extended them although neither was a *Daily News* staff member.[20]

Raymond Swing, Mowrer's Berlin counterpart during the early war years, experienced a much less settled career in the twenties and thirties before finally achieving a full measure of success as a radio news commentator after 1936. Able, imaginative, and restless, Swing kept both his private life and his journalistic career in a recurrent state of turmoil. After expulsion from Germany and a brief roving assignment for the *Daily News*, he secured a post with the War Labor Board. At the war's end, he worked for a year for the liberal journal, *The Nation*. He was anxious to return to Europe and took a position as Berlin representative for the *New York Herald*. Swing found postwar Germany's cultural climate lively and stimulating, and he made friends with leaders of various political factions. Berlin in the early twenties was the center for news of the Soviet Union and a base for correspondents en route to observe the experiment under way there. Swing joined Floyd Gibbons and others in such an expedition. He had met some Russian Communists, including the journalist Karl Radek, in Berlin; but he was surprised to find Moscow conditions worse than he expected. Swing was unimpressed with the Russian regime and with the Asian Communists he met, but tried to write a balanced, objective assessment for his paper. However, the *Herald*'s violently anti-Communist owner, Frank Munsey, destroyed his dispatches. A visit by Munsey to Berlin convinced Swing that the publisher's attitude toward his foreign service was insulting.

Swing was offended further when the *Herald* assigned a less experienced but strongly anti-Bolshevik reporter to cover the 1922 Rapallo Conference. He applied for a position to Clarence Barron, the owner of the *Wall Street Journal*, whose interest in German economic conditions had impressed him. Barron, who had earlier approached Swing, now hired him, and he served the *Wall Street Journal* from 1922 to 1924 from a base in London. Uncomfortable with the *Journal*'s conservatism, Swing was solaced by the opportunity to learn more about European and American economic relations in weekly staff conferences at *The Economist*. He settled pleasantly into London life with his second wife, Betty Gram, whose name he shared, and his family. His work left him time for literary and musical composition, while his reports were published in *Barron's Business Weekly* as well as in the *Journal*. His political and intellectual circle included philosopher Bertrand Russell, whose experimental school the Swing children attended for a year although Swing found Russell arrogant and anti-American.

In 1924 Swing resigned over an editorial difference with Barron and, wishing to remain in London, signed on at a reduced salary as second man for the *Philadelphia Public Ledger–New York Post* service. Eventually, however, he attained the top position and remained in London until the service was disbanded in 1934. By then, Swing felt that his experience had prepared him for wider responsibilities, but bad economic times limited his opportunities. After canvassing other openings in Europe, he returned home as a Washington correspondent for *The Nation*. Here, ironically, his views proved too conservative for his editors. In 1936 he became New York correspondent for the *London News Chronicle*. That, too, proved unsatisfactory since its editors were more interested in "spicy" than in serious reporting. He also served briefly as correspondent for *The Economist*.[21]

Wythe Williams, whom the war had made into a capable, serious newsman, also had difficulty settling into a regular postwar position. Ending his work for the *New York Times* in 1918, Williams served for a time as European correspondent for *Collier's* magazine. In 1919 he took the position of Berlin correspondent for the *London Daily Mail* but soon returned to Paris, where he headed the *Philadelphia Public Ledger*'s new bureau. Simultaneously, he contributed some fine interpretive articles to the *Saturday Evening Post* between 1925 and 1927. In 1927 he covered the League of Nations in Geneva for the *New York Times*, then moved to Berlin in 1929 as bureau head. Williams entertained few illusions as to the league's effectiveness as an agent of international peace, and he became increasingly discouraged over the resurgence of nationalism and the failure of statesmen to contain or confront issues realistically. In the face of rising reaction in Germany, he left for London in 1931 to join Hearst's International News Service. He returned to the United States in 1937.[22]

Meanwhile, after a postwar visit to the States, Edgar Mowrer had returned to Rome as bureau chief for the *Chicago Daily News*. Mowrer and his wife Lilian flourished in the cultured and intellectual circles of the ancient capital. Full of enthusiasm for schemes for international government propounded by an Italian writer, Gaetano Meale, Mowrer had also been stirred by Woodrow Wilson's League of Nations proposal. Because he was discouraged about his literary career, Mowrer poured his energies into promoting international understanding. His first book, *Immortal Italy* (1922), extolled the glories of that nation's ancient culture to present-minded Americans. Covering a series of international conferences served to heighten his appreciation of the persistent strength of nationalism and to temper his idealism. With a journalist's luck, he returned from a trip to Greece on the train carrying Mussolini to power in Rome, and he secured a newsworthy interview. While reporting Italy's relations with Albania, he was offered that new nation's crown by its acting foreign minister—the only foreign correspondent on record to have received such a proposition! But by 1923 Mowrer was disgusted with Mussolini's Italy. His brother Paul helped him arrange a transfer to Berlin.[23]

After a brief London posting in 1919 for the *Chicago Tribune*, George Seldes was transferred to Berlin, with responsibility for central and southern Europe as well. From that base he interviewed Gabriele D'Annunzio in Trieste and carried out a variety of other assignments, including a series of autobiographical interviews with Isadora Duncan. A radical by heritage and persuasion, Seldes was highly critical of Germany's Socialist government and of the Allies' deference to German imperial and military interests. During a year and a half in the Soviet Union, he found much to criticize in the new experiment as well. He later wrote that he went to Russia "an enemy of the Communist regime" and returned "perhaps an even greater enemy, but a more enlightened one." Although the stories of Russian censorship and religious intolerance he smuggled across the border satisfied Colonel McCormick, eventually they led to Seldes's expulsion. Seldes was not unsympathetic toward the Soviet effort to remake the nation, but he was too much the libertarian and individualist to accept the Communists at their own evaluation. He returned to Berlin in 1923.[24]

The following year Seldes moved to Italy, but within a few months he was expelled by the fascists for exposing the murderer of the Socialist

Giacomo Matteotti. Mussolini's bribery and coercion of the press angered Seldes. He was further embittered by the failure of most American journalists and of Colonel McCormick, who had backed him against Soviet pressure, to support him against Mussolini. After brief assignments in the Middle East, Mexico, and a short return engagement in Europe, Seldes, convinced of the blind ignorance of his employer and the venality of much of the rest of the press, retired from the foreign news service.[25]

Meanwhile, Floyd Gibbons, whose wartime daring Seldes had admired, remained as head of the *Tribune*'s Paris-based European service. His own proclivity for headline-hunting combined with lack of financial and intellectual support from McCormick left Gibbons, in Seldes's view, with little to do but produce dramatic news stories without too much concern for their accuracy. Seldes concluded that Gibbons lacked any concern for the underlying causes of events. Amid the new school of journalists interested in serious analysis and interpretation, he wrote, Gibbons remained "the police reporter of Chicago in excelsis." After occasional excursions in pursuit of headline stories—for forty-seven days to observe the Polish-Russian conflict near Warsaw, to Russia to cover the 1921 famine, to Australia and Africa—Gibbons returned home in 1925 and left the *Tribune* the following year.[26]

THE GOOD LIFE

Paris in 1925–27, according to William L. Shirer, offered a "golden time [when] one could be wonderfully carefree in the beautiful, civilized city, released from all the puritan, bourgeois restraints that had stifled a young American at home." Yet what Europe offered aspiring journalists remained very much in the eye of the beholder, depending upon motives and circumstances. Certainly the attitudes of the Bells when they reached London in 1900 had been highly ambivalent. Bell had no doubt welcomed the advancement that the leadership of Victor Lawson's new overseas service offered him; but the role was new and ill-defined. Mary Bell was dismayed that London food prices were so far above Chicago's that it was impossible to survive on her husband's salary of thirty-five dollars per week. Her "explosion" and threat to quit within a few weeks of their arrival undoubtedly also reflected other tensions of transition. She was appeased by a raise of fifteen dollars per week for Edward and probably by the passage of time and increased familiarity with her new home.[27]

The network of associations upon which Bell's success and reputation eventually rested had taken years to build. The efforts of many other Americans and, even more importantly, the shifting fortunes of Europe and the United States all contributed to the ease with which young Bill Shirer could slip into the "golden" life of Paris in the twenties. Even this could not be taken for granted, for Wythe Williams was soon complaining that Paris had become "an important center for unimportant things," with little news to relay except for an occasional divorce scandal or the carryings-on of visiting American legionnaires and other tourists.[28] And with the Depression after 1929 conditions would deteriorate further.

Clearly it is dangerous, if not impossible, to generalize about the styles and circumstances of life enjoyed by a highly individualistic group of American journalists over a period of nearly forty volatile years of European history. Yet it would be equally wrong to overlook the influence of their experience on their perceptions of themselves and their trade, of the nature of American society and the role of the United States in world affairs, or of the shape and direction of European developments. Although they by no means abandoned their Americanism, as would become clear in the 1930s, almost inevitably they became internationalists. From the perspective of Europe they could more readily see that America's accomplishments and security depended not upon herself alone, but upon an international framework of mutual interest and interdependence.

British suspicions coupled with Victor Lawson's orders required Bell and Wile at the outset of their London years to concentrate on human interest stories with a distinctively American slant. This led them to cultivate the acquaintance of a wide variety of American residents in London. Among these were not only other journalists, but businessmen, artists, writers, wealthy expatriates, and the continuous flood of tourists, visiting athletes, performers, and others. Wile, who arrived with a pro-Boer, anti-British bias, found a generally warm reception among the English despite some condescension toward the United States. He discovered that Charles T. Yerkes, whom he had covered for the *Record* in Chicago, had already electrified—or "Americanized"—the London transit system. C. C. Barker, the "Yankee match king," was a member of London's long-standing American business community. In a few years he would be joined by H. Gordon Selfridge, from Marshall Field and Company in Chicago, who would revolutionize British marketing by introducing American department store techniques. Wile interviewed Mark Twain and heard Charles Frohman, the American theatrical producer, observe that London reminded him of New York City because he found so many Americans there. Wile covered the visits of American tennis players and oarsmen, much as Wythe Williams a few years later would find American Olympic athletes good copy. In addition, Lawson had negotiated access to the war dispatches of the *London Daily Chronicle* to supplement his reporters' news from South Africa, which brought Bell and Wile into direct contact with British newspapermen. By 1909 Bell had established connections which enabled him to exchange tips with British journalists.[29]

Early in their European tours, Bell, Wile, and other neophyte correspondents probably consorted most comfortably and frequently with their own peers. Such relationships could become highly congenial, convivial, and cooperative, as Wythe Williams also discovered; but they remained competitive in important respects. Scoring a "beat" on rival correspondents in reporting a major or a colorful event was considered a mark of ability or ingenuity. Even the best of friends could drink together while simultaneously planning to outdo each other in pursuing a promising lead. Bell reported in 1911 that the *New York Times* correspondent had tried to establish a monopoly of the coveted passes for the Westminster Abbey coronation of George V. Yet in Berlin, Wile found British and American journalists in 1903 substituting for each other to allow for vacations. While covering for a *London Daily Mail* reporter Wile wrote the story that induced Lord Northcliffe to tempt him away from the *Daily News* in 1906. Often, however, such stories were submitted in the name of the absent reporter to avoid calling attention to the practice. In Berlin, too, Wile found an American colony similar to London's, "a typical cross-section of Yankee life in Europe." By 1912 foreign correspondents in most major capitals had formed their own social and professional societies. It was such a group that rallied on behalf of Wile's *Daily News* successor when its members believed he had been undercut by Raymond Swing.[30]

Paul Mowrer's literary interests had led him initially toward artistic rather than journalistic or government circles in Paris. Not until he sensed the rising temperature of international politics in 1912 did he begin to cultivate the political connections that would later serve him so well. Mowrer was inevitably involved with other *Daily News* staff members, as well as those who worked for most of the major European and American papers or news services. And Wythe Williams, moving from London to Paris in 1913, found himself, superficially at least, in much the same circumstances as before. The American colony in Paris was small but wealthy. Tourists and journalists met regularly at the popular bars and bistros, but the Café Napolitain had substituted for the Savoy. Williams noted later the theme song of the expatriate community: "Oh, when I say I'm homesick, I mean I'm sick of home." Tourist, society, and similar light stories were in demand at the *New York World*, too; only fashion news was added to his usual list of assignments. And it was Williams's secretary, not his editor or other journalists, who suggested his first serious political interview, with Georges Clemenceau.[31]

Rome, Vienna, and Geneva (after World War I) had comparable cosmopolitan communities, as Edgar Mowrer, Dorothy Thompson, and other correspondents discovered. Until he mastered Italian, Edgar Mowrer necessarily depended heavily on Italian journalists for his information—which may have affected his understanding of the nation's circumstances. Most American newsmen lacked fluency in foreign languages. Lawson and Bell even held that well-trained, able, and ambitious young Americans, familiar with the interests and circumstances of their readers, could report foreign news more effectively than "a lazy and untaught continental." The record of the *Daily News* in the end upheld this conviction, although its most successful correspondents had—or soon acquired—considerable familiarity with the culture, politics, and society of their host countries.[32]

Colonel Robert R. McCormick of the rival *Chicago Tribune* carried xenophobia much further and with less happy results. Anxious that his reporters maintain a "strictly American" point of view, he moved them frequently from country to country lest they absorb the prejudices and assumptions of a foreign home base. Ironically, this policy must have increased their initial dependence upon native speakers and more experienced colleagues, thus lessening their independence. When George Seldes reached Rome in 1924, he found that his predecessor for the *Chicago Tribune* had been a pro-Fascist Italian, as was another correspondent representing the *New York Times* and the Associated Press. Seldes also discovered an Italian anti-Fascist on his staff; the quality and political leanings of his Italian assistants were evidently of little concern to McCormick.[33]

David Darrah, who replaced Seldes in Italy, found the Foreign Press Association of Rome thoroughly dominated by the Italian government, many of its members bribed by or otherwise beholden to Fascist officials. After London and Paris, Darrah felt the atmosphere of Rome restrictive and claustrophobic, more like that of a "large-sized provincial town" where life went on "in restricted circles and behind closed doors and, for the most part, among the upper cliques." All the more, then, he welcomed the fraternal association with American and British counterparts at the Anglo-American Union Club or at lunch in the Zinc Bar at Garguilo's.[34]

In Vienna and Geneva, the social and political climate in the 1920s was more congenial. When Dorothy Thompson reached Vienna in 1921 she found a city rich in culture and nostalgia for the empire. The capital of the former Austro-Hungarian Empire was also the base for news gathering from most of the Balkan nations. It maintained, despite its loss of power and prestige, a social and political style far beyond its objective means. Thompson fell in readily with a cosmopolitan circle of diplomats, artists, politicians, intellectuals, and a small band of correspondents who met at the Café Herrenhof and the Café Atlantis. In 1922 she married a Hungarian lawyer and writer, Josef Bard, a former associate of her mentor, Marcel Fodor. Sigmund Freud attracted many foreigners to Vienna, and when George Seldes spent a year in the city in 1926–27 he found that almost every correspondent there had "bumped his head into the new psychology." Seldes himself spent many hours as a guest in the home of Freud's erstwhile disciple, Alfred Adler, and was strongly influenced by the association to assert his own independence in breaking with the journalistic establishment from which he had long felt alienated.[35]

John Gunther reached Vienna in 1930, after Thompson had left for Berlin. He, too, sought out Fodor whom he later credited with teaching both him and Thompson most of what they knew about foreign correspondence. The city so enthralled Gunther that he worked on and off for years on a novel with a Viennese setting and with a small group of journalists as the central figures. In the late thirties, he submitted for publication a manuscript titled *Ring Round Vienna* which had one character clearly based on Fodor, but fear of possible libel suits by some other readily recognizable characters helped block its publication. Years later, in 1964, he published a novel titled *The Lost City*, which was evidently drawn from the same materials. It pictured the "fraternal" life of the correspondents' community, where "such a lot of journalism was a reciprocal process of barter, picking your friends' brains," and rendering "value for value received." Louis Fischer, another correspondent, described Gunther about this time as "big and made bigger by baggy suits, jovial, friendly...good company." Gunther enjoyed the good life and the companionship of interesting, influential figures and had a knack for clear, journalistic writing and for character delineation which—although not enough to make him the successful novelist he always aspired to become —helped him to capture public attention and to emerge as the most widely recognized correspondent of his generation.[36]

Gunther's Vienna colleagues, as they appeared in the novel, saw themselves as a "hard-working, respectable lot, with children growing up and never enough money to go around." They were more conventional than "the boys in Paris," but by no means dullards. Gunther's chronic need for more money to maintain the lifestyle he fancied earned him the resentment of some of his less flamboyant colleagues. He began to write magazine articles to supplement his salary to enjoy the comforts of life. His energy and ability to soak up information were extraordinary. Vienna is the "fatteningest town there is," he wrote one of his colleagues; "I am expanding like a melon in July." Junkets through the Balkan states offered colorful, if not always very important, stories. "I had a good time in Bucharest," he wrote Webb Miller in 1930, "trying to figure out whether the precious [King] Carol was sleeping with [Queen] Helene, Ileana, Marie, [Magda] Lupesco [*sic*]. . . or the fat porter at the Athena Palace Hotel."[37] For Gunther, as for Thompson and others, Vienna was a pleasant assignment and a good training ground for future eminence. Before long, however, more serious concerns would appear.

Geneva, where reporters gathered for the sessions of the newly created League of Nations, was both cosmopolitan and parochial. Diplomats and journalists from the league's member countries, as well as some nonmembers, mingled here; and correspondents accredited to other capitals often attended league sessions when leaders of the governments for which they were responsible were to appear. John T. Whitaker, arriving in 1932 to cover the sessions for the *New York Herald Tribune*, found the league a "fools' paradise of liberalism" and a hotbed of intrigue as nationalists and internationalists jockeyed for position or attempted to manipulate the press. Some foreign journalists, he discovered, were also government agents. Still, there were many outstanding reporters in the group; at different times virtually all the leading American correspondents covered one or another of the league sessions. "The most gifted of all," in Whitaker's view, was the *Chicago Tribune*'s Jay Allen. Allen kept a photograph of "'Simple' Willie Stephens, the idiot boy in the Hall-Mills case" pinned over his desk, as a reminder of his "average reader."[38]

Whitaker found an atmosphere of "easy camaraderie" among the reporters in Geneva. After competing for news stories each day they met in the city's bars and restaurants in the evening, pooling resources yet respecting each other's "off-the-record" materials. Private as well as national self-interests hinged upon league deliberations. Armament manufacturers and military organizations found it expedient to have agents in attendance. George Seldes noted that Wythe Williams and other journalists worked hand-in-hand with these men, sharing information for mutual benefit. Despite their doubts and disillusionments, young journalists such as Whitaker, Edmond Taylor, and others who had too long been isolated in a single country or capital encountered in Geneva the realities and complexities of international politics.[39]

In a variety of ways, postwar Berlin may have offered the liveliest and most interesting European assignment for American reporters. The struggles of the young Weimar Republic to establish a democracy in the midst of a defeated and embittered Germany, the remnants of imperial society on the one hand and the presence of a powerful socialist party on the other, the persistent political influence of the military and the uneven, disturbing growth of the fledgling Nazi movement all contributed to an uneasy but exhilarating life. Berlin also offered a window on much of eastern Europe with its mélange of ancient national rivalries and new, prideful, but pathetically ill-equipped states. It further served as a center for news of the Soviet Union, the most disturbing phenomenon of the decade. But the city offered rich attractions of other kinds as well. Its artistic and intellectual life was as rich or richer than ever before, and its contributions in theater and in the new mass medium of the era, film, were among the most significant to be found. In addition, its night life reputedly was wilder and its social mores less restrained than those of any other European capital.

It was little wonder, given these circumstances, that Raymond Swing yearned to return to Berlin from London in 1924 and was disappointed when the *Public Ledger* chose Dorothy Thompson to head its bureau there. And Edgar Mowrer, transferring the same year from his beloved but now besmirched Italy, found in Berlin the combination of cultural wealth and intellectual stimulation that encouraged him to produce by the end of the decade some of his shrewdest interpretations of the European scene. Somewhat to his surprise Mowrer found Germany, partly because of its "loony atmosphere...anything but an unpleasant spot to work in." Settling into a two-story apartment, with Dorothy Thompson subletting the floor above, the Mowrers responded quickly to the "zany," ambivalent character of Weimar Germany. Mowrer found the Germans' passion for learning and abstract thought as appealing as he did their genuine interest in other countries. The scars of defeat were everywhere apparent, yet he concluded by 1928 that the nation had a real chance of achieving the democracy he believed most Germans desired.[40]

Berlin had the distinction in the twenties of having the only two American news bureaus on the continent headed by women. Dorothy Thompson held that position for the *Public Ledger* from 1924–28, when she was succeeded by H. R. Knickerbocker. And Sigrid Schultz represented the *Chicago Tribune* in Berlin from 1919 and headed its bureau from 1925 until she was expelled in 1941. But Mowrer and Knickerbocker were undoubtedly the stars of the American journalistic community in the late twenties. Knickerbocker was already winning recognition as an acute observer with a low tolerance for administrative detail.

When Knickerbocker departed for a long Moscow assignment, Albion Ross, his assistant, was astonished to be left without instructions for running the Berlin office, except to consult Edgar Mowrer if he needed help. Inexperienced and with only a German office boy to help him, Ross rushed to Mowrer whom he found ensconced in an impressive *Chicago Daily News* office over a café at the corner of Unter den Linden and Friedrichstrasse. Mowrer was generous but so brilliantly idiosyncratic that he intimidated the unassuming Ross. Paul Mowrer had earlier sized up his younger brother as "a bubbling caldron of miscellaneous philosophical and literary ideas. He must bubble over every few minutes or he would burst." In 1935 Gunther described Mowrer in his diary as "the most persistently engaging conversationalist I know...passionate, gloomy, explosive with biases (of the right kind), overwrought, and very sweet when he relaxed.... I think he is the best educated American I have ever met, Vincent Sheean possibly excepted. He is, unlike Sheean, a severe moralist. There is a touch of Lincoln in Edgar; and of Shelly [*sic*] and of Mohammed."[41]

But of the American journalists in Berlin, Louis Lochner perhaps entered most fully into the life of the city and the nation. Lochner's family connections familiarized him with many of Weimar Germany's leading figures and with such carryovers from the imperial past as the kaiser's grandson, Prince Louis Ferdinand, "a close friend." Lochner's interest in the arts brought him contacts with another significant stratum of Berlin life. He became a friend and literary agent of Maxim Gorki, who wrote a preface for Lochner's book on Henry Ford's peace mission.[42]

In addition to doing routine work for the Associated Press, Lochner interviewed nearly every leading artist, performer, or political leader who passed through the German capital. Under an assumed name, he reported on the German musical scene for *Musical Arts*. Over the years he interviewed conductor Wilhelm Furtwängler, cellist Gregor Piatigorsky (a personal friend), Ottorino Respighi, Mrs. Fritz Kreisler, Max Reinhardt, and Luigi Pirandello. In politics, Lochner was equally ubiquitous, interviewing at various times such figures as Gustav Stresemann, Hjalmar Schacht, Franz von Papen, Konstantin von Neurath, President Hindenburg, and the wife of Marshal Józef Pilsudski of Poland. He chatted with Cardinal Pacelli, the future Pope Pius XII, at a luncheon of the Foreign Press Association, and was impressed by the cardinal's breadth of learning. He noted the passage through Berlin of a succession of American visitors and performers, notably Paul Whiteman—who "came, saw and conquered" and was "dippy about Berlin," which in turn was "nutty" about his jazz—as well as Nicholas Murray Butler, the president of Columbia University, and tennis champion Bill Tilden.[43]

Amid these encounters, the Lochners managed to sandwich in regular visits to the opera, concert halls, theaters and films, as well as a continuous round of teas and suppers. For nearly twenty years Lochner sent a steady stream of letters to his American relatives describing this rich, if exhausting, round of activities. Although he frequently complained of overwork, it is far from clear where his work left off and his social life began. What is obvious is that Lochner loved his work and left a copious record of upper middle-class life in the years surrounding the rise to power of the Nazis. He had little time or need for visits to the Adlon bar or the other haunts which attracted the usual gatherings of correspondents.[44]

London remained the premier prestige assignment, however, by tradition and general consent the acme of the profession, although the advent of radio and the proliferation of news sources had undermined its technologically strategic location. Gunther had managed to leapfrog from Vienna to London for the *Daily News* in 1935 on the strength of his growing reputation and restiveness. He remained only a year, long enough to complete the draft of *Inside Europe* which ended his career as a journeyman correspondent. But in his short stay he proved a worthy successor, socially if not journalistically, to Edward Price Bell. He cultivated high society and hobnobbed with an assortment of the political and social elite that would have made Bell envious and that accurately mirrored the new status accorded leading foreign correspondents.

Vincent Sheean indicated the possibilities of the London post in congratulating Gunther in 1935. A London correspondent's job was "the grandest there is in journalism, I think," Sheean wrote. "I always used to hanker after it, vaguely and hopelessly, the way a dog yowls for the moon.... The correspondent of an important American paper is a Personage: he is treated quite differently from his equal colleague on the continent; his self-respect occasionally blooms out a little too much and becomes frog-chested, but anyhow it's a wonderful thing for the innards .... I'd rather have that job than be managing editor of a paper.... You'll have a grand time in London. With Rebecca West and Lady Oxford (to name but two) eating out of your hand the town will be yours." This was a far cry from Bell's 1910 complaint that "certain distinguished Englishmen will extend their hospitality to almost any kind of hobo from America but strictly draw the line at a newspaper man."[45]

Constantine Brown, a long-time *Daily News* correspondent, pointed out to Charles Dennis in 1927 that different news gathering techniques were required in different countries. In France it was always possible to purchase directly any information wanted, but the British required a more subtle approach. In London, membership in the right club was essential, held Brown, who may have been interested in justifying his expense account. In such surroundings he had been able to play bridge regularly with Prime Minister Stanley Baldwin's private secretary.[46]

If the life of an American correspondent in Europe had its full share of excitement, color, pleasures, and temptations, it was not, however, an unalloyed delight. The satisfactions of observing history in the making were, no doubt, real enough; but there was a great deal of drudgery, boredom, and alienation to offset the brilliant moments. Sheean, a freer spirit than many and consequently unable or unwilling to settle anywhere for long, noted the boredom and cynicism that affected many correspondents after a time. He and his fellow neophytes in the early twenties had been "avid for experience, interested in everything"; but most of the veterans seemed already tired and discouraged, "like a pack of jaded dramatic reviewers, familiar with the play, but profoundly uninterested in the material." Hampered by official or unofficial censorship and repelled by the shortsighted, unimaginative behavior of statesmen and nations, the horrified Sheean after two years of Europe dashed off to Morocco to begin a free-lance, travelling career.[47]

Another disillusioned correspondent was George Seldes, angered by the controls publishers imposed on their reporters' efforts to expose financial and political manipulations behind the scenes of official policy and routine news. Seldes accused many of his colleagues of corruption or tacit cooperation with the international political and economic elite. He conceded that a few of the younger correspondents were more analytical in their approach than the majority—naming in particular the Mowrers, Knickerbocker, Walter Duranty, and W. H. Chamberlin (the latter two correspondents in the Soviet Union primarily). But the rest he found mired in routine and indifference, taking advantage of the freedom from close supervision by their home offices. Most of them contented themselves, he thought, with casual treatment of important issues and "never had a thought in the world outside the production of news." Seldes's biting comments suggest an alternative to the glamorous stereotypes:

> Some of my colleagues drank themselves to death, several reformed, some made love to each other's wives, one committed suicide, several were married or divorced or psychoanalyzed, most of them shot dice or played poker, one made a fortune in foreign real estate, two wrote poetry, one collected shoes, nearly all tried their hands at plays and novels—in short, they were very much the same as the American diplomatic, consular, military and commercial groups to be found in all foreign countries. . . .
>
> Generally speaking, the majority of foreign correspondents in my time, were men who took no sides, who did "straight" reporting, spent most of their time in their offices, wrote few think pieces, kept themselves neutral in all political storms, never entered entangling alliances (except amorous) in European countries, and maintained pretty well the American provincial attitude of sneering down everything foreign.[48]

If Seldes's assessment was harsh, it depicted only one side of the correspondents' experience. It was not, in many ways, an easy life and the casualties were numerous. Money was scarce but the temptations to extravagance were many. Family life was difficult, with liaisons, divorces, and remarriages frequent. Children led a somewhat rootless existence or had to be sent home to America for school. Trips to the United States were rare and brief, and alienation both from American and from Europe was a familiar response. Few could have remained unaffected by so unsettled an existence. That their circumstances undermined their "Americanness," as some editors and publishers seemed to fear, was doubtful. But they were Americans with a difference, with a new perspective on themselves, their work, and their native land. Given the nature of their lives and duties, these special points of view began to manifest themselves quite early.

If the correspondents developed toward each other a mutuality based upon common circumstances and concerns—despite inevitable rivalries or differences—they experienced considerably greater ambivalences toward other groups with which personal or occupational ties involved them. The United States, their home and that of their families, stirred many memories or associations both warm and otherwise. Some had left home reluctantly or inadvertently, others eagerly or at least readily. Still, few could avoid at least occasional moods of nostalgia, curiosity, or anticipation and reassessment. More often, the very nature of their work bore in upon them the fact that their employers and superiors in the home offices held very different assumptions and expectations than their own.

With these remote associates, upon whose cooperation they depended but whose understanding of their own special needs and interests they seldom could take for granted, the correspondents were bound in an essential but inherently uneasy relationship. The longer they remained overseas and the more confident and experienced they became in their work, the greater was the likelihood that they should feel divided from—and unappreciated by—their American colleagues. The longer they remained in Europe, the surer they became that they were involved in a serious turning point in the fortunes of the continent and of the United States as well. The more confident their judgments of the European scene became, the more inevitable were the differences separating them from editors at home. The very structure of their lives ensured that they should come to consider themselves a group apart, at odds with their home country, their employers and superiors, and even with their European hosts.

4

Initiation
Europe from Impressions
to Analysis

■ That one people's reaction to another is strongly influenced by its own self-image has been suggested by historian Akira Iriye; and the perception seems equally applicable to individuals.[1] American journalists approached Europe with a variety of purposes, plans, and expectations in mind, so it is hardly surprising that what they found upon their arrival and their reactions to these early encounters varied considerably. That Europe in the twenties differed in many respects from its prewar patterns, and that the 1930s were separated from both of the earlier periods by fundamental social, institutional, and psychological changes is obvious. So is the fact that an American reaching London at any of those times would have found a different set of circumstances than would have faced him had his destination been Rome, for instance, or Vienna. In the light of such diversity it may seem futile to look for any common responses. And yet, and perhaps not so surprisingly, certain similarities and shared themes can be found both in the correspondents' early impressions and in their more mature views.

These areas of agreement or convergence in understanding are highlighted and possibly exaggerated by limiting our attention at this point largely to the 1920s. There is justification for so doing, however, in the fact that the decade brought an influx of alert young American reporters across the Atlantic. It also saw a marked growth in the range of observation and the critical capacities of the older correspondents as well. With a new self-consciousness of their own special circumstances and vantage point, American journalists now readily accepted the responsibility of interpreting European affairs for their American readers.

Occasional analytical comments on Europe and Europeans had been scattered through the correspondence and copy of prewar reporters, to be sure. But preoccupation with establishing connections and routines, with scoring "beats," and with convincing still-dubious employers of the value of their services probably discouraged more thoughtful, far-ranging observations. Furthermore, the knowledge that their editors were interested chiefly in eye-catching spot news or in touching human interest vignettes hardly encouraged more ambitious efforts. True, the dean of turn-of-the-century American correspondents, George W. Smalley, had published a volume of *Anglo-American Memories* upon his return to New York. But these essays, gleaned from his years of reporting, were chiefly chatty reminiscences of British elite political and countryhouse society, revealing more about Smalley's and his American readers' interests than about the richness of his opportunities for observation. During the war Frederic Wile had written books on the Germans and the British while Carl Ackerman, Berlin correspondent for the United Press, authored *Germany: The Next Republic?;* but these, although more analytical than Smalley's, were highly colored by wartime preconceptions.[2]

PREWAR IMPRESSIONS

Edward Price Bell had been touched by English political life, London's poverty, and "practical altruism" at Toynbee Hall on his visit in 1896,[3] but when he returned as correspondent for the *Chicago Record* in 1899 he was preoccupied with his new responsibilities. At the outset Bell felt nearly overwhelmed. The British government offered no assistance to foreign correspondents, and other newspapermen were of little help. Even the arrival of his wife and baby daughter and of Frederic Wile did little to ease Bell's problems. However welcome, the presence of a young family brought additional complications and responsibilities, while the need to edit copy passing through London from correspondents on the Continent and in Africa and Asia made further demands on his time and energies. From the first, Bell had had doubts about the London assignment, despite his appreciation of the opportunity it offered. It was a venture into the unknown, and he worried over the financial hazards it entailed as well, no doubt, as over the possibility of failure. Only repeated reassurances by Lawson and Dennis, an early salary increase, a scaling down of the foreign service, and Bell's own energy and determination to succeed combined to see him through an extremely trying time.

Soon he was establishing contacts with London hotel managers to secure access to their guest lists. With an instinct for establishing well-placed connections, Bell arranged an interview with statesman Joseph Chamberlain and cultivated the influential English editor, W. T. Stead, and the American ambassador, Joseph H. Choate. He developed cordial relations with British journalists and government officials, as well as with members of London's international community. In addition, executing Lawson's instructions for furnishing the Trafalgar Square bureau, as well as greeting and assisting influential visitors from Chicago, took much of his time.

At the same time, Bell's widening circle of London acquaintances involved him in an active social life that richly served his personal and journalistic needs. If, amid a seemingly endless round of activities, he relied heavily on interviews with important figures for his own stories, he can hardly be criticized for that. What is remarkable is the extent to which, despite distractions, he managed to evolve out of the constraints and resources of his position an ambitious conception of foreign correspondence and to communicate it to his associates. Bell soon developed a distaste for the easier pace of his fellow journalists who gathered their stories in the sociable atmosphere of the city's bars and cafés. These, he wrote Dennis in 1906, were "the curse of continental correspondence. Here the journalists gather and eat and smoke and drink and dream."[4]

In the decade between his arrival in London and that of Mowrer in Paris, Bell came to believe that Europe held, in addition to casual human interest stories and news of immediate popular appeal, more significant issues, ideas, and experiences than American journalism had yet discovered. And he suspected, too, despite discouragement from Chicago, that American readers would welcome such material despite the distance separating them from the life of Europe. To a friend at home, Bell had already expressed the wish that "more of our people would come abroad ...with a feeling of sympathy for other nations and a determination to gather knowledge and inspiration from their travels. It is easy to quarrel with usages not our own; it is better to bring insight to bear upon them and thus...to understand them. Thus we please ourselves and enrich ourselves and cause to rise among other peoples a more favorable impression of Americans." Bell urged his *Daily News* colleagues to consider, "What were the Emperors, Kings, Queens, *elite* doing? What the Government? Who were the outstanding personalities and what did they come to? What are the *people* feeling, thinking, doing? What was the national story from the peak to the pit of the country's life?"[5] The advice combined his own early leaning toward high-level contacts with a broader, more ambitious conception of what foreign correspondence might become.

If Bell grasped more fully than most prewar journalists that Europe challenged serious understanding and interpretation, a number of his colleagues were struck by features of life that differed sharply from those with which they were familiar at home and which provoked their curiosity. On his initial visit to England, Bell had recorded his impressions of the "compact" buildings and the absence of skyscrapers in Liverpool. To this young midwesterner, "compact life, compact activity" had registered an obvious characteristic whose meaning he was already pondering.[6]

Frederic Wile spent a good deal of his short stay in London among members of the American community. He was impressed by the extent of the American presence there and his own initially anti-British sentiments probably encouraged such associations. In less than a year Wile was transferred to Berlin, so he had little time to develop lasting associations or conclusions. Later two impressions remained in his memory: British condescension toward Americans and widespread drunkenness in the nighttime London streets. Wythe Williams, who reached England a few years later, found London and Europe generally moving "at a slower pace than the growing United States," and commented afterwards on the "tranquil, easy-going life of the city."[7]

Wile spoke no German when he reported for duty in Berlin. Trained in Chicago and London, he was among the first to test Bell's and Lawson's thesis that success as a foreign correspondent depended less on familiarity with the language and culture of one's assigned country than upon a thorough grounding in the methods and objectives of the *Daily News* service. Despite his regard for Wile as a friend and colleague, Bell continued to send advice from London. According to Bell, Wile found the German capital "somewhat of a virgin field" so far as news gathering was concerned, "more like London was before the A.P. awoke to a desire to cover everything." Germany proved to be a satisfying assignment and "a happy country" for Wile, although as a Jew he was sensitive to a deep, if not obvious, anti-Semitism. He also observed the dominance of business and military interests and reported frequently on preparations for war which he later termed "of long standing, extensive, systematic and transparently purposeful"; but he could arouse little interest in the subject on the part of either American or British readers. In 1908 Viscount Northcliffe commissioned Wile to write a book on the Germans, whom he later described as "a hearty, healthy race of intelligent, patriotic, tolerant, hospitable, home-loving, music-worshipping folk who also ate ravenously, and sometimes audibly, and drank freely, but capably." Reminiscing long after his retirement, Wile still puzzled at the "mystery" of why this admirable people had succumbed to militarism.[8]

Wile was succeeded in his Berlin *Daily News* post by Albert C. Wilkie, who in turn was followed by Raymond Swing under circumstances described earlier. Swing had the advantage of fluent German and, despite the unpleasantness surrounding his appointment, he settled into Berlin comfortably enough. At first he found the city less interesting than Paris or Munich, but its politics full of "energy and assertiveness." He had ample time to enjoy life there because his assignment consisted largely of supplying human interest features and greeting visiting Chicagoans. As he gained familiarity with the German scene, however, Swing became aware of more serious matters. Like Wile, he found evidence of military preparations and alerted Chicago to them but failed to impress his editors with their significance. Swing's inability to place substantial, important stories irritated him. His personal life was complicated with the coming of the war because he had married a French woman who had recently presented him with a son. Bell feared that the tense situation might cause Swing to leave the *Daily News*; instead, his wife returned to the United States and, ironically, the coming of war eased Swing's discontent by allowing him more important reporting responsibilities. By no means hostile to the Germans, Swing tried to present their position accurately—and incurred Bell's criticism for so doing. By 1916 his success in evading censorship had attracted the suspicion of the government. Relations between the American embassy and the American press in Berlin had become difficult. By the time German-American relations were broken off, Swing was more than ready to return home.[9]

One of the most perceptive early observers of twentieth-century Europe was certainly Paul Mowrer. Mowrer threw himself into the life of Paris, relishing the exuberance of its street life, theaters, operas, and concert halls. He attended meetings of a group of "vers-librists...longhaired and ragged and velvet-clad freaks," and he met such figures as Anatole France and Socialist Jean Jaurès. He interviewed Marie Curie and Sarah Bernhardt, eliciting from the latter the opinion that American women seemed bored because they did not have enough to do. In search of feature stories to satisfy Lawson, he examined such topics as French landscape design, woman suffrage, a labor university in Belgium, "England's Militant Women," American tourists—including a visiting professional baseball team—and, of course, the obligatory fashion stories with special attention to the new harem skirt. He vacationed in England and met Bell for the first time, describing him as an "incessant, often brilliant" conversationalist. Mowrer's wife and his mother, who visited them, enjoyed Parisian cultural life as much as he. His literary interests, perhaps, made him especially sensitive to other cultures and peoples, to the need to defer judgments and observe widely and carefully. He roamed the countryside, vacationing at the seashore and in the mountains. Eventually, the Mowrers bought a farmhouse outside Paris for weekend use.[10]

Meanwhile, Mowrer was increasingly unhappy with the "tourist bureau" functions he was expected to fulfill. The *Daily News* offices were across from the Café de la Paix, "luxuriously filled, like a club...with palms and Oriental rugs and leather armchairs." The American tourists Mowrer encountered considered Europe a "playground," while he was coming to see the continent as a tinderbox. Despite orders "not to concern myself too much with European politics," Mowrer was beginning to do precisely that. Local wars in North Africa and the Balkans seemed omens of more serious imperial rivalries. When he answered instructions to collect French jokes for the Chicago funny papers with a suggestion that a reporter be sent to the Balkans to observe conditions there, however, Mowrer was pleased to receive the assignment himself. The trip confirmed both his impression that all was not well with Europe and his reputation as a serious reporter. His reports were well placed in the *Daily News* with a coveted by-line, and in Paris he received an invitation to write articles on the Balkans for *L'Illustration*.[11]

Mowrer's concept of himself, of his ambitions, and of human nature in general were changing under the influence of such diverse exposures. He returned from the Balkans more skeptical of human motives and more aware of the fragile qualities of peace and civilization. He also had begun to question not his love and dedication to literature, but his exclusive commitment to it. "I doubt," he commented in an undated note written probably sometime in 1913, "if I am meant to write fiction. May not the powers of imagination which seem to impel me to it be just as valuable in other forms—in the article, the essay, the book of imagination or of thought?" When he returned for a brief visit to the United States in 1914 Mowrer learned still another lesson, the fleeting character of journalistic fame. No one discussed his Balkan stories or the European situation; attention was focussed on the Mexican border where American troops were pursuing the colorful Pancho Villa.[12]

Even more intense in responding to Europe than Paul Mowrer was his brother, Edgar, who visited Paris in 1911 while still a student and returned there in 1913 hoping to make his way as a writer and literary critic. Edgar faced few of life's experiences mildly, and Paris called forth his most passionate feelings. "Paris was civilization, the first I had ever seen," he recalled later. His letters to his mother at the time bear out his recollections. "It took me nearly a week to get accustomed to Paris. The streets run in all possible directions and frequently curve about. Everything is lovely," he wrote initially. A month later, his enthusiasm still sparkled while his observations had become more discriminating. "I am becoming enamored of Paris," he conceded. The pursuit of pleasure there might not always be "absolutely admirable," but he appreciated even the "old bloody selfish kings" who had slaughtered their subjects but saved the forests and parks for their personal pleasure. Parisians, Edgar found, were "simple people...almost enigmatical" in their freedom of behavior, which Americans tended to repress, and in their love of art and culture. Some might think them decadent, he conceded, but the strength of their patriotism was undeniable.[13]

Edgar moved from Paul's apartment to the Latin Quarter where his brother remembered him shopping for breakfast each morning in a blue bathrobe. Study at the Sorbonne was "the center of life" for him. He became intrigued with metaphysics, the "solidarism" of Charles-Bernard Renouvier, and the "vitalism" of Henri Bergson. He practiced the flute, wrote poetry, and flourished in the company of students and expatriates. Never hesitant to express his views, he found in contemporary art the "dissolution of past cultural patterns and...[a] search for new ones." France quickly became a "second home" for Mowrer. Despite growing international tensions, he settled in happily until the war intervened. But he also had begun to react against "irresponsible aesthetic experimentation." Europe's cultural scene, paralleling its politics, seemed "an amusing, fascinating, fermenting chaos that juggles with the great ideas of the past with a sort of feverish grace—but still a chaos."[14]

PRIVATE LIFE

With the return of peace in 1919 and the arrival of a younger, more self-assured generation of reporters, comments on the character of European society and culture, like comparisons with the United States, became more frequent. American interests aroused by the war undoubtedly encouraged such speculative and interpretive writing. Certainly editors and publishers at home showed greater receptivity to thoughtful, as well as merely colorful or entertaining, reporting. And the eager junior journalists seemed almost to have reached Europe primed with questions, expectations, and assumptions, confident of their ability to record significant impressions and reactions.

They did, however, defer to the ablest of their seniors; and Paul Mowrer, strategically located in Paris, with a distinguished record of war reporting and close ties to French governmental and literary circles, offered a highly visible role model. Mowrer had become disillusioned with the failure of reason and idealism to guide public affairs in resolving the tangle of national interests and ambitions that surrounded the Versailles settlement. Refreshed by a visit home, Mowrer returned full of plans for a more highly developed, sophisticated foreign news service. He undertook a trip through eastern Europe to report on American relief missions in Austria and Poland and to assess the conditions and prospects of the new Balkan nations in the region he had visited before the war. His reports from this journey won Mowrer the respect of serious readers while suggesting to younger journalists some hitherto unnoted possibilities for fame and accomplishment.[15]

Balkanized Europe, based on Mowrer's travel reports, deals primarily with the economic and political obstacles to continental peace, stability, and progress; but he wrote also of social and psychological factors complicating, when they did not utterly defeat, the search for compromise between divergent interests. Age-old ethnic and national jealousies remained strong, he noted, to a degree incomprehensible in the United States. The break-up of the Austro-Hungarian Empire in the name of national self-determination had inflamed more than it alleviated traditional enmities and suspicions. Such resentments were further aggravated by threats and propaganda from the new Soviet government in Russia and by Great Power interventions from the West. Even the American Red Cross relief missions to eastern Europe had encountered xenophobic reactions inexplicable to naive humanitarians. Mowrer concluded that European tendencies to succumb to Bolshevism were waning and would fade faster with the return of stable conditions, but the long-range picture he painted was hardly an encouraging one.

In a separate *Atlantic Monthly* article he noted still another complicating factor, "the revival of anti-Semitism in Europe since the close of the war and its curious repercussions even in the United States." Terming tales of Jewish plots to dominate the world "ingenious fantasy [that would] not bear analysis" and the work of "conservative chauvinists" in the West, Mowrer still saw a basis for the widespread hatred of the Jews in eastern Europe where they had lived for centuries without assimilating. The identification of some Jews with Bolshevism, he thought, further aggravated racial antipathies. He could see no solution to the anti-Semitism either in Europe or America except in a clear choice by Jews, either for a "single allegiance" or for removal to Palestine "under the flag of Israel itself."[16]

Although *Balkanized Europe* was well reviewed in America it was not a popular success. Not only were Mowrer's observations and conclusions disturbing, but his approach and style were somewhat heavy-handed—a measure, perhaps, of the seriousness with which he viewed the European scene and of the responsibilities of foreign correspondence as he conceived it. Such shortcomings may have encouraged Victor Lawson somewhat later to publish reports from quite a different kind of Balkan trip. Negley Farson's proposal to cross Europe by boat to report on the life and conditions of the people he met along the way sounded more like the old-fashioned human interest journalism Lawson so prized. Indeed, it was. Farson had the down-to-earth, observant, yet good-humored eye, and the easy-going, readable manner that Lawson had long been urging his staff to cultivate. His interest was in people more than politics, and his style was that of a rough-and-tumble, liberated Richard Harding Davis.

Farson's *Sailing Across Europe*, published in 1926, appeared first as articles in the *Daily News*. They pulsed with the variegated life of the postwar continent keenly observed from the deck of a riverboat passing leisurely through its midst. From young Germans doing calisthenics along the river banks and feverish industrial activity at the Krupp works and the Ruhr, Farson deduced "the inevitable comeback of this [German] people. Germany seemed a nation in training." Yet there were homeless drifters in the woods near Nürnberg, nomads and youthful wanderers trying "to walk out of this [industrial] age." Vienna cafés, Budapest, "the most adorable, bewitching, and intoxicating city in Europe," and interviews with high American and Hungarian officials all passed under Farson's catholic view and were set down in readable, animated prose.[17]

In the Balkans, Farson found the makings of ethnic and national conflicts: Russian refugees, charming, generous peasants "scratched and inoculated" by dynastic rivalries. "One feels almost certain that the Balkan problem would not be a problem if the local Bismarcks and so-called diplomats of Paris, London, and Berlin, could only find a new plaything," he wrote. He described good, simple people and wicked politics; Rumanians who had returned to their native land from America and regretted the change; corruption and "diseased ideals" in the cities and courts while virtue reigned in the countryside; and bribery and subservience where low wages and miserable living conditions drove men to seek every possible advantage. It was a colorful catalog, accurate if limited in scope, and tolerant in its affirmation that seemingly perverse and inexplicable customs could be understood in the light of the circumstances underlying them. Farson entertained his readers and opened their eyes, but he did not demand too much of them. He also encouraged their complaisance by remarking that Sinclair Lewis's critiques of materialism in the United States seemed mild from the perspective of Bucharest. Farson, too, had once laughed at America, he noted; but after seeing the Balkans he would never do so again.[18] Europe might be lively and colorful, but America's superiority was unquestioned.

Another book of early impressions, Edgar Ansel Mowrer's *Immortal Italy*, appeared in 1922, striking an equally personal, even rhapsodic note. Mowrer had been intrigued by the contrast between American materialism and technocratic virtuosity and the variety, life, intellect, and rich tradition of the Old World. In an opening chapter entitled "Where Dreams Come True," he listed the many ways in which Italian life was richer and more fulfilling than that of the United States. In language that might have been the envy of a chamber of commerce publicist or a writer of travel brochures, he managed to turn even acknowledged Italian deficiencies into assets. Italy was undoubtedly poor and overpopulated, yet even its tenements were often better built than the homes of the American rich, and there was an almost organic unity of man and nature lacking at home. Italians might appear amoral, but their realism and strong family feeling were preferable to the seemingly stronger "moral sense or respect for public opinion" so widespread in the United States.[19]

Italy's demerits were easily seen; the virtues of its openness to life and pleasure, its frankness about sex, its lack of false shame, might be less apparent. But for Mowrer these qualities, added to the ever-present evidence and influence of its rich history, made Italian life "indescribably delicious." As he progressed in his writing, he became more critical, conceding that Italians tended to be boastful, subject to flattery, egoistic and nationalistic. Yet their "lack of constraint" and insistence upon freedom in their private lives was "inexplicably attractive. . . . Here men are free, free to be idle, vicious, drunken, selfish, careless of others; but also to be sincere, free to think and act above or below the level of group opinion, as their own minds dictate and their own limitations permit." Political life in postwar Italy troubled Mowrer, enough, in fact, so that two years after the publication of this book he was ready to leave the country; but his outpouring of affection for the Italians and their culture revealed both his personal responsiveness and his reservations about his own native land.[20]

No other American correspondent of the 1920s devoted an entire book to consideration of the European scene, and even Paul Mowrer's and Negley Farson's volumes were essentially extended newspaper series. Yet few reporters could fail to observe, ponder, and react to the diverse features of a society which they found on the whole so pleasantly different from America. Scattered through their published writings and more copiously in their correspondence can readily be found evidence of their responses—both at the time and in afterthought. Raymond Swing, returning to Berlin in 1919, found the city friendlier and more relaxed under the Weimar government than he had remembered it earlier. There was a flowering of artistic creativity and spirit into which he and his family entered happily. Most complete and perhaps unself-conscious were Louis Lochner's letters regaling his American family with his satisfaction in the busy social and cultural rounds of his life in Berlin. At times, Lochner even felt called upon to apologize for his way of life, as when he wrote in 1928, "my week brings so much variety that I sometimes fear you who read my accounts must think we are enjoying one continuous holiday, forgetting that . . . work . . . at the office is often exceedingly hard."[21]

John Gunther's reports struck a practical note. Paris was "the cheapest capital in the world," he pointed out in explaining why so many young American artists congregated there. In an article titled "What Paris Really Needs is a Good 5-and-10," he noted the abundance of small neighborhood shops and superb restaurants but found prices of food and necessities high and lamented the absence not only of Woolworth's, but also of convenience food stores and inexpensive restaurants. Gunther held it "undeniable that European life is softer, smoother, more mellowed, more deliberate" than life in America, where there was "no place to sit down." Governments were more responsive in Europe, Gunther felt. There was greater freedom to express oneself, no Prohibition, no Mann Act. "Maybe as a result youthful immorality is infinitely less frequent, or at least less blatant than it seems to be in the United States." Somewhat later Gunther noted the biased and limited news of the United States carried in central European newspapers. Crime, scandal, and public personalities commanded attention, and American politics was badly covered; but, then, European papers got most of their news directly from the American press.[22]

Features of European society most widely noted by the correspondents included freedom for experimentation and exploration, whether in ideas, alcohol, or sex; the value placed upon art, culture, and leisure; the variety of its history and its cultures; its relaxation and realism in contrast to America's moralistic idealism; and its respect for considerations other than material success and progress. Variations on these themes appear with almost predictable regularity in both the contemporary and retrospective writings of every correspondent from Dorothy Thompson in Vienna to William Stoneman in Stockholm, who found the Swedes "a highly civilized, modern-minded people who ran their country, their industry and themselves better than we managed to do at home," and who found his time there "a mild and charming introduction to the life in Europe at its very nicest," or to David Darrah in Rome where "the abundance of life was . . . bewildering and its buoyance seemed irrepressible." William L. Shirer found London less pleasant a few years later, its residents "insufferable" in their condescension toward and resentment of Americans. When Edmond Taylor, who had discovered in 1925 an alternative to American materialism in European artistic circles, returned as a reporter in 1928 he found society more humane, relaxed, and historically aware than at home. With an "old-fashioned attachment to the human and the personal" it was like being in "an earlier, more human America."[23]

France awakened Leland Stowe to many dimensions of life he had failed to appreciate at home. He and his wife visited the museums, cathedrals, and chateaux, and he tried to make up for lost time by reading history and economics, having little time for literary studies. Stowe later termed himself "not only a slow grower . . . but a late bloomer (to the extent that it happened)." But despite an often hectic schedule, his zest for life ensured that he made the most of the opportunities that came his way. On a 1929 trip to Madrid, he wrote his impressions to his sisters. The countryside had been "very arid and quite desolate for miles upon miles —much as I imagine Arizona would look." Madrid was surprisingly modern: "It contrasts with Paris, because restaurants are so scarce there." He had noticed that many Spanish women wore only a bit of lace over their beautiful, thick hair. The Spanish were the noisiest people Stowe had ever encountered. "You almost have to shout to be able to talk in a café. . .at first it is pretty tiring on the nerves. The young men appear especially rowdyish and boisterous, annoyingly so. You can't picture them being serious about anything for very long."[24]

Albion Ross, reaching Paris from New York at the very end of the decade, repeated the experience of his predecessors. "I reckon that my life began on a morning in March," before the church of St. Sulpice in Paris, he wrote. "Suddenly the world seemed possessed of many dimensions and I felt dizzy, as perhaps newborn infants do." Ross was shocked, too, at the quality of French automobiles, as he had assumed until then that American technology was the world's best.[25]

But it was left to Edgar Mowrer to emphasize a quite different aspect of European life—the extent to which the Continent was beginning to resemble the United States. In a volume that appeared in 1928 with the title *This American World*, Mowrer pointed out that America was, after all, a child of European civilization and had drawn heavily on its parent. Now, Europe was weakened and America strong; and although both the Continent's elite and its radicals might "bitterly resent American plutocratic ideals and standardized mediocrity," the masses "fall ready victims to the lures of American life," its "luscious" material benefits. To Europeans already concerned about the dangers of "Americanization," Mowrer held out solace. Europe could recoup strength and wealth by following the lead of the United States. American self-confidence and "reforming zeal" might offend, but the "old European culture is decrepit. Its vitality seems to be running away in a sort of diabetic self-destruction." In any event, there would be limits to the Americanizing process, although Mowrer's discussion of them may not have been as consoling as he thought. The power of the "democratic masses, techniques [and] materialistic ambitions" was too strong to be resisted, however hard Europe might try. But such forces were, after all, European in origin; little wonder their appeal was very nearly as potent there as across the Atlantic. Germany was likely to succumb rather readily and most of eastern Europe would pose no serious difficulties to the Americanizing forces, Mowrer thought. Technology and mass education were spreading a single civilization, "however thinly," over the globe. "Finance and democracy, technique and science" were supreme. America was their embodiment and must therefore lead.[26]

Not all American journalists shared the enthusiasm with which the majority greeted European society and culture. There were critics and dissenters, some clearly more thoughtful than others. Floyd Gibbons, who left Europe in 1925 for a career in radio at home, conceded that life in Europe excelled in "simpler pleasures"; although poor and fearful of the future, people lived "better and easier on what they have" there. Yet Gibbons, despite the glamorous life he enjoyed abroad, concluded that there is "no place like the United States," where "folks is folks, not classes."[27]

Ben Hecht, who worked for the *Chicago Daily News* in Berlin from 1918 to 1920, quickly tired of the "Pandora's box of Europe." Postwar Germany provided some dramatic experiences, but too much "inhumanity" and too many "zanies." Hecht's "young cynicism lost much of its grin" as anti-Semitism and political instability embittered him. He asked for a recall, saying that he was bored and preferred Chicago.[28]

Samuel Spevack, born in Europe, returned there in 1922 from New York—where he had imbibed the notion of European superiority—as correspondent for the *New York World*. In 1926 the *Saturday Evening Post* published an article by Spevack proclaiming "Four Years in Europe Made Me an American." The New York intelligentsia believed, he wrote, that "Europe is the place to live"; it has "culture...everything America has not." Despite having a correspondent's independence, comfortable conditions, social status, prestige, and sense of observing history in the making, Spevack was disillusioned by Europe. The war had made the Continent "a League of Nations of tired old businessmen.... Europe in 1926 is and must be composed of money grubbers...absorbed in the problem of food and a patched roof." Nor was the vaunted culture to be envied; Europe offered "no culture not obtainable in America, while it deprives you of the new culture America is producing.... America alone offers culture." America had drawn away the best European artists, writers, and scientists. "Europe is standing still. It is looking backward." In Berlin, the housing shortage, the need to file endless police reports, the officious bureaucracy, all rankled. American jazz had conquered Germany, and the Germans were too exhausted to resist. "Jazz becomes the escape from the general stagnation, from the cold sogginess of the Prussian soil, from the creaking measured heaviness of existing." Nor was Germany alone: Paris had "fifth-rate opera houses with fifth-rate singers [and] mediocre concerts," and Italian singers were no better than American. Only two reasons remained for living in Europe, said Spevack: "dipsomania and laziness."[29]

Spevack's critique was echoed by George Seldes, who returned to the United States in 1927 discouraged not only by the state of journalism but by the spread of unrest, totalitarianism, terror, and reaction. Turkey, Seldes noted ironically, was at least one country in which terror and dictatorship were accompanied by constructive acts.[30] Already by the 1920s some American correspondents, if not necessarily Seldes, were beginning to look homeward with increased respect and longing as they contemplated Europe's circumstances.

PUBLIC LIFE

Seldes's discontent derived more from Europe's political and economic plight than from its social or cultural features. Postwar continental politics generally shocked and frustrated correspondents, highlighting American values and assumptions lying not far beneath the surface of their fledgling cosmopolitanism. Despite their disappointment with the United States, most reporters, even those who had matured professionally on the seamy corruption of urban government at home, were unprepared for the relentless, life-and-death clash of interests and national rivalries they found in the Old World. Reactions ranged from hasty idealization of the men and movements seeming to offer new directions for a war-weary, disillusioned age, to cynicism and disgust at entrenched selfishness, greed, or reaction. Although they may not have recognized it, most of the journalists were too deeply imbued with progressive American assumptions about the virtues of compromise and adaptation to change to come easily to terms with Europe's ingrained, distrustful politics. And those who did, such as Paul Mowrer, risked their credibility with their editors and readers. Yet there was an unexpected beneficial aspect of the gulf separating American and European political sensibilities. More skeptical than when they faced its cultural largesse, the correspondents cast a more critical eye on the Continent's political and, to a degree, its economic life. Thus some of the most thoughtful reporting of the twenties was done in the area of national and international politics.

Paul Mowrer set the pace. *Balkanized Europe*, which he had conceived in part as a response to John Maynard Keynes's *The Economic Consequences of the Peace*, probed further and more perceptively in its political and economic than in its social commentary; Mowrer's data gathering techniques were evidently more systematic and less impressionistic in the former area. He noted that the Versailles settlement had divided eastern Europe into hostile, jealous and suspicious nations when the region desperately needed economic cooperation and integration for survival. Disputes between Great Britain, France, and Italy further aggravated an already disorderly situation, while the spectre of communism spreading from the Soviet Union heightened the prevailing fear and uncertainty. Concluding that communism could not offer most Europeans an acceptable solution to their problems, Mowrer sought to discover the basis upon which some form of stable equilibrium might be achieved.

Solutions, he insisted, must be grounded in a realistic assessment of circumstances. The League of Nations offered in principle the machinery for conciliation and compromise but was too weak to act effectively. Conversely, ideas of national economic self-sufficiency that appealed both to old resentments and to the pride of independence in many new countries were simply impractical. Meanwhile, militarism, mass psychology, and the new techniques of opinion manipulation were roiling the already troubled waters. Mowrer concluded that an answer must eventually come either through "hegemony or federation." He found a "strong vitality" and a widespread spirit of reform, and he predicted a growing role for the state in whatever solutions might emerge. Mowrer anticipated a strong recovery for Germany, which would initially at least add to the unsettling, disruptive forces at work. He offered no specific recommendations, except for a strong appeal that the United States join the League of Nations to add its weight and prestige to the search for an accommodation of interests.[31]

In Italy, Edgar Mowrer was attempting at about the same time to make sense of an extremely complicated and fluid political situation. Mowrer's political instincts were volatile, reflecting his uneasy personal combination of powerful emotions with keen analytical powers. His response to the rise of Benito Mussolini's Fascist regime in 1923 showed unmistakable signs of ambivalence, although in that he was hardly alone. He had shared some of the values that Mussolini professed—a strong desire to see Italy achieve the stability and recognition she deserved and an aversion to communism which he saw as a deadly threat to the future of democracy and of civilization itself.

In *Immortal Italy*, Mowrer had termed the Fascists a "wild faction whose methods are at best illegal, at worst abhorrently barbarous"; but he had also worried that Italy's Socialists were "the most consistently radical party in Europe." Out of the confusion, conflict, and violence marking postwar life, Mowrer optimistically hoped that "a new Italian spirit" was arising. "Despite many appearances the real foundations of national life are much more solid than before the war," he wrote. The energy, patriotism, and rebellion of Italian youth might lead them in the direction of expansion and "brutal egoism" in the absence of "discipline, discipline, discipline and wise tolerance." But, in keeping with the book's enthusiastic tone, he concluded, "I have faith in Italy."[32]

Shortly after Mussolini seized power, Mowrer discussed Italy's future under fascism in *The Forum*. At the outset he appeared laudatory, but there were facts and questions that his keen perception would not permit him to overlook. He began by arguing that Italians had never desired "real self-government" and were satisfied with only its "bare semblance." Socialism had paralyzed the state and terrified the business classes who were supporting Mussolini out of fear. Fascism merely substituted "the dictatorship of a political party for a feeble pseudo-democracy." It had emerged as the most interesting political movement of the time, and if the decline of democracy continued worldwide, it might "become the type of the new Middle Ages." Acknowledging that Italy's economy and politics had begun to stabilize before the Fascists had seized power, he still held that Mussolini's dictatorship, although "brutally illegal," was "economically salutary." The Fascist "hand grenades, clubs and castor oil represent a guarantee against labor troubles," he wrote.[33] If the regime remained in power, Italy's future was hopeful.

The seemingly ambiguous nature of the new Fascist government puzzled Mowrer, as it did many others. There was no denying its authoritarian elements, yet Mowrer refused to classify Mussolini as a "reactionary." The latter favored the widest possible scope for private enterprise but was unwilling to tolerate contests between labor and capital that threatened the national economy. He was "a dictator who had risen by means of a party, but now...is determined to legalize his position and gradually merge the party into the newly organized constitutional life of Italy." The regime, Mowrer suggested, was "a kind of Tory democracy or benevolent Rooseveltian idea of prosperous masses, individualism, militarism, and a strong state all harmonized." Mussolini himself had stated that Italy and the United States had much in common, and that "many Americans, including the mayor of Philadelphia, are spiritual fascisti."[34]

Yet Mowrer could see problems for Italy on the horizon. He discounted Mussolini's expansionist rhetoric in the absence of power to support it, but he saw "blind nationalism," violence, and the restriction of freedom as the price of the restoration of order. The dictatorship paralleled communism in its contempt for popular rule, and its own logic pointed to future complications. Once in power, the party would prove difficult to satisfy; there would not be enough "fat jobs" for all the expectant Fascists. An inherent conflict would emerge between the dictatorship and its capitalist, "free economy" commitments and supporters. As discontent spread, still stronger measures would be required to contain it. Even as he acknowledged Mussolini's regime a "patent despotism," Mowrer could see no alternative for Italy but chaos. He left Italy in 1924, disappointed and disgusted long before many Americans—both in Europe and America—had awakened to the tawdry, fraudulent character of the regime. Having taken fascism's measure there, Mowrer was well prepared to recognize it in Germany a decade later.[35]

George Seldes visited Italy briefly for the first time in 1919. His roving assignments for the *Chicago Tribune* then took him through central Europe and to the Soviet Union before he returned in 1924. By then the shape of the new regime was becoming clearer. Seldes found American correspondents in Rome largely silent on its misdeeds, influenced by censorship, bribes, and intimidation, or by cynicism and the belief that their superiors were not anxious to risk by angering the Fascists the subsidies and favors that greased their operations. The Fascist attack on foreign journalists reached its height in 1926, at the time of the trial of Matteotti's murderer; but between 1925 and 1928, Hiram Motherwell, Mowrer's Chicago *Daily News* successor, and a few other reporters managed to expose some fraudulent government activities.[36]

When American reporters were assigned to democratic nations, they were on more familiar ground, yet even here the difference between politics in the United States and Europe struck them forcibly. Among the veterans such as Paul Mowrer or Swing, familiarity with the Continent's problems and close acquaintance with some of its leaders fostered sympathetic understanding not always shared by their younger colleagues. Both Mowrer and Bell were suspected from time to time by their editors, readers, American government officials, or by their own colleagues of being pro-French or pro-British, respectively. There may have been more truth to some of these suspicions than they were aware of, since each prided himself on maintaining a high level of professionalism in his work. A subjective element in one's judgments could not, in any case, be avoided completely, whether it stemmed from personal preferences and predilections or from familiarity or freshness in confronting a story. Mowrer felt it his responsibility to present as accurate an account as he could of the French viewpoint on national or international affairs, while Swing acknowledged that he had learned much about British and international affairs from fellow staff members of *The Economist*.[37] To less experienced journalists, however, postwar continental politics often seemed merely disreputable and hypocritical. These correspondents were as ill-prepared for the national and class antagonisms that the war had aggravated as they were for the dominant role still played by the old elite or for the complexities of European radicalism and reaction.

Even the veteran Wythe Williams, who served in Berlin, Paris, and Geneva in the course of the twenties, found postwar Paris "glittering" but "vulgar," its excitement like that of a "mounting fever." He watched with interest the development of Europe, which now was losing power rapidly in comparison with the United States. Years later he reflected on the "collective muddling by inept statesmen," the "cul-de-sac" of reparations, the "blunder" of France's occupation of the Ruhr, Germany's bitter resentment and continuing militancy, Italy's "narcissist Napoleon," and the futility of the League of Nations—"a comfortable first-class club" for the Great Powers. Great Britain had stumbled along, preoccupied with its own affairs, and the French, in his view, had been the greatest obstacle to peace. Their program of "beating Germany down" had produced the opposite result, so much so that the success of Nazism might have been labelled "manufactured in France."[38]

In a series of articles written in the mid-twenties for the *Saturday Evening Post*, Williams tried to explain the European political scene. He wrote on the return to power and prominence of French leaders such as Joseph Caillaux and Edouard Herriot, who were more sympathetically inclined toward the Germans. He argued that the "necessary alliance of French iron and German coal" was more important than all the talk of treaties, alliances, and reparations dominating the headlines. He pointed out that the League of Nations was not where the "real leaders" of Europe did their negotiating and that, for all the talk of disarmament, none of the European powers was prepared to risk its own security. He noted also that the French were unlikely to repay their war debts without more persuasive pressure from the United States. He reminded Americans that Europe was, after all, very different from the United States and could not be understood in the latter's terms. International power politics were not as Americans imagined them. "Close frontiers, different languages, clashing systems of education—all make for individualism and ultranationalism" in Europe. The "bloc system" of politics or of cartels in the economic sphere fostered intense rivalry: "It contains no thought of brotherly love. Its aim is simply to conduct burial services over hostile parties." The multiparty system and, especially in the Latin nations, "racial individualism" made "political teamwork and party discipline" impossible. American party politics followed quite different principles, Williams thought.[39] Whether his readers were enlightened or merely had their doubts and suspicions confirmed by Williams is impossible to say. At the very least, they might well have concluded that understanding Europe was not an easy matter.

Vincent Sheean's reaction to the European politics he found upon his arrival in 1922 was swift and negative. When his Venetian landlord explained the ways of the bands of young Fascist toughs harassing the city, Sheean likened them to the Ku Klux Klan and recognized an "ominous" sign, although he understood little of the movement or its background. Assuming the post of correspondent in Paris, Sheean was prepared— without any real experience as he later recognized—to render judgment on the performance of the nation's leaders and policies with all the confidence that the cold impersonality of his typewriter and, no doubt, his deadline, gave him. His interest in politics grew with familiarity, a pattern he thought differed from most of his colleagues. They reached Europe burning with "beliefs and enthusiasms," but "ended in callous indifference toward all human effort." Briefly awed by the prestige of Raymond Poincaré, the prime minister whose weekly press conferences he covered, Sheean soon came to detest his harsh, unyielding determination to punish the Germans to the utmost. "It was monstrous to think that this little man, whose intellectual resources were hardly more than a combination of prejudice and syntax," Sheean recalled, "disposed of the destinies of many millions of people."[40]

Covering the Lausanne Conference in 1923, Sheean observed the British and French, "those loyal allies...intriguing against each other for Turkish favor." Italy's occupation of Corfu, like France's of the Ruhr and Britain's resistance to Irish independence, all convinced Sheean of the hypocrisy and selfishness of the European powers. Nor did the League of Nations offer hope. The "boredom and futility of Geneva," where ambassadors droned on while their governments settled matters elsewhere, irked Sheean. He was tempted to conclude that, "There seemed a good deal more sense in the suggestion in the air—sometimes from Moscow, sometimes from Rome—that you had to begin by altering the composition of the material, its chemical formula." After three years, he prepared to leave "the pesthouse of Europe," having lost faith both in journalism and politics. He no longer respected the politicians, "because I had seen them squirming and dodging about, the poor powerless ferrets, trying to find a way out of the system in which they were imprisoned. In this doomed house, there was no hope." Although he would return many times and ultimately die in Europe, the steady, depressing round of the regular correspondent's responsibilities were not for him.[41]

Politics in postwar Germany, a former empire struggling to become a republic in spite both of its history and its defeat, offered American journalists unusual opportunities for observation and speculation. Wythe Williams contributed some articles on German affairs in the same 1925–28 *Saturday Evening Post* series in which he considered France and the League of Nations. In a comparative mood, he argued in 1925 that, while Latins tended to believe only what they knew was true and Anglo-Saxons often believed what they wanted to officially (although unofficially they might know the difference), the Germans also believed what they wanted to, "but with a dismaying and characteristic thoroughness." Germany was consolidating her "state of mind" and strength under the Dawes Plan which had eased the burden of reparations. Confidence in her leadership role was returning. Prosperity was evident in Berlin, and the German motion picture industry was threatening America's place in that new and influential field. With peace and prosperity, the Germans were in a position to determine their future course, for republicanism or empire. But, whatever the direction chosen, Williams thought militarism would not dominate it. The war had determined that: "it had proved that we need not lie awake nights fearful of a German-ridden planet. . . . Germany has abandoned Weltpolitik, the military conquest of the world. She still believes she can become the world's economic leader. She is still determined to acquire by this means the famous place in the sun."[42]

Williams conceded that there was another, less optimistic, view of Germany which in fact saw her spoiling for revenge. Her army was already rebuilding to become one of the world's finest, and a secret army, the "black Reichswehr," trained future officers in defiance of the principles of disarmament. The French army, now reduced in numbers, still gave a "thrill," Williams wrote, "but the German war machine gives a chill." Doubts and apprehensions as to German intentions still flourished among the Allies. But Germany "remains Germany. She may never again be the arrogant, steel-clanging Germany of before the war, but already she refuses to take everything lying down." After all, this was a nation of "ancient discipline and modern spirit, and, next to the United States, she possesses the greatest materialistic civilization of any nation of the world." The time had come for the Allies to make peaceful concessions. Germany was determined to be treated as an equal, and deserved to be. Williams suggested the likelihood of a forthcoming showdown and the advisability of concessions on the status of Upper Silesia and Poland.[43]

Berlin in the twenties was also a base for Dorothy Thompson, H. R. Knickerbocker, and Edgar Mowrer, among others. Each of the three later wrote at least one book accounting for Hitler's rise to power and the collapse of the Weimar Republic. Since each was an intelligent, sensitive observer, their collective comments shed light both on the German political scene and on American interpretations of it that is difficult to match for clarity or power. Mowrer, in particular, wrote some of the most thoughtful reports to appear before the debacle of 1929. His Italian experience had alerted him to potential sources of stability or instability. Admitting later that he had never fully understood the Germans, whom he considered "genuinely hospitable" and "mildly 'daft,'" he was still attracted by their love of learning and culture. He concluded that millions of Germans wanted "nothing better than the democratic republic," provided they also were accorded equal status with other nations. Yet he conceded that the forces opposing democracy were strong and that the emergence of the republic had been "more or less an accident." He contradicted Wythe Williams in holding that Germans had a genuine interest in other nations, but agreed that American bankers were pouring too much credit into the German economy.[44]

In 1925 Mowrer pointed to the prevalence of anti-Semitism and monarchist sentiment. Later, in a lengthy *Harper's* article he discussed the Dawes Plan which he thought had created a solid foundation for Germany's political and economic recovery. The nation was sound, and reparations had been scaled down to reasonable proportions. Some critics of the plan still opposed reparations as being beyond Germany's capacity to pay without serious damage to its economy, but Mowrer disagreed, holding that the plan entailed specific guarantees and procedures to minimize such consequences. The real issue, he suggested, was the war guilt clause of the Treaty of Versailles which assigned Germany full responsibility for the conflict. After ten years, this clause had been discredited. The Allies would do well to make a gesture of goodwill by abandoning it and by further relaxing "this monotonous stream of reparations."[45]

Mowrer pointed out in 1927 that Germany, in spite of Versailles, had resumed its Great Power status—a fact that he ascribed less to "deliberate German effort than [to] the growing belief on the part of others that Germany is a...necessity." The reality of the German presence had outweighed the fears and jealousies that had attempted to restrain her. France's effort to "perpetuate the fortuitous and ephemeral" had failed because, among others reasons, it was now recognized that the French and German economies were substantially complementary. Britain had aided a potential customer, while the United States had assisted both with technological and financial reorganization. The Germans, of course, had contributed their share. "[Prime Minister Gustav] Stresemann succeeded in appealing to the steady perseverance, fundamentally sound nerves, and incredible patience of the German people and in making them realize that time was on their side.... The helpless pariah of 1918 has come back."[46]

Returning to the same theme later, Mowrer offered an assessment of "Germany After Ten Years" with, as it turned out, appropriate warnings about the dangers of analyzing contemporary developments. The German revolution had been an essentially conservative one, he argued, "an act of a people that instinctively and by education prefers 'quiet and order' to political freedom.... [It had been a] respectable, orderly, self-controlled, decent, middle-class revolution." Germany had steered through dangerous waters, fending off attacks from both the Right and the Left as well as surviving disastrous inflation and achieving—most remarkably of all—"the mastery of its own emotions" by resisting self-righteous temptations to resentment and hostility. Mowrer felt sure that the Germans, having successfully dealt with so many problems, would continue on a constructive course. He reported estimates that some 80 percent were convinced republicans and concluded that it was "a foregone conclusion that the German Republic will stand."[47]

Still, Mowrer saw persistent, serious problems. The nation was "cluttered up with time-honored junk left from the *ancien régime*": monarchist and militarist ideals clashed with republican values and institutions; an archaic political structure fostered conflict between eighteen federal states and the central government; an ineffective parliamentary and political system blocked the achievement of responsible majority party government. A strong Communist party and an "insolent" Reichswehr, a prestigious traditional social caste system, and a tendency toward popular docility and exaltation of the state combined to pose formidable obstacles to Mowrer's own optimistic predictions. He added a list of other troublesome items: conflicts of power and principle over the relation of the state to economic affairs; the submergence of individualism in a widespread exaltation of the state; and a superpatriotic element yearning for a "dictator"—despite the fact that Germany and, indeed, Europe itself was becoming too small for nationalism "and is beginning to know it." "In considering the future of Germany," Mowrer concluded, its fundamental "hostility to individualism must be permanently kept in mind." Despite the optimistic beginning of the analysis, it was cautious and balanced. Mowrer's own ambivalence about Germany was mirrored in his portrait of a nation uncertain of itself and its future.[48]

In 1929 Mowrer moved from political analysis to a broader cultural perspective. Germany, Mowrer wrote, felt a strong need to be distinctive, different from others in its cultural orientation. The traditional "kultur" had broken down at the end of the war and Germans since then had been trying for some kind of "mental tuning-in on the modern world." Yet they also yearned for the old, romantic, aristocratic values; and perhaps some of that spirit might still prove valuable in a "wise synthesis" that could save Germany from complete loss of its historic personality in a new, homogenized industrial order. The world was becoming "Americanized...that is, industrialized on a superficially democratic basis," Mowrer wrote. Perhaps Germany, in this perspective, might have a useful and distinctive role to play in offering some kind of mediation between Western science and Eastern mysticism.[49]

However carefully he assessed the roadblocks barring the path to future peace and freedom in Europe, Mowrer could not avoid the perhaps characteristically American hope that reasonable solutions might be found. In 1930 he published a small book titled *Sinon, or the Future of Politics* which drew upon the ideas of his Italian mentor, Gaetano Meale, for a study of political power and the "crisis of the modern state." Here Mowrer moved beyond his journalistic function in advocating an international confederation to replace the current national system.[50] The volume's picture of a world at a crucial stage, with nationalism, science and technology, human aspirations for liberty and equality, and the ingrained drive for political and economic domination all seeking new forms or combinations reflected Mowrer's judgment on a decade of Europe's turmoil and change.

In 1928 Raymond Swing also offered an overview of European political directions. There was a kind of "radicalism" in Europe, he told the readers of *Harper's*, that Americans totally failed to understand or appreciate. It had little to do with standard political labels or American fears of communism or socialism, although these movements formed the left wing of what Swing generally had in mind. What had been happening, he argued, was a widespread "redistribution of wealth through political action," virtually irrespective of party or ideological lines. In England, both Liberal and Conservative parties had been attempting to achieve greater equality of incomes through modifications in the tax structure. The Tory government of Stanley Baldwin had redistributed more wealth than the Soviet Union, through pension, insurance, and educational legislation. "England is a nation virtually unanimous in its adherence to radicalism [of this kind], differing only as to methods of applying it." And the same might be said of most of western Europe. Swing speculated that the war had deterred the United States from noticing or copying the advance of British social legislation, and the mass consumption of the twenties offered Americans a privately managed alternative. But America, however satisfied with its own way of doing things, should not misinterpret developments elsewhere on the basis of political slogans that obscured, as much as they explained, reality.[51]

The significance of observations such as Swing's and Mowrer's lay as much or more in the attitudes they revealed as in the facts and explanations they offered. The interpretations they presented were pointed and thoughtful. They saw events as aspects of larger historical movements, evidences of broadly based changes not alone in Europe but in an even larger international context. They offered a truly cosmopolitan perspective, acknowledging the depth and distinctiveness of cultural variations while setting them in a broader context of common concerns. Correspondents who wrote in such terms had moved far beyond interest in scoring "beats," reporting human interest or local color items, and high living. They were reaching for a fuller understanding of the world they had discovered when they crossed the Atlantic. They were exploring the outer limits of journalism in the synthesis and analysis of international affairs for a concerned, enlightened public.

Ten years' familiarity with European life had encouraged these correspondents to undertake the difficult task of explaining one continent to the other. If initial impressions had sometimes been hasty and superficial —telling more about the observer than about the observed—time, curiosity, and intelligence brought a depth of insight and sensitivity that repaid their efforts. Not all, of course, achieved equal maturity. Some, reacting violently or cynically, had turned away after the initial exposure. Others had settled for the "good life" of freedom and irresponsibility with little thought for serious matters. A few had recognized an occasion and a challenge. They had seen themselves and their careers in a new light. They had discovered a need for a foreign correspondence more thoughtful, probing, and analytical than that of the past. Pioneers such as the Mowrers, Swing, Wythe Williams, and Dorothy Thompson achieved enough success and recognition with this new approach in the twenties to encourage their younger colleagues. The next decade would see the emergence of the Gunthers, Stowes, and Shirers. In 1929 Paul Mowrer became the first foreign correspondent whose work was acknowledged with a Pulitzer Prize.

These men and women were, in fact, among the few expert observers of international affairs whose information and opinions could be tapped not only by the general public but by American government officials and interested business and other leaders as well. Their new status was already presenting them with opportunities not yet fully comprehended, but whose dimensions and ramifications they were testing. Interestingly enough, it was in their relations with their immediate institutional superiors—their editors and publishers—that the correspondents found the greatest difficulty in winning the consideration and respect to which they now felt entitled.

5

Between Two Worlds
The Correspondent's Roles

◼ By the 1920s institutional arrangements for collecting, transmitting, and disseminating foreign news had evolved into patterns of reasonably common practice. Individual reporting styles and the policies and objectives of different press services inevitably varied. Still, sufficient agreement on ends and means existed so that correspondents moving from one service to another readily understood their new assignments. Not only did the technical, economic, and organizational features of foreign news reporting set fairly regular guidelines, but informal comradely and competitive exchanges between reporters created a widely shared set of standards for the correspondent's role. Correspondents had gained enough self-assurance to see possibilities for widening the scope of their work even as they rankled at attempts, from whatever direction, to confine or infringe upon it.

Two issues threatening this newfound sense of identity and purpose challenged the correspondents to seek ways of strengthening its claims. The expansion of government censorship and propaganda, only partially relaxed in peacetime, hampered access to dependable news sources. And efforts by editors and publishers to regulate reporters more closely after the permissive war years emphasized the many ways in which the latters' work was hostage to the methods, assumptions, and control of home offices. To escape such restrictions, correspondents were forced to devise more ingenious ways of eluding the nets set to restrain or entangle them. To justify their desire for wider editorial influence they sought alternative ways of enhancing their recognition and prestige.

The effort to win greater independence and a wider audience presented correspondents with serious problems. Powerful social and economic forces on both continents were driving society toward increasingly centralized, tightly regulated forms of organization. Except in wartime or for stories of extraordinary interest, home offices often edited, cut, or even rewrote—sometimes drastically—material submitted from the field. Considerations of space, economy, and editorial priorities or bias all influenced these decisions, making them a frequent source of transatlantic dispute in the twenties and thirties as American opinion swung heavily, although by no means entirely, away from the international concerns the war had aroused.

A small group of journalists, no matter how dedicated, could scarcely have resisted such a massive opinion shift on their own. Other developments, however, were working in their favor. The internationalizing influences which had already shaped their own personal lives and careers remained too powerful to succumb entirely to postwar nationalism and isolationism. Amid such conflicting influences the correspondents were strategically placed. Their expertise had already begun to win them recognition in government and business circles. By the 1920s the bureau chiefs and star correspondents of most American papers were assured of byline treatment for any major story they submitted, although second-line reporters and stringers still had to content themselves with anonymity except in unusual cases. Despite all obstacles, therefore, leading correspondents had some basis for confidence that in due course the broader recognition and influence they aspired to would be theirs.

Not all correspondents, to be sure, held such high ambitions. True to the old, freewheeling individualism of the trade, many still pursued it for the hedonistic satisfactions their freedom from close supervision allowed. Those who did hope for a larger role as international relations experts and advisors, however, found a new model and rationale for their work in the concept of professionalism. Their efforts to promote the professional ideal and otherwise to win recognition for their interpretive skills are the subject of the following two chapters.

REPORTERS AND EDITORS

The growing attention American editors and publishers had paid to international affairs since the beginning of the century already implied an enlarged idea of the foreign correspondent's role. The creation of overseas services had reflected their dissatisfaction with past international reporting. Still lacking, however, was agreement on the kind and quantity of foreign news editors and their readers would accept. Disputes had flourished over this matter for years, as the exchanges between Victor Lawson, Charles H. Dennis, and members of the *Chicago Daily News*'s European staff revealed. The issue, set aside to some extent during the war, was revived quickly enough when peace returned.

The self-conscious pride in their work shared by many members of the *Daily News* overseas staff may account for the fact that their records seem to have been more fully preserved than most. It is easier, therefore, to follow the debate over functions and responsibilities as reflected in their writings than in those of other journalists. The quality of the *Daily News* staff and particularly of its leaders, Bell and Paul Mowrer, coupled with Victor Lawson's erratic support for his foreign service, may have fostered open discussion of responsibilities less fully debated elsewhere. Other journalists, even when they did not follow the *Daily News* pattern, acknowledged the quality of its service. For example, when Cyrus H. K. Curtis of the *Philadelphia Public Ledger* undertook in 1919 to establish his own foreign service, he and his staff clearly took the *Daily News* as their model.[1]

There were, of course, differing patterns and styles in editor-correspondent relations. The *New York Times*'s reliance upon European nationals as reporters has been mentioned previously. In the late 1920s and 1930s the *New York Herald Tribune* extended its overseas operations with a staff of talented young journalists such as Leland Stowe, John T. Whitaker, and Ralph Barnes. But its owners lacked the steady commitment to sustain their service through good times and bad. Like its not-so-friendly rival, the *Daily News*, the *Chicago Tribune* assembled a group of able, resourceful, and highly individualistic reporters. But its publisher, the crusty and autocratic Colonel Robert R. McCormick, did little to encourage them to conceive of their careers except in response to his own ideological preconceptions.[2] Meanwhile, the press associations left their employees little scope for imaginative or analytical work. The charge to be first in relaying the hard news of the day encouraged efforts to establish wide connections and to anticipate the next headline or human interest story; but scoring a beat or developing leads to a future one were the chief, if not the sole, measures of accomplishment for press association reporters. Louis Lochner in Berlin enjoyed a rich association in political, intellectual, and artistic circles, but his assignment discouraged analysis and interpretation. To write more freely on the German musical scene Lochner published in a specialized journal under an assumed name.[3]

Even as Edward Price Bell begged his Chicago superiors for clearer instructions, he sensed new possibilities for foreign correspondence as a contributor to international understanding. He urged Lawson to allow London to become a "training school for developing correspondents," and he promoted the placement of his disciples in other capitals. He relayed Chicago's calls to restrict cable wordage, but he resented the limitations imposed, complaining that Lawson sometimes seemed "better pleased when he does not get stuff than when he does." And when Charles Dennis chided correspondents for veering "too far away from the news," Bell responded that this was the result of orders not to duplicate spot news stories.[4]

Bell's thinking had already evolved beyond simple obedience or protest. As early as 1901 he indicated to Dennis that he saw new possibilities for journalism. "All we have to do," he wrote, ". . . is to graduate a staff of men worthy of the idea and we shall have the most picturesque and the most substantial news service in the world." He acknowledged that the average reader might want to know "more about the bungling on Blue Island Avenue if it has novel features. . .than about the latest complication in some bundesrath or reichstag or diet, unless the complications really get somewhere—and complications never or rarely do." But he urged Wile, on a Chicago visit, to press for fuller coverage of international news since Chicagoans needed better understanding of events. "You see the ordinary American editor," he wrote in 1904, "cannot rise to a world point of view. . . . He needs his skull expanded."[5]

Like Mowrer and Swing, Bell disliked "tourist bureau" work. When Wile left the *Daily News* for the *London Daily Mail* in 1906, Bell seized the opportunity to tell his employers that Lord Northcliffe, Wile's new chief, paid his staff better, brought them back to London for frequent consultation, and allowed them time enough to think seriously about their work. The prestige that the war brought Bell further enlarged his vision of foreign correspondence. Spurred by the idealistic moralism of the era, he saw international journalism as a potential force for world peace and understanding, moving beyond mere reporting toward participation in the shaping of public policy and opinion.[6]

Paul Mowrer had also developed ambitious ideas about the place and potential of international journalism. He knew that peace meant a lower priority for foreign news but complained that correspondents found it hard to keep "a keen edge on" when their stories were edited drastically or failed to appear at all. He protested that Lawson's renewed requests for stories of colorful Americans overseas was "simply impossible and is . . . going to kill our foreign service." If the publisher were serious about that expectation, he should fire his experienced staff and start over. "The idea that people who are not interested in foreign affairs can be so interested by our writing 'entertainment' instead of serious information and opinion is erroneous." Those who wanted foreign news at all wanted serious news; there was a "duty to the public which should be kept in mind—a duty of educating and informing the people on foreign affairs."[7]

Although they did not see eye to eye on all matters, Bell and Mowrer joined in resisting a return to prewar patterns. Bell conceded that, "During the war we forgot direct American interest. We wrote war and war and more war. We also got badly tangled up in European politics. Further, we became deeply inoculated with the virus of overwriting." But when reprimanded for editorializing he replied that readers welcomed more provocative material and that "long resident men like Paul Mowrer . . . and myself ought to have considerable freedom of interpretation." Bell and Mowrer wanted not only relief from what they considered petty restrictions but also the ability to influence editorial policy on international affairs. Before he left Europe in 1922 Bell negotiated an arrangement with Lawson giving him something like free-lance status and the assurance that his interpretive work would find a place on the editorial page. Mowrer even earlier had requested roving European "diplomatic correspondent" status, with two articles on foreign affairs provided each week for the editorial page. The *Daily News*, "already famous for its foreign news service," he had argued, still lacked the essential elements of synthesis and interpretation which his articles could supply.[8]

While Lawson retained control, Bell and Mowrer received at least part of the recognition they felt their expertise merited. Bell was permitted to mount an elaborate series of interviews with leaders of the major powers, eliciting their views on world peace. Mowrer was recalled to Chicago for consultations and, although his request for regular editorial page exposure was denied, he was named Bell's successor as head of the European service. Returning to Europe early in 1922 Mowrer told other *Daily News* correspondents that he had relayed complaints about the inadequate attention paid to their reports. He had countered Lawson's call for limited cable wordage by requesting more front-page foreign news coverage, especially since "our prestige is now so firmly established." Mowrer urged others to deal with pressure for human interest and American-oriented stories by recognizing that "there is no part of the world in which the United States has not at present real interests—economic, moral, cultural, diplomatic, social, political. We should...analyse...these interests and write about them." In response to Chicago's parochial stance, he also proposed more reports on "social problems and experiments especially when analogous to our own social problems in America." He assured the others that coverage of important international events was still called for; and, in terms reminiscent of Bell, Mowrer asserted that "ours is fundamentally an interpretative service, the aim of which is to explain to our readers not so much *what* has happened as *why* it happened, *what* it means, and, above all, what it may lead to."[9]

During the early twenties Mowrer attempted to influence the *Daily News*'s editorial policies, criticizing its treatment of the League of Nations and urging it to recognize that substantial progress was being made in Geneva. He objected that a *News* editorial on France's occupation of the Ruhr ignored information he had already reported. He submitted a proposal for settlement of the reparations issue, requesting editorial support for the position he advanced, and was gratified when his recommendations received a favorable response in Chicago. He pressed steadily for closer coordination of the editorial and reporting staffs, with editorial policy to be based on information supplied by experienced correspondents.[10]

Mowrer remained the *Daily News*'s senior European correspondent for twelve years, until 1934. He received the first Pulitzer Prize awarded a foreign correspondent in 1929; five years later he was recalled to Chicago to become the *Daily News*'s managing editor. Yet Mowrer never was able to dominate the paper's foreign service. Resistance in Chicago was strengthened with the death of Victor Lawson in 1925. Whatever his shortcomings and idiosyncrasies, Lawson had taken pride in the foreign service. Reporters like Bell and Mowrer had capitalized upon that pride to extend their work far beyond their employer's original conception; and Lawson had allowed them considerable leeway, despite fits of economizing. His death left effective control in the hands of Dennis and a group of associates much less friendly to the foreign service. Dennis, after serving as managing editor for more than twenty years, was conservative and self-assured. His determination to assert his authority seemed to the overseas staff to outweigh any loyalty he may once have felt to the Lawson policies. Only the succession of Walter A. Strong, Lawson's son-in-law, to the publisher's chair encouraged the correspondents to hope that in time and with Dennis's eventual retirement they might increase their influence.

Recognizing his need for assistance, Dennis brought Hal O'Flaherty, one of the European correspondents who had served in Stockholm and succeeded Bell in London, back to Chicago as foreign affairs editor. The choice of O'Flaherty, a member of the casual school of overseas reporting, ensured Dennis's control. Mowrer thus found himself with considerable personal prestige and influence among his peers, but with only marginal ability to promote the foreign service. It is easy, in the light of this experience, to understand the tribute Mowrer later paid to Lawson. Crediting his long-time employer, perhaps in retrospect, with sharing his own philosophy, Mowrer wrote movingly, "Few men. . .had done more to establish high standards of journalism. . . . To give his. . .readers unbaised analysis of foreign events which they were not qualified to interpret for themselves, he had allowed us to build up the great *Daily News* foreign service. The. . .reporting he encouraged was literally without favor. . . . He never attempted to tell reporters. . .what they should find out."[11] Mowrer and his colleagues soon discovered that dealing with Dennis and his allies would be a different matter.

Dennis injected himself actively into foreign service affairs. While he seldom criticized Paul Mowrer directly, he was not so restrained in his dealings with others. He complained that the foreign service was too political and too little interested in colorful stories and novelties. What readers wanted, he once wrote Mowrer, were more stories like one from Hiram Motherwell in Rome "about the song bird discovered singing at night in the Coliseum." In 1926 Dennis wrote that "the great mass of our readers are not likely to reason deeply regarding foreign matters. The. . . American bumptiousness of the *Chicago Tribune* in its foreign dispatches goes over big with them." He did not want reporters to ape their Chicago rival, Dennis protested, but they might at least recognize the reality of its appeal.[12]

In particular, Dennis was outspoken in dealing with Edgar Mowrer, whose "bumptiousness" in its own way matched the *Tribune*'s. Repeatedly, Dennis deplored the lack of human interest stories from Berlin after Mowrer took over in 1924. He complained about Edgar's editorializing on the state of German democracy and insisted that the merits of reparations arguments must be assessed in Chicago, not in the field. Yet Dennis did not hesitate himself to suggest a viewpoint for Mowrer's reports. He called for emphasis on "the enormous benefits which the Dawes Plan unquestionably has bestowed on Germany and the German people," to off-set Senator Robert LaFollette's appeal to German-American voters in the 1924 presidential election. Several times Dennis protested Mowrer's highlighting military and imperial influences in Weimar Germany, writing that "...we wish to state facts and point out tendencies rather than to pass judgments sweeping and untimely"; but he did invite Edgar to submit further reports based upon more complete analysis of the subject. Dennis also charged him with "unnecessary pessimism" about the prospects of German democracy.[13]

Mowrer was too unsympathetic to the difficulties Germans faced, treating them in his reports "rather as laboratory specimens than as human beings," Dennis felt. "The German Republic has not fallen, but on the contrary, so far as I can discern, continues to grow stronger," Dennis wrote sarcastically. But again he invited Mowrer's considered response: "Do not hesitate to prove that I am wrong in this if you can do so by quotations from your articles or in any other manner." Dennis's challenge in this instance may have stimulated Mowrer's subsequently more even-handed assessment. In any case, the editor mixed his criticisms with praise and invitation to reasoned response so that Mowrer—not an easy man to disagree with—made no public protest. Indeed, in his memoirs he stressed the freedom accorded by the *Daily News* editors, saying that they had insisted on first-hand reporting and assumed that the man on the spot was always right.[14]

Dennis also attempted to influence Carroll Binder, who replaced Motherwell in Rome in 1927. When Binder, a young Quaker protégé of Walter A. Strong, had expressed reservations about his assignment to a totalitarian regime, Dennis waved the issue aside. But knowledge of Binder's position may have provoked him to write later, "Personally, I believe...the Italian government by its strong and constructive policy expects to gain material benefits, perhaps even in colonial territories, peacefully.... In any event, it is clear that Italy is more and more taking a leading part in European affairs.... As I have said before, we believe that the present government knows best what is good for the Italian people and we have no wish to criticize it, our only desire being to reflect its activities and correctly interpret its purposes." Binder responded tactfully that he was appraising the situation and that, indeed, "Italy's laboratory has something to contribute to the solution of America's problems." He would report constructive features, he assured Dennis, although he had found more negative than positive lessons to be learned. Those who praised Mussolini, Binder wrote, had not scratched beneath the surface of censorship and phony propaganda. He hoped to continue the "dispassionate view of this truly remarkable experiment" in the best *Daily News* tradition. He criticized the news coverage provided by the press associations and by the *Chicago Tribune*'s David Darrah, urging continuation of the *Daily News*'s "superior interpretation." Regardless of what Dennis may have made of this, by the time his Rome assignment ended Binder shared the dissatisfactions with Chicago's editorial policies expressed by Paul Mowrer and others.[15]

For all their discontents, Bell, Mowrer, Binder, and other *Daily News* correspondents probably knew that their situation was at least relatively favorable. They sometimes complained that better wages or conditions existed elsewhere, but they seldom complimented competing foreign services. With the early exception of Frederic Wile, few seem to have left the *Daily News* voluntarily. Raymond Swing, for example, found it impossible to work for Munsey's *New York Herald* after the war and was uncomfortable with the *Wall Street Journal* and the *Philadelphia Public Ledger* in London; and Swing's complaints were not attributable solely to his prickly disposition.[16]

Similarly, George Seldes became increasingly disillusioned with the superficial work of Floyd Gibbons, who headed the *Chicago Tribune*'s European staff, and with Colonel McCormick's ideas and policies. Seldes found venality and lack of courage widespread among the American press in Europe. Publishers paid their reporters minimal wages and often got the quality of work and commitment they paid for. Out of ignorance or indifference, Seldes thought, most editors permitted foreign correspondents greater freedom than they would have enjoyed at home, the chief exception being in their coverage of the new Soviet government where rabid antibolshevism virtually barred attempts at balanced, sober evaluation. One *Chicago Tribune* correspondent, Donald Day, was allowed to file "fake" anti-Communist stories from Latvia for years without any checkup, Seldes recalled, since they agreed with McCormick's political bias. He observed also that the AP, UP, Havas, Reuters, and other news services showed little interest in accurately covering Mussolini's Italy, and he found the Paris editions of both the *Chicago Tribune* and the *New York Herald Tribune* accepting bribes from the Italian, Polish, and Rumanian governments.[17]

Despite the factors which caused Seldes's disillusionment, the attractions of a Chicago connection for young midwesterners coupled with the attractions of Europe drew able correspondents, along with some notorious characters, to the *Tribune*'s European staff. Some, such as Seldes and Vincent Sheean, became disgusted and moved on. Others, Sigrid Schultz and Edmond Taylor, for example, were happy to settle in Berlin or Paris despite McCormick's views and his inclination to move people around. Still others, such as William L. Shirer, may simply have welcomed freedom from close supervision and their employer's indifference to their own personal views. So long as they submitted lively copy, they had little to worry about, although Seldes earned a reprimand when he reported, contrary to McCormick policy, that Germany's publicly owned railroad system was not in imminent danger of collapse.[18]

With the rise of nazism as a powerful political force in the 1930s, McCormick began to police his staff more closely. Edmond Taylor noted that McCormick read his Paris dispatches carefully enough to criticize his translations of French documents. As Taylor became more critical of the Nazis, he found it necessary to couch his reports very carefully in order to get them into print. Once, for example, he resorted to the tactic of emphasizing the failure of Hitler's economic planning program in order to slip in other criticisms of the regime. As he awakened to the deeper significance of European events, a process which he described as a "trek out of the coonskin world of Col. McCormick to the frontiers of contemporary reality," Taylor joined a growing number of journalists who, in direct conflict with McCormick's isolationism, advocated collective security in the face of totalitarian aggression.[19]

As the temperature of international politics continued to rise in the thirties, Taylor found himself increasingly "bombarded" with criticism from Chicago. Eventually he was dismissed for flouting the *Tribune*'s isolationist line too flagrantly. He later conceded that he had sometimes let his anti-Axis sympathies influence his writing and acknowledged that the necessity of clearing his reports through McCormick's suspicious scrutiny had probably helped him control his own enthusiasms in favor of "hard-minded, detached" copy.[20] Whatever the talents or weaknesses of his correspondents, McCormick's method of dealing with them discouraged the development of any esprit de corps or sense of mutual responsibility. When Taylor began to feel an obligation for more serious reporting it was to colleagues of other press services, not to his *Tribune* associates, that he turned for support.

When the *Philadelphia Public Ledger* established its own foreign service in 1919, publisher Cyrus H. K. Curtis hired Carl Ackerman, an experienced correspondent, to head its European staff. Ackerman recruited Wythe Williams for Paris, Clarence Streit for Italy and southern Europe, and—through Williams—Dorothy Thompson for Vienna and later Berlin. Raymond Swing and H. R. Knickerbocker eventually also joined what was an extremely capable staff. Efforts to recruit from the Associated Press proved less successful. His first Berlin reporter, a former AP man, earned Ackerman's criticism for "sending news bulletins instead of special articles" and more detailed "interpretive and descriptive" materials. In Rome, Ackerman at first negotiated with Sylvester Cortesi, an AP representative with twenty-five years' experience, but concluded, "An A.P. man cannot be remade, I fear!" He then tried, but failed, to woo Edgar Mowrer away from the *Chicago Daily News*.[21]

Ackerman favored a style of correspondence similar to that of Bell, whom Curtis had also tried to recruit, and Paul Mowrer. This approach, however, quickly brought him into conflict with the *Public Ledger*'s editor, John J. Spurgeon. Spurgeon took strong and frequent exception to Ackerman's work, complaining that too much editorializing and too little human interest news was reaching Philadelphia. "Too Much Russia Too Much World Politics Too Little American News...," he cabled at one point. At another, he implored Ackerman to "get rid of the notion that the only news Americans are interested in is what the various European governments are doing.... *Please*, for the love of Mike, try to think of news in the human sense. Give us something about the people. We are fed up on Russia, Bolshevism, Czechoslovakia, Poland and what the various Prime Ministers are doing and saying to one another...please stop trying to save the world. Let the poor old guy totter along for a few months unaided by the Public Ledger...cut off your subscription to the Soviet Workers Press Service."[22]

Ackerman had asked for criticism and guidance from home, but this was not what he had in mind. He complained to Curtis that "the curse of European news and of the American newspapers...is the placing of a premium on sensation and scandal and the discouraging of originality, reliability and accuracy." He protested that his articles were rewritten by an editor who thought he understood London conditions better than reporters in the field. Other newspapers, he noted, found it best to trust the judgment of the man on the spot. He suggested that he be named foreign editor with full responsibility, reporting directly to Curtis; when this ploy failed Ackerman resigned.[23] Promising as the *Public Ledger*'s foreign service had seemed, it failed to develop effectively. Well before it was closed down under pressure of the Depression in the early 1930s, many of its leading correspondents had left.

At the same time that the issue of reportorial and editorial responsibility was being argued at the *Public Ledger*, it was raised pointedly and publicly in the case of an established and respected newspaper, the *New York Times*, by Walter Lippmann and Charles Merz, two *New Republic* staff members. In August 1920 Lippmann and Merz reviewed in detail the *Times*'s coverage of Russia for three years following the revolution of March 1917. Their findings constituted a blistering indictment of the *Times*'s reportorial and editorial staffs for a pervasive anti-Soviet bias that had distorted its coverage. Not only had the *Times* slanted its assessments of events, but where field reporters had submitted information and observations contradicting the editorial line, these had been played down or ignored. News captions, too, had exhibited "clear and flagrant examples of the invasion of the news by editorial opinion."[24]

Lippmann and Merz had singled out the *Times*, they said, not because it was more biased than other papers but because of its reputation and influence. By implication, their criticism was aimed at the accuracy and reliability of journalism as a whole. The Russian Revolution had not been an easy story to cover, they conceded. Censorship and propaganda had distorted the usual channels of communication, reliable information was not easily come by, and emotional and ideological biases inevitably colored responses. But the overwhelming importance of the event made it all the more crucial that a responsible press exercise restraint. "A great newspaper is a public service institution," wrote Lippmann and Merz. "It occupies a position in public life fully as important as the school system or the church or the organs of government."[25]

By such standards, the *Times* had fallen far short. "From the point of view of professional journalism the reporting of the Russian Revolution is nothing short of a disaster," they concluded. The news had been "dominated by the hopes of the men who composed the news organization. . . . [T]he news about Russia [was] a case of seeing not what was, but what men wished to see. . . . The chief censor and the chief propagandist were hope and fear in the minds of reporters and editors." The *Times* had demonstrated "boundless credulity, and an untiring readiness to be gulled . . . a downright lack of common sense." Some correspondents had proven untrustworthy because of their personal sympathies. "A reporter is not entitled to hold an assignment when his sympathies are in question," Lippmann and Merz argued. "[E]ven so rich and commanding a newspaper as the Times does not take seriously enough the equipment of the correspondent...something more than routine reporting is required.... The Russian policy of the editors of the Times profoundly and crassly influenced their news columns." To reform the press, Lippmann and Merz looked to the journalists themselves. "Power to define and enforce professional standards must come from within the profession," from the "corporate tradition and the discipline of the newspaper guild."[26] Although there is no direct evidence that their critique was discussed by Bell, Mowrer, or Ackerman, its demand for quality, judgment, and accuracy clearly paralleled their own concerns.

Conflict between the editorial and reportorial roles was chronic, probably unresolvable. Each group, generally speaking, had its own outlook, sense of priorities, and responsibilities. The conflict flared beyond ordinary proportions at times of rapid change, when new political or ideological issues thrust themselves forward. Correspondents in Europe or Asia, where such new forces were most dramatically in evidence during the interwar decades, had to react to change more rapidly than did those at home. It was virtually inevitable then that they should feel their editors and readers to be out of touch with important developments. Meanwhile home offices readily concluded that reporters were exaggerating events. Whether the issue was communism in Russia, fascism in Italy, war debts and reparations, international trade and tariffs, the rise of nazism, or collective security, the opportunities for disagreement between the continents were legion.

Perhaps the most dramatic instance of divergence between the outlooks of correspondents and their editors occurred with the event which most radically altered the perspective of the reporters themselves, the Spanish Revolution of 1936–39. Until then, most newspaper people had remained sufficiently disengaged from the Continent's political and ideological camps to view its conflicts and controversies dispassionately. The uprising in Spain and the intervention of Mussolini and Hitler on the side of the Nationalist rebels, however, converted many American journalists from doubtful observers of the European political scene to outright partisans in a confrontation of forces presaging, in their view, an immanent world conflict. In trying to rally American opinion behind a beleaguered and disunited democracy, correspondents jumped far ahead of many editors and large segments of American opinion. The involvement of the international Communist and Catholic establishments on different sides of the struggle further complicated the controversy both on the field of battle and in the trenches of public opinion. And correspondents, having at last found a cause with which they could fully identify, were frustrated to find that their editors and readers, more remote from the Spanish arena, were less persuaded and less open to persuasion of its vital importance than were they themselves.

One correspondent who felt the conflict more severely, perhaps, because he had earlier managed to remain personally disengaged, was the *New York Times*'s Herbert L. Matthews. From Paris and Rome, Matthews had surveyed coolly the posturing of the democracies denying peaceful adjustments and equal partnership to Germany and Italy while concealing their own selfish purposes behind a façade of liberal rhetoric. An assignment to Madrid, however, converted Matthews from a cynical onlooker to an ardent partisan. Convinced that the international attack on the Spanish republic foretold an even larger conflict in the making, Matthews was eager to inform and arouse Americans to the insight he had gained.[27]

Matthews was constantly at odds with his editors over his treatment of the Spanish conflict. He blamed in particular the "bull pen" of night editors and copyreaders whose partisanship led them to edit his dispatches. They treated his copy with "suspicion, anger, and, at times, disbelief." They omitted some of his reports entirely, deleted references to German and Italian participation, and buried his stories on inside pages. At the time, he considered these actions malicious, but Matthews later concluded that, however wrong, they reflected the sincere beliefs of the editorial staff. There was no personal vindictiveness toward him, he realized. Publisher A. H. Sulzberger had, in fact, defended him from attacks by the Catholic Press Association and other partisan groups. Yet Matthews thought Sulzberger and Edwin L. James, by this time the *Times*'s managing editor in New York, had been "seriously, carelessly, and thoughtlessly mistaken" in their approach to a controversial issue. The *Times*'s policy was to have reporters covering the war from both sides and to give roughly equal space to each. Such a mechanically even-handed approach, Matthews felt, failed to provide truthful coverage. In this instance, editorial caution reflected pressures at home that Matthews, in the field, did not face.[28]

The tension between correspondents and editors over Spain was not limited to the *New York Times*,[29] although Matthews discussed it more openly than many others. The crucial nature of the Spanish conflict, which for the first time brought an open and active alliance of the dictatorships, struck even many hardened journalist veterans more forcefully than it did those more remote from the arena. Not until the Munich Crisis of 1938 would the imminence of war diminish the gap in perspectives between correspondents and their home offices. Then, the growing sense of crisis would cause editors to rely on the expertise of their tested reporters, thus lessening the tensions between them. But in the nature of the relationship, the differences could never completely disappear.

THE COSTS OF CORRESPONDENCE

A second persistent source of contention between correspondents and publishers involved cost controls. Again, perspectives inevitably differed; correspondents bridled at orders to condense or mail important news stories while business offices suspiciously eyed expense accounts and cable costs. The latter had been a sore point for years. The creation of the press associations had enabled editors to instruct their staffs to minimize spot news and use the slower, cheaper mails for all but the most pressing stories. The application of this policy brought problems, however, since reporters and editors differed in their assessment of important news. Editors often compounded the difficulty by inconsistently chiding correspondents when the associations beat them in relaying especially newsworthy items. Reporters, for their part, questioned editorial priorities and resented penny pinching. Again, because the records of the *Chicago Daily News* are more accessible, it is convenient to view the issue primarily from that perspective, although there is little reason to think that conditions differed markedly elsewhere.

Within a few months of his arrival in London, Edward Price Bell complained to Charles Dennis that other American press services were not required to "skeletonize" (cut and abbreviate) their cable materials so drastically as he. As early as 1902 Bell reported monthly cable wordage from thirteen locations. In April 1905, with the *Daily News* attempting to reduce its overseas wordage, his monthly statement indicated 9,597 words sent from eleven centers, with 2,689 words from St. Petersburg, 2,042 from Berlin, and 2,720 from London. The July report for the same year showed a total of 13,047 words sent at a cost of £84 4*s* 11*d*. In September Bell explained that the 4,444 words he had cabled from London were an unusually high amount because of the Marshall Field wedding and the need to fill in for lack of news from Scandinavia and Hungary. Repeated warnings from Chicago kept the matter at the forefront of Bell's thinking. When Victor Lawson in 1906 subscribed to the *London Standard*'s news service to supplement his own, Bell, fearful of competition, hastily assured Lawson that his own correspondents were already outperforming the *Standard*'s staff.[30]

World War I quieted disputes over cable costs, but they cropped up again in the twenties as the relaxation of international tensions reawakened disagreements over priorities. Even before the war had ended, Paul Mowrer was protesting orders to cut back on the flow of news from Paris. A suggested limit of 2,000 cable words per day from Europe would leave only about 500 for Paris, he complained in 1920. If this limit held, he wrote Bell, he would consider "using the by-product of my labor elsewhere—for example, in magazine articles." Mowrer wrote Dennis that mailed reports were seldom satisfactory and few foreign services were still relying on them; mail also implied low priority and such stories were often therefore cut drastically or not printed at all.[31] Excessive reliance upon skeletonized cables caused difficulties, too, requiring reconstruction of the message at the receiving end, filling in missing words, and elaborating truncated messages into a coherent story. Even with experienced operatives this meant virtually limitless opportunities for misunderstanding. Complaints, explanations, reprimands, and rationalizations on both sides filled the correspondence between Chicago and the field.

When Mowrer assumed leadership of the European staff in 1922 the size of the operation remained, despite postwar cutbacks, much larger than it had been earlier. This is indicated by Dennis's instructions in 1923 that the monthly cable quota must be reduced from 48,000 to 38,000 words, since the foreign service was costing the *Daily News* some $250,000 per year. Although Mowrer resented Chicago's cost-cutting measures so strongly that he threatened to resign, he soon found ways to turn them to advantage by urging the use of mail stories to develop longer, more interpretive articles.[32]

Again, in the 1930s financial stringency dictated reductions in cable usage. In 1929 Paul Mowrer wrote Carroll Binder in Rome, suggesting a limit of between 600 and 700 words for "very big" stories, with 200 words or less for less important ones. Mowrer noted that more than business considerations alone were involved, warning that it was important not to lose the initiative or "let the foreign service run dry." Binder may have been unusually loquacious, but many correspondents obviously failed to adhere to their theoretical limits. When Binder moved to London in 1931,

Mowrer again warned him that cable usage was running at unacceptably high levels. Rome had sent twice its allotted 5,000 words the preceding month; Berlin (where Edgar Mowrer was in charge) had exceeded its 6,000-word quota by an additional 11,000. London, meanwhile, had sent 23,000 instead of 6,000—more, Mowrer pointed out, that had been sent during the London Naval Conference. In hard times, even Mowrer did not object strongly to a 1932 order to cut the total cable budget from $80,000 (which had been exceeded by $10,000 in 1930) to $64,000.[33]

Reporters' salaries and expense accounts offered another fertile area for disagreement. Complicated by shifting rates of international exchange, the uncertain costs of data gathering, rumors of extravagance and high living among correspondents far from home office supervision, and sloppy record-keeping, the subject lent itself to endless dispute. The issue of salaries and raises had arisen repeatedly. Bell preferred to mention the subject obliquely, merely noting the salaries paid by competing British and American papers. When Wile left the *Chicago Daily News*, Bell pointed out that Wile's $50 per week salary had not been adequate for "the finest newsman in Germany" who would now receive more than £1000 per year. The following year Bell's own salary was raised to $100 per week, far less than that of correspondents no more able than he. Not until 1914 did Bell's salary reach $150 per week and it took the war to push him to $10,000 per year; by then he received an additional $6,000 for the expenses of the London bureau office. In view of his experience, duties, and expenses, this was not an extravagant sum.[34]

Indeed, it appears that *Daily News* foreign correspondents' salaries were modest in comparison with those paid by the Associated Press, the *New York Times*, and a number of British papers. The evidence is sketchy at best, and the *Daily News* may have supported its staff more generously than some other papers; but the correspondents frequently complained that they provided superior service at considerably less cost than the *New York Times*, in particular, incurred from its correspondents. Paul Mowrer in Paris, with less experience than Bell, seems to have been about equally well (or poorly) paid before the war. When he negotiated the hiring of Raymond Swing in 1913, Mowrer wrote Bell that Dennis had offered Swing $200 per month. On the strength of his own recent Balkan reports, Mowrer indicated that he planned to ask Lawson for a raise from the $250 per month he had been receiving for the past two years and on which he found it difficult to keep his family in comfort.[35]

When Edgar Mowrer became a *Daily News* correspondent in Italy in 1915 he was paid only $60 per month, for what may have been considered part-time work.[36] By the time he reached Berlin, Edgar had acquired experience, self-confidence, and reportorial scorn for home office accounting procedures. Instructed to reduce bureau expenditures, Mowrer took the offensive. He wrote to Dennis, "Having for the last two months been gradually going into debt, I have been obliged this month to add an extra $250 for living expenses. This represents the lowest supplement to my salary upon which I and my family can live here and maintain the News service at a proper level of efficiency. If you desire I can furnish a vast deal of information on this subject, but perhaps—indeed, I believe—you understand the situation as well as I."[37]

As Mowrer suggested, the finances of a major overseas bureau were not a simple matter. In addition to correspondents' salaries and cable charges, there were other items to be attended to. Office supplies, furnishings, and rent had been a subject of special interest to Victor Lawson from the first; they represented the one area in which *Daily News* correspondents had found their employer extravagant. The worm had turned, however, by the 1920s as the business office began to supervise affairs more closely and cut back on the facilities and amenities it provided the bureaus. A clue that Lawson's era was ending appeared early in 1924 when Dennis asked Paul Mowrer if the Paris office really needed to continue receiving nine copies of the *Daily News*.[38]

When Edgar Mowrer took over the Berlin office, he requested authorization to improve its furnishings and heating facilities. Rugs were worn, wallpaper shabby, and the coal stove both unattractive and inefficient—the office temperature in October hovered around sixty-two degrees Fahrenheit. In December, with improvements still not authorized, Mowrer taxed Dennis on a sensitive point: perhaps his predecessors had not complained of the cold since they warmed themselves frequently at nearby bars. This reference to the foibles of earlier correspondents produced the desired authorization, but within a few months Mowrer was defending the size of his staff and payroll to Chicago. He replied that he was providing top-quality interim coverage of Russia and paying an additional twenty-five dollars a month for scientific coverage, and he added that he was the only correspondent of a large newspaper without at least one or two full-time assistants, essential for the kind of coverage Dennis expected. The editor was not easily persuaded. In 1927 Mowrer was again criticized for employing "too many people to do needless things for you and to furnish us with second and third rate articles," but Dennis excepted Edgar's own work from the comment.[39]

Paul Mowrer was more businesslike than his brother. He protested what he saw as petty harrassments from Chicago, but he agreed in principle that overseas operations should be carefully managed and accounted for. Complaining to Bell in 1913 at the absence of systematic accounting procedures, he claimed in his three years in Paris to have run a bureau nearly twice as large as had existed before at two-thirds of the cost. Lack of adequate records, however, made it impossible for him to document his effort. In 1924 Mowrer took advantage of a report on accomplishments of the European service under his direction to indicate dissatisfaction with the tight, if not parsimonious, budget allotted the foreign service. He himself was only able to complete his work, Mowrer wrote, by taking advantage of a "large and helpful acquaintance" in France and through a "system of work which enables me to use every bit of my energy to good purpose." For his own work, as well as for supervising the entire European service, he had a staff consisting only of one "first-rate secretary and one cheap office-girl." By contrast the *New York Times* had four correspondents assigned to Paris, as did the *Philadelphia Public Ledger*, while the *Chicago Tribune* had three. The monthly office expense of the *Times* was nearly three times that of the *Daily News*, Mowrer claimed, cable tolls included. In 1929 Mowrer wrote Binder that the *Daily News* was considering instituting an annual audit of overseas bureau books. The practice was common among other businesses with overseas branches, Mowrer explained, and had been followed in the London bureau for years. He welcomed its extension to the Paris office.[40]

Some reporters felt it justifiable to entertain at a standard suited to the sometimes-quite-high company they kept. Others were simply slovenly or opportunistic in their bookkeeping. Some borrowed heavily from employers or friends and a few got themselves in trouble on this account.[41] It was probably true, on the other hand, that business offices had no very clear idea of what the position of foreign correspondent involved. In any event, when reporters found it impossible to sustain themselves at a level they felt suitable they turned to magazine articles as a source of additional income. The practice of selling news and analysis to several papers or journals had not been uncommon earlier, and it persisted into the more highly structured postwar period when, in fact, the audience for serious international reporting had grown.

Paul Mowrer published several volumes of poetry during his tenure in Paris, as an expression of his own literary and esthetic bent much more, no doubt, than for profit. As his political antennae developed, he also began to seek outlets for these newly acquired skills and interests. His prewar tour of the Balkans provided the first opportunity for extended political analysis. It not only earned him recognition in Chicago, but also led to an invitation to publish some articles in a French journal. Mowrer secured Dennis's approval and was probably more than compensated psychologically by the invitation for the fact his fee was turned over to the *Daily News* at whose expense the trip had been undertaken. After the war Mowrer began to explore additional outlets for the materials and understanding that he had accumulated. He discussed with Bell the advisability of soliciting European publications to reprint stories already prepared for the *Daily News*, noting that such arrangements would increase the prestige of the foreign service and the visibility of its correspondents. Mowrer was the first of the postwar European correspondents to attempt an extended work of sociopolitical reporting and analysis, the articles derived from his second eastern tour which became *Balkanized Europe*.[42]

The fact was that a corps of outstanding reporters was now able to produce more informative and interpretive material than American newspaper editors and their readers were ready to pay for. Mowrer was only one of several correspondents, however, who discovered an outlet for their serious work in the American journals of opinion that appealed to educated and internationally minded readers. Both their need for funds and their desire to reach a wider audience combined to drive correspondents beyond mere news reporting.

CENSORSHIP AND PROPAGANDA

As correspondents tried to win greater influence over the presentation of international news, they also faced infringements upon their activities from another direction—governmental efforts to restrict or regulate access to information sources. Before the war, governments had largely ignored international correspondence instead of attempting to shape it; yet even then some American newsmen had expressed concern at the influence wielded by foreign agencies, public or private, over their sources. When war introduced considerations of national security, mobilization, strategy, and patriotism, officials had responded quickly; both military and civilian authorities initiated censorship programs. More slowly, a variety of techniques were introduced to manipulate news content in order to influence public opinion. Wartime correspondents, coping for the first time with such techniques on a massive scale, had found ways of evading, penetrating, or otherwise circumventing restrictions.

Peace brought relaxation but never abandonment of the new forms of public opinion control. The stakes of international politics had become too high, and the advantages promised by the ability to mold public attitudes too obvious for a return to easy prewar ways. The appearance of new regimes and ideologies threatening the established order and, in turn, threatened by it, provided additional incentives for public opinion management. A more assertive community of foreign correspondents now faced an array of public and private vested interests, with both sides well aware that the ability to manipulate opinions entailed significant political and economic advantages. Western European governments guarded their secrets and fostered favorable public attitudes almost as successfully as did the new Soviet regime. Private political and economic interest groups were also attempting to influence public opinion, although in the correspondents' view government news management efforts were more threatening. As might be expected, the totalitarian systems in Italy and Germany acted most forcefully in this regard. Other right-wing governments, such as in Hungary or Spain, also attempted to control information, but their attempts were not effective, nor their importance and interest great enough to concern American reporters.[43]

The first extensive postwar effort at government news manipulation occurred in the press's encounter with Benito Mussolini. When George Seldes reached Rome in 1924, he found the government bribing foreign correspondents with free cable and radio service in exchange for favorable coverage. Seldes was astonished when the editor of the *Chicago Tribune*'s Paris edition urged him to accept similar favors. He soon discovered that the Paris edition was competing with its *New York Herald Tribune* counterpart for advertising from the Poles and Rumanians as well as the Italians, in exchange for friendly treatment. After Seldes was expelled from Italy, correspondents who remained had to bow to the system or resort to roundabout measures to smuggle out unapproved stories. Their situation was further complicated by the necessity, in deference to the sensitivity of American Catholic readers, of dealing cautiously with the Vatican.[44]

David Darrah, replacing Seldes in 1927, began with the assumption that he could take a "detached...disinterested" stance toward the government, but soon found that this seemingly straightforward objective was "not only impossible but illegal." Darrah discovered a Fascist, whom he thought a "patriot and idealist," on his staff and useful for establishing government contacts. He found the intellectual life of Rome unlike that of any other Western capital. An ideological pall hung palpably over the city. Café life was dull. Even the Foreign Press Association was dominated by the government, which paid its rent, provided translators who were often spies, and packed its membership in order to control its election of officers. Like Seldes, Darrah found the senior Associated Press correspondent, an Italian long considered an authority on local affairs by most Americans, thoroughly subservient to the Fascists. Darrah was by no means so aggressive a reporter as Seldes. Yet he, too, eventually got into trouble. He was kept under police surveillance and his office was frequently rifled. He received support, however, when the Paris *Tribune*, to which he reported, was threatened with loss of its Italian advertising. He was instructed to inform the Italians that any attempt to influence his reporting would lead to the withdrawal of *Tribune* representation in Rome.[45] In 1935 Darrah was at last expelled.

Hiram Motherwell of the *Chicago Daily News*, one of the few correspondents who had backed Seldes against the Italian authorities, also encountered difficulty after getting a report critical of Italian finances past the censors. Carroll Binder, who replaced Motherwell in 1927, found that he had used a number of Italian tipsters to whom he, like other American correspondents, had paid considerable sums. Binder thought that competition was driving up the price of information and that "backstairs" stories, "these tales from queer people," were unreliable. Shortly however, he found that a young anti-Fascist staff member named Renzo Rendi was a valuable source of information. Binder thought it possible, nonetheless, to achieve a relatively balanced "dispassionate view of this truly remarkable experiment" by combining reports of constructive achievements—of which he found a few—with other information. He criticized other American reporters for superficial coverage and for kowtowing to the authorities in return for favored spot news. Yet before he left in 1929 he, too, found it necessary to make compromises, courting favor by transmitting government propaganda in order to slip what he considered more important information past the censors.[46] William Stoneman followed Binder to Rome for the *Daily News* and continued to attempt balanced reporting in the face of pervasive pressures. Shortly after Stoneman's departure, Renzo Rendi was jailed by the government, and neither Stoneman nor the paper were able to win his release.[47]

Mussolini's censorship and propaganda machine was western Europe's most egregious in the twenties, but the record of other governments was far from admirable. After his return to the United States, George Seldes wrote a stinging critique of "censorship, propaganda, intimidation and . . .terrorism" and their effect upon the press. There was a concerted effort by foreign governments to influence public opinion in the United States and Great Britain, Seldes held. Americans, who knew "pathetically little" about Europe, were being persuaded by the combined influence of foreign governments, bankers, and American officials to channel funds into southern and eastern European countries where a "refined. . . subtle, sometime Machiavellian" propaganda and censorship system cloaked the prevailing tyranny and promoted the idea that democracy was not suited to local conditions. Despite some resistance, most reporters and newspapers were bribed or otherwise silenced, Seldes charged, while American diplomats feared to back up independent newsmen. The strongest protection for correspondents, in Seldes's thoroughly soured view, lay in the fact that most editors were still too indifferent to foreign news to question their reporters' work closely. He feared that as American international involvement grew, such benign neglect would yield to greater pressure from editorial offices.[48] By then Seldes had broken completely with the journalistic establishment, but his charges clearly were not without foundation.

To consider the full range of censorship and propaganda activity in Europe between the wars would require at least a volume. For our purposes, however, the correspondents' observations on their own personal experiences suffice. Their experiences with the system as it evolved in Nazi Germany after 1933 further document the range of pressures they faced and the devices to which they resorted in attempting to cope with such an unprecedented situation. In December 1932 Edgar Mowrer published *Germany Puts Back the Clock*, his searching analysis of the factors underlying the nation's crisis. Mowrer's journalistic sense of timing proved acute, for within a month Adolph Hitler was appointed reichschancellor and began consolidating his control. Mowrer's criticisms of the Nazis immediately attracted fire from the new regime. He was placed under surveillance and his associations were closely monitored. Efforts to discredit him were followed by an official declaration naming him persona non grata and by a government boycott of the Foreign Press Association of which he then served as president. Members of the foreign press rallied to Mowrer's defense, but his situation was untenable and he was forced to leave Germany.[49]

Louis Lochner, who had presided over the Foreign Press Association previously, resumed that post after Mowrer's departure when it seemed symbolically desirable that another American be named. Despite his earlier reputation as a radical, Lochner had cultivated connections with the Nazis, as well as with monarchists and the military. As Berlin head of the Associated Press he had little opportunity and, apparently, little inclination to express political views of his own. On this account he may have seemed well suited to bridge the gap between the Nazis and the foreign press. His political education began almost at once, however, and continued until he left Germany in 1942. For the remainder of his tour of duty Lochner faced a combination of pressures and persuasion that tested his endurance and ingenuity along with those of many other American correspondents. His letters and his autobiography reveal a great deal about the ways in which Hitler's government squeezed and manipulated the press.

Lochner first arranged a series of informal meetings between the foreign press corps and Nazi officials, hoping to open lines of communication. He discovered, however, that the government was already recruiting German employees of foreign news bureaus to spy on their employers. Telephone tapping and other espionage attempts were commonplace. The Foreign Press Association, long noted for its banquets at which government spokesmen discussed policy matters with the press, found that under the Nazis one of its chief functions had become that of holding farewell dinners for members expelled from the country. The German government harassed Lochner because of his Jewish friends and associates but apologized after considering the danger of alienating the Associated Press. News gathering, nonetheless, became increasingly difficult. Many of the AP's local correspondents and stringers severed ties, fearing an American connection might bring trouble for them. Official news releases could not be accepted at face value, but the means for verifying them were limited. By 1934 Lochner felt the Nazis were "drawing a chain around the foreign correspondents." "We are sitting on a smouldering volcano," he wrote Kent Cooper, president of the AP. Unlike some other reporters, Lochner did not feel threatened personally. The Ministry of Propaganda's hostility had not ruptured his friendly ties with other government offices; connections in the military, economic, and foreign affairs departments gave him protection and lines of communication to official sources.[50]

The Nazis alternately courted and squeezed foreign journalists. They were offered observation tours to persuade them that all was well, then denounced by the propaganda minister, Joseph Goebbels (whom Lochner termed "Wotan's Mickey Mouse"), for not accepting the party line. On one such trip, to check out rumors of a munitions plant explosion, Lochner and others were arrested by the secret police and held for forty-five minutes. In 1936 Lochner was threatened with expulsion, but was backed by Ambassador William Dodd and the entire American colony which elected him president of the American Chamber of Commerce. To his family and to Kent Cooper, Lochner complained of the difficulties of carrying on under such trying circumstances; but, a newsman at heart, he found satisfaction in occasional successes. These included scoring a beat in reporting Hitler's renunciation of the Locarno Pact thirty-six hours before the official announcement, and having tea with Charles A. Lindbergh—despite the latter's hostility to the press—on the strength of his friendship with their mutual host, the Crown Prince Wilhelm. Lochner even managed to turn his troubles in Germany to account at home by asking AP headquarters not to edit his copy, since he was forced to choose his words carefully and alterations made in America might create difficulties for him with the authorities.[51]

The Nazis' intensive public opinion management dramatized what had been occurring less openly elsewhere and focused attention on the implications of organized thought control. As early as 1934 Leland Stowe wrote ominously that "public information. . .is on the retreat," and he questioned whether, should another war break out, Europeans would have "any modest conception of both sides of the issues in advance of this second twentieth-century reversion to mass suicide?" Although Germany and Italy were obviously the chief offenders, Stowe held that the French press had always received both government and private subsidies and was substantially controlled by military and munitions interests. French radio, however, was not so deeply involved with propaganda functions as were the Italian and German systems. In the latter countries, film production also faced government control or censorship. These facts had far-reaching implications, Stowe argued in relating them to other developments of the era: "Among the foremost refinements of the twentieth century must be listed this systematic and wholesale manufacture of opinion. Streamlined chassis have to be planned, plotted and molded in advance. So does the production of a mass idea, mass prejudice, or mass emotion."[52]

Dorothy Thompson went still further in pointing out that the first target of recent antigovernment coup attempts had been, not military or finance headquarters, but radio stations. A failed coup in Austria had reacted in part against the government's use of radio to spread lies about the opposition leadership. Domination of information channels by power blocs created problems, Thompson argued, not only for news gathering, but for the very basis of democracy itself. Government by consent of the governed had, thus far, depended upon individual reason and access to diverse information sources. Powerful authoritarian movements now challenged this conception by reinterpreting it. They, too, rested their claims to legitimacy on the doctrine of consent, but coupled powerful programs of mass persuasion with other rigid controls to create a new totalitarian system. Building upon the recognition by Freud, Sorel, Pareto, Bergson, and others of the power of irrational forces in human behavior, they had discovered new and threatening ways to command public allegiance. Thompson noted that the German Ministry of Propaganda relied not on censorship alone, but upon the licensing of newsmen, tests of racial and ideological purity, and the minute regulation of news content to establish its control. In Russia, private ownership of radios was not permitted. Elsewhere, too, techniques of persuasion which had often been initiated by business and applied by all nations in the course of the war were now being organized into highly integrated and effective systems of thought control. Truth was defined as what was useful to the state, and propaganda was a method of using ideas as weapons against enemies of the state.[53]

As the thirties unfolded, reporters were exposed to a range of techniques for manipulating public opinion that expanded more rapidly than they could outmaneuver them and that clearly imperiled the integrity of their work. By 1939, in the period between the formal declarations of war and the beginning of large-scale hostilities the following spring, Edmond Taylor in Paris had devoted an entire book, *The Strategy of Terror*, to discussing government efforts on both sides to disconcert, discourage, and divide enemy opinion. Leaflets, leaks, rumors of increased—or lowered—tension, and calculated alternations of rhetoric between the conciliatory and the hostile all convinced Taylor that a turning point had been reached in the management of public opinion and morale. He stressed the pivotal significance of the new techniques although he disclaimed any ability to describe or delineate their character adequately.[54]

It was little wonder that those seriously concerned with the future of journalism and of democracy should have felt deep concern at such developments in control and censorship. And it may, in the end, have been a sense that modern techniques of opinion control by those hostile to freedom menaced all that they cared for that led so many newsmen to abandon journalism for government service as the Second World War approached. In military and civilian intelligence, propaganda, public information, diplomatic service, and similar functions, the former correspondents could turn the weapons of information management, whose awesome power they had felt, directly against the enemies who had first mobilized them.

At the time, however, realization of the full import of the emerging patterns of opinion management came slowly, even to correspondents who found themselves treading the new ideological battlefields. Herbert Matthews, facing the censorship and propaganda in both Italy and Spain, still insisted upon the correspondent's responsibility for accuracy. Censorship could prevent the sending of news at a particular time or from a given spot, but it could not force correspondents to report falsehood. Reporters, not censors, he insisted, must take responsibility for erroneous stories and mistaken judgments.[55] In view of the many obstacles, distortions, and pressures with which newsmen were faced, this was too simple a statement, yet it contained an important element of truth. In stressing the reporter's ultimate responsibility for his copy, Matthews was not merely upholding an embattled, impossible ideal. He wrote in the light of decades of journalistic experience with censorship and propaganda and with the techniques newsmen had devised for circumventing or mitigating them. No one could argue, with a second world war in prospect, that journalists had coped successfully with the rapidly proliferating technology of opinion management. Yet over the years, in peacetime as well as in war, they had found ways of evading controls and at least occasionally piercing the fog of secrecy and misrepresentation. Experienced reporters had learned to question official releases. Ingenious and determined ones had discovered indirect ways of gathering and transmitting news that evaded the authorities. It is no more possible to detail the variety of measures used by correspondents to escape the net drawn around them than it is to specify the multitude of methods deployed against them. There were positive ways of cultivating and exploiting information sources, as well as negative ones of evading restrictions.

Bell, Mowrer, Williams, and others during the First World War had cultivated British and French officialdom as well as American embassy personnel. News bureaus in Mussolini's Rome had found it helpful to employ Italians with connections among the powerful Fascisti. Sigrid Schultz, working night after night in the *Chicago Tribune*'s bureau in the Adlon Hotel, had found it an admirable listening post when government officials dropped by for a chat on their way home from official functions in the upstairs ballroom.[56] Louis Lochner's network of relationships with influential Germans of all political stripes proved a source both of valuable information and of personal protection. Wythe Williams had established a group of informants while in Germany, and he continued to find them helpful after he returned home in 1936. His connections included members of Hitler's entourage even after he became editor of the *Greenwich* (Connecticut) *Times* and a radio commentator. From this unlikely vantage point, Williams later claimed to have predicted the German invasions of Denmark, the Low Countries, and the Balkans and to have issued reports on the state of German aircraft production based on information derived from these "secret sources." Ironically, he even got into trouble with American authorities in 1940 for using such information to support his advocacy of American military preparedness.[57]

There were dangers as well as advantages in reporters' close identification with and dependence upon favored sources. Bell and Paul Mowrer faced criticism for reflecting interested European, rather than presumably independent American, viewpoints. Their indignant rejection of such charges, although sincere, was not entirely persuasive. Too heavy dependence upon a few sources could produce bias as readily as reliable insights. Familiarity with the European scene was obviously helpful, but it could widen the gap between the perceptions of correspondents and their readers. Thoughtful reporters were themselves sensitive to this problem, although they usually dismissed it with sneers at the ignorance and provincialism of American readers. Bell had begun early to point out to Victor Lawson the value of periodic home visits for a correspondent's perspective, and he noted in 1904 that the Associated Press, the *New York Sun*, and the *New York Times* called their people home from time to time "to get brightened up."[58]

Colonel McCormick, fearing the "Europeanizing" of his foreign staff, kept his reporters on the move lest they become contaminated with the biases, attachments, and "un-American" influences of any particular locale. Whatever its shortcomings, this approach did encourage one technique of censorship evasion upon which all correspondents and news services came to rely when restrictions were severe and the news value of a story particularly high. George Seldes attributed to Floyd Gibbons the phrase "Tell the Truth and Run"—which Seldes later appropriated as the title of his memoirs—as a description of the hit-and-run method of relaying a politically dangerous story and moving on to another country before the authorities could discover its source and apprehend the sender. Useful for a quick scoop, the trick did not lend itself to the development of an important story over time, and obviously it could not be used repeatedly by the same reporter or from the same location.

Consequently, correspondents developed less dramatic but equally effective means of getting officially banned news across borders controlled by sensitive governments. The mails were slightly less subject to government supervision than were cable, telegraph, and radio channels, but they too were not reliable. Still, a certain amount of material could be smuggled out via these means by using codes or burying sensitive data in messages ostensibly devoted to other matters. Sometimes a story could be carried by a friend or colleague, or even by the correspondent himself on a trip outside his base country. Such reports could be published anonymously or under another reporter's name, to protect the source.

As the Nazi censorship net tightened around him, Louis Lochner managed to send a message to the AP's Kent Cooper by none other than Prince Louis Ferdinand of Hohenzollern. In 1936 Lochner was able to inform Cooper of German assistance to the Spanish rebels by way of an AP colleague from Paris. Perhaps the most ingenious method reported for eluding the censor was that used by Herbert L. Matthews in Spain. Taking advantage of the relaxed character of Spanish censorship, Matthews managed to get his stories to Paris for the *New York Times* by simply having the Paris office telephone him at home during the hours when the censor went out to dinner![59]

Such ruses give some inkling of the ingenuity correspondents could muster in defense of their trade. Defying governments no doubt added to the element of adventure, as it did to that of risk and danger, associated with their work. But there were other considerations at work as well. Those who were serious about news gathering—who refused to be bribed, coddled, or intimidated by self-serving governments and interest groups, who felt a responsibility to inform and stimulate understanding among their American readers—acted on an assumption that journalism had a role in modern society that took precedence even over the claims of government itself. Consciously or unconsciously, they were claiming the prerogative of experienced professionals to define and apply the standards they deemed appropriate to the service they rendered. Correspondents who took such a stand and who earned the respect of their peers and of the public in trying to uphold it faced powerful, pervasive opposition. In assuming the risks such defiance involved, they reaffirmed their confidence in the value of their work. Risking what they did abroad to gather the news, it was natural for them also to challenge the authority of those at home who published it.

6

Toward Recognition and Professional Status

■ Hedged in on the one hand by editors and business managers and on the other by powerful efforts at opinion manipulation, reporters lacked an independent base. But their strongest resource, their accumulated knowledge and expertise, was beginning to command respect. Such recognition, in fact, made their dependent status all the more galling, helping to convert resentment of home office insensitivity into outright contempt. The idea of foreign correspondence as a profession with its own rights and responsibilities appealed to some of the more thoughtful members of the group as a basis for claiming quasi-independent status. Others began to reach beyond newspaper work for alternative channels of communication to the public. Both approaches expressed the correspondents' conviction that their expertise and understanding had become too important to remain at the mercy of ill-informed third parties. Edward Price Bell, Paul Mowrer, and Walter Lippmann were among the few who openly applied the terms *professionalism* and *profession* to international reporting, but others clearly showed their adherence to a similar standard. The professional ideal offered both an acknowledgment and a challenge. It dignified their skills and knowledge while offering them a criterion of effective performance.

THE PROFESSIONAL IDEAL

Traditionally, professions are defined by several distinctive features: a body of specialized learning, a structured system for training and testing members in the acquisition of this knowledge, and a strict, enforceable code regulating its application for the benefit of society as a whole. By none of these criteria could foreign correspondence properly qualify for professional status. Although journalism schools offering specialized training in certain—chiefly technical—functions had begun to appear early in the century, none devoted significant attention to international relations, foreign languages, or the political, economic, or cultural subjects upon which correspondents depended. In the early stages of other professions such as law or engineering, entry had depended upon apprenticeship systems such as that which operated in journalism, so that this objection might have been overridden. But there remained the fact that no clearly defined and prescribable body of information, practice, or tradition existed to equip a correspondent for the varied assignments he faced. Bell had devised an informal system of advice and supervision that Paul Mowrer carried even further. No doubt the chiefs and senior correspondents of other overseas services operated in similar ways. But in the end the individual correspondent lived by his wits, his energy, and his imagination. He learned as much, perhaps, from his competitors and from friends or associates outside the journalistic sphere as from his superiors. No formal, regularized program of training, practice, and advancement suited the uncertainties, irregularities, and sudden changes of pace or direction that characterized foreign correspondence.

Correspondents were even less capable of setting and enforcing standards of ethical, socially responsible behavior. Rather, they were subject to the whims or biases of employers and to the policies, pressures, and persuasions applied by those from or about whom they sought information. To make matters worse, such pressures were heightened by the exigencies of time, the need to meet cable or publication deadlines, and the premium in important matters on scoring a beat over their rivals. In the face of such hurdles, it may appear quixotic that experienced reporters thought seriously of defining a professional ideal. Indeed, to many of the old rough-and-ready types, as well as to some of their younger, adventure-seeking colleagues, it probably did.[1] But for those who found new importance in their work, or to whom America's new international role had become clear, the professional ideal despite its difficulties exercised an appeal that measured both their frustration with the existing system and their hopes for a more influential role.

Those who pleaded the case for professionalism can also be understood as offering a rationalization for a rapidly disappearing quasi-independent status in an age of encircling corporatism. This yearning for professional status was not, after all, an isolated effort. A wide range of functional social and economic groups, including engineers, business executives, social workers, advertising and public relations personnel, and many others were similarly claiming special expertise and status in the face of the powerful bureaucratic movement permeating many levels and sectors of modern life. Curiously, having left home in part to preserve their sense of individuality, foreign correspondents now confronted the same centralizing forces which were reshaping society there and which were already crossing national boundaries to bind people in larger ties of mutual interdependence. Even as the correspondents heralded the international character of this development at one level, they struggled to limit its impact on their personal lives and careers at another.

Early in the century Bell had formulated a rough notion of foreign correspondence as a profession. War had sidetracked such ideas by fostering competition for quick news delivery, strengthening government controls, and emphasizing patriotism or ideology at the expense of balanced reporting. War, however, had also raised the consciousness and commitment of foreign correspondents. Men such as Bell and Paul Mowrer were now prepared to argue for a greatly enlarged vision of the nature and responsibilities of foreign correspondence. Both were eager for more ambitious roles, even for a share in the formulation of editorial policy. Bell, about to leave Europe in 1922, negotiated an assignment that enabled him to hobnob with powerful leaders and to work for world understanding and peace.[2] Mowrer, destined to remain for another decade, devoted himself to improving and extending the influence of the foreign service there.

In May 1920 Mowrer sent Lawson and Dennis a list of suggestions for reorganizing the service in response to Chicago's renewed requests for human interest stories and "picturesque" materials. He conceded that there was a place for such items but urged concentration on more serious matters. "The basic aim of our foreign service," Mowrer argued, "should be to inform the American people regarding all important *social, political, economic* and psychological developments." Democratic government relied on informed public opinion and journalism must strengthen that opinion. American readers wanted "careful, serious news" such as the *Daily News* had provided, Mowrer insisted; and he pointed to growth in the number and circulation of thoughtful weekly magazines as evidence. It was more important, he continued, to provide first-class news to those who truly appreciated it than to attempt to please everyone. The *Daily*

News could retain a loyal following by addressing important issues and events as they were evaluated by its trained correspondents. It could furnish "a sounder, finer service than has yet been seen in America," Mowrer wrote. He ended with a plea: "Our men are simply itching to do their best, provided they are given a high aim, and a feeling of mutual support and encouragement."[3]

There was no direct response to Mowrer's suggestions, although Dennis approved his proposed tour to survey postwar developments in southeastern Europe. Mowrer's observations on this trip encouraged him to prepare a second proposal which he forwarded to Bell for comment. Citing his Balkan reports, Mowrer argued that such materials, "partly informative, partly editorial," should become a regular feature. As "Diplomatic Correspondent" with a decade's exposure to world issues, Mowrer wrote, "I believe that I can succeed in giving the *Daily News* a feature that will be unique in American journalism." For years the paper had supplied its readers "not merely with features which amuse, but with features which instruct and educate, or which are a public service." Domestic interests, understandably, had preoccupied Americans in the past, but henceforth "we must also give serious attention to foreign affairs...for which as a people we are at present less well equipped."[4] Chicago's reaction to Mowrer's implied criticism of its editorial approach was ambivalent. His request for special status was denied but he was named to succeed Bell as head of the European service.

During his remaining twelve years in Europe, Mowrer failed to win management's support for his ambitious program of interpretive journalism. Still, by personal example and judicious guidance and supervision, he assisted in maintaining the service at a level which made it the envy of others. In 1924 he submitted a report to Lawson on his tenure as chief of the European staff, spelling out the improvements instituted under his leadership. The report was the closest thing to a statement of his concept of a professionalized foreign news service that Mowrer had an opportunity to present. He may have intended it as another round in his campaign to win Chicago over to his vision of comprehensive, analytical foreign correspondence. If so, he was soon disappointed, for Lawson's death later in the year ended whatever opportunity there may have been for further strengthening the *Daily News*'s foreign service.

Mowrer's report addressed both the issue of economy, which concerned Dennis and Lawson, and that of effectiveness, which interested Mowrer himself so deeply. He had urged correspondents to utilize radio transmission, cheaper than cable, for important stories and to mail longer, more analytical reports intended for serial publication. He had reduced cable costs by using less busy, less expensive filing hours, and he had instituted a cable quota system, long demanded by Chicago, limiting reporters to a specified number of words each month. Careful planning had enabled him to strengthen news coverage without adding personnel. He had provided advice, carefully prescribed assignments, and regular supervision for the less experienced correspondents, while allowing their knowledgeable seniors much greater latitude and discretion. Reporters were urged to send stories by way of Paris, where Mowrer could edit them to regularize the flow of news, if need be. He had encouraged close cooperation between correspondents, for "exchanging tips, information and opinions; of pooling common experience and knowledge for the benefit of the many concerned in any given assignment...making reliefs and carrying out changes with a minimum of loss of continuity and efficiency; and in general...heightening the esprit de corps of the service." He had developed a group of "mobile correspondents" for emergency assignments outside the normal beats. And he had circulated home office suggestions and "personal news of the service, and news of American foreign policy" to all bureaus, while sending copies of his telegrams and letters to correspondents back to Dennis each week. The picture that emerged from this summary of activities was of a carefully coordinated and supervised service, dedicated to comprehensive, systematic, and thoughtful presentation of the news. As proof of its effectiveness, Mowrer noted that the number of papers subscribing to the *Daily News*'s foreign service had nearly doubled in the preceding year.[5]

Mowrer's work for a more responsible foreign correspondence coincided with an examination by Walter Lippmann of the role of the press in modern society. After wartime service with Military Intelligence and the planning staff for the Versailles peace conference, Lippmann had joined the *New York World*'s editorial staff. Over the years he had concluded that the traditional democratic reliance upon a free press and an informed citizenry was increasingly threatened by well-organized private interests. Large-scale concentrations of economic power, armed with new techniques of advertising and mass marketing, were overpowering the free exchange of ideas characteristic of a more equalitarian, individualistic age. Still further, new findings in individual and group psychology challenged long-standing assumptions as to the rationality of human behavior and decision-making.

In a 1922 book, *Public Opinion*, Lippmann discussed journalism in the light of these sweeping changes. In his view, the press suffered many of the conditions that were sapping society's ability to control its increasingly complex institutions:

> ...the troubles of the press, like the troubles of representative government, be it territorial or functional, like the troubles of industry, be it capitalist, cooperative, or communist, go back to a common source: to the failure of self-governing people to transcend their casual experience and their prejudice, by inventing, creating, and organizing a machinery of knowledge. It is because they are compelled to act without a reliable picture of the world, that governments, schools, newspapers and churches make such small headway against the more obvious failings of democracy...violent prejudice, apathy, preference for the curious trivial as against the dull important, and the hunger for sideshows and three-legged calves.

To mobilize social intelligence more effectively, Lippmann proposed the creation of networks of experts in government, education, and other sectors to organize information with which administrators could make rational decisions. Citizens, lacking interest in and access to detailed information, could then limit themselves to ascertaining that full and fair procedures for decision-making based upon all relevant considerations had indeed been followed.[6]

Lippmann's call for an elite to mobilize the quantities of data increasingly required by a highly integrated society was an extension, as he recognized, of developments already under way. His analysis tended to discredit newspapers as reliable information sources because they depended heavily on public favor and were easily manipulated or controlled by powerful interests. What Lippmann did not consider or, if he did, did not find sufficiently impressive to discuss, was the fact that journalism itself was responding to the specializing tendencies he found elsewhere—developing its own specialties and experts, among whom, of course, were the foreign correspondents. Paul Mowrer, who thought himself such an expert, dismissed Lippmann's discussion briefly in a note to Dennis as "surprisingly barren." But Mowrer's reaction may have been disingenuous, struggling as he was to establish his own professional credentials. He was also devoting a good deal of thought to the subject of public opinion and foreign policy.[7]

Mowrer's ideas were set forth in two statements issued in the course of more than a decade, a 1923 book titled *Our Foreign Affairs* and an essay on "The Press and the Public," printed in 1934 by the League of Nations' International Institute of Intellectual Cooperation. In the latter, he considered the part played by daily newspapers in efforts to "educate the people...and to further the cause of peace," and conceded that newspapers were not primarily educational vehicles. Rather than careful analysis of important issues such as books or journal articles might offer, newspapers presented "a more or less skillful, more or less arbitrary selection of events snatched hastily from current life to be reported and spread before the reader with a minimum of delay." Those papers devoted to "the fair and serious presentation of political, economic, scientific and artistic events must be prepared to sell few copies," he acknowledged, while those with large circulation "devote[d] their pages primarily to photographs and...crime, sex, sports and cinema actors, with, by way of international interest, frequent chauvinistic attacks on foreign nations." Public-spirited editors, however, were seriously concerned with this situation. Much emphasis and ingenuity were being poured into arousing public interest in important subjects by vivacious presentations of their human interest angles. Mowrer himself set little store by such tactics. In terms that may well have been directed to the *Daily News* editors as well as a wider audience, he argued that a "new and far better formula" was emerging. His own answer to the problem of quality rested finally on the capacity of highly skilled, experienced specialists to select and interpret the news. "Given a free country with a high level of education and independent thought," Mowrer insisted, there was "no reason why a public-spirited publisher cannot produce an honest, independent newspaper with enough readers to make it fairly successful and to enable it to command the services of competent journalistic specialists."[8]

The foreign affairs reporter, Mowrer held, must be a specialist in international politics and economics. He must investigate all sides of each question. "He must not talk merely with the diplomats and politicians, he must study documents and situations by himself, at first hand." Not only was he responsible to report events but also to explain their significance to readers who might not see how developments far afield related to their own lives. Mowrer emphasized the "ethical ideals of the modern journalist." Although not all achieved the ideal of honesty and objectivity, its influence "in the ranks of the entire profession" ran "far deeper than is commonly supposed." "A journalist may be a fervent patriot, an enthusiastic party member, a faithful employee," he asserted, "but at the same time, in his strictly journalistic function, his first loyalty is not to country, party, or paper, but to his readers." Newspapers were already raising the level of public understanding by giving readers accurate news on which to base their opinions. The way to get "true news [was]...to have competent journalists and create a demand for their work." Such journalists needed public understanding and support; theirs was a "delicate situation," between the pressures of powerful interests and the dangers of falsehood or distortion. Their chief hope lay in public recognition of the journalists' code of honor: "loyalty, first of all and above all, to the public, to the readers of the newspapers, who are entitled to the truth and whose confidence it is dishonorable to betray."[9]

To illustrate, Mowrer considered the issue of journalism's responsibility to promote peace. The press should not be expected to promote even the best causes, he argued; "a newspaper is not a peace society." Its duty was simply to report facts. "When politicians, statesmen and peoples think, speak and act peaceably, they further the cause of peace. When they do not, it is hardly the fault of the newspapers if their columns are therefore filled with alarums." As long as journalists reported "the demonstrable truth, no matter how unpleasant," they deserved public confidence and, of course, that of their editors as well.[10] Given his own experience of limited support from a newspaper widely considered among the best in its international coverage, Mowrer's advocacy of journalistic responsibility and professionalism may seem unrealistic. In view of the economic, political, and ideological buffetings to which the press has been subject since he wrote, it may even appear quixotic. Yet the ideal he espoused clearly influenced the work of many of his peers.[11] As a standard of accomplishment and aspiration, the idea of foreign correspondence as a profession—granted its limitations—set the ideal for a generation of journalists whose work brought the field new dignity and recognition.

INTELLIGENCE AND DIPLOMACY

Well before the expertise that foreign correspondents commanded had gained general recognition, editors, businessmen, and even government officials had begun to tap these special sources of intelligence. Journalists combined the opportunity and the incentive for information gathering across a wider range of topics than any other group. This had been true at an early stage, if we may once again take the experience of Edward Price

Bell as illustrative. As head of a news service extending through the major European capitals and beyond, Bell was in an excellent position to glean items of interest and importance. In 1905 he passed on to Charles Dennis reports that the Russian czar was stirring up trouble in the Balkans "to show he is still around," after the disastrous war with Japan and the recent revolution. Later, Bell relayed word of British backing for France at the time of the Moroccan Crisis and confidential news about the invasion of the London commercial arena by H. Gordon Selfridge, the former Chicago department store magnate. By 1908 he was able to advise Dennis concerning the background of current Anglo-Japanese negotiations and the attitudes of both powers toward the United States. When Paul Mowrer reached Paris in 1910, he discovered that "echoes of respect for [Bell's] knowledge of affairs in London" had already crossed the English Channel.[12]

War enormously increased the number and value of news items, as well as the eagerness of editors and government officials for whatever tips and secret information could be uncovered. Frederic Wile and Raymond Swing may have encountered difficulty before 1914 in persuading the *Daily News* of the significance of German war preparations, but thereafter American newspapers were avid for virtually any rumor, "break," and confidential—or merely credible—background intelligence they could secure. According to Bell's biographer, by the war's end British press and government leaders both frequently turned to him for news or for confirmation of news they had obtained elsewhere. In preparing to return to the United States in 1922, Bell asked the aid of former Ambassador George Harvey in arranging interviews with Lord George Nathaniel Curzon, Joseph Chamberlain, and Winston Churchill. He wanted, he wrote, to be in a position to answer as authoritatively as possible questions that President Coolidge and Secretaries Hughes and Hoover might put to him.[13]

Bell's experience provides an early example of the information an alert reporter could assemble by carefully cultivating sources over a period of time. The war taught editors the value of such connections, both for news and for background to guide editorial policy and plan future coverage. Conditions in the twenties tended to reinforce their appreciation of and reliance upon it. Not only did they have more experienced correspondents upon whom to draw, but the twistings and turnings of European politics and the active, if often informal, involvement of the American government in international dealings increased the value of reliable private sources of information.

Long before Bell retired, Paul Mowrer's situation in Paris had begun to match his in London. During the war the two had exchanged military and political intelligence, helping each other understand how events were viewed in the two capitals. Mowrer, at one point, sent Bell the name of a French embassy staff member in London to whom he could turn for reliable information. Returning from his second Balkan trip in 1920, Mowrer advised Dennis that the *Daily News* could take a fairly optimistic editorial stance toward Europe: the threat of bolshevism was receding and conditions were somewhat better than had been generally reported. Replying to criticisms relayed by Dennis in 1922 that his stories reflected a strongly pro-French bias, Mowrer defended the accuracy and reliability of his work. His information was based on "inside" but not "official" sources, he wrote. If his critics really wanted to know what the French people were doing and thinking they would do well to "leave off *The Nation* and *The New Republic*, and...read more carefully the dispatches of the *Chicago Daily News*." He met periodically with Ambassador Myron T. Herrick, but Herrick knew less than he about American or French politics, Mowrer asserted. The ambassador tried to pump him for information, while all Mowrer got in return were requests for help in preparing speeches.[14]

In 1923 Mowrer reported having received two offers, from a French and an American company, to provide them with confidential political reports. He claimed to have turned down twelve thousand dollars per year for such work and was doubtless pleased to point to this evidence of recognition. Later Mowrer recalled having refused a contract offered by the Japanese government for a monthly report on the "state of American opinion." Other newsmen, he stated, had accepted similar offers and thus placed themselves on the Japanese payroll. When Mowrer was named head of the *Daily News* European service he received a note from Arthur Sweetser, an American serving the League of Nations Secretariat, proposing an informal exchange of information. Mowrer forwarded the note to Dennis and cryptically noted that a similar arrangement already existed. Mowrer personally covered the naval disarmament conferences in Washington in 1921 and London in 1929, and from Washington, he wrote Dennis that he had dined with Herbert Hoover, who wanted to learn what he could do to promote the conference's success. Eight years later, however, Mowrer incurred Hoover's displeasure by stressing the importance of recognizing French interests. Mowrer and Bell supported different sides at the 1929 conference. Bell, an ardent Anglophile, advised Hoover, while Dwight Morrow and other American conference delegates were more receptive to Mowrer's views. Mowrer heard that Hoover had complained to the *Daily News* and tried to have him discharged—recognition of a most impressive kind. And, indeed, Dennis, while critical of the foreign service, seldom had anything but praise for Mowrer himself. In 1923 he wrote that Lawson had been so impressed with Mowrer's analysis of the reparations problem that he wanted the *Daily News* to endorse it editorially.[15]

Mowrer's range of contacts and connections was certainly extraordinary, but it was not unique. As gatherers, exchangers, and interpreters of international news, with access to private and informal as well as official sources, foreign correspondents had no equals; and access to intelligence fed on itself by attracting to them individuals and organizations seeking information. Raymond Swing, for instance, upon a return visit to the United States in 1917 found his familiarity with Germany of special interest to Colonel Edward House, President Wilson's advisor. House employed Swing as a private informant and messenger to France, Spain, and Switzerland to explore conditions for a negotiated peace. This secret assignment troubled Swing as inconsistent with his journalist status and ended by getting him into trouble with House when his reports contradicted official positions.[16]

Reaching Berlin in 1924, Edgar Mowrer found himself in an extremely lively news center. He described his position to Dennis in terms indicating its possibilities both for news gathering and information exchange: "Since I have come here I have become an artist in finance, economics, and social etiquette, spending vast quantities of otherwise valuable time out of office hours with bankers, counts, manufacturers, etc. . . . I wonder if you in Chicago really realize the enormous influence the United States might wield in Europe if they would, all the good the *Daily News* is doing, and even more, which it might do?" At the time of the election of Paul von Hindenburg as president of the republic in 1925 Mowrer reported confidentially that Parker Gilbert, the American reparations agent, had warned that the election results would greatly complicate matters. Mowrer later recalled many conversations with American bankers interested in learning about Germany's prospects but "deaf to warnings by newsmen like me" about dumping loans on the Germans. His ties to German intellectuals also produced invitations to speak at German universities and write for various journals.[17]

Other examples show how correspondents' access to information and sources enabled them to supply information to a variety of interested recipients. Bell and Paul Mowrer had seen from the outset that exchange of information among correspondents increased their effectiveness, and Mowrer had tried to regularize such exchanges upon assuming leadership of the European service. Meanwhile, of course, correspondents of various papers and press associations had been exchanging tips and data as friendly rivals for years. When Dorothy Thompson married Sinclair Lewis and returned to the United States to launch a regular public affairs column for the *New York Herald Tribune*, she called upon another Vienna veteran, John Gunther, for an update on Austria. Later, Gunther himself drew heavily on the knowledge of many of his correspondent colleagues for materials for *Inside Europe*. And Raymond Swing in London in the early thirties learned enough about Britain's financial situation from associates and friends to write several articles on the gold standard which his editor refused to print for fear of influencing the stock market.[18]

Given their circumstances, it was virtually inevitable that some correspondents would move beyond the mere exchanging of information with government officials to at least marginal participation in diplomatic activity itself. Correspondents often had a wider circle of acquaintanceship and greater familiarity with local conditions than did diplomats. Their private status also gave them a latitude of action frequently not available to officials. Journalists, in fact, made such admirable go-betweens, private agents, and spokesmen that diplomats were tempted to cultivate and use them in situations where formal channels were inadequate. Reporters seem usually to have welcomed such opportunities, either because they provided additional information sources or as flattering acknowledgments of their own expertise. Presumably, both parties benefited from such arrangements; but little consideration seems to have been given to the possibility that they might threaten correspondents' independence and freedom of judgment. Raymond Swing, however, felt sufficiently uneasy with his intelligence assignment for Colonel House while a *Daily News* correspondent to report the situation to Paul Mowrer. Mowrer himself seems to have cooperated actively in a number of minor diplomatic undertakings in the twenties while insisting to Dennis that his periodic meetings with Ambassador Herrick involved no "official" commitments to the embassy. He told Dennis that he had provided information to the staff of the American minister to the Netherlands and had helped to arrange a meeting between French Foreign Minister Aristide Briand and

Soviet representative Maxim Litvinov. And when the French occupied the Ruhr he drafted a call for more active American intervention for use by Ambassador Herrick.[19]

Aside from Swing and Mowrer, few correspondents indicated doubts or reservations as to the propriety of such diplomatic involvements. This is not necessarily surprising. The relationships in question developed quickly and under the pressure of events. On their face they seemed beneficial to both parties concerned, although we cannot discount the possibility that in their eagerness to impress others correspondents may have exaggerated their influence and connections. Still, the ties that reporters cultivated with important public or private figures, however helpful for gathering data and gaining perspective, were potentially capable of coloring their judgments and raising difficult conflicts of interest.

Bell, a correspondent with extensive personal and journalistic connections, engaged in several activities that raised questions concerning his objectivity. His support for the Allies led him to become an ardent advocate of America's entry into the First World War. Sensitive to criticism of United States neutrality, he openly defended the American position in letters to the English press, while expressing the view that the United States would eventually join the Allies. After conversations with Colonel House and Ambassador Walter Hines Page, Bell also sent an open letter to President Wilson advocating American involvement. Bell's public expressions of opinion were criticized by Dennis, who refused to publish the letter, and by Swing in Berlin who felt his own position threatened by the partisan actions of a colleague. In England, however, Bell's letters won him additional popularity and respect, especially since his predictions proved accurate.

Private status coupled with official connections enabled Bell to act as an informal ambassador to the British people at a time when American officials were unable to speak publicly. Given the immanence of American belligerence, any threat to the reputation of the *Daily News* in Berlin was more than offset by the popularity it gained in London; but Bell's actions nonetheless constituted an instance of overt journalistic partisanship. A second incident, from which he emerged less happily, occurred in 1929 in connection with efforts to arrange a meeting between President Hoover and Prime Minister Ramsay MacDonald. Bell allowed himself to be quoted in the press as saying that meeting plans, which he was actively fostering, had been completed when in fact they had not. This premature action embarrassed both governments and damaged his reputation for accuracy as well. It would seem that in Bell's case, partisanship and influence blinded a correspondent to the dangers of mixing journalism with diplomacy.[20]

A less compromising but equally revealing instance of the ease with which journalists could become involved beyond the limits of their responsibilities found George Seldes in the midst of delicate negotiations between British and Irish Republican leaders in 1919. Seldes's superior in the *Chicago Tribune*'s London office was John Scott Steele, a naturalized American citizen born in Ireland. Steele's balanced coverage of Anglo-Irish relations had earned him the respect of both sides. He was pressed into service as a go-between for the British and Irish leaders who at one point even met in the *Tribune* office. Steele sent Seldes with a secret message to Republican headquarters in Dublin, where he went as a reporter for an American paper with an influential Irish clientele. Seldes returned with a reply for the British and with new material on the Irish nationalist movement for his readers as well.[21] Since the mission suited both parties Steele and Seldes in this case probably did not jeopardize their independence, although under other circumstances their activities might have provoked serious problems.

That they were recognized as knowledgeable sources of information by highly placed Europeans was understandably satisfying to correspondents at a time when they were struggling for similar recognition from their own employers. At a testimonial dinner in London in 1919, an admiring British colleague termed Edward Price Bell an "unofficial ambassador between the two great English-speaking races"; and Junius Wood, another *Daily News* correspondent, commented that "more than any other writer of his time...Bell was a newspaper reporter at the ambassadorial level."[22] Some years later John Gunther observed that men such as Bell, the Mowrers, and Swing had become "personages of real importance in the political life of Europe." An American correspondent, Gunther continued, "not only reports a country to his newspaper, he also represents his newspaper to that country; he is a servant, in an intimate sense, both of his publisher and of the government under which he works."[23]

Such ties, influence, and responsibilities had their dangerous, as well as their exhilarating, side. Under pressure, they might tempt reporters to forget that their independence, as well as their knowledge, was an essential element of the professional status to which they aspired.

139

POWER STRUGGLE

Another effort by foreign correspondents to gain influence, if not control, over the *Daily News*'s management and editorial policy occurred early in the 1930s. Carroll Binder, a young reporter with ties to Walter A. Strong, Lawson's successor as publisher, had been assigned to Rome in 1927 to gain experience, evidently with some expectation that he would return to Chicago as a member of the editorial staff. The understanding was not explicit, but word of it reached Paul Mowrer who wrote Binder to congratulate him and offer assistance. Binder, who expected to spend only a portion of his three-year European "sentence" in Rome, arranged to stop in Paris for a briefing with Mowrer en route to his new assignment.[24]

While in Rome, Binder exchanged ideas with Mowrer on a wide range of journalistic and foreign relations topics. Mowrer confided in Binder his ideas on the foreign service and his hope for Strong as an avenue to a more enlightened editorial policy. He praised Binder's dispatches and sympathized when they were mangled in Chicago—a chronic complaint. Binder also corresponded directly with Dennis and Hal O'Flaherty, the foreign affairs editor in Chicago. Anxious to prove his worth as a prospective editorial staff member, he chafed at their criticisms and their handling of his copy and complained when they printed Associated Press or other news reports he believed less accurate than his own. Before the end of his Rome assignment, Binder openly shared the reservations about Dennis already held by Mowrer and others. He confided his concerns to Mowrer, who advised him to prepare a memorandum with his ideas on "the best editorial practice" for submission to Strong.[25]

Early in 1929 Binder wrote Mowrer that his planned return to Chicago was beginning to seem less attractive. He was unsure of Strong's wishes, and the prospect of serving as an editorial writer without "room for individuality" under Dennis's control was not appealing. Strong was not intervening to change editorial policy as had been expected, and there were reports that Dennis's rigid methods made the *Chicago Tribune* seem "a veritable haven of intellectual liberty" by comparison. Binder hesitated to take up the matter with Strong directly, he wrote, while Dennis remained in command. But without assurances that a different kind of editorial page was planned, at least for after Dennis's retirement, he was not eager to go home. He enjoyed an interim assignment in Moscow and hoped to move from there to the London bureau, but was chagrined to discover that Dennis and O'Flaherty were planning to send Gunther instead. At Mowrer's suggestion, Binder asked Strong for a meeting to clarify his status. Noting that both the *Baltimore Sun* and the *New York World* had sent editorial writers abroad for study, Binder suggested that American newspapers were beginning to place a higher value on "informed comment on foreign affairs."[26]

After further exchanges with Mowrer, Binder sent Strong his ideas for a revamped editorial page. Describing his two years' service under Mowrer as "the happiest and busiest" of his life, Binder raised the key issue by saying that he preferred to remain abroad rather than serve as a member of Dennis's editorial staff which he and others considered one of the paper's weakest elements. In a lengthy memorandum, he argued that the editorial page should appeal to "that thoughtful but influential minority of Chicago readers whom we alone can serve and whose loyalty constitutes a peculiar asset of the paper." It should contain "editorials written by experts who command respect for their knowledge, their brilliance and their moral leadership." Binder continued, "I advocate a page which will be read by those who care about good government, sound morals, informed explanation and comments on contemporary political, social, literary and scientific developments at home and abroad—comment so loud and interesting that it will be talked about in Chicago and quoted in the press of the world." This could only be developed by a trusted lieutenant with full authority to act independently yet in harmony with the "considered group judgments" of his associates. Binder pointed to the Pulitzer papers as having consistently good editorial pages supervised by editors with "plenary powers," such as Walter Lippmann of the *New York World*. Lippmann had a "full and well paid staff of topnotch men" arguing out the issues on their merits and providing fresh viewpoints in their special areas.[27]

In conversations and correspondence over many months, Binder had already spelled his ideas out to Mowrer, who must have agreed enthusiastically. The foreign editor should report directly to the chief editor and publisher, should participate in discussion of editorials on international matters and write many—if not all—of them, should control space allocations as between Associated Press and *Daily News* foreign service reports, should be responsible for selecting foreign service personnel, and should represent the newspaper at important conferences. He should be free to travel when necessary, and naturally, he should be an acknowledged expert on foreign affairs. The description read as if it had been written with Paul Mowrer, if not Binder himself, in mind.[28]

How many of its details were considered in Binder's meeting with Strong, held later that August, is impossible to say. Binder went from that meeting to relieve Negley Farson in Moscow but returned to Paris early in 1930, visiting the Mowrers. Talk evidently centered around the London assignment, which Binder still coveted and for which he enlisted Mowrer's support against the claims of John Gunther, whom he considered "much petted in Chicago." Not only were Binder and Mowrer unhappy with Dennis's allocation of bureau posts but Mowrer was under attack by Dennis for being "too pro-French." Along with office politics and personalities, the two correspondents must have discussed larger issues, for Binder admiringly wrote his wife, "Paul's mind is so richly stored and his experience so varied that I never weary of sharing its wisdom." Mowrer's theory of "history, international relations and the mainsprings of human power," which were thoroughly grounded in a realist perspective, seemed to Binder—despite his own Quaker background—"exceedingly profound."[29]

The outcome of Binder's conference with Strong, meanwhile, remained unclear. Through Mowrer's intervention or otherwise, Binder received the London assignment. In correspondence with Strong and others implying that an agreement had been reached, he continued to criticize Dennis's editorial page. He also warned Strong against undue emphasis on anticommunism and suggested more constructive treatment of race relations, employee stock ownership plans, and other topics. He complained to O'Flaherty of inadequate facilities, as well as of repeated conflicts between editorials and the news reports, including "a flat-footed contradiction of a *Daily News* foreign service cable" on British tariff policy. To Strong, Binder continued to indicate his interest in an editorial position on the basis discussed at their meeting. Strong made no firm commitment, however; and Binder wrote Edgar Mowrer that the situation was "depressing."[30]

In February 1931 Paul Mowrer cabled from Chicago, where he had gone for consultations, that Strong definitely wanted Binder in daily contact with him looking toward "gradual readjustments" in editorial policy. Mowrer urged "acceptance in [the] common interests." Later he wrote that there had been a "hard fight, but Strong is 100% with us...and I think we have won out." By March, Binder was convinced that Strong agreed with him and that he could return to Chicago enthusiastically. Before his departure preparations could be completed, however, word came of Strong's death, and all plans were thrown into confusion. Binder and Mowrer immediately launched a furious letter-writing campaign to Dennis, Mrs. Strong, and others, attempting to specify and itemize the position and terms Strong had offered. The opportunity to establish a powerful editorial position for the foreign service seemed about to vanish even before it had been won. When Dennis called Binder to Chicago and acknowledged Strong's offer without specifying his responsibilities, Binder countered that his agreement with Strong had been "subject to trial" and a meeting of minds. He would be happy to work with Dennis, but Strong had promised him participation in editorial policymaking on national and local levels, in addition to foreign affairs.[31]

Upon his return to Chicago, Binder found soon enough that Dennis had no such plans for him. Dennis had greeted him cordially, he wrote Paul Mowrer, and talked of plans "for preserving the present management of the paper." But Dennis not only showed no signs of retirement, he had been galvanized into action. He proposed that Binder concentrate on domestic affairs, including such topics as taxation, transportation, and unemployment, in order to "sell himself" to the public as an expert on such matters. Meanwhile Dennis showed no interest in Binder's foreign experience and, indeed, had given him a desk next to that of the real estate editor! Dennis had joined the other editors in belittling the foreign service as a "luxury," of interest "only to college professors." Binder had won a concession that half his time could be devoted to foreign affairs, but neither Dennis nor anyone else really cared. "First class local news" was to be the order of the day. Binder thought Dennis liked him personally, and he held on in hopes of eventually influencing policy. But, he wrote, "Walter's project and the high hopes entertained by you, Edgar and Negley of systematic cooperation for the strengthening of the foreign service and the paper seems [*sic*] still born." Things soon went from bad to worse. Ignoring his promise, Dennis scolded Binder for wasting time on foreign "sideshows." Bell further discouraged him by stating that Strong would never have followed through on his commitment had he lived. "Factionalism and senile decay" flourished everywhere.[32]

Once again, the balance of Binder's fortunes seemed to swing wildly. In August 1931 Colonel Frank Knox, a newspaperman whom Binder thought a "man of vigor and charm" with respect for the *Daily News*'s tradition, bought control of the paper. Further economies were planned, but Binder wrote that Knox recognized the foreign service as an asset.

143

The former was given special assignments and invited by Knox to participate in editorial conferences. Waste and inefficiency were to be eliminated, Binder reported. Despite severe cuts he hoped that "the vital parts" of the foreign service could be saved. The Mowrers, Farson, Stoneman, and a few other outstanding, well-paid reporters, Binder held, were more important than the "present costly organization." Knox respected the service and would preserve it, barring further economic problems.[33]

Binder had shown Mowrer's dispatches to Knox to counteract stories that Mowrer had been a "pampered pet of WAS [trong]...." "Present a VARIED correspondence by all means," Binder wrote then to his friend. All should not be political, he continued, and above all Mowrer must not give up hope. "Don't spurn visiting firemen.... Our kind of people must stay on the job to keep the CDN basically right as I believe she can be kept." He stressed that "NOT A SALARY HAS BEEN CUT HERE," although many people had been let go. Expenses were being reduced, layout and printing improved, and the editorial page, although still under Dennis, was changing. Binder was advising Knox on editorial matters and writing foreign affairs editorials. Editorial policy was becoming more "liberal and enlightened." In comparison with the *Tribune*, "we go far beyond what popular opinion favors in the way of [debt] revision." Editorials might sound "ultranationalistic in Paris but here they are considered advanced" in the light of widespread hostility to the French.[34]

By 1933 Knox had travelled to Europe, been "wined and dined by Negley and Paul," and begun to rebuild the foreign service. As assistant to the publisher, Binder maintained a difficult relationship with Dennis, who continued to rewrite his editorials. Knox's meeting with Mowrer had counteracted another effort by Dennis and his allies to undercut the Paris correspondent. When Dennis resigned in 1934, Mowrer himself was brought home to assume the position of managing editor. And in 1936 Binder became foreign editor on terms in keeping with his concept of the office.[35] It seemed that at long last the foreign service had achieved the status and power its leaders had hoped for and that their chance to put their conception of a finer, more professional international reporting system into effect had been won.

But it was not to be. The continuing ravages of the Depression forced further retrenchment. Knox's own political interests, leading ultimately to his vice presidential nomination on the Republican ticket in 1936, diverted his attention from international issues. And the *New York Times*, meanwhile, had begun the long-overdue upgrading of its own overseas staff which would enable it, with ample financial support, to achieve pre-eminence as the decade progressed.[36] Although the *Daily News* continued to attract outstanding reporters and to function with distinction through the climactic years of the Second World War, the heyday of its foreign service was, in fact, past by the time Binder and Mowrer reached Chicago.

BRANCHING OUT

If efforts to establish an independent, professionally oriented foreign correspondence within the established structures of American journalism fell short of the mark, other developments were more encouraging. Not only had highly placed outsiders acknowledged the reporters' demonstrated skills and experience, but other forms of recognition and approval were appearing. Correspondents found magazines both in Europe and America interested in printing interpretive articles and reports they were unable to place with their own papers. Previously, reporters had been able to find publishers for their literary efforts. Paul Mowrer and Clarence Streit published poetry, and John Gunther, Vincent Sheehan, and others appeared in print as novelists. These works were of uneven quality and, however dear to the secret hearts and suppressed ambitions of their authors, were probably not very lucrative either. What was more, they were only incidental to the work that had become the focus of the correspondents' career and competence. Only a receptive audience for their journalistic writing could acknowledge the expertise they had achieved or the influence and status to which they aspired. Such an audience emerged slowly in the twenties and then more rapidly in the thirties as economic and political upheavals brought Europe, in a series of convulsive episodes, closer and closer to a general war. Public interest in the United States gradually awakened to the dramatic, threatening changes abroad. Growing recognition, in turn, helped foreign correspondents increase the influence they could wield with newspaper editors.

After the First World War, a flurry of books and articles by correspondents who had observed its political, military, or economic ramifications answered the public's desire to learn more than wartime censorship had revealed.[37] With the peace settlement and America's assumption of a new role as nonaligned and ostensibly disinterested participant-observer, public interest in European affairs declined, if the dearth of extended book and magazine treatments of the subject is a reasonably accurate measure of the market's demand. Paul Mowrer's *Balkanized Europe*, despite its virtues and its favorable critical reception, may have suffered by appearing just as American interest in Europe's problems was on the wane. Mowrer's dissection of the complexities of Europe's politics, economics, and nationalistic psychology and his conclusion that the Versailles settlement had further complicated them were hardly calculated to appeal to an increasingly distracted audience. For several years after 1920, in fact, the list of American publications dealing with European affairs in an analytical fashion was notably short. Newspaper series such as Negley Farson's colorful catalog of sights along the Rhine-Danube route, Paul Mowrer's and Vincent Sheean's adventures among the Rifs of Morocco, or Bell's interviews with the chiefs of state of the major powers might capture attention; but little of a more serious nature was attempted.

Gradually, however, reality intervened. The touchy issues of war debts and reparations, German inflation, Mussolini's new experiment, and French occupation of the Ruhr inevitably raised questions among thoughtful Americans that their daily quota of headlines and press association reports could not answer. Thoughtful reporters found opportunities to publish their views on key issues and events in journals such as *Harper's, The New Republic, The Forum*, and even in that bastion of middle-class opinion, *The Saturday Evening Post*. By the late twenties, correspondents such as Wythe Williams, Dorothy Thompson, the Mowrers, and the indefatigable John Gunther were finding receptive audiences for their assessments of European affairs.

The emergence of Adolf Hitler from the wings to the center stage of history converted America's limited interest in Europe into a consuming hunger for knowledge of the sources and implications of the increasingly troublesome crises threatening across the Atlantic. Even then, the shift in receptivity came slowly and unevenly. Hitler's assumption of power early in 1933 coincided almost exactly with the appearance of Edgar Mowrer's *Germany Puts Back the Clock* to mark a revival of public interest in sustained critical analysis. Mowrer's book was followed the next year by Leland Stowe's *Nazi Means War* and H. R. Knickerbocker's *The Boiling Point*.[38] Meanwhile, extensive magazine and newspaper coverage of the Nazi regime attested to rising concern at the puzzling, disturbing changes that came with increasing frequency.

By 1934 what the American market would bear in the way of interpretive journalism was being tested on many fronts. The New Deal at home had become the subject of a steady stream of reportorial analysis. International politics, with its own new names, programs, crises, and challenges to accepted belief or behavior, lagged in interest only by comparison with the dynamism of the domestic scene. If correspondents were ever to burst through the institutional constraints confining them to subordinate status, this was the time to do so. And, in fact, some of the more adventurous foreign correspondents evidently were thinking exactly along these lines.

First, two individualists who were never comfortable within the organizational framework of foreign correspondence published autobiographies in which the combination of personal style, adventure, colorful associations, and sense of involvement with history-in-the-making captured the public's imagination and personalized its image of a world in upheaval. *Personal History*, by Vincent Sheean, a Literary Guild selection for 1934, offered a brilliant, evocative record of personal involvement and disillusionment with a decade of revolution and upheaval on three continents. Negley Farson's *The Way of a Transgressor* (1936), was a travelogue of adventure, observation, and engagement at many levels in Europe and the Soviet Union, with side glances at the Middle East and Asia, by a correspondent so immersed in the lively events of his time that he seldom rested long enough to reflect upon or order them into any kind of meaning.[39] The popular reception accorded these American odysseys across a global stage suggests a growing audience for lively descriptions of the international scene.

Neither Farson nor Sheean carried his story far beyond the level of individual observation and response. It was reserved to another 1936 bestseller, John Gunther's *Inside Europe*, to join political analysis, psychological insights, and lively writing in a readable, provocative picture of the forces and personalities dominating the continent and impinging ever more menacingly on American consciousness. Having conceded his inadequacies as a novelist, Gunther had for years struggled to find a formula for popular writing about the international scene that could bring him the financial independence and freedom he desired.[40] *Inside Europe* succeeded, perhaps more than he expected. Its triumph released Gunther from the constraints and dependencies of a workaday correspondent's existence. He had captured public attention as an individual writer, free of his newspaper connection. He had created a model for independent reporting that, repeated and extended through the succeeding

147

volumes of his *Inside…* series, secured him wealth, celebrity status, access, and audience for a remarkable career as an expositor of a new sense of America's involvement in world developments.

After *Inside Europe*, access to print and the other media over and beyond the daily news columns opened to foreign correspondents as never before. For a select few, such access brought for the first time if not the possibility of financial independence, at least, alternative sources of institutional and financial support to undergird claims for professional autonomy. For Gunther, certainly, independent status, subject only to his ability to continue selling his books, had become a fact of life. Vincent Sheean also managed to support himself on royalties as a free-lance reporter and author of grippingly personal interpretations of the unfolding international crisis, as well as from novels and short stories. In a different fashion, Dorothy Thompson retired from foreign correspondence to establish herself as a columnist and commentator on national and international affairs for the *New York Herald Tribune* in 1936, thereby securing a national reputation.[41] Foreign affairs reporting needed only the outbreak of war and the United States' active participation in it to stretch its influence and acceptance to their utmost.

As the crisis of the 1930s intensified, media other than print were increasingly pressed into service to bring America closer to world affairs and vice versa. Some had been used on a casual, incidental basis earlier, but public interest now justified their systematic organization to bring news and interpretations of the news to concerned audiences. Speeches or lectures by foreign correspondents on home assignment had been an occasional source of exposure at least since Floyd Gibbons had returned home to publicize the war effort for the United States government. Edward Price Bell, after his London assignment, had lectured in the Middle West in 1923 to promote the *Daily News* and its foreign service. Vincent Sheean had lectured across the nation in 1928–29 and again the following year. Carroll Binder, contemplating his own return from London in 1932, had opened discussions on terms and conditions of possible lectures with a Chicago agency even before he began packing his bags.[42] Other correspondents in the course of their return visits may have made similar explorations.

The upsurge of concern over the direction of world developments after 1933, however, encouraged lecture bureaus to expand programs bringing citizens in towns and cities across the nation into direct, face-to-face contact with reporters who spoke as eyewitness observers of the dramatic events. Among the early entries into the lecture field was Leland Stowe, whose first organized lecture tour in January 1934 ran for a two-month period and included five possible topics including disarmament, the revival of German militarism, and Franco-American relations and culture contrasts. In the course of the tour Stowe delivered twenty-four lectures to audiences in the East and Midwest, ranging from the Ad-Sell Club of Omaha, Nebraska, to the United States Military Academy at West Point. In 1935 he offered a second lecture series, speaking to thirty-five audiences in the course of about three months.[43]

The lecture tour offered an opportunity for correspondents to augment their incomes while allowing them to share their knowledge and views on issues they felt were insufficiently understood at home. It enabled newspeople long absent from the United States at a time when important changes had occurred there, too, to satisfy their curiosity, renew their contacts, and sharpen their feeling for the audience toward which their overseas reports were directed. They learned what Americans felt about events abroad and what they wanted or needed to know. Editors and publishers seem to have accepted and perhaps even favored such arrangements. They, too, gained from more opportunities for direct contact with their correspondents, while the publicity and exposure the latter received probably compensated for the scheduling complications involved.

The experience of Stowe, one of the most enthusiastic and effective of the correspondent-lecturers, illustrates the nature and value of the new medium. After 1934 his tour was repeated almost yearly, with a varied list of topics. Few other correspondents could have matched Stowe's list of engagements, and certainly few equalled his lively, down-to-earth, and informed presentations. By the late 1930s the clubrooms, lecture halls, civic auditoriums, and high school assemblies of the United States were regularly being exposed to recently returned foreign correspondents bringing a sense of immediacy and personal perspective to the puzzling, threatening news.

Still another new medium, radio, was by this time beginning to assume an important role in the transmission and interpretation of news from foreign as well as domestic sources.[44] It was natural that journalists already engaged in news gathering should have been tapped at an early stage to supply radio news with its raw materials as well; but rivalry and competition between the established medium and the new obstructed what might otherwise have been a natural process of collaboration. Still, foreign correspondents searching for new outlets and sensitive to new opportunities were not long in finding their way to radio. Raymond Swing had made some broadcasts for the British Broadcasting Corporation while still a reporter in London. Upon his return to the United States in 1934, he became a regular commentator on news from the United States for the BBC. Later, he found a position with the National Broadcasting Company which, with the deepening international crisis, projected him into a new career as a commentator and analyst whose nightly programs were followed intently by a growing audience.[45]

Radio brought a sense of immediacy and participation in remote events and experiences that print could not convey and that answered the emotional and intellectual needs of an audience unaccustomed to sustained treatment of distant topics. Such a response was experienced by Leland Stowe. He had written in depth of the 1929 negotiations over war debt reduction and reparations and had followed the controversies these issues engendered during the bitter Depression years. In 1933 Stowe was asked by NBC officials to interpret this touchy matter to Americans, whose resentment of European failures to repay the obligations was souring international relations at a particularly sensitive time. Stowe broadcast several times over the next few years, but his most notable program was the 1933 war debt discussion titled "Americans and the Man Next Door." He carefully tried to explain the outlook of the average Frenchman in personal terms understandable to American listeners. The broadcast was evidently effective. Congratulatory messages poured in not only from friends, family, and associates, but from strangers across the United States who had heard the program and responded to its power. Even the French Foreign Office approached him for copies of the script, to be used to persuade government censors that radio could be useful in supporting national interests.[46]

Almost inevitably, as these examples indicate, the knowledge and abilities of journalists encouraged the radio industry to draw them into its orbit. But it was not until the Austrian Anschluss in 1938 that the Columbia Broadcasting System managed, through the efforts of its young European representative, Edward R. Murrow, to enlist leading newspaper correspondents in the major continental capitals for a continuing country-by-country report of news and analysis.[47] With this development and the evolution of international crisis from an episodic to a virtually chronic fact of life, the pattern of overseas radio news was established for the future. In the long run, the emergence of the new medium would have far-reaching consequences for the form, content, and audience of international journalism. In the short run, it constituted still another acknowledgment of the skilled understanding that foreign correspondents could offer an increasingly interested public. Their long struggle for acceptance had prepared them for the time when those skills would be tested as never before.

Despite growing acknowledgment of the importance of foreign correspondence for a world increasingly international in its activities, interests, and potentialities for conflict, its practitioners could still make no claim to have established firmly its professional status. Try as they might, they had failed to win sufficient control over their materials and methods to protect themselves from institutional and external constraints. During the years when international reporting was winning recognition, a drive for professional status had emerged within journalism. An early step had been the establishment of the first school of journalism at the University of Missouri in 1908 and the awarding of the first degrees in the subject the following year. The first journalism textbook had appeared in 1911, followed by the formation of an American Association of Teachers of Journalism the next year. In 1912 Columbia University established its own journalism school, destined to exercise leadership in developing critical and theoretical studies of the field. Columbia awarded the first Pulitzer Prize in 1918, with funds provided in the will of Joseph Pulitzer to recognize outstanding work by journalists.[48] Despite all this, foreign correspondence as a journalistic specialty had been minimized when not completely ignored. Now the growing importance of international journalism, as well as, no doubt, the interest of students in a particularly attractive, colorful sector of the field, led gradually to efforts—however incomplete—to acknowledge its importance.

In 1929 the first Pulitzer Prize awarded to a foreign correspondent, Paul Mowrer, gave formal recognition to the specialty, as did similar awards to Leland Stowe and H. R. Knickerbocker the following year. In 1930 the Columbia School of Journalism named Carl Ackerman, an experienced foreign correspondent, as its new dean. Beyond such gestures, however, formal training for international reporting made little progress. Even more than was true of general journalism, the skills, knowledge, and experience upon which excellence in foreign correspondence ultimately depended were too diverse to be reduced successfully to a single curriculum. Still further, as interest in international affairs spread among a wider circle of able young Americans, recruits with a variety of educational backgrounds, abilities, and interests entered the field. Given the institutional structure of journalism, it was impossible to restrict entry to any specifically approved channel or course of training. For better or for worse, foreign correspondents continued to be drawn from a broad spectrum of aspirants whose interests, abilities, aggressiveness, or merely good luck brought them to the attention of editors and bureau chiefs.

The failure of foreign correspondents to achieve formal professional status was, in any event, less significant than the fact that the best of them displayed the skills, understanding, and judgment that the ideal denoted. If their efforts to influence editors and elude the domination of powerful interests were frustrated, their aspirations made them more thoughtful, more critical, and more effective journalists nonetheless. And if their achievements did not win them quite the power, recognition, or influence they desired, they did earn growing admiration and respect. As events unfolded along the dangerous lines many correspondents had foreseen and warned against, it was to them that the public and the media turned for explanations and perspective. If the "golden age" of foreign correspondence arrived in the 1930s and 1940s, its foundations had been well laid in the teens and twenties.

7

Europe in Upheaval
The 1930s

■ The economic collapse of 1929 and its aftermath presented correspondents with challenges and opportunities which demanded every resource of energy, experience, insight, and understanding they possessed. From the relative calm that had led even doubters such as Edgar Ansel Mowrer in 1928 to anticipate a gradual accommodation of differences and an orderly evolution of democratic institutions, Europe plunged into a maelstrom of tensions, terrors, and hostilities that spiralled in less than a decade into total war. The crisis brought journalists risks and dangers, together with a degree of recognition, influence, and eventually—for some—even power that they could scarcely have imagined earlier. By 1940 foreign correspondents had become familiar figures in American editorial and governmental offices, lecture halls, radio broadcasting studios, publishers' conference rooms. Trench-coated and fedoraed, their images appeared in picture magazines, newspapers, and on film. Soon they would be accorded special recognition, the hero's role in an Alfred Hitchcock film, *Foreign Correspondent* (1940)—unfortunately for the durability of their image in the public mind, not one of his best. And their years of preparation had readied them for new, more influential duties.

In the depths of the Depression, however, all this lay in the future. More immediately palpable was an awful anxiety that the frail foundations of Europe's peace and democracy were tottering toward collapse. For some senior correspondents, worn by struggle, frustration, and accomplishment, it was time for departure. A decade or more of confronting Europe's political and economic troubles, of contending with hostile or suspicious officials and disinterested editors had taken its toll. The joys the Continent had offered upon their arrival had turned stale; and its disadvantages—its tired, fruitless politics, its cynicism and despair, its seemingly intractable bitternesses—loomed larger in their thoughts.

Some had left Europe even before the crash. Dorothy Thompson's interest in Europe did not flag, however, after her return home in 1928. She frequently crossed the Atlantic to gather materials for articles and lectures. George Seldes left Europe in 1929; but free-lance journalism, a string of books and articles criticizing the press, and eventually the editorship of an independent newsletter attested to his continuing commitment to journalism. Raymond Swing returned to America reluctantly in 1934 and tried a variety of positions, in print and in the new medium of radio, without notable success until the Munich Crisis of 1939 produced a regular sponsor for his NBC news broadcasts. The year 1934 also saw Paul Mowrer's assumption of the managing editorship of the *Chicago Daily News*. After more than twenty years abroad he was more than happy to change bases. Like the *Daily News*, the *New York Times* had brought its chief European correspondent, Edwin L. James, back home as managing editor in 1932.[1] As the old guard passed, however, its successors were already in place, well trained and ready to carry on. With reporters such as John Gunther, Leland Stowe, H. R. Knickerbocker, Herbert L. Matthews, and Edmond Taylor, the American press would have few apologies to make for its performance during the coming years.

EUROPE AT THE BRINK

Paul Mowrer reached home, "tired of Europe...tired of watching French and British mistakes, and the Germans getting ready for war." He welcomed freedom from police restrictions, freedom for discussion, scope for individual initiative. He was eager to express his ideas without the need to preserve a reporter's balance and objectivity. In 1929 Mowrer had described French-German relations in highly optimistic terms. For more than a year France and Germany had been growing together "diplomatically, culturally, and especially economically." The trend would continue, he had predicted, eventually leading to resolution of such troubling issues as reparations, the Rhineland, and disarmament. Briand and Stresemann had strengthened ties between the two nations, which were also well suited to complement each other economically. If French conservatives resisted accommodation and preferred an Italian alliance,

Mowrer found liberals more comfortable in association with the German republic.[2] Clearly, the three years between this article and his departure from France had jarred Mowrer's expectations severely.

Nor was Mowrer alone in finding hope on the European scene, even as the clouds gathered across the horizon. Negley Farson, ever the romantic, still saw vitality and interest wherever he turned in Europe. In 1928 he visited Spain, Ireland, and the Soviet Union, observing signs of life and enthusiasm everywhere. Earlier, in Italy, Farson had concluded that Mussolini was invigorating the nation and imbuing it with a "new sense of self-respect." The beauty of the country, he wrote, more than compensated American girls who had married into Italian nobility; "it contained more of life itself than they would have got out of some stucco palace on Long Island Sound." The inclusiveness of Farson's tastes was evident in his 1928 return to Russia where, despite Moscow's somber atmosphere and the widespread fear of police surveillance, he still detected more vibrancy of spirit than in either the United States or Great Britain. Farson's enthusiasm tended to be short-lived, however; within a few years he was settling into a four-year London assignment and finding there the "good sense of values" for which he claimed to have been searching throughout all his travels and which he had first hailed in his initial visit to the country some twenty years earlier.[3]

The initial impact of the Depression did not seem wholly negative to a scarred and frustrated veteran such as George Seldes. The fall of the de Rivera regime in Spain and the refusal of American bankers to extend further loans to Mussolini in 1931 led him to hope that the "twilight of the dictators" might be approaching. They had been heavily subsidized by American banks, but a dictatorship's elaborate mechanism of police, spies, military forces, and other commitments was expensive. Democracy was much more economical, Seldes argued, and bankers who held the ultimate power of the purse might at last recognize this. "The dictatorship of the future," Seldes argued, "is that of the American dollar. Politicians and bankers may use it for the restoration of democracy or the prolongation of terrorism throughout the world. The signs favor the former."[4]

Such hopeful signs as correspondents could find in Europe after 1929 were, however, few and strained. To most observers, the prospects appeared dark and the resources for meeting them unpromising. Lincoln Steffens had spent much time in Europe and the Soviet Union in the twenties, finding there "more intelligent hope for change" than in America. But he had concluded by 1927 that possibilities for significant change had dwindled, and he returned home welcoming "the vigor and ever-changing movement" of his native land in contrast to the "fixity" of Europe "where nothing new is doing." Another veteran, Edward Price Bell, returned to Europe to cover the London Naval Conference in 1930 and the London Economic Conference three years later. Yet even this long-standing Anglophile was struck by the changes he found. He refused an offer to stay on as a regular *Daily News* correspondent in 1933. "Europe is sick. It makes me sick," Bell wrote. "Quarreling, intrigue, hate, poverty, constant uncertainty as to what may happen.... The color, the interest, every suggestion of romance or appeal has gone out of this place for me."[5]

A more far-reaching critique of European culture had been supplied by Edgar Ansel Mowrer in his 1928 book, *This American World*. Responding to protests by European intellectuals at the "Americanization" of the Continent, Mowrer had tried to put American-European relations into perspective by examining the sources and nature of America's growing influence and of Europe's susceptibility to it. Despite his love of European culture, Mowrer's analysis was far from encouraging. Europe's culture had lost its vitality, he believed. The Continent now seemed to lack even the ability to reconstitute itself. Not only had America's military, economic, and technological prowess made her the center of attention and influence, but her consumer culture—automobile, films, slang, chewing gum, and other appurtenances of modern mass society—was sweeping across the ocean as well. Mowrer pointed especially to two sources of this shift: the breakdown and decay of the old, aristocratic society and its standards; and the rise of bourgeois, industrial culture in which, ironically, Europe had shown America the way. Although elite values lingered on in Europe, they had lost the support of powerful institutions and survived chiefly among isolated and embittered minorities. Meanwhile the masses and even the rising generation of leaders were attracted by the powerful, tempting forces emanating from across the Atlantic. Mowrer traced Europe's weakness to its nineteenth-century materialism and held that the recent war had amply demonstrated the divisions, destructiveness, and futility which had overtaken a once-proud civilization. In their effort to resist change, Europeans had, indeed, produced a new alternative in the form of fascism; but Mowrer dismissed this as the work chiefly of "dispossessed aristocrats," "embittered middle class victims of European disorder," "capitalists with bundles of axes to grind," or "adventurers fond of heads to break." Americanization would continue, he predicted, in part because its elements were themselves essentially European in origin, a product of the Continent's own industrialization. The chief alternative was communism; but it was new and not fully tested while America had reached its zenith in power, if not in maturity and sophistication.[6]

Other correspondents were reaching similar conclusions. In September 1931 Leland Stowe broadcast a radio commentary from Geneva to America for NBC, a program which he claimed was the first by a permanent American foreign correspondent overseas. Stressing the common interest of both continents in strengthening their economies, Stowe called for more active leadership by the United States. European capitalism was in decline, he noted. "Only France and the Soviets have strengthened their positions in the last five years"; Britain no longer exercised "the supreme balancing force in Europe." Unless the economic crisis was brought under control within two years, Stowe quoted a European source, "Europe may be the victim of the greatest social upheaval she has ever known." Another informant had stated, "Nothing can be done without America. The first move must come from the United States."[7]

Like Stowe, others were questioning Europe's capacity for self-renewal. Louis Fischer was lecturing to American audiences in 1927 on "The Eclipse of Europe." After the death of Briand, Edmond Taylor felt a new responsibility for more serious and critical assessments of French leadership and institutions. And George Seldes, despite his earlier hopes, was alarmed by 1931 at the growing militarization and aggressiveness evident in a number of countries. Meanwhile Wythe Williams anticipated an early confrontation based on the underlying strength of Germany, despite its "chaotic" politics and difficult economic situation.[8]

Dorothy Thompson also found conditions in Germany far from reassuring. German youth, she wrote in 1931, were ready for drastic change. Years of insecurity and uncertainty, coupled with their refusal to accept responsibility for the war and its consequences, led them to reject the status quo. Viewing the Weimar Republic as "a symbol of failure" and defeat, they did not want the monarchy back yet they were strongly nationalistic in outlook. They opposed communism but were even more critical of American materialism. Their ideal was some kind of medieval community, characterized by absolute loyalty and obedience. Since the Depression the Social Democrats had lost support to the Communists, Thompson continued. Hitler and the Nazis, by contrast, were offering something to answer every complaint. Although she found the Nazi program "half-baked," Thompson took it seriously enough to consider its prospects should Hitler attain power. Its radical elements would be dropped, she felt sure, as had been the case with Mussolini in Italy. Middle-class determination to suppress the working class, the build-up of armaments, and Nazi exploitation of anti-Semitism would prevail. The only hope for alleviating the situation lay in improved relations with France or an economic upturn. Two years later Thompson was questioning the very idea of a "postwar" era. The old conflict between defenders of the status quo and revisionists was simply continuing with different weapons, "deadlocked, but as hostile as ever." Europe was approaching "a state of total disorganization...a mass insanity." Reviewing the decade, she placed the failure to undertake serious revision of the post-Versailles political relationships at the heart of the problem. French adamance, British and American hesitancy, and German determination to achieve revision had blocked all possibilities for compromise. Patience was wearing thin and pressures threatening the Continent's peace were straining out of control. Unless a commitment to political reorganization was undertaken soon, Thompson warned, war was likely.[9]

From Vienna, John Gunther confirmed the general picture of entrenched stubbornness and stagnation. In 1931 Austria had elected a moderate coalition government; but a proposed German-Austrian customs union, which Thompson had seen as a first shot at treaty revision, had been blocked by the Allies. Now Britain and France were pressing for economic cooperation among the Balkan nations, favoring tariff reduction and the elimination of reparations to strengthen the region, whose instability threatened all Europe. Gunther held, however, that political and ethnic hostilities would defeat any rational economic measures since the peoples involved hated each other so that they would sink separately before agreeing to swim together. Allied efforts to prevent German participation in the settlement were equally unrealistic, he thought, since Germany was the natural trading partner of most of the nations involved. The necessary basis for a workable settlement was some kind of Franco-German understanding; and Gunther warned that it must come soon.[10]

Perhaps the tension and frustration of an intractable problem, as much as its complexity, began to wear at Gunther's nerves as he contemplated his own situation. He had confided to his notebook in 1931: "My CDN work [h]as slipped badly recently. The Cen[t]ral European financial crisis leaves me technically unequipped, and emotionally uninterested. I still read too [*sic*] papers with avidity. I would hate to miss a really good story.

But the old glow and surge and kick and sting of newspaper work is gone, all gone. Well, I always said I would quit at 30. Soon now!" Gunther clearly had other plans. Perhaps, too, he sensed that the complexities of European finance and politics, however important they might be, were no more exciting to his readers than they were to him. Americans, amid the pressures and concerns of their own depression, were not overly concerned with bad news and dire warnings from Europe. Whether as a gesture of despair and frustration, a reaching out to a new audience at a new level, a reversion to old-time "local color" writing, or simply out of a need for fun and relaxation in difficult times, Gunther met the crucial year, 1933, in a somewhat different mood. A month after Hitler's assumption of power, he was regaling readers of the *Saturday Evening Post* with an article entitled "Cabbages for Kings," on the head waiters of Europe and their dealings with members of high society and royalty. In November he wrote to Frank Knox, "The longer I live in Europe the better American I become. And the more I see of dictatorship the more attractive seems the good old American liberal democratic ideal. . . . If the Germans keep on running wild, there is going to be a war sure—and it may break out here."[11] Europe's plight had become so severe that frivolity or despair seemed equally logical responses.

HITLER'S GERMANY

Writing to his daughter in April 1933 Louis Lochner listed some of the problems that the installation of a Nazi government the month before had brought him as head of the Associated Press in Germany. Only six months earlier Lochner's weekly letters had begun for the first time to mention political matters. Not that he had been unaware of political developments. On the contrary, his work required contacts with a broad range of political leaders and organizations. Now, however, personal concerns were dominated by politics, by the demands of work and, finally, by the sheer necessity of holding on until the eventual rupture of relations between Germany and the United States led to his expulsion nearly nine years later. It was a remarkable experience, and Lochner's letters provide a window on the early days of the new regime as seen by a reporter whose politics were sometimes naive, but whose involvement was total.

"I don't suppose anybody in America can realize what it means to go through a revolution—and that is what the present upheaval in Germany is," Lochner wrote. "One must establish entirely new connections, adopt new methods of treating the news, get acquainted with new laws...and cool one's heels for hours while the men are getting organized." Not only were there delays occasioned by "victory marches, delivering speeches against Jews and Socialists, and outlining programs for the future," but Lochner feared that on patriotic grounds German news organizations would win government help in squeezing out American competitors.[12]

The Lochners had recently celebrated their child's first communion, making a point to invite their German, and particularly their Jewish, friends as a gesture of solidarity. The Associated Press was already under pressure to fire its Jewish employees. Lochner had refused and was anxious to make a counter statement: "...I felt that somewhere...someone must try to build a bridge between the past and the present, and between the Jews and even the Nazis. We as Americans can be helpful in a manner in which perhaps no Germans dare." The Lochners had held two parties, including in their guest lists both Jews and members of the Steel Helmets. Things had gone well, Lochner reported, and "both camps saw that there are decent people to be found even among political opponents." Putzi Hanfstaengel, the Harvard-educated head of the government's foreign press section, had attended one party, as had Sigrid Schultz, Berlin correspondent of the *Chicago Tribune*. The Lochners had told Hanfstaengel that they did not approve of all the policies of the new government.[13] Such gestures, however well intended, were of course futile. They suggest that Lochner still did not take the Nazis quite seriously. If so, he soon discovered that the changes were more sweeping and fundamental than he had supposed.

A month later, Lochner wrote that the Nazis continued to "rush along ...without counting the costs or estimating the consequences." They had, however, made an effort to persuade correspondents that there was nothing to rumors of harsh treatment accorded Germans who had been arrested. Reporters had been taken to a retention center and permitted to question prisoners. Conditions were better than they had been initially, Lochner reported, although the men were being held in "protective arrest" for an indeterminate period. Lochner also noted Nazi book burnings and commented that members of the United Evangelical Church were the "only bunch who seem to have had the backbone not to submit to the Nazis altogether." He was somewhat encouraged by the conciliatory tone of a Hitler speech on foreign policy. It seemed obvious that Hitler wanted no war while he was consolidating his power; but Lochner wondered whether, "when you instil [*sic*] military traditions in a people," war would not inevitably come. He continued to cling hopefully to his old ties and loyalties and arranged a meeting between the kaiser's grandson, Prince Louis Ferdinand, and a "very distinguished statesman." In the light of the hundreds of thousands of prisoners already rounded up into concentration camps, he ridiculed Propaganda Minister Joseph Goebbels's claim that the Nazis had created a "Germanic democracy."[14]

News gathering became increasingly wearisome. "You have no idea," Lochner wrote in July, "how difficult it is to get news nowadays. One must establish communications with all sorts of people; because the official news sources are so one-sided, and often there is something that the German papers simply are not allowed to report." A "gigantic...fight" over their position toward the Nazis was under way within the Protestant churches. To further complicate Lochner's struggle to understand what was happening, American visitors were besieging him with questions, assuming that he knew much more than he felt free to tell. Meanwhile, various Nazi officials and foreign diplomats were also cultivating the foreign press while seeking information. In August, Lochner met with the chief of the secret police in an effort to secure the release of a Jewish correspondent. And, in the hope of persuading German officials to moderate their policies, he pointed out to them that they were provoking anti-German feeling elsewhere. By September, Lochner needed a rest. He travelled with his wife to Czechoslovakia, where he wrote that they were recovering from a "Brown Shirt complex—we just could not stand the sight of them any longer.... And then those fierce anti-semitic speeches!" By November, Lochner wrote from Berlin, "It is no longer a pleasure to work here, for the foreign correspondent is blamed for everything that goes wrong abroad.... I never dreamed I'd have to become an American nationalist, but fail to see why I should be biffed on the bean for not saluting Nazi fashion."[15]

Lochner continued cultivating the Nazis for access to news. "I am naturally doing everything in my power," he told Kent Cooper, "to build up solid connections for AP with the new regime, and think I can say that I enjoy the confidence of the Nazis quite as much as I did that of the former administration. The Wolff people even claim that I am 'persona gratissima' with the new powers that be, but...despite my ideals of western democracy I try to be fair and objective."[16] Lochner thought it was more important for the AP to stay on the scene than to risk expulsion. New York should not complain, Lochner wrote, if he sent few stories critical of the Nazis. To avoid the censors and get news through, he was carefully basing stories upon official releases. Luckily, he added, local and national releases were not always identical, which gave him some leeway. An outright challenge to the German authorities would only end his usefulness.

Until the fall of 1933 Lochner seems to have hoped that Hitler might ease his policies or that he might be replaced by the army and the monarchists. The correspondent's efforts both to cultivate the regime and to report its activities as fully as possible involved him in some awkward, if not contradictory, situations. Lochner was still able to write that, despite its anti-Semitism, Nazism was a "Messiah movement" with some "wonderful sides to it." "There is also something great and noble in the ideas and ideals of a 'Volksgemeinschaft'—a real community of interest between all classes of society," he thought. The "youthful enthusiasm" of the movement he attempted somehow to balance off against its greatest failing, the abandonment of "western concepts of justice." A photograph taken of Lochner and other journalists at an interview with Hitler proved useful for getting special treatment from the Nazis. Events had, meanwhile, drawn the small American community in Berlin closer together. Lochner often saw Ambassador William E. Dodd, with whom he had established a relationship of mutual confidence; on Christmas Day the Dodd family visited the Lochners. By 1934 Lochner had reluctantly concluded that Hitler would survive indefinitely and that war was increasingly likely. "One nation after another is getting ready for it," he wrote. "Here in Germany the whole psychology is one of the inevitability (of course because the other fellow is at fault!) of war. Poor Europe."[17]

By this time, Lochner had succeeded Edgar Mowrer as president of the Foreign Press Association. Mowrer had resigned when the Nazis made him persona non grata because of his book, *Germany Puts Back the Clock*. Published early in 1933, it had reviewed events leading to the election of November 1932, when the Nazis, although failing to win a majority, had remained the leading political party. Examining democracy's collapse in Germany, Mowrer found evidence of weakness at many levels. He began with the Social Democrats, who had played a key role in the establishment and the life of the republic but had failed effectively to resist von Papen and Hindenburg in 1932. Fearing a confrontation with the Right and the military, on the one hand, or of playing into the hands of the Communists on the other, they had allowed themselves to be outmaneuvered. They and other supporters of the republic so feared the Communists that they had appealed to the army and acquiesced in the return to power of monarchists and reactionaries. The German republicans, Mowrer charged, had been "the first...to throw away nearly full power in so few years." Their "supine passivity" had allowed the state "to be flouted and bribed with impunity by generals, ex-sovereigns, nobles, judges, officials and sturdy adventurers."[18]

From consideration of recent blunders, Mowrer turned to examine the record of German liberals and democrats under the republic. Postwar enthusiasm for democracy, which had offered a basis for success, had dissipated and disintegrated under successive liberal failures. Instead of purging Germany of its reactionary, traditional elements the liberals had timidly made concession after concession. They had inadvertently "left a bridge over which the old figures came streaming...so soon as they realized they had nothing to fear." Conservatives, meanwhile, had never accepted the republic. They had allied themselves with the Junkers and had attacked social democracy, even though it had saved the nation from communism and the trade unions and had actually subsidized industrial and financial growth.[19]

Beyond political jealousies and breakdowns, Mowrer discovered still broader obstacles to the success of the republic. The elaborate structure of the Weimar constitution, an ill-matched combination of "a democratic machinery of the most complicated...and perfected sort" with long-standing, traditional regional governments and loyalties, was a system that never gave German democracy "a fair chance." Allied policies had created still further obstacles. Intransigence over reparations, war debts, and the war guilt issue, coupled with lavish American loans for economic expansion and social services even as German capitalists continued to exploit workers and undermine democracy, had complicated Weimar's problems. Despite all this, the republic might have survived, Mowrer held, had not democracy been in fundamental conflict with key elements of German culture: "...Germany never really accepted liberalism," he argued; rather the Germans craved a paternalistic, organic social order. Liberal individualistic, rationalist, and materialistic values were ill-suited to the German longing for purpose, order, and direction. And liberalism suffered further from its inevitable association with erstwhile enemies, still seemingly vengeful, unrelenting, or indifferent.[20]

Mowrer's argument was informed by his years of close and curious observation. If somewhat contradictory and unsympathetic in its analysis of German democracy, it acknowledged the odds against which democrats had had to struggle. And it recognized the Allies' responsibility in failing to support those elements in German life and leadership upon which democratic society had depended. In the face of these combined failures, Germans had turned toward leaders who seemed to offer what the republic lacked, a sense of direction, order, and unity, a belief in the greatness and destiny of the nation. The Depression had completed the process of undermining faith in the Weimar government; militarism and reaction had claimed the future. Hitler's assumption of power focussed an attention upon Mowrer's report that it might not otherwise have achieved; but the book's provocative analysis merited the favorable response it received—outside Germany. Its timing and intelligence made *Germany Puts Back the Clock* the first work of sustained analysis by an American foreign correspondent to attract widespread, respectful attention.

Mowrer's colleague, H. R. Knickerbocker, had preceded him with a book entitled *The German Crisis*, published in mid-1932. Based upon a series of newspaper articles, Knickerbocker's work had combined a description of the German scene with an effort to persuade Americans that their own interests were at stake in Germany's political upheaval. A "prolonged civil war" or the "collapse of capitalism," at least in Germany and perhaps more widely, might result from Hitler's drive to power, he had argued. Economic and political pressures were driving the Germans away from democracy toward the radical extremes on the Right or the Left. The collapse of Germany would affect its neighbors as well. And Americans held a huge stake in Germany's future in the form of very heavy investments, some 38 percent of the total foreign investment. Further growth of inflation and unemployment or Allied insistence upon tariff restrictions that hampered Germany's ability to export would only hasten the debacle.[21]

Knickerbocker presented eyewitness descriptions of conditions among the poor and unemployed in Berlin's working-class district, the extravagant nightlife of the capital's café society, the prosperity of the Zeiss glassworks at Jena, the Rhineland—still fearful of French invasion—as well as interviews with prominent Nazis and industrialists. Despite extremes of wealth and poverty, Germans as a whole were living better than they had in the early twenties, he argued; but the situation was deteriorating. Contradictions and extremes prevailed at many levels. The nation was "industrially the strongest power in Europe...financially the least secure...politically the most divided," and it harbored socially "the most explosive possibilities." Knickerbocker had found the Germans, however divided politically, united against further reparations and for treaty revision. Any German government would necessarily "yield to the current of defiant nationalism" sweeping the nation. The "Age of Hitler" had thus come to Germany, whether or not the National Socialists actually assumed control. The ranks of the Austrian's followers already included a broader range of classes, interests and individuals than did any other political party. In all this, Knickerbocker emphasized America's stake in Germany's future. Not only had American investments poured into the nation in extraordinary amounts, but the economic stability of all Europe ultimately was threatened. "To 'wash our hands of Europe' is a comfortable dream but three to ten billion dollars is an expensive bath," he warned. With Germans united in resisting further reparations and Allied restrictions, continued investments on the Continent would become, in effect, "investments in a battlefield." America's interest lay in assuming the role of peacemaker and architect of compromise, assisting Europe toward a peaceful resolution of long-standing disputes and away from an impasse that could be resolved only by revolution, war, or communism.[22]

Well received in Europe, *The German Crisis* won little notice in the United States. In 1934, after Hitler seized power, Knickerbocker issued a second volume, *The Boiling Point: Will War Come in Europe?* Drawn from observations and interviews during a swing through major European countries, its tone was cautious but ultimately pessimistic. "Europe is in uniform. Will she go to war?" Knickerbocker opened. He found some reassurance in the fact that Danzig, under Nazi leadership, had made peace with the Poles for the first time in thirteen years—possibly an augury of better German-Polish relations. Meanwhile, Polish-Russian amity was encouraged by mutual apprehensions over Hitler's intentions. In Czechoslovakia, where he interviewed both the president, Tomáš Garrigue Masaryk, and Foreign Minister Eduard Beneš, Knickerbocker also received at least mild reassurances. Masaryk, perhaps voicing his hopes more than his actual opinions, said that Americans seemed more alarmed than he was. Beneš held that peace had at least a 50-50 chance; if war could be avoided for five years it might be averted altogether. Austria, the next on Knickerbocker's itinerary, offered somewhat less encouragement. At the time under Chancellor Englebert Dollfuss, the nation seemed safe from the Nazis; but, "if Dollfuss goes, the Nazis come." Meanwhile, the Germans were biding their time and hoping that internal divisions would precipitate a crisis. The Hungarians, Knickerbocker found, would welcome a German takeover of Austria since in such a readjustment they expected to regain the territories and peoples lost at Versailles. In Italy, Knickerbocker interviewed Mussolini, whom he termed more knowledge-able about the prospects of war and peace than any other European leader. The Duce thought German rearmament inevitable and a general arms race highly likely.[23]

Knickerbocker took special note of Germans living outside the borders of the Third Reich, for whose reincorporation into the nation Hitler was pressing relentlessly. The issue directly threatened such post-Versailles nations as Poland, Lithuania, and Czechoslovakia; but nowhere was it potentially more explosive than in the Saar, scheduled to vote in 1935 on the question of its return to German rule. For the sake of "a pinprick" France was encouraging resistance, but with no real hope of keeping the Saar separated from Germany, and thus was needlessly and foolishly souring the inevitable outcome. Meanwhile the French relied heavily on their new "great wall," the Maginot Line, to hold off the Germans for at least ten years; yet their generals admitted that the line could be out-flanked. French Foreign Minister Jean-Louis Barthou thought Austria the likeliest spot for conflict, but the French and the British people opposed war and their governments were unwilling to risk military engagement. The immediate danger of war, Knickerbocker concluded, was not great, since Hitler, too, was still unprepared; but the strengthening of Germany's armed forces would alter the power balance significantly within three more years. Germany was already "morally rearmed" in its determination to recapture continental primacy. And the arms race, "the Olympic games of death," was launched beyond recall. Disarmament was no longer possible, insecurity was rising, and the future was unpromising.[24]

All eyes swung toward Germany in the months after the Nazis seized power, as both Europeans and Americans tried to deduce the direction in which the new regime would lead the nation and the world. Another journalist who attempted to evaluate the German scene was Leland Stowe, who spent September and October of 1933 in Germany. His reports, based entirely upon German sources, were quickly published in London under the blunt title, *Nazi Germany Means War*. In a brief introduction, Stowe observed that, even for an American correspondent with no direct ties or interests involved, the journalist's goal of impartiality had been hard to achieve amid the rapid and extreme changes Germany was undergoing. He began by contrasting Hitler's recent avowals of peaceful intent following Germany's withdrawal from the League of Nations with the militant, threatening language of *Mein Kampf*. To assess these contradictory statements Stowe then turned to the test of observation.[25]

His visual impressions had been immediate and powerful: "more uniformed men on the streets and in the public places of Berlin than I had seen in any foreign city from London to Constantinople...more parades and marching troops in three weeks than I had seen in Paris in nine months...rousing military bands at eleven o'clock in the morning... long columns of boys and girls in their teens, uniformed and carrying flags...great swastika or imperial flags hung out everywhere." From such sights, Stowe turned to describe the various uniformed groups which, in addition to the regular army, he calculated as totalling over one million men, "discipline *in excelsis.*" The Nazi S.A. and S.S. forces, with their own air and cavalry units, were already being synchronized with the regular armed forces. Despite official disavowals, they carried weapons and held military maneuvers, although German officials preferred to compare them with American football teams or the Boy Scouts. The German Labour Corps, recruited from the ranks of the unemployed, superficially resembled the New Deal's Civilian Conservation Corps but was organized quite differently, for different purposes. It was trained in military maneuvers from the official Reichswehr manuals and its members were supplied with arms. Stowe also described measures undertaken to mobilize and bring under Nazi discipline associations of automobile owners, youth groups, and societies of aviation enthusiasts, all bases for training and indoctrinating the German people in ideas of racial superiority and national destiny.[26]

As for the aims of national mobilization, Stowe noted that the announced intentions of Nazi leaders from *Mein Kampf* onward clearly included regaining territories lost at Versailles and expanding the nation's borders to incorporate all peoples of German descent in an empire that would include Austria and large parts of Poland and Czechoslovakia. Such a power would inevitably dominate Europe. And even as they lamented the inadequacy of Germany's territory to contain her population, the Nazis were deliberately fostering population growth to increase their numbers. Such actions and policies left little doubt as to the future prospects for Germany and Europe.[27]

No knowledgeable persons expected war within the next few months, Stowe wrote; yet none had denied that "another European catastrophe" lay directly ahead unless ways were found of averting it. Germany was not ready for war, but armament plants were being expanded and the manufacture of airplane motors would soon be possible. Two to five years of additional preparations would probably be required before Hitler could confidently pursue the course toward which both his words and his actions pointed. Resistance to the Nazis, ineffective before they took power, was even feebler now. Stowe found the Germans decent, kind, friendly, and clearly fearful of the future toward which the Nazis were leading the nation; yet their love of order and authority, and their susceptibility to nationalistic appeals, left them readily exploitable for aggressive ends. "Psychologically, spiritually and physically," Stowe concluded, "the Nazi dictatorship is designed...to create a nation of warriors and a civilian population trained to follow blindly in their wake." Checks might come in the form of an internal economic collapse, discrediting Hitler's regime or—more likely if far from certain—firm resistance by the French, Italians, and British that might convince Hitler to adopt a more reasonable stance. Failing such obstacles on the basis of which justifiable German demands for treaty revision might be accepted, war would surely come, however soon or late.[28]

For an American edition, Stowe added a concluding chapter, "If War, What About America?" A reporter, he wrote, could not formulate policy or offer specific solutions, yet a clear policy was needed and public discussion of America's role was essential since the United States inevitably would be affected should war come. The issue of neutrality must be openly considered and debated. Few experts, Stowe held, believed that neutrality of the pre-1914 variety was likely to be effective. Should Americans once again choose to remain neutral, they must face the fact that such a policy would be costly. The United States would have to give up its adherence to freedom of the seas by invoking a boycott against aggressor nations; profitable wartime trade would also have to be abandoned. Either way, a European war would cost America heavily in sacrifice of men or of wealth; Americans must consider the alternatives carefully.[29] For Stowe the time had come for his countrymen to acknowledge that Europe's troubles could no longer remain of remote or local interest only. His report, published in December 1933, was the first to detail Hitler's systematic militarization of the German people and their institutions, from the Nazi party and the police to labor unions, youth, education, and the legal system. It offered a striking, chilling glimpse of a nation in the throes of becoming a totalitarian military machine.

Dorothy Thompson also reported the steady drive towards militarism, rearmament, and authoritarianism. In a May 1933 *Saturday Evening Post* article, "Back to Blood and Iron: Germany Goes German Again," Thompson held that, in its recent elections, Germany had been the first nation to abandon democracy by popular choice. "More than fifty percent of all Germans politically minded enough to exercise the right of suffrage...deliberately gave away all their civil rights, all their chances of popular control, all their opportunities for representation." Germany had already recovered great power status before the Depression, Thompson argued; reparations had been scaled down, the economy had prospered, and pressure against the Versailles settlement had already rendered it virtually dead. Yet Hitler's propaganda campaign of "envy, hatred and ignorance" had nonetheless appealed to "a vast dream wish," a "mass flight from reality." Discovering in the "disinherited middle classes a truly revolutionary element," Hitler was now driving to accomplish the Nazi aim, "to make Germany safe for war." Only in the light of this objective did the Nazi program of terror, persecution, repression, and revenge make any sense. Furthermore, the "rage, hatred, bitterness and cruelty of the Nazi outbreak" suggested that its roots lay deep within the national psyche. Germany was "on the warpath," and the future looked dark for Austria, Poland, and the rest of Europe.[30]

Later, Thompson considered Hitler's attack on the Jews. Noting that anti-Semitism and race prejudice were not confined to Germany, she still termed the Nazi program "a sort of social atavism, a return to the darker side of the Middle Ages." Its extreme character, she thought, was provoking a reaction around the world and especially in America. "After all, if it be true, as Hitler insists, that a nation can consist only of blood brothers like an Indian tribe, then our whole American history is just one long folly." After a 1934 trip to Europe, she described economic and political strains within the Third Reich and the effectiveness of Hitler's propaganda techniques in dominating public opinion. During this visit Thompson had been expelled by the German authorities and barred from further entry. Her outspoken commentary had incurred official anger and the Nazis now felt strong enough to defy whatever criticism their action might provoke elsewhere. Henceforth, foreign correspondents were on notice that the German government would tolerate only those who held their peace or parroted the official line.[31] By then, many of the ablest and most clear-sighted correspondents had concluded that the odds for war were such that only the most extreme and unprecedented measures could prevent it.

Those who remained in Germany found themselves subjected to increasingly severe pressures. Even Louis Lochner, despite his official ties, was not immune. He continued to relay tidbits of information indicating the existence of submerged discontent among the German people, but he had concluded by mid-1934 that there could be no peace in Germany or in Europe "until the great Adolf has either radically changed his policies or chooses to disappear from the political parquet." He covered the Olympic games at Garmisch-Partenkirchen in 1936 and the first flight of the dirigible Hindenburg and Charles A. Lindberg's visit to Berlin during the same year; but aside from such assignments Lochner's family reports from Germany had lost most of their zest. He did not actually fear for his life, he wrote Kent Cooper, but he was threatened with expulsion in 1936. The American Chamber of Commerce of Berlin elected him its president in 1935 as a gesture of support, and in 1939 he was awarded a Pulitzer Prize in recognition of his years of steadfast service. True to his responsibilities and instincts, Lochner remained at his post until the outbreak of war between Germany and the United States in 1941. He continued to cultivate his connections—winning, in the process, the suspicion of some who felt he consorted with the Nazis too willingly. But his enthusiasm had obviously evaporated. Only a sense of duty, family ties, and, perhaps, a reporter's indefatigable curiosity sustained him.[32]

It was in 1934 that William L. Shirer reached Berlin from earlier Universal News Service assignments in Austria, the Far East, and France. He immediately joined the correspondents' group meeting at an Italian restaurant, the Taverne. Among its members were the *New York Times*'s Guido Enderis and Albion Ross, Wallace Duell of the *Chicago Daily News*, and Sigrid Schultz of the *Chicago Tribune*. Lochner seldom joined them, Shirer noted, but under the circumstances prevailing in the German capital foreign journalists must have hung together even more than was normally the case. Shirer soon found himself receiving visits from Jews who hoped, mistakenly, that he could help them escape to England or the United States. A liberal by conviction, Shirer bridled at a situation which required him, as a news syndicate correspondent, to limit his reporting to "the facts." When Hitler occupied the Rhineland in 1936 Shirer erupted at the "sand in the eyes" talk of peace with which the dictator masked his ultimate purpose. It was, Shirer believed, "pure fraud," and furthermore, "if I had any guts, or American journalism had any, I would have said so in my dispatch tonight. But I am not supposed to be 'editorial.'" When his fellow correspondents agreed that French intervention would bring Hitler's downfall, Shirer checked with his London office on how the British were reacting, only to find that they were trying to restrain France. Unhappy in his Berlin post, Shirer was rescued by Edward R. Murrow, who hired him in 1937 for the new CBS radio news service. He was assigned to Vienna in time to cover Hitler's invasion. His radio career was thus ironically launched with the help of the dictator whom he had observed with detestation during his Berlin days.[33]

Albion Ross, whom Shirer encountered in Berlin, had begun his intellectual and his political education in Germany as a student before the Nazi takeover. Ross later remembered that he had found German youth living for the moment, with the feeling that "all moorings had been loosened." Living with an anti-Nazi family, Ross awakened to a new set of realities. Nothing in his American past had prepared him to recognize the significance of the "Jewish question" as it was then being raised. Observing the lives of Berlin's working-class poor, Ross felt a strong sense of identification with them. Rootless and uneasy himself, he saw in the German workers "the neurosis of the modern world, the hidden hatred of fate that made each one's life an empty existence, as another face in an anonymous mob." Later, on repeated visits along the Polish and Slovakian frontiers, Ross steeped himself in the life of the peasants, in whose communal existence and direct contact with the soil he found a more satisfying sense of reality. He recognized also its less attractive aspects: provincialism and suspicion of change, limited horizons, and susceptibility to manipulation by bigots and nationalists. Ross saw the Depression as evidence of Europe's loss of direction and Germany's reactions as those of a people desperate for a sense of purpose and progress. Hitler played effectively upon these emotions, liberating the nation from frustration and offering a seemingly meaningful alternative to stagnation and decay. "I saw the rising of a nation from dead rot and despondency," he wrote; and more leaders of Hitler's ilk could be expected so long as modern society failed to offer men the order and meaning their lives demanded. Ross's sympathy for the Germans' situation heightened his understanding of Hitler's appeal for them; but when he was beaten by a Nazi mob for buying at a Jewish store, any possibility that his sympathy would extend to the new leader vanished. He became involved with an "anti-Nazi Confessional Church group" and was soon welcoming opportunities to travel outside Germany. He had become convinced that "straight news," without explanation or interpretation, gave readers an inadequate appreciation of complex and crucial events.[34]

In an experience paralleling Ross's, Edmond Taylor found a brief assignment in Germany in 1934 enough to clarify his view of the Nazi threat. In Paris his doubts as to the virtues of democracy had been stirred by the vagaries of French politics. Early in 1934 he was sent to report on the situation in Germany. Taylor went with an open mind, intrigued to learn more about the German experiment with economic planning and half-persuaded by some French friends that the Nazis were more socialist than nationalistic. Familiar with the criticisms of colleagues like Edgar Mowrer, Knickerbocker, and Sigrid Schultz, who had sized up the Nazi movement before it reached power, Taylor claimed a reporter's right to draw his own conclusions. They were not long in coming. Married to a Jew, Taylor was immediately confronted with the realities of aggressive anti-Semitism. Conversations with German Jews convinced him that the threat under which they lived was quite real. He saw more on a visit to a model concentration camp and confronted the terror directly when he was broken in on by the gestapo. This taste of the "new Germany" was enough to transform Taylor from a "critical observer to an outspoken adversary" of the Nazis. He, too, was convinced that Hitler's regime spelled trouble unless the Allies took strong, united measures.[35]

THE ALLIES

If the news that American journalists sent back from Germany and eastern Europe was alarming, what they reported from the Allies was almost equally discouraging. The politics of the European democracies had appalled some American journalists throughout the twenties. British insularity, French intransigence, and the inability of the Allies to agree on a common approach to the German problem had seemed in sharp contrast with European cultural and intellectual verve. Lacking the historical perspective to interpret their observations sympathetically, American reporters often reacted to European politics with easy cynicism or with unexpected appreciation for the political system of the United States, with all its shortcomings. A decade of observation had supplied much of the needed perspective, yet the Depression and Hitler's rise seemed to confirm earlier doubts that post-Versailles Europe had the vitality or flexibility to meet serious new challenges. Vincent Sheean, who had left Europe partly out of disgust at the self-centered nationalism and corruption he observed, was less indignant but equally critical after having girdled the globe visiting China and the Soviet Union. Returning to the United

States in 1928, Sheean had found even its "barbarism...a much more comforting spectacle than...European civilization in decay." There was, he wrote, a "total absence of the national hatreds that control existence in Europe."[36]

Herbert L. Matthews responded to French politics much as Sheean had. He saw corruption—"seething rottenness under the thin crust of respectability" and "deliberate and shameful efforts of French politicians to disguise the facts"—in short, widespread indications of "moral decay." Yet Edmond Taylor, in Paris during the same years, interpreted conditions rather differently. Perhaps reacting against Colonel McCormick's view of the "unregeneratedness" of Europe, Taylor found himself, after Briand's death in 1932, increasingly aware of the difficult, complicated nature of France's problems and less inclined therefore to be critical of its leadership. But Taylor's conclusions did not differ greatly from Matthews's. He found the French government, educational system, and other key institutions backward, dominated by wealthy interests and powerful pressure groups. And the leaders, drawn as many were from outdated sectors of society, were powerless to deal with the prevailing corruption. In the end, Taylor acknowledged, French politics raised grave doubts as to the future of democracy.[37]

Writing as France prepared in 1936 for another election amid continued hard times and rising pressures from both the Left and the Right, Leland Stowe tried to explain to American readers the conditions that guided the average French voter, "Jean Deaux." France was still basically an agricultural country, Stowe stressed. The French were "born to small horizons; taught to cherish little things." They still thought of governmental problems in personal terms and hesitated to give much power to the state. They were confirmed democrats, opposed to dictatorship, yet Stowe conceded that the extreme Right and Left might be strengthened at the expense of the center in the coming election.[38] Even after the Popular Front won the election, American journalists continued to anticipate a Fascist takeover of the Third Republic. Interviewing Socialist Premier Léon Blum, who emphasized the French worker's independence as a bulwark against fascism, Edgar Mowrer noted the equivocal foreign policy Blum's cabinet felt obliged to pursue in the face of Fascist pressures both from within and without. And George Seldes, writing in 1937, suggested the likelihood of Fascist attacks upon the French government, weakened both by Communist and right-wing militarist discontent.[39]

If France seemed at times perilously close to paralysis, the view from London for American journalists appeared rather to be one of blind unwillingness to face the realities and pay the price of effective foreign policy. Before he left England in 1934, Raymond Swing had noted the British government's imaginative response to the Depression through "a series of drastic national actions which demonstrate how a modern democracy can cooperate with destiny in times of danger." A number of measures, including abandonment of the gold standard, tariff measures, and subsidies had eased the impact of the Depression and encouraged an economic revival, although conditions remained desperate in northern England and Wales.[40]

British foreign policy, however, showed less imagination and realism. A combination of disarmament and disengagement, Negley Farson reported, rendered the British ineffectual, either in resisting Fascist pressures or in pushing the reluctant French for concessions to Germany. Hitler's reoccupation of the Rhineland, according to Farson's successor, John Gunther, shocked British opinion and revealed the weak, divided character of Allied policy. Britain had been unwilling to support France's demand for a German withdrawal and the resentful French now refused to back the British against Italy in the Mediterranean. By 1937 Gunther was reporting that the British, despite considerable pro-German and pacifist sentiment, recognized the need to rebuild their military forces, to strengthen their ties with France, and to take a more active international role.[41] Yet it would be two more years before the Chamberlain government, faced with the bankruptcy of its temporizing policies, was finally forced to undertake the commitments it and its predecessors had so long resisted.

ITALY AND THE ETHIOPIAN WAR

The rise of Hitler and Germany's resurgence in the early thirties had diverted attention from the dictatorship of Benito Mussolini who, by comparison, had begun to seem an almost respectable figure on the troubled European scene. After consolidating his power, he had undertaken a massive effort to win favorable public opinion in the United States and elsewhere. The Fascist campaign of bribery, censorship, and coercion had substantially silenced unfavorable reporting; and Mussolini's colorful behavior made him a subject of interested, if not always friendly, comment. He appeared to have brought order and at least a modicum of progress to the notoriously unstable Italian state. He had pleased the Allies by taking the initiative that they were unwilling to assume in countering early German designs upon Austrian independence. Only a few "old hands" managed from time to time to pierce the haze of complacent commentary with which Mussolini was surrounded. Thus Hiram Motherwell in 1929 had suggested that the logic of fascism might eventually impel Italy toward expansion and war. And George Seldes, revisiting Italy in 1931, met a number of reporters eager to smuggle out forbidden news and documents. But Seldes's report was suppressed at the urging of the British foreign office, while the French government was no more anxious to see it in print. Not until 1936 was Seldes's *Sawdust Caesar* published, and by then Mussolini had revealed himself as something other than a genial, bombastic statesman or poseur.[42]

In October 1935 Mussolini attacked Ethiopia. Immediately, of course, he became front-page news, the subject of much journalistic speculation and interpretation. Motherwell held that Ethiopia was only the beginning, rather than the completion of Mussolini's expansionist ambitions. With ancient Rome as his model, the dictator aimed at nothing less than to establish himself eventually as the emperor of a domain encompassing much of the Balkans as well as the eastern Mediterranean. By splitting England and France, he would nullify any possible opposition and block League of Nations intervention. Only the unforeseen rise of Hitler, with whom Mussolini had already clashed, Motherwell thought, posed a likely obstacle to the Italian's long-cherished ambition. For his old adversary, George Seldes, the dictator's attack on Ethiopia confirmed the logic of the Fascist impulse, which Seldes found inherently and incurably imperialistic. The Ethiopian war, Seldes believed, was Mussolini's last gamble for survival in the face of Italy's economic stagnation.[43]

Reporters who spent less time brooding over Mussolini's significance found the assault on Ethiopia interesting, but less ominous. John Gunther reflected some of the lurking admiration that still colored American views in terming the Italian leader a "turncoat, ruffian, and man of genius," an intellectual, a good administrator moved more by his recognition of Italy's need for "glory" than by economic considerations. Herbert L. Matthews saw Mussolini primarily as a nationalist whose policies commanded the support of his people. He believed, too, that Italian rule would benefit the backward Ethiopians. Matthews was sympathetic toward the Italians and critical of the ineffectual protests of the French and British governments, which he saw as hypocritically censuring Italy for measures not fundamentally different from those pursued in building their own empires. Considering himself a "realist," he was unswayed by the moralism with which the democracies cloaked their defense of the status quo.[44]

Matthews covered the war in Ethiopia, welcoming it at first as an adventure, an exciting change from the boring "daily grind" of Paris. As the conflict bogged down after the initial Italian victories, he experienced the tedium and discomfort of war in an unfriendly, impoverished, and barren land. Matthews, however, remained unshaken in his belief in an Italian victory. He later complained of being labelled a Fascist sympathizer at a time when the majority of the American press, carried away by misplaced enthusiasm for an underdog, had misled its readers as to the chances for Ethiopia's retaining independence. Matthews subsequently conceded that he had seriously misjudged Mussolini, but he continued to admire the conquest of Ethiopia as "a difficult job superbly done."[45]

Webb Miller, who shared Matthews's disgust at the hypocrisy of European statesmanship, saw early that a news story was about to break in Ethiopia. Through Italian connections, he reached Eritrea where the Italian forces were massing for an attack. There he found Floyd Gibbons, a friend of Mussolini's since Gibbons's *Chicago Tribune* Paris days. The veterans, Gibbons and Miller, not only beat most other correspondents to the scene of action, but Miller used his knowledge of cable transmission patterns to get a report of the Italian invasion to New York ahead of his rivals. Like Matthews, Miller concluded that an Italian victory would benefit the Ethiopians, morally indefensible although the invasion might be. He was repelled by the "savage, uncivilized" country where filth, disease, and disunity prevailed. He compared the Ethiopians unfavorably to American Indians after the arrival of the Europeans. The Indians at least had had a high "moral and physical development"; but among the Ethiopians Miller discerned few, if any, redeeming qualities.[46]

New York Herald Tribune correspondent John T. Whitaker, who felt his experience as a political reporter in America had equipped him to assess international politics without illusions, was transferred from Geneva, which he termed the capital of idealism, to Rome, the center of cynicism, in 1935. Whitaker professed a "prejudice" against fascism, which he saw as distracting from rather than contributing to the solution of Italy's domestic problems. Mussolini was dangling meaningless glories before the Italian people, "bewildered by the complexities of modern government, frightened by the inexorable monster which the machine has become, and left neither trust in man nor faith in God" after war. Fascism, Whitaker wrote, had no real program, it represented a "revolt against reason." Yet it appealed nonetheless to peoples such as the Italians and Germans who "cry out unconsciously for some idealism."[47]

Whatever his reservations as to fascism, Whitaker had no qualms about getting on close personal terms with Mussolini's son-in-law and foreign minister, Count Galeazzo Ciano. It may have been through this connection that he won permission to cover the war in Ethiopia. Once there, Whitaker's encounter with the Ethiopians—colored perhaps by his southern background and perspective—influenced his outlook on the war. He despised the Ethiopians "for their disease, lechery, and venality," concluding that they were "wholly wanting in the virtues ascribed to them by the sentimental propagandists of England and America." Shocked by the filth, superstition, and dishonesty he found everywhere, Whitaker was impressed, however, by some black Somali Mohammedan soldiers whom he found displaying "at one and the same time courage, loyalty and politeness—a combination of virtues rare in any civilization." Still, he concluded that the Italian conquest of Ethiopia, despite the inefficiency and corruption which had bogged down the campaign in its early stages, was probably justifiable. "Perhaps the Italians with quinine and mercury could give the Ethiopians sound bodies and, with stern military policy, the tranquility" to make the most of themselves.[48]

THE LEAGUE OF NATIONS

The failure of economic sanctions against Italy further undermined such respect for the League of Nations as remained among American journalists. In the twenties, Wythe Williams, George Seldes, and Vincent Sheean, among others, had expressed disgust at the efforts of armaments industry representatives, as well as of the French and British governments, to manipulate the league for their own short-term advantage. Williams had come to see the league as "a comfortable first-class club" of the Great Powers, who in the absence of the United States "connived" at Geneva to preserve their tattered primacy. He concluded that it was just as well the United States had not joined the league, although he still thought it "a step forward in civilization." It offered small nations a forum in which to air their concerns, and it had accomplished some worthwhile measures for control of the international drug and white slave traffic. William's concern for the league's effectiveness led him to join in efforts to strengthen its position. Together with Frederick Birchall, managing editor of the *New York Times*, he undertook a campaign to move the league's headquarters from Geneva, where they believed it was isolated from the problems and conditions of the real world, to Vienna. Later, Williams tried to promote the idea of an international peacekeeping force, a "permanent roving body" that would report on world trouble spots and represent the league at centers where conflict and disorder occurred. He discussed the proposal with peace activists in the United States and even opened an office in Europe to mobilize wider support for the plan.[49]

Favorably disposed as he was toward the league, Williams nevertheless came to believe that the press, out of sympathy for its objectives, had been too lenient in reporting its shortcomings. Others such as Herbert Matthews saw little in the league but false rhetoric or idealism until accumulating evidence of the breakdown of the Versailles settlement awakened their appreciation of even the flawed virtues and potential of the international organization.[50] The league in the twenties had failed as a vehicle either for moderating the terms of Versailles or for promoting compromise and accommodation among the Great Powers. Its helplessness in the face of Japan's invasion of Manchuria and subsequent withdrawal from the league in 1933 was further underscored when Hitler withdrew Germany's delegation the same year. With Mussolini's successful defiance and the Allies' failure to agree upon effective measures for resistance to aggression, the last vestiges of league effectiveness and credibility were destroyed.

John T. Whitaker had found Geneva and the League of Nations in the early thirties an attractive but misguided showplace of naive liberalism. Dependent upon Great Power cooperation to meet any challenge, the league faced the Japanese with "timid banter" and delay. Whitaker sensed that fear and insecurity were undermining any possibility of united action; he was witnessing, he thought, the "collapse of democratic leadership" and the "bankruptcy of internationalism." When the league failed to act effectively against Italy, Whitaker concluded that its collapse was "miserable and complete." Returning to Geneva from Africa, his disillusionment was total. "What had they done to my League," he wrote. Any remaining idealistic dreams of the future of world democracy had to be scuttled, for "the world was drifting back to 1914."[51]

Edmond Taylor, covering the League of Nations at the time of the

Italo-Ethiopian conflict, was one of a group of correspondents for whom sanctions and collective security in the face of aggression became crucial issues. Taylor later conceded that Wilsonian internationalist idealism, manipulated by a "sanctionist lobby" of league officials, propagandists, and other interested parties had fostered unrealistic hopes of what the league might accomplish. Mussolini's defiance of sanctions only fed the conviction of these journalists that a more effective defense of collective security must be forged. Although Taylor hesitated to advocate military pressure upon Italy, he was contemptuous of the league's inability to face the issue. Others, he later remembered, were even more ardent than he in their "fierce" conviction that "the master issue of the day—our challenge to make the world safe for democracy" had at last emerged clearly. Among these correspondents several impressed Taylor particularly. Edgar Mowrer's "avenging extremism," as Taylor recalled it, "reembodies the fire, the incorruptibility, and a bit of the fanaticism of a New England Abolitionist." Mowrer's intensity was matched, if at a less explosive level, by the "prairie idealism" of the *New York Times*'s Geneva correspondent, Clarence Streit, who held a "gentler, more optimistic, and slightly hazier dream of brotherhood." The United Press's Wallace Carroll had been "the most conscientious reporter among us," Taylor wrote, "the most sober analyst, in general a much-needed balance wheel." But regardless of temperament or ability, a bloc of "fierce" "sanctionists" had formed among the ostensibly cool, cynical, and uncommitted American journalists.[52]

Taylor acknowledged that Europe's and the league's crisis had led some correspondents to shift their stance from professional neutrality to advocacy, if not outright partisanship. As the Continent drifted palpably and at an accelerated pace toward military confrontation, objectivity, whether grounded in cynicism or in aspiring professionalism, seemed increasingly unrealistic and irrelevant. Taylor noted that his new commitment required special efforts to avoid letting his sentiments color his reporting too heavily. And he did not pretend that he had succeeded in striking an even balance between his personal feelings and his journalistic responsibilities. Taylor agreed with Williams and Whitaker that the press had raised false hopes concerning the league in its early days, but it had also lent itself to "anti-League" campaigns by nationalists, the armaments industry, and others. "Despite—or because of—the cynicism upon which we have been suckled," Taylor wrote, "we proved in many ways to be amazingly innocent." From "idealogical apathy" journalists veered swiftly into "salvationary politics," swinging from disillusionment to hope and back again all too readily. Questioning the value of a profession whose editors and readers seemed little interested in the truths they thought they had discovered, correspondents sharing Taylor's views found "a new dignity" in "bearing witness to the evilness of evil." They tried "to become in reality those brave watchdogs of the truth and the frontiers of the news that our promotion departments advertised us as being," only to find criticism at home from those who preferred not to be jarred out of their comfortable thoughts by new and disturbing truths.[53] Not only the League of Nations, it appeared, but Europe, the peace of the world, and—somewhat less obviously—the character and future of international journalism had all reached a crossroads.

For Clarence Streit, who had reported from Geneva since 1929, the personal and professional ramifications of Europe's crisis loomed especially large. A convinced democrat, lover of peace, and advocate of international cooperation, he felt deep loyalty to the goals and ideals for which the League of Nations stood. Whitaker thought Streit "the most distinguished" of the Geneva correspondents, "but he wore the League like a heart on his sleeve." Yet as an experienced observer, Streit was well aware of the league's shortcomings. By 1934 he was already drafting what would eventually become a book offering an alternative plan for international union, a confederation of democratic states structured and empowered to provide the framework for a workable confederation of nations.[54]

Meanwhile, the fears and forebodings of correspondents such as Streit, Taylor, Whitaker, and the others were within sight of full realization. The Munich Crisis of 1938 demonstrated the incapacity of the Allies to honor their commitment to the Versailles settlement or to the principle of collective security as embodied in the independence of Czechoslovakia, while the German invasion of Poland precipitated the general war that both the League of Nations and the futile appeasement policy had aimed to avert. Even before those climactic events, the desperate, drawn-out civil war in Spain had begun, testing the effectiveness of the newly forged Rome-Berlin axis and demonstrating again the inability of the Western democracies to mount effective resistance to the subversion of democracy and the aggressive designs of dictatorship. For the foreign correspondents, too, Spain proved a turning point. Their love for Europe and their disillusion with its politics, their rediscovered faith in America and their new-found internationalism were transmuted in the fires of the Spanish conflict into an active commitment to the preservation of international democracy. Professionalism for its own sake, however admirable an ideal, no longer appeared an adequate journalistic response to a world on the verge of collapse.

8

Spain and Beyond

■ Civil war in Spain, which broke out in July 1936, hard on the heels of Mussolini's attack on Ethiopia, marked a distinct turning point not only in Europe's drift toward a general war but also in the attitudes of American correspondents toward their own nation's role and toward their personal commitment and responsibilities as well. The international catastrophe that many had thought virtually inevitable since Hitler's consolidation of his grip on power now appeared imminent, if not already in its opening stages. The rapid lineup of Italy and Germany in support of the Spanish Nationalist insurgents seemed to presage the division of the Continent into two distinct camps, the reactionary aggressors and the pacifically minded—if feckless—democracies. True, the blind neutrality of the British and French governments, on the one hand, and the active commitment of Europe's Communists and the assistance offered by the Soviet government to the Spanish Loyalists, on the other, blurred the lines of distinction. But the brave, determined defense of the Spanish republic in the face of what came to be overwhelming odds was seen by a number of reporters as the first, exemplary rallying of the forces of democracy against the totalitarian menace.

In such a perspective, the remoteness and detachment of the United States almost inevitably was called into question. Europe's earlier quarrels and fumblings had dampened calls for American involvement in continental diplomacy, but now the sharpening lines of division and the mobilization of forces committed to freedom and self-determination seemed to present a compelling cause from which the United States could not abstain. Only in America, it seemed, could be found the strength, the vigor, and the commitment to lead an effective resistance against aggressive totalitarianism. Yet the United States continued to remain apart, strangely reluctant to involve itself.

The events of the climactic years 1936–39 require little retelling here; they have been treated widely elsewhere, and notably in works by the journalists who observed or participated in them.[1] For our purposes, the significance of these years lies less in the events themselves than in their effect on the outlook and careers of the correspondents. The demand for America's commitment seemed to be paralleled by a similar call upon the journalistic profession itself. As the frailty and futility of the League of Nations had provoked some reporters to rally around the cause of collective security, so the ordeal of the Spanish republic aroused a new sense of responsibility to alert distracted democrats everywhere to the threat now facing them. To their concerns for the future of democracy, Spain now added an appreciation of the ruthlessness and ingenuity with which the dictators could deploy hitherto little-understood powers against their opponents—powers that included new forms of opinion manipulation as well as unorthodox military tools and tactics. In the eyes of a number of American reporters, a crisis long in the making—a social and cultural as well as ideological, political, and military confrontation—was coming into close and immediately threatening focus. Not only was the Europe which they had loved threatened with destruction, but also the America they had left behind but never completely abandoned and toward which their thoughts increasingly turned seemed itself imperilled as never before.

Journalism, under such conditions, took on a new urgency and importance. Not only events, but their context and significance must be set forth in graphic terms. Loyalties and emotions had been touched as seldom before. The model of the cool, disinterested reporter—to whatever degree it had influenced the behavior of the community of American correspondents in the past—seemed less appropriate to the new occasions. Professionalism seemed increasingly measurable in terms of commitment, rather than in the quixotic categories of impartiality and objectivity that had once appeared so admirable. In the face of imminent, pervasive danger, these correspondents felt compelled to position themselves and their fellow Americans on the side of the embattled democracies whose shortcomings and foibles they had so long scorned.

For American reporters these were, inevitably, busy times—filled both with satisfaction and discouragement. Each turn of the political and propaganda struggle brought new developments to cover and interpret, even as it added to the respectful interest with which their work was received. Their warnings, long discounted at home as the outpourings of slanted, perhaps even un-American, imaginations began at last to find a more appreciative audience. Americans who, from the Spanish Civil War onward were awakened to the reality of danger, had long had access to the correspondents' descriptions of the international scene. Now they turned with rising interest to those whose efforts they had hitherto taken so lightly.

Recognition of these efforts, when it came, was sudden, sweet, and comprehensive. For convenience, it may be dated from the reception accorded John Gunther's *Inside Europe* in 1936—the first work of international analysis by a foreign correspondent to win an enthusiastic public reception in the United States. Certainly there already had been evidence of public interest in the growing attendance at the lecture tours correspondents had been offering since the early thirties. And later there would be more official recognition. Yet, for our purposes, two events of 1936, the outbreak of war in Spain and the publication of the Gunther volume, mark as well as any the sudden rise of American concern for the gathering European crisis.

INSIDE EUROPE

John Gunther's success as the first correspondent author of a popular book of international political description and analysis was an instance of the happy combination of a man and a time. For more than a decade, Gunther had travelled widely and reported on central and eastern Europe from his base in Vienna. His assignment required periodic trips through the Balkans, and the *Daily News*'s system of sending its correspondents to other capitals to fill in for vacationing or otherwise absent bureau chiefs had served him well. Gunther's ambition to become something more than a routine correspondent had driven him to make the most of every opportunity that came his way for travel or for widening his acquaintanceship in newsworthy or knowledgeable circles. He was a direct beneficiary of Paul Mowrer's long struggle with the *Daily News* management to build the foundations of a strong, professionally oriented news service.

Yet Gunther had never been content to be a mere cog in the machine.

Independent and energetic, he had frequently dealt directly with Chicago instead of through Mowrer, technically his superior. Neither Gunther's nor Mowrer's papers show evidence of any considerable correspondence between the two; it may be that with regard to Gunther Mowrer pursued the policy he had recommended to Chicago, that of letting a productive, reliable reporter pursue his own path. Yet Mowrer had shown some resentment at Gunther's demands for special consideration with regard to expenses and assignments and his success in getting Chicago to approve them. Mowrer may have been influential in winning the envied London assignment for Carroll Binder over Gunther in 1930, although Gunther eventually succeeded Binder there in 1935. In any event it was probably Gunther's almost uncanny sense for the kind of lively, readable news stories that Chicago welcomed, rather than favoritism, that accounted for whatever preferment he received.[2]

Such special consideration, if any, was clearly insufficient to satisfy Gunther. Sociable, restless, and ambitious, he loved to live well and to mingle in high society. On a reporter's meager salary, even with an added expense account, this was a prescription for constant tension; he had been driven almost from the beginning to supplement his income by writing magazine articles. As a prolific writer he had thus gained further recognition while at the same time extending the scope of his knowledge. By the time he reached London in 1935 Gunther had a wide circle of friends, acquaintances, and connections distributed across Europe.

Since at least 1932 he had been exploring the idea of a book "exposing" the inside stories and gossip of European politics. He had contributed that year to such a volume, prepared by a number of correspondents, but by 1935 he felt capable of undertaking a more ambitious effort alone. Disciplining himself strictly on a regimen that nevertheless included his responsibilities as chief of a major news bureau, to say nothing of what can only be described as a hectic social life among the British upper crust, Gunther produced his manuscript. He drew, of course, upon his own ample collection of articles and notes, and he leaned heavily, as he acknowledged, on information supplied him by his correspondent colleagues.[3]

The reception accorded *Inside Europe* was unmatched in the previous experience of the foreign correspondence community. Its success was immediate and virtually complete. It jumped to the top ranks of American best-seller lists almost at once and remained there for several months. At year's end it ranked sixth on the nonfiction lists, close behind Negley Farson's colorful autobiography, *The Way of a Transgressor*, whose popularity was further evidence of rising public attention and interest. Earlier, the Mowrers' several volumes of political and economic analysis had been well received by a small audience but had failed to arouse the general public. More recently, Vincent Sheean's autobiography had shown that a popular market existed in the United States for well-written, fast-paced descriptions of international adventure. The excitement of the early New Deal was passing and the threatening clouds that had gathered on the international horizons had evidently begun to stir American curiosity. Gunther's approach offered exactly the mixture of information, explanation, gossip, and glamor for which curious American readers were evidently ready.

Gunther had consciously chosen to emphasize the element of personality in politics. The book's viewpoint, as Gunther wrote, was that "the accidents of personality play a great role in history."[4] And Europe in the thirties had conveniently provided him with a stage swarming with colorful, intriguing characters. Yet, within his framework of descriptions of the lives, loves, politics, and peculiarities of many of the Continent's leading personalities, Gunther had managed to pack a good deal of solid information about Europe's political and economic scene. Perhaps even more significant than the facts themselves was the collective impression they offered of a continent racked by deep hostilities and conflicts, confronted by an unprecedentedly powerful totalitarian challenge, whose traditional rulers blindly groped for responses to a crisis whose dimensions they did not fully comprehend.

Gunther's readers learned much that was important and much that was trivial as well: from Pierre Laval's taste in neckties and Edouard Herriot's favorite Lyon restaurants to the role played in French politics by the regents of the Banque de France and the Comité des Forges; from the literary connections of Sir Samuel Hoare's wife's grandaunt to the power base and the significance of Prime Minister Stanley Baldwin; from the inhabitants of Magda Lupescu's chicken coops to the dependence of Rumania on Germany for a market for her grain. As an education in both the high and the low politics of the Continent, the book offered much that was both valuable and interesting.[5]

It had its limitations, however. Gunther's familiarity with the Western democracies, the ramshackle residue of the Austro-Hungarian Empire, and the Balkans left him more at home in those regions than in Germany, Italy, or the Soviet Union where, necessarily, he depended heavily on what he could glean from others. Consequently, although Hitler's Germany dominated the foreground—and provided much of the background, as well—of his stage, the dynamics of neither the German, Italian, nor Soviet Russian totalitarian systems were treated adequately in his gossipy, cocktail conversation approach. Scandinavia and the Low Countries were omitted altogether, while Austria was allotted more than forty pages, almost as many as those devoted to Britain. Lupescu received the better part of a chapter; Winston Churchill came close to being overlooked entirely. Spain was discussed with barely a hint of the calamity in the making there. Still, for a book aimed at a wide audience, *Inside Europe* fulfilled its purpose admirably. It piqued its readers' interest, humanized and made comprehensible some of the men and movements dominating the daily headlines; and for those who chose to probe more deeply, it provided at least some hints as to where to begin.

With a strong assist from Adolf Hitler and Benito Mussolini, John Gunther had achieved at last what a generation of American foreign correspondents had been striving to accomplish. He had captured the attention of the American public and directed it toward events in Europe in whose making the United States was becoming ever more deeply involved. After 1936, reporters overseas would seldom be able to complain that Americans were not reading reports, however much the public may have varied in its interpretations of what it read.

SPAIN

In view of later developments, the revolution that overthrew the Spanish monarchy in 1931 attracted surprisingly little attention in the American press. On the fringe of Europe and no longer a great power, Spain had largely been considered a sideshow by reporters accredited to the major capitals. They had passed through in the twenties on their way to cover the Rif wars in North Africa, or later on brief holidays from their assignments they went to soak up some sun and to comment occasionally on the peculiar features of Spanish politics or culture. In 1933 the ubiquitous Gunther had described the outlines of the new republican regime for *Harper's*. The republic defined democracy in social as well as political terms, he had written. Dominated by intellectuals and lacking in experienced leadership, it still seemed to have brought the military, the Church, and the nobility under control and to have established a reasonably mod-

erate and successful regime. If there were contradictions in his evaluation, Gunther did not recognize them, nor did other leading
correspondents devote enough attention to the new government to expose
its weaknesses and vulnerabilities.[6]

With the outbreak of rebellion, the focus of journalistic attention rapidly swung southward, however, and within a short time regular correspondents and free lances were vying with one another to report from the
scenes of action. Although Spain was to offer an emotional focus and
rallying point for a number of journalists, none became more caught up
in its drama than Herbert Matthews, the *New York Times*'s hitherto detached and determinedly self-preoccupied correspondent. Fancying himself a "realist" Matthews had scorned the pacifist rhetoric and the futility
of the League of Nations and had expressed understanding, if not admiration, for Mussolini's invasion of Ethiopia. Now, from the perspective of
Spain, he began to see the Italian dictator in a new light. The Duce's alliance with Hitler as well as the commitment of Italian troops and resources to aid the Spanish Fascists converted Matthews into an outspoken
advocate of the Loyalist cause. The Spanish war "gave meaning to life,"
he later wrote, "it gave courage and faith in humanity; it taught us what
internationalism means, as no League of Nations or Dumbarton Oaks
will ever do. There one learned that men could be brothers, that nations
and frontiers, religions and races were but outer trappings, and that nothing counted, nothing was worth fighting for, but the ideal of liberty." A
book titled *Two Wars and More to Come*, published in 1938 while the war
still raged, revealed the extent of Matthews's conversion. Placing the
Ethiopian and Spanish wars squarely in the context of the world confla-
gration he now expected, Matthews wrote, "Of all the places in the
world, Madrid is the most satisfactory.... It is indeed the hub of the uni-
verse, for the immediate fate of this world of ours is being settled right
here." Terror and brutality had been resorted to by both sides, but that
carried out under the Loyalists had been exaggerated. There could be little doubt, Matthews held, that Spain was in the throes of a "genuine social revolution" and that the Loyalist government had solid popular
support.[7]

The Spanish war was like a "vortex into which a struggling world is being sucked," he continued. The spread of fascism beyond Italy and Germany was "an ugly thing to behold." Having staked his regime on the
outcome, Mussolini was committed beyond the possibility of withdrawal.
Germany and Russia, although they were supplying equipment, were less

fully engaged. Despite stories to the contrary, Matthews denied that Russians were fighting in the International Brigades. Communists of many nationalities were assisting the Loyalists, he acknowledged, as were Liberals and Socialists of many stripes. Although Russian war materiel and staff assistance had played a crucial part in the defense of Madrid, Matthews saw Soviet influence as already waning. He was particularly impressed by the participation of American volunteers. They were few in numbers, but their willingness to fight signified a new commitment. Most of all, Matthews was struck by the heroism of Madrid's defenders and by the world implications of the struggle. "Here is courage, ideals, patience, fortitude," he enthused. "I am not a Communist or a Fascist, a radical or conservative, a Catholic or an anti-clerical, but I take off my hat to these people." The war had a "long, long arm and it is reaching out for all of us," be believed. "The day of judgment is coming."[8]

With the virtues of hindsight, Matthews later concluded that the Spanish republic had been a "colossal failure," although a "noble effort" to establish democracy among a people unprepared for it. He had learned things less favorable to the Loyalists and the International Brigades but he remained convinced that their cause basically had been just. More than anything else, his Spanish experiences caused Matthews to question the nature of the journalism profession itself. He attributed the failure of Americans to rally strongly to the Loyalists' cause to the bias and influence of the American Catholic church, on the one hand, and on the other to the shortcomings of the American press in general and of his employer, the *New York Times*, in particular. The Church had at the outset opposed the Loyalists as atheistic Communists and had brought enormous pressures to bear on the American government and press to discredit opposing views. The *Times*'s copy editors, who happened to be Catholics, had accepted at face value information dispensed by Nationalist propagandists and sympathizers while downgrading reports favorable to the Loyalists.[9]

Matthews's critique of his editors has since been largely substantiated. What he failed fully to consider, however, was the strength of the pressures mounted by conservative Catholic and non-Catholic elements on behalf of the Spanish rebels. In the face of an organized campaign of pressure and propaganda not only the *Times* but the United States government itself struggled with difficulty—and far from successfully—to establish policies that would be both fair and responsive to the conflicting interests at stake.[10] More than most Americans saw at the time, but as

Matthews had begun to recognize, the war in Spain was an omen of changes ahead both for government and for journalism in an era of increasing ideological polarization.

Matthews was only one of a number of correspondents deeply affected by their Spanish war experiences. In addition to the expanded coverage provided by the press associations, a bevy of special reporters including such notables as Ernest Hemingway, Martha Gellhorn, and Vincent Sheean descended on the peninsula and were soon sending out reams of copy. Matthews travelled for a time with Hemingway and Gellhorn, and over lunch in Barcelona he discovered that Sheean shared some of his views on the conflict's larger significance.[11]

Sheean, who had travelled the world since his early days in Europe, found in Spain the one bright spot on an otherwise depressing continent. The world was refusing to face up to the problem of the Jewish refugees from Nazi persecution; the British and French were engaged "either through stupidity, cowardice or something more infamous in the network of treachery" that was undermining democracy. In 1938 Sheean wrote that Britain and France were "fatally weak, legalistic without being honest, and undecided without being fair." Only in Spain did he feel a part of "the struggle of common humanity against the black forces" that everywhere threatened it. That that struggle would sooner or later engulf not only all of Europe but America as well, he had little doubt. And when it came it would be "an imperialist war, fought for no principle except that of Empire." The democracies had already shown that they would fight only to save their own skins.[12]

Other correspondents shared Matthews's and Sheean's view that the Communists, influential as they had been in assisting the early defense of the republic, played a minor role in the Loyalist government. The bravery of the Loyalist armies, the gallant, unselfish commitment of American and other volunteers, and the lies and cruelty exhibited by the Nationalist forces were the chief topics of comment by American journalists. Even John T. Whitaker, once a confidante of Mussolini and now assigned to the Nationalist forces in Spain, had little but contempt for the rebel leader, General Franco. Whitaker later noted that the Germans and Italians, too, had been disgusted with the Nationalists. Whitaker's admiration for the Loyalist cause led him to denounce its abandonment by the British, French, and American governments.[13]

Leland Stowe, recalled to New York by the *Herald Tribune* in 1935, returned to Spain on at least two occasions. For Stowe also, Spain acted as a catalyst. Since the *Herald Tribune* refused to send him, he accepted an assignment from the Committee for Medical Aid to Spanish Democracy in 1937 to visit the war zones and to lecture on behalf of the committee's fund-raising efforts. As did most other correspondents, Stowe quickly identified with the Loyalists. His outspokenness cost him money, since the fund-raising lectures so angered his regular lecture bureau that his annual fall tour was reduced on the ground that his fund raising had precluded return engagements in certain areas.[14] But money was not all that Stowe lost in Spain. An enthusiast by nature, he had always made a special effort to write as objectively as possible, delineating Europe's problems and indicating the measures and costs the United States must accept should it choose to preserve its neutrality in the approaching conflict. After Spain his stance changed noticeably. Without abandoning his journalist's eye for the telling incident or human interest story to convey the immediacy of a situation or the pertinence of an experience, he exchanged the role of the objective reporter for that of the committed observer-advocate.

For Stowe as for others it seemed that Spain held a special and compelling message. Freedom and democracy, taken for granted in America, were under siege in Europe. After more than a decade of ineffective defense, democracy's adherents were at last beginning to rally militantly to its side. In the face of the totalitarian menace that shaped the issues of the late 1930s, considerations of professionalism and objectivity that had concerned correspondents a decade earlier now seemed remote and abstract.[15] With an audience more eager than ever for their explanations, they had a story to tell that lacked little in drama, intrigue, heroism, villainy, or suspense. With the situation in Spain, American foreign correspondence entered its prime. Its experience and equipment were without parallel. Its subject matter had begun to stir the emotions and its message now could be seen to drive straight to readers' deepest traditions and convictions. As the intensity and pace of events increased, there was little time or incentive to ponder any questionable implications or consequences of the new situation. Who could, or should, have given consideration to theoretical issues such as the dangers involved in too close an identification with one's subject matter? From detachment, correspondents were moving swiftly toward engagement in the international struggle to save democracy.

AUSTRIA

Early in 1938, while much of the rest of Europe was preoccupied with Spain, Hitler at last moved on Austria. The Austrians were totally dependent upon others for their security, but the French and British once again were unwilling to risk anything in Austria's defense. And Mussolini, whose possible intervention had stopped Hitler from seizing control four years earlier, was now Germany's ally, heavily committed in Spain and in no position to uphold Austrian resistance.

Throughout the early thirties, John Gunther, from his post in Vienna, had been watching developments in Germany and assessing their implications for the feeble Austrian state. Early in 1933 he had begun a series of articles for *The Nation* that he continued on a regular, almost monthly, basis for more than a year. From Vienna he could also observe the Balkan nations whose fraility and insecurity rendered them, like Austria, sensitive to every chill emanating from Berlin. In May 1933 Gunther had considered Hitler's rise to power, attributing it to the vengeful Versailles treaty and to the accidents and intrigues that had marked the tortuous path of German politics subsequently. He had pointed out that Austria was already under severe pressure as a result of the Depression and its own internal divisions. Its chancellor, Engelbert Dollfuss, was ruling by decree with the parliament "dead" and the press gagged, while both the Socialists—whom he had attacked—and the right-wing Heimwehr—on which he depended—threatened at any moment to overthrow him. A small domestic Nazi movement, obviously inspired and supported by the Germans, added another menacing element to the mixture.[16]

Hitler's policies were deliberately creating terror and "confusion amounting almost to chaos" throughout eastern Europe, Gunther reported. By September, he had concluded that Hitler was intent on conquering Austria with a combination of propaganda, political and economic pressures, and subversion. When Dollfuss had outlawed the Nazis in June they had replied with a campaign of terror and bombings to frighten off tourists, with propaganda leaflets dropped from the air, with violent radio attacks, and with a general stepping up of the "war of nerves." Although a conservative anti-Marxist, Dollfuss was now recognized by the Socialists, Gunther wrote, as the only man who could hold Austria together in the face of such pressures.[17]

After an interlude in Berlin, covering the trial of the man accused of setting fire to the German Reichstag, Gunther returned to Vienna. In

February 1934 he reported again on Dollfuss's desperate efforts to withstand the relentless German onslaught. He found Dollfuss too lenient with the Nazi troublemakers, and he also questioned the chancellor's reliance on Mussolini, an undependable ally, in Gunther's view. The Duce was not anxious for war and Hitler could be counted on to provide no pretext for Italian intervention. The Germans would violate no treaties but would see to it that the takeover, when it came, appeared as a purely internal matter. By this time Gunther had concluded that only firm measures could stop Hitler: "The only treatment a Nazi understands is a mallet on the head." Vatican backing for Dollfuss, the possibility of an alliance with his enemies, the Social Democrats, or the return of the Hapsburgs were all possible counters to pro-Nazi sentiment; meanwhile, Austria's economy was worsening steadily.[18]

In March 1934 Gunther reported Dollfuss's attack on the Social Democrats. Their power center in Vienna's working-class district had been surrounded and shelled by the army; a call for a general strike had failed. The official excuse for the coup as an anti-Bolshevik measure had been absurd, although many Austrian conservatives did, indeed, think the Socialists a serious threat. Despite his discomfort at Dollfuss's violent measures, Gunther noted that the Austrian government had treated prisoners reasonably well and there had been few casualties; destruction was not so great as it might have been. Evidently, having concluded that the chancellor was the nation's only hope, Gunther was willing to countenance measures he would otherwise have found indefensible.

Two months later he offered a fuller explanation of Dollfuss's actions. Crushing the Socialists had consolidated the chancellor's power by ensuring the support of the conservative Heimwehr. With his enemies reduced to helplessness, and with the backing of the Vatican and of Mussolini as well, Dollfuss had withstood the Nazi threat. Hitler was, at least temporarily, turning down the heat, although Gunther thought that the Nazis could well afford to bide their time. To maintain his position, Dollfuss would have to make concessions either to the Socialists or the Nazis, each of whom, Gunther estimated, commanded the support of about 40 percent of the population. The chancellor's "fascist coup d'état" had won him some time, but very little else.[19]

In July 1934 Dollfuss was murdered by Nazis who broke into the chancellery wearing Austrian army uniforms. Much to Hitler's surprise, however, the Austrians managed once again to block a German takeover. Dollfuss dead had proven as powerful as Dollfuss alive, Gunther wrote.

The Social Democrats had rallied to the government as they could not have to Dollfuss, and the Austrian Nazis had proven weaker than their propaganda suggested. Gunther admitted having been fooled himself, but pointed out that the "gangsters" might well strike again. For the moment, however, the chief lesson of the attack had been that "a Nazi putsch in Austria means war."[20]

While Austria was staving off the Germans, Gunther reported that the Balkan nations were responding to Hitler in ways that boded ill for democracy and peace. A new government in Bulgaria, he told *The Nation*'s readers, represented a step in the direction of fascism as much as Dollfuss had in Austria. Imitation führers were cropping up throughout the region and, to survive the rising pressures, moderate forces were being pushed farther and farther to the Right. Czechoslovakia was the least likely to go Nazi, Gunther thought, but the Germans exercised enormous influence as a market for the grain of Rumania and Yugoslavia. The Rumanian king and Iron Guard were already leaning toward the Germans. If Austria were to fall, it would be all the more difficult for other nations to hold out.[21]

In 1935 Gunther moved to London and—after *Inside Europe*—to the United States. But like Dorothy Thompson who had preceded him in the Austrian capital, he retained a sentimental attachment to the city which he had termed "the most delightful" in Europe. In 1935 he had described his life and work there, noting the pleasant, friendly life of the journalistic community, centered around the *stamtisch* at the Café Imperial where reporters met twice daily for coffee, gossip, the newspapers, and an exchange of tips. At the time of the *Anschluss*, William L. Shirer was enjoying the pleasures of Vienna in his new capacity as correspondent for the new CBS international radio service. In close touch with his superior, Edward R. Murrow, Shirer helped to mobilize newsmen in the major capitals for the historic first international news "round-up" as Hitler's diplomatic, propaganda, political, and military tentacles closed around hapless Austria.[22] Shortly thereafter, Shirer regretfully transferred his base of operations to Switzerland to protect his family and ensure his freedom to broadcast.

Even correspondents not regularly assigned to Vienna but who had spent time there were deeply touched by Austria's fall. Following the abandonment of Spain, the failure of the democracies to rally to Austria's defense seemed to them still another betrayal of freedom and of a nation and city to which they felt a sentimental attachment. This mood of double loss was well mirrored in a verse Leland Stowe published in February 1938 in the *New York Herald Tribune*, "Farewell Vienna":

> So, Vienna, too, is dying.
> Call the spadesmen for her grave!
> We, who gave her to the tyrants,
> Bury what we would not save.
>
> We shall bury joy and laughter
> Thrust the bones of freedom deep
> Into earth that once was kindly,
> Turn our backs—and let them sleep....
>
> She was but a lovely lady,
> This Vienna we have known.
> Give her ravagers full license!
> Send her back to earth and stone!
>
> Let her die, since none will save her.
> But let her mortal wounds be clean.
> If her days are dimmed with anguish
> Death shall find her face serene.[23]

CZECHOSLOVAKIA AND POLAND

Scarcely had Austria been incorporated into the Third Reich when Hitler turned his attention to Czechoslovakia. Here, the picture was more complicated since the Czechs themselves had a competent army and had earlier signed mutual defense treaties with France and the Soviet Union. These complications indeed may have contributed to the fact that Hitler faced strong opposition from within the German military and was forced to accomplish his objective in two stages, moving into the Sudetenland with the full acquiescence of the French and British in October 1938 and seizing the remainder of the enfeebled Czech nation in March 1939. The prolonged crisis over Czechoslovakia, with the meeting of the British and French prime ministers with Hitler and Mussolini at Munich and an extended period of uncertainty as to the final outcome, aroused and divided the American people as no earlier crisis had. For the American correspondents it presented the fullest opportunity yet offered to reach a concerned and curious audience. At the same time it fulfilled their worst fears that the democracies would fail to face effectively the now unmistakable threat, while confirming their sense that the free and pleasant Europe they had enjoyed and loved was on the verge of collapse.

Shirer, at his new base in Geneva, found himself "depressed...beyond words" by the sellout of the Czechs at Munich. Too "sick at heart...to work seriously at my profession," he lacked the spirit to go to Prague to cover its fall the following March. Raymond Swing, however, travelled to Prague and found there a whole community of foreign correspondents, including Knickerbocker, Whitaker, Sheean, and *Manchester Guardian* correspondent Marcel Fodor. Swing, who was now doing radio broadcasts, pointed out to his listeners that by occupying all of Czechoslovakia, Hitler had extended his empire for the first time to include a non-German people. In so doing, Swing argued, he had "thrown away his moral case" and completely discredited the Allies' appeasement tactics. Earlier, John Gunther had suggested that the Munich sellout encouraged the Japanese to attack in China by convincing them that they no longer needed to fear Western opposition there.[24]

After the fall of Austria, Edmond Taylor began to think about making the study of propaganda methods that eventually became *The Strategy of Terror* (1940). Increasingly at odds with his isolationist editor, Colonel McCormick, Taylor was drawn to the ideas of those who had formed a "coherent picture of the Nazi menace," among whom he included his colleagues William L. Shirer and Edgar Ansel Mowrer. On a post-Munich trip through the Danube countries, Taylor was able to observe both the growing Nazi influence in the region and the consolidation of anti-Nazi opinion as well. Torn and confused by the conflicts swirling around him, and dismissed at last from the *Chicago Tribune*, Taylor took refuge for a time in psychoanalysis. From this, and the shock of the fall of France, he emerged, he thought, a "more dedicated, as well as a more disillusioned, democrat," both a "franker nationalist and a more authentic internationalist."[25]

Meanwhile, the German-Russian pact, Hitler's attack on Poland, and the Allies' declarations of war had completed the transformation of Europe's political and ideological landscape. The war which correspondents had been anticipating at least since 1933 had at last materialized. H. R. Knickerbocker, for one, had even predicted a forthcoming German-Soviet alliance as early as 1937. Despite the bitter hostility that had long divided them and that "formed the principal background of Europe's fear of war," and despite Hitler's vociferous anticommunism, the two governments were contemplating "friendship—even alliance—with the end in view of dividing Poland and perhaps more of Europe between them!" Knickerbocker had written. Faced with the possibility of such cynical Machiavellianism, he concluded that "if Europe has any lesson to give America, it is that in a world of gunmen, a good citizen must go armed."[26]

For Vincent Sheean the lessons of Europe's collapse were only slightly different. England in 1938 he found "a mixture of bewildered weakness and courageous perfidy," desperately trying to avoid the fact that "the river that flows beneath this [London] bridge contains the water of the Ebro, and there is blood in it (some of it English blood). Austria, Czechoslovakia, China, Ethiopia, Spain: they are all around, as near as Billingsgate, as inexorable as the river's movement to the sea." Sheean questioned whether the New World should attempt to rescue the Old, "since those who have been its guardians for centuries are sunk in such coma decay [*sic*]?" France was "wavering into timorous reaction, half Fascism and half sheer cowardice." Yet when the crisis came, he knew, it would be hard for America to remain indifferent. "Interest and emotion will propel us into action and in all likelihood we will save them again...even though we know that they have deserved their fate to the fullest." By 1939 he sensed an "obscure but persistent consciousness of gathering doom," which as yet the "fashionable world" refused to acknowledge. And, from Paris in the spring of the following year, he made perhaps the most pessimistic observation of all: "...of all the things sacrificed in the holocaust at Munich in 1938, the most precious was the trust of democratic peoples."[27]

As the European war clouds massed, journalists were among the front ranks of those rallying the American people to prepare for an active role in democracy's defense. John T. Whitaker, Raymond Swing, and Edgar Mowrer contributed to a symposium titled "Calling America" in a special 1939 issue of *Survey Graphic*. Swing, convinced that a war more serious than World War I was on the horizon, argued that democracy was endangered at home as well as abroad. Something more than neutrality was now required to assure America's safety, he wrote. In the modern world it was necessary to prepare a defense against propaganda and infiltration as well as against outright military attacks. In a war of clashing ideologies, the only defense would be "a still better idea properly understood and clearly discernable to the rest of the world." The world was changing rapidly, Swing warned, and America must be prepared to change too, while holding fast to her basic principles. Mowrer, noting that liberalism with its underlying assumptions of progress, reason, and equality was losing ground rapidly elsewhere, urged that "liberal democracy must become militant or perish."[28]

When war came in September 1939 American correspondents were more than ready. Not only had they acquired the experience and perspective with which to comprehend it, they had been justified in the warnings and anticipations they had been sending home for nearly a decade. The evil which they had identified and described had now fully manifested itself, and opposition to it was at last gathering. What remained to be determined was what the relationship of the United States to that opposition was to be. The Europe the correspondents had loved was collapsing around them. America, from which they had distanced themselves geographically and intellectually for so many years, now seemed to offer the only hope for preserving the best of both worlds. And journalism, too, to which they had committed their own lives and fortunes, was caught up in the central conflicts and issues of the time.

9

An Ocean Away
Views of America

■ The experience of living in the midst of another continent and culture inevitably raised questions for American reporters concerning the society they had left behind but with which they retained strong personal and career ties. Perceived differences between the United States and Europe implicitly, if not overtly, had motivated many in their decisions to live overseas. Their initial impressions of Europe inevitably had been strongly colored by what they thought of the United States. Individual attitudes varied widely, but some patterns can be detected even in the responses of this highly individualistic group. Self-centered or cynical American careerists were not miraculously transformed overnight into high-minded professionals by overseas assignments. Adventurers and romantics tended to discover the freedom and glamour they had sought. Aspiring writers and esthetes revelled in the cultural riches of Europe, confirming as they did so their initial critiques of America as a materialistic intellectual wasteland. Much as they deplored or ridiculed the crudity of the thousands of tourists who followed in their wake, the correspondents shared at least one fundamental experience with their fellow Americans in Europe, that of finding essentially what they had gone in search of.

Differences manifested themselves in time, however. As correspondents remained on, extending their acquaintanceships and deepening their familiarity with Europe in ways that tourists never could, their perspectives inevitably altered. Europe and its problems began to command the foreground of their consciousness even as their image of the United States receded into memory. Although they seldom came to think of themselves as true Europeans, it did not take long for many to reach the conclusion that they understood a great deal about Europe that most Americans did not. At the same time, they were challenged to explain the United States to curious Europeans; in attempting to do so they were forced to consolidate and codify many of the attitudes and impressions about home that they had brought with them.

One consequence of this process appeared early as a gap between reporters' ideas of news suitable for publication and their editors' conceptions of what the American public wanted to read. Correspondents had challenged the persistent editorial demand for gossipy human-interest news; yet this probably colored their views of the United States, nonetheless, confirming suspicions that Americans were insensitive to the political, intellectual, and cultural currents they themselves found so important in Europe. Correspondents had reacted to this gap in perceptions in various ways. While it heightened the cynicism of some, others found it a spur to their efforts to achieve a more comprehensive, informative foreign news service. Some used it as a basis for requesting more frequent home leaves. The lecture circuit, as we have seen, was in part a response to the perceived distance between perspectives on the news at home and in the field.

The increasing frequency of these home visits coincided at least roughly with drastic changes in the social and political climate of both Europe and America. The rise of Hitler dramatized the failure of the European political system which American journalists had long found the least impressive feature of the Continent's life. Meanwhile, in the United States the New Deal seemed to be reviving the nation's politics after the long, dry twenties, even as social and cultural life exhibited refreshing new influences. Changes on both continents provided an irresistible stimulus to reconsideration of European and American conditions. America in the thirties became much more hospitable and interesting to her foreign correspondents than she had been earlier. At the same time, it seemed more important than ever that the nature and sources of Europe's weakness be understood by a people who were at last showing signs of concern.

The experiences of the correspondents themselves provoked still further comparisons between the two worlds whose differences and divergences their careers spanned. So they all were tempted, and especially the more imaginative among them, to speculate and write about America.

Their European sojourn lent a special flavor to their understanding. If it did not always sharpen their insights, it colored their perceptions and encouraged them sometimes to minimize similarities between the two continents or to exaggerate America's support for the values they found so deeply threatened across the Atlantic.

Before the First World War, foreign correspondence had contributed little to serious consideration of either European or American conditions. Yet even then occasional comments by reporters reflected their awareness of characteristics and divergent values distinguishing the two continents. Thus, Edward Price Bell had written in 1907 on the American character for a British publication, addressing the question "Is Every American Potentially a Rascal?"—a question suggested by scandals in the United States and perhaps also by the flood of American tourists pouring into the United Kingdom. He had tried to explain what he conceded might at times seem an apparent, if not necessarily basic, rascality on the part of his fellow countrymen. The Americans' experience had tended to make them "non-political, non-social...intensively and exclusively economic," Bell had written. Frontier opportunities had fostered individualistic, exploitive attitudes. Politics had been left to the lazy and dishonest. However, Bell assured his readers, America was awakening to the unfortunate results of this outlook, and "scoundrelism" was now happily on the wane.[1]

Bell assured critics that Americans admired British achievements and that the nation had abandoned its earlier isolated state. Once, Bell's father and his farmhands had ridden off excitedly to see the first railway train passing through southern Indiana. Now America's eyes and ears were open to the world. "When internal America was like another planet, it mattered little what anybody in Europe said about the country; the words were lost in the...untravelled waste. Today when a great newspaper or a great man speaks, it is into the very ear of the whole American world."[2]

Paul Mowrer tended to be both more critical of the United States and more sensitive to the peculiar qualities he had discovered in Europe. Mowrer answered pressures for local color stories by sending a number of small articles on national character as found on both sides of the Atlantic. He included descriptions of American tourists and of an American baseball team in Paris, together with discussions of the late age of marriage in France, "England's Militant Women," and, in an effort to make as much as possible out of an often irksome assignment, an article titled

"Love Formal Gardens: French, Unlike English and Americans, Prefer Artificial Landscapes." After a trip home in 1914, Mowrer described some of the impressions aroused by the sight of Chicago's skyscrapers. In some ways, he wrote, the tall buildings seemed to reflect aspects of the American character. They might be, as some critics suggested, economically or sociologically unsound, but they appealed to the American imagination and served as "symbols of the dizzy and ever-ascending idealism of the American people."[3]

Prewar foreign correspondents, however, seldom indulged in such imaginative or speculative commentary. Not until the war dramatized the growing interdependence of the United States and Europe did issues of national character and culture and their implications for international relations begin to force themselves upon journalistic consciousness.

AMERICA IN THE TWENTIES

Much of the interest which American reporters focussed on the United States in the twenties stemmed from its political and economic relations with post-Versailles Europe. America's failure to ratify the treaty or to join the League of Nations seemed to many correspondents both irresponsible and unrealistic. Some were already troubled by the unhealthy state of postwar European politics. Only a relatively powerful and disinterested leader, it seemed, could exert the influence needed to persuade still-suspicious and self-concerned Europeans to compromise their differences. Still further, it was clear to thoughtful reporters that the United States could not avoid substantial involvement in continental economic affairs. Given America's new economic preeminence and Europe's precarious circumstances, the former's seeming refusal to recognize that successful economic relations called for more than casual political commitments as well seemed highly unrealistic. When Frederic Wile after the war scheduled some home lectures under the title, "John Bull and Uncle Sam," the point he emphasized was that "America is in world affairs for keeps and...the path of our own best interest lies straight in the direction of a warm and friendly cooperation with Great Britain."[4] Yet the United States, preoccupied with its own economic well-being, seemed bent on enjoying the fruits of its successes and confident that it could do so without assuming any international responsibilities. American nationalism, materialism, antiradicalism, and refusal to accept responsibility seemed from across the Atlantic to confirm the charges of self-centered materialism that journalists and others had made earlier.

In an essay titled "Jingo Democracy," written after a postwar home visit, Edgar Ansel Mowrer summarized his reactions to the nation he had not seen for half a decade. "The American people, under the absurd threat of bolshevism, which not one in fifty understands," Mowrer wrote, "has tied and gagged itself to an extent incredible to the less democratic peoples of Europe." Reaction, "sentimental humbug," and "bloated jingoism" could be seen in the race riots and the Red Scare. Prohibition, another American phenomenon that attracted Mowrer's scorn, appalled most of his fellow correspondents as well. Victory "had been too strong a drink" for the teetotallers of the United States, which had accepted the strictest prohibition with enthusiasm during the war. Mowrer attributed America's rejection of President Wilson and the League of Nations to rampant nationalism that favored a "strong and predatory United States" or, alternatively, demanded total isolation from international problems. Americans lacked both understanding of "the overwhelming role of power in human affairs" and a true sense of history. "The more a people (or an individual) is familiar with its past, the more 'objective' its judgments are likely to be." After President Coolidge, in an interview, asked him not a single question about Italy, Mowrer left the White House wondering "what kind of joke God had played upon the American people."[5]

In a 1926 *Forum* article Mowrer argued that America's interest in economic expansion implied an equal, if still unacknowledged, need for political relations favoring "development with the minimum of risk." In the light of the recently announced Dawes Plan for the reorganization of Germany's postwar debt structure, he complained that American leaders were deceiving the public as to the extent of the nation's stake in international economic stabilization. Under the terms of the plan, the United States had become "financially, that is, vitally, interested in the economic prosperity and political tranquility of the industrial heart of Europe," Mowrer pointed out. Leaders might speak of "no political commitments," but when American loans were endangered the government would have to react. Much as the United States might disavow any desire for power or empire, such professions were simply unrealistic. Refusal to face openly the facts of political and economic interdependence could only lead to "results that we did not anticipate and that fill us with dissatisfaction and displeasure." Only by shoring up Europe's shaky political and economic foundations could America ensure its own future prosperity and growth. The Dawes Plan was only the beginning; it must be followed by "definite action to protect the interests we are creating for ourselves on the Mother Continent!"[6]

Other reporters made similar points both in public and private statements, yet their arguments seemed not to be heard at home. Mowrer feared that he might be considered an expatriate crank, and others no doubt felt similarly.[7] Divergent perspectives separated most Americans at home from those assigned to keep them in touch with international developments. That the divergences could exacerbate the sense of alienation already felt by some correspondents can be seen in the case of Raymond Swing, a veteran of many years' European experience who returned home temporarily in 1924. Overseas opportunities were scarce at that point, and Swing, who preferred to remain in Europe, found it necessary to seek alternatives at home. Letters to his wife, Betty Gram Swing, written during the spring of 1924, show that reacquaintance with his native land confirmed a number of his earlier reservations.

On his first day in New York City Swing wrote that he was "caught up already in the atomic dance of America." His initial conversations "added to the general jazz of street and sky, and my real underneath inner intimate acquaintance with my native country, group themselves on my horizon as a gigantic, star-written NO." If Swing's impressions confirmed his worst expectations, they also reminded him clearly of what he valued about Europe: "...the calm, contemplative hours, the pleasant, unrushed communion of spirits between us, the freedom to appraise, weigh, measure and judge all the merits and demerits of affairs and values." He concluded, "[M]y dear, you are right: we can't have it in America."[8]

As he encountered difficulties, Swing began to shift ground a bit. They would have to be prepared to accept a smaller salary than he had been receiving, he reported. And there were some situations in Europe that might reconcile him, however partially, to remaining in the United States. "Any American job would be a hardship, but no hardship is so hard as dull work even in Europe. I should, I believe, prefer being in Iowa to being an AP man anywhere." The New York musical scene, however, convinced him that his brother Herbert, a singer who had been training in Europe, would do better to remain there. "The place simply reeks of disease," he wrote. Herbert "would never have the cash to besiege that indomitable babylonic fortress. His other recourse is to settle down to a comfortable existence, teaching in some American city, singing in a wealthy Presbyterian church, doing an occasional local concert or tour, bellowing out the bass solos for oratorio societies of the district, and dying a prosperous citizen who never had a career. If I were he, I should take out my papers in Berlin or even Roumania, and live as an artist."

Commercial radio, in its early stages, provided Swing with still another glimpse of the American scene. He had listened for two hours

> to the wierdest [*sic*] jumble of conglomerations you can imagine. I heard: Mlle. LeBlanc, Maeterlinck's wife, read French poetry, Bishop Lawrence speaking to the Harvard Club on the benefits of colleges, a lecture on hunting the rhinoceros, music ranging from Bach on the piano, Meyerbeer on the organ, a tenor doing Gounod, to a celebrity telling how hard he worked making his last film, a jazz band in continual tribulation, and the blow-by-blow report of the McTighe-Stribling fight—this from Pittsburgh. You switch from one wavelength to another like moving from one mind to another, and one understands what God must be like. Only I hope he is more patient with each one of us than I was at that instrument. These are the first creakings of what in full motion will be a phenominal [*sic*] advance into miracles and "miracles."

Politics Swing found even less promising. The Teapot Dome revelations were arousing only slight response among the people, who joked about them, wondered how much was true, then proceeded about their business. "A few people are downright hurt by the revelations, wounded that their country should be so filthy; a few are downright indignant that anyone should be hounded by the political scandal mongers. Nobody else cares. I tell you, America is in her special post-war psychosis, having a good time as hard as she can and not willing to take stock of where she is going or what chaos is storing for her in the future."

By this time Swing was even ready to consider an opening with the United Press, if only it would get him back to Europe. "If we get a European job at all, we must count ourselves lucky," he concluded, "even if it involves your stacking up the dishes for me to wash when I get home at night. So much the better. Nine-tenths of the world is impoverished, let's join 'em and share with 'em if need be. God knows I should rather be poor than be rich and carry around on the top of my neck the well ventilated bird cages which most Americans wear under their bonnets." Fortunately, in view of Swing's state of mind, an opportunity to remain in England did appear; and when he finally returned to the United States some years later both he and the country were in happier moods. In the meantime, however, his disaffection was only an extreme case of the criticisms being expressed by many correspondents.

Paul Mowrer, his own career more firmly established than Swing's, spent much of the twenties pondering the responsibilities of his profession. Among other concerns, he felt it incumbent upon foreign correspondents to awaken Americans to the realities of international politics and to encourage them to recognize the implications of their financial and technological predominance. In 1924 Mowrer published *Our Foreign Affairs: A Study in the National Interest and the New Diplomacy*, which was a carefully reasoned plea for Americans to open their eyes to "the principal trait of the new era, which is the henceforth unavoidable political, economic, and moral interdependence of the nations."[9] Circumstances called for a reconsideration of the national interest, now threatened by an outdated isolationism and moralism, Mowrer argued. Whatever the earlier justification for such values, they no longer served America well.

Anxious to persuade as well as to criticize, Mowrer paid his respects to the past. "Our customs and our institutions are indeed good; they fit us. Our motives, generally speaking, are really high-minded." But a less parochial, less timid, and more realistic world view was now called for. He hoped that a better educated, more sophisticated public opinion would acknowledge the implications of America's extensive international economic and political interests. With the guidance of a more responsible press, a more respected foreign service, and an actively concerned intellectual elite, the United States, he believed, could face its news responsibilities.[10]

Mowrer's plea was that rational assessment of the national interest should replace emotionalism and moralism in the making of American foreign policy. Americans needed to adopt a more self-critical outlook. It was natural for nations to be self-satisfied, he conceded, but it was at least equally important for them to recognize the values and interests they shared with others. The United States had much in common especially with Europe, from which many of its peoples and traditions derived. America's achievement of first-rate power status meant that the nation must shun emotionalism and "the psychology of fear." The country's chief weakness was "neither moral nor material, but psychological—the hesitancy to make contact with other nations, even when such contact is clearly in our interest," for fear of losing moral superiority or succumbing to the "machinations of foreign diplomacy."[11]

Mowrer argued that American foreign policy traditionally had been based on considerations of interest as much as on ideology. This approach was sound and simply needed to be adapted to the new circumstances of life. America's dependence upon international trade, as well as its newly achieved creditor status, made its economy sensitive to world conditions. For its own sake, then, the nation must cooperate with others in creating the basis for a peaceful, orderly world. Because foreign policy in a democracy depended upon an enlightened, thoughtful citizenry, Mowrer recommended close study of the background and formation of other nations' policies and urged that Americans demand better international affairs coverage in their newspapers. He realistically did not expect all Americans to be equally interested and informed; however, he suggested that well-informed citizens take the lead in stimulating discussion through their churches, chambers of commerce, and similar agencies—all efforts aimed at fostering a more active, critical public opinion which could bring pressure to bear upon political leaders.[12]

Our Foreign Affairs was well received by American reviewers, but it flew too strongly against the winds of public taste and custom to win a large audience. Nearly thirty years later, political scientist Hans Morgenthau wrote Mowrer that he was still assigning the book to students,[13] but in the short run Mowrer's hope of significantly influencing American opinion was disappointed.

The earnest thoughtfulness which the Mowrer brothers brought to their analysis of the international scene set their work apart from that of many of their colleagues. They were clearly among the first to feel that the interpretation of social and cultural matters called for more than the briefest treatment possible in the daily news columns. Paul's *Balkanized Europe* had been matched by Edgar's *Immortal Italy*. Now, *Our Foreign Affairs* was followed in 1928 by Edgar's *This American World*, an interpretation of the cultural and intellectual, even more than of the economic and political, relations between America and Europe. In Berlin, where he was conveniently positioned to observe the ongoing struggle between the old and the new elements of European culture in a highly unstable environment, Edgar Mowrer had been both fascinated and repelled by what he saw. His mercurial intellect and his lively concern for tradition, order, and the life of the mind made him sensitive to most of the cultural currents of the day. He knew that many Europeans were fearful of what they perceived as the encroachments of a new technocratic barbarism—which they associated either with the Soviet Union or with the newly powerful

United States—undermining the foundations of Europe's traditional order. Mowrer himself shared many of their concerns.

This American World was written in part to explain the United States to his European friends, in part to relate developments on both sides of the Atlantic to their underlying causes, and in part, perhaps, to provide Mowrer himself with some reassurance as to the future of democracy. His work constituted an uncomplimentary, yet not entirely hostile, view of American civilization. Mowrer acknowledged at the outset that the Old World was "losing its grip" while America had become "apparently the most important single factor in the shaping of contemporary history." A new world culture, "something mankind is learning to call American" seemed "destined to contemporary supremacy," he began. But Mowrer had his own doubts and questions concerning the shape of the new order. "If there be any civilized tomorrow to [*sic*] a society rooted in intellectual democracy and plutocratic industrialism, the United States should see it first," he continued. "If there be none, then the world's hopes must needs rest unsatisfied until the period of Americanism is over."[14]

Americans, Mowrer believed, were in many respects poorly equipped to lead the new civilization; they were even reluctant to do so, preferring to go their own way and ignore the outside world. They acted, Mowrer complained, like "overgrown children, careless, incurious, infantile, resentful of admonition or reproof." Peter Pan, not Abraham Lincoln, best represented this quality of the national mind. For all their talk of progress, Americans were smug and satisfied with the status quo, "a nation of adult children, somewhat aware of the absurdity of this condition, but liking it, and striving desperately to avoid becoming anything else." Immaturity characterized not only the American outlook on international affairs, but its approach to education, ideas, morals and leisure as well.[15]

Yet for all that, Mowrer argued that the American people were not notably less mature than Europeans. The latter deferred to their intellectual elite, their "cultured classes"; in the United States, however, the tone was set by "really undeveloped masses." American society reflected the dominance of the "normal," or average, rather then the "best." Despite this weakness, Mowrer thought Americans better equipped than Europeans to face the conditions of modern life. They had developed "that powerful puerility, clever mastery of machinery, gregarious adoration of numbers and standardization, mass anonymity, which make for almost violent efficiency in this disillusioned yet marvellously organized modern world."[16]

America, after all, had been founded by the finest and most adventurous of Europeans, Mowrer reminded his readers. The best of European culture had been transplanted there and had flourished until the westward movement and the frontier spirit had exercised their levelling influence. Even then, traces of longing for "something symbolized by Europe" had never wholly died out; "we hankered subconsciously for the only civilization our race had known and on whose crumbs we were continually though sparingly nourished." In time, success and prosperity had brought America once again into closer contact with the outside world. A new leisured, educated class had begun to emerge, one naturally sympathetic to European cultural traditions and sources. The war had introduced many more Americans to European standards; "they tasted a subtle drug; looked in the windows at a life that is not all work and sports and uplift; heard melodies more exciting than the American C-major hymn to progress." Such changes might, after all, point the nation toward a richer, more vital, cultural and intellectual life.[17]

For all its diverse ethnic origins, the United States was, according to Mowrer "the most homogeneous and solid [society] in the whole world," made so by its frontier experience, its commitment to equal opportunity, and its enormous resources. Despite a strong strain of anti-intellectualism and conformity, Americans were no more materialistic than other peoples. True, economics had been the sphere of their greatest triumphs, but they had sought adventure and accomplishment as well as mere subsistence; and democracy required that the general welfare, not simply individual advantage, ultimately be served. Americans valued wealth as a measure of excellence, not for its own sake. What America offered that the masses everywhere found appealing was this vision of opportunity open to all, this "generous materialism." As Mowrer wrote, "The American mediocracy is hindered by no tradition, no loud voices and unsettling intellectuals, and no hampering material privations, from creating a society in its own image." Its appeal was "the strongest apostolic force in the modern world," perhaps the only one capable of competing with communism for the loyalty of the masses.[18]

With America now in its moment of triumph, Mowrer found a swelling chorus of internal criticism of its democracy. "People with leisure find America dull; democrats complain of plutocracy; discontented workers charge it with injustice; unsuccessful burghers of the older stocks denounce it as increasingly foreign and Jewish; old-fashioned Puritans name it godless; cynics label it 'bosh-and-boss' rule; artists with unsatis-

fied hopes pronounce it unproductive; intellectuals sneer at it as uncivilized; philosophers with ideals find it soulless." After such a litany
Mowrer could only conclude that contemporary America offered cultured men little "save as a spectacle and a hope." It might become "a
more powerful, more humane, more educated, more democratic and
more glorious Rome," if mass education, religion, and modern technology led it toward a more decent, balanced, and sensitive society.[19] But in
the light of his catalog of its shortcomings, the hope seemed faint indeed.

Needless to say, *This American World* received little favorable notice
west of the Atlantic, but soon after its publication Lillian Mowrer wrote
Dorothy Thompson that Edgar was receiving warm praise in Germany.
Invitations were pouring in from cultural societies and universities, and
he was planning to speak both at Heidelberg and Stuttgart.[20] Although
Mowrer's critique was characteristically sharp, it echoed virtually every
complaint or criticism of the United States uttered by his fellow correspondents over the preceding decade. None made the case so forcefully
and comprehensively as he. And few attempted, as he did, to see America
and Europe in such a broad cultural and historical perspective. Yet Mowrer's outlook did not differ greatly from that of many of his colleagues. A
decade of Europe had enabled them to find satisfying life-styles and
promising career opportunities, but it seemed to have mellowed little, if at
all, the reservations they held about America.

Yet their criticisms, even when as severe as Edgar Mowrer's, remained
tempered by hope—perhaps by a peculiarly American faith in progress
and reason. Their own essential Americanness was revealed in the determination and exuberance with which they pursued success and recognition, as well as in their impatience at the cynicism, fatalism, and rampant
nationalism they had found so widespread in Europe. For all their scorn
of American materialism, they had never hesitated to press their employers for salary increases, or to solicit advice on the Great Bull Market over
which the American plutocrats presided and in which the insensitive
American masses were swept up. For all their love of Europe's life and
culture, few were under illusions as to its strength and durability. They
saw how fragile the bonds were that held the post-Versailles order in an
uneasy peace. This knowledge undoubtedly strengthened their belief that
the United States had a constructive role to play in preserving stability.
When the economic collapse after 1929 undermined the none-too-firm
foundations of European democracy and stability, the correspondents
had quickly recognized the signs of impending crisis and collapse. As the

long-feared disasters overtook Europe, the view toward the United States brightened rapidly.

THE THIRTIES

Once America's own social and economic problems appeared to be being seriously addressed, even if not solved, public interest in the strange and disturbing news from overseas increased. Even with Depression-tightened budgets, editors and publishers were more willing to pay travel expenses home for the sake of face-to-face explanations of Europe's troubles. Radio news and commentary were beginning to attract a growing audience. The popular news magazine, *Time*, was gaining a growing readership although it maintained no regular staff in Europe and its European news columns still consisted chiefly of materials drawn from the *New York Times* and *Herald Tribune*, rewritten by its own highly biased foreign editor.[21] Newspapers and lecture agencies were finding American audiences eager to hear from those who could speak at first hand of the events and conditions behind the evidently deteriorating international scene.

Vincent Sheean, on a 1928–29 lecture tour, was one of the first of the reporters to form more favorable impressions than had prevailed earlier. His reactions, he later wrote, were, if not entirely objective, at least "comforting." The "American type," Sheean observed, was childish in some ways but likable nonetheless. Americans were woefully uninformed, even uninterested, in international affairs. But Sheean was nonetheless attracted by their "lack of class consciousness, meanness of spirit, and general grubbiness, the dislikeable characteristics of the European bourgeoisie." He found "a total absence of the national hatreds that control existence in Europe," and even American barbarism was "a much more comforting spectacle than. . .European civilization in decay."[22]

Among the first to recognize the opportunity to reach the American public by radio and the lecture circuit was Leland Stowe. Pleading that depression, even more than prosperity, called for mutual understanding and forbearance, Stowe's 1933 NBC radio broadcast, "Americans and the Man Next Door," had suggested a lesson that might be drawn from the world crisis, that "all men are *much more ONE* than we ever realized before. That men, whatever their nationality, yearn for the same simple things—for an honest livelihood, and a fair chance for their children." Americans and Europeans should declare a "mental armistice," an end to harsh words and feelings. Stowe took direct aim at the parochial, self-righteous American nationalism he and his colleagues had so often decried. He cited the words of George Washington, patron saint of the isolationists, "A nation which gives way to feelings of love or hatred for another nation becomes the slave of its love or hatred," to argue that it was in America's self-interest to maintain cordial relations with others upon whose welfare and good will her own security ultimately depended.[23]

In an article intriguingly titled "Who Is Killing America's Good Name?" Stowe in 1932 had described aspects of American life that, he argued, were causing Europeans to lose confidence in the United States. Noting the failure of the United States to provide the energy, ideas, and leadership expected of it, Stowe found that "Europe's basic respect for American ruggedness, American youth, American forcefulness, is ebbing away." The appearance of traits familiar to Europe—"doubt, distrust, defeatism and fear"—across the Atlantic was "even more undreamed-of, inexplicable and disheartening than our material state of depression. It is a sad thing to say for an American," Stowe continued, "it is also humiliating.... Europe looks at America without spite and without bitterness."[24]

Stowe wrote a friend that he admired some of President Roosevelt's early actions, but questioned his steadiness and commitment to principle. Some of the president's advisors were "soothsayers," the National Recovery Act offered a doubtful answer to the nation's economic ills, and the country seemed to be flirting with "incoherence to regain prosperity at any price, even the price of moral principles." Yet he believed that fundamental changes were in order. "For 100 years," he wrote, "Americans have glutted themselves upon always expanding national resources, but the hog days and hog mentality have got to end. How, without more suffering, I don't see.... We are too vast a country, too big a people, too divided in our sectional self-interests; too childlike in our optimism and too lacking in balance and self-discipline. Sometimes this spectacle of America today is enough to make one bleed. It wouldn't seem so disheartening if it did not mean so much to you."[25]

Stowe's first American lecture tour, in the winter of 1934, was designed to capitalize on interest in his book on Nazi Germany. He returned to the United States somewhat awed at the prospect of public appearances as an expert on a great many matters about which he felt less than well qualified. Still, he was eager to learn whatever he could about the New Deal and the state of the nation. The results of the tour added to his confidence on at least one count. He wrote his family that he had received many compliments on his presentations. The chairman of the Chicago Council on Foreign Relations had indicated that Stowe's session there was the best the council had had all year. The lecture agency wanted him back the next year and, an additional satisfaction, his success would mean larger lecture fees. He was somewhat encouraged by what he learned about the nation as well. Dorothy Thompson had held out hope of a "fight to remake America," and others, too, had been "full of the change in the people beyond the Alleghanies [*sic*]." It seemed that a "new American life...is just beginning," he wrote his parents, "and I believe the writing profession will supply some of the most important leadership."[26]

After returning to France, Stowe addressed a business audience at the American Club in Paris on changes in the United States between 1929 and 1933. The differences, he said, made him feel like the proverbial "man from Mars." The contrast was one between a "mixture of materialistic greed, arrogance and cocksureness," and a United States where people were open to new ideas, "where a lot of false gods had fallen away; and people were glad to have an opportunity to walk on them." The old leadership had failed, and the nation was feeling its way toward a new compromise between plutocracy and democracy. Stowe was cautiously enthusiastic about Roosevelt and the New Deal as offering a middle way between extremes of right and left; but he warned that a larger role for government, a "self-imposed restraint" upon the old "freedom to get rich," would be the price of recovery and stability. Soon Stowe was proclaiming that the "real revolution" was to be found in the United States, and that Washington had become "the most interesting city a man can visit."[27]

In 1935 the *Herald Tribune* recalled Stowe to New York, but he continued his annual lecture tours for most of the decade. He added to his repertory such topics as "Rediscovering America" and "What Europe Teaches About America," neither by any means uncritical. In these talks he acknowledged American friendliness and hospitality, the general availability and high quality of consumer goods, and the national talent for voluntary organization. On the other side of the ledger he listed American impatience with tradition and gradual change, boorishness, and resistance to long-range planning—an "un-American" notion. Stowe believed that Americans, unlike Europeans, had no sense of responsibility to the state. "Here we have no real idea of service to our country. The young German is sent out to collect bones and bottles for the state...to the young American we say: 'You can get yours, kid. Your whole future is your own to do with as you please.'" The United States could learn much from Europe in such areas as law enforcement and observance, social legislation, high standards for education, respect for the knowledge and experience of public officials, public morality and integrity, he believed. He balanced Americans' deficiencies against their "Seven Great Virtues": energy and enthusiasm; a capacity for teamwork; great curiosity; ingenuity and inventiveness; hospitality and generosity; adaptability; and self-confidence.[28]

Stowe believed that the Depression placed a heavy responsibility upon America for world leadership, and he questioned whether the nation was as yet ready to assume it. At least until 1936 he held it both possible and desirable for the United States to avoid military involvement in Europe. The neutrality laws might take the profits out of the armament trade, thus lessening economic motives for involvement, Stowe told his listeners; but he warned that such a policy would entail enormous restraint and self-discipline. Later, the Spanish Civil War and Hitler's increasing aggressiveness led him to reject the idea of neutrality.[29]

Other correspondents returning to America in the early thirties responded, like Stowe, more warmly than they had earlier. Raymond Swing was "despondent" in 1934 when the collapse of the *Philadelphia Public Ledger*'s foreign service once again left him without a European base. Returning to the United States to join *The Nation* as its Washington correspondent, however, he found a livelier and more stimulating environment than had greeted him a decade earlier. His experience and his new affiliation made him particularly sensitive to the possibility of "fascistic elements" in America, both in the New Deal itself and in some of its most prominent critics. The early New Deal programs, Swing later wrote, "reeked of authoritarianism." Nevertheless, he assured readers of the British *Fortnightly Review* as early as February 1934 that the New Deal was neither Fascist nor Bolshevik and that "the basic situation in America, at least ideologically, was sound." His attention was soon attracted to men like Huey Long, Gerald L. K. Smith, and Father Charles E. Coughlin, about whom he wrote articles for *The Nation* which were later published in *Forerunners of American Fascism*. Swing found that Long's program contained strong liberal elements, and that the Kingfish himself was entirely ignorant of European affairs and not at all inspired by the dictatorships there.[30]

Whatever his problems in readjusting to American life, Swing evidently found the experience stimulating. He told John Gunther, who was himself in the process of relocating there, that America's energy was infectious; it caused him to need an hour less sleep at night than he had in Europe. Jobs for former correspondents, too, were more accessible than they once had been. Gunther could get any New York job he wanted, Swing thought; he himself had had "three or four nibbles within a week of landing." Gunther agreed that he had never seen such energy. "It's in the air," he wrote his wife. Europe seemed "extremely small and unimportant and remote" in comparison. Gunther's impressions were ambivalent, but vivid. Upon sailing into New York he wrote, "The buildings looked like Carcasonne...a mountainous pyramid of towers and castles shouldering themselves out of the mist.... I saw the American flag, which made me weep." Yet, after a few days, he reported, "The city seemed too monstrously unreal and strange and confusing. The enormous leaping towers on all sides were, I admit, exhilerating [*sic*], but if you stare up at 600 feet of building it makes you...seem pretty small. New York has vastly changed. Radio City makes you want to cry and weep with a mixture of incredulity and awe. The new buildings are all pale amber or silver."[31]

Impressions bore in upon Gunther from all sides. After an evening in a New York bar he wrote, "Repeal [of Prohibition] has changed, enlightened, enlivened New York enormously. Don't let anyone tell you that alcohol isn't a major factor in a community's civilization." He commented on food, too: "I can't begin to tell you how good American food is. So far, though, I haven't had much but bacon and corned beef.... All servants in America now say 'Sir' and are excessively polite." Continuing on his way to Chicago, Gunther found that, "Pullmans are horrible; the food was good; whisky and soda comes in tiny little 1/4 pint bottles. American beer is very pawky." By comparison with New York, Chicago seemed "squat and dumpy," but there were compensations to be found at the World's Fair. Sally Rand's fan dance was "quite thrilling" and the performance at the Folies Bergères was "very nude and very fine." "We have grown up over here," Gunther thrilled, "and we certainly do things wholesale. This show goes on *four* times a night, each show about an hour long and different."[32]

Gunther found the *Chicago Daily News*'s Frank Knox cordial but too preoccupied with national politics to be interested in what he had to say. Knox expected him nevertheless to attend daily lunches with the top staff, much to Gunther's disgust, and lined up a number of speaking engagements for him. Hal O'Flaherty, the foreign editor, did not impress Gunther: "very limited, cheerful, cautious, and frozen in routine." His old rival, Carroll Binder, pleased him even less: "He is a complete yes-man and shit. . . . Autographed portrait of Mussolini on his wall." He was delighted at a reunion with Paul Mowrer, now the *Daily News*'s managing editor. Mowrer and his wife, the former Hadley Hemingway, had "a duplex flat in the loveliest taste and greatest luxury; they have FOUR bathrooms and two nigger servants. . . . Lake Superior whitefish, and don't ever let me utter another peep about. . . Dover sole. . . . My God, you should see American peas; they are as big as marbles; and apples, they are as big as watermelons." Gunther concluded that there was very little real interest in matters European. He had "wowed" the Council on Foreign Relations, which was used to hearing serious discourse, with gossip about King Alexander of Yugoslavia, Magda Lupescu, Dollfuss, and others.[33]

There was much to report to his wife. "I must make a list of the things that most bedazzle me. Free matches. Smooth silent powerful lifts. The room girl makes up your bed only once a day in the hotel. All service orders by phone. The loveliest and most beautiful goergeous [sic] and capacious closets. Bathtubs [sic] that fill and flush instantly. A downtown club with a swimming pool on the 27th floor. The girls, all the girls, with ankles and waists as thin as noodles. Shoes are not cleaned in the hotel. Taxi drivers who talk to you about 'the situation over there,' and, My God, last night I drove home in one [taxi] that played MUSIC! The rudimentary wine lists and the lousy beer." Yet, there remained another, less pleasing side of life in America even for Gunther, the bon vivant: "I was feeling pretty swell about being a regular contributor for *Harper's* and *Vanity Fair* but I have now discovered that no Americans have time to read any magazines. Even folk who might be expected to follow that sort of thing very closely. . . had never seen any of my *Harper's* stuff."[34]

Whatever the drawbacks of the American scene, its fascination and the possibilities it held out of supporting himself independent of the pressures of day-to-day reporting, combined with his determination to launch a new phase of his career, convinced Gunther that the time had come to return home. Within two years, his *Inside Europe* completed, he returned to make the United States the base of operations for his future reporting. Among the *Harper's* articles with which Gunther had found few Americans familiar was "Slaughter For Sale," which was written in 1934 and dealt with the activities of the international munitions industry. The topic had attracted the attention of other correspondents seeking to uncover the roots of international conflict and to assess influences on the operations and prospects of the League of Nations. Gunther described data that would soon be cited by the Nye Committee of the United States Senate and indicated that American as well as European manufacturers had profited from the sale of arms and other militarily useful items to nations on both sides of the recent world war and other conflicts. Such revelations still surprised inexperienced and idealistic Americans, although Clarence Streit had noted long ago the joint interests and wartime collaboration of French and German industrialists.[35] Journalists who had covered the League of Nations had also noted from time to time the maneuvers of the munitions industry to influence the league's disarmament efforts.

Among the more outspoken and persistent critics of munitions profiteering was George Seldes who, after his return from Europe, had been sent by the *Chicago Tribune* to Mexico. Observing the pressure exerted by American oil interests to protect properties they had acquired from earlier, corrupt regimes, and disgusted by the press's efforts to hamper discussion of the facts, Seldes concluded that the time had come to separate himself from orthodox journalism. Resigning from the *Tribune*, he soon launched a new career as a free lance and attacked in a long series of articles and books the machinations of industry and the press to conceal their dishonest operations.

Seldes's unorthodox upbringing, his observation of totalitarian regimes in Italy and the Soviet Union, and his experiences with the press at home and abroad convinced him that powerful forces in the capitalist system, as well as in the dictatorships, were working to suppress democracy. Covering the Spanish Civil War in 1936–37, he found further evidence of the failure of democratic governments to defend the principles they professed, of their inability to resist organized economic, political, and religious pressures. Even in America, he felt, he could only pursue his calling to report the truth from outside the structures of organized journalism. By the decade's end, he was preparing to produce his own newsletter, *in fact*, attempting to counter the distortions and misrepresentations of the orthodox press.[36] No other American correspondent in the course of the decade presented so comprehensive and radical a critique of capitalist culture in the United States or elsewhere. Seldes's divergence from his fellow correspondents became even more pronounced after 1939 as they identified increasingly with the American government's leadership of a second crusade to make the world safe for democracy, while he remained an outspoken critic.

As the approach of a second great international confrontation seemed to drive Seldes farther to the Left, so it began to push others in the opposite direction. Sensitive to the spreading new totalitarianism which had kept Europe in turmoil for nearly two decades, some correspondents, such as Raymond Swing, feared that right-wing forces were sapping the strength of American democracy as well. Edgar Ansel Mowrer, on the other hand, was one of those whose intellectual and political conservatism grew with the years. Upon returning to the United States in 1933, Mowrer was even more critical than he had been a decade earlier. He found the nation stunned by the Depression, its self-confidence lost—a country which "God had abandoned." Mowrer thought labor union efforts to maintain wage levels in the face of economic stagnation nothing but another example of the "national fixation on something for nothing." He rejected the proposition that business leaders could be held responsible for the Depression, and he felt that the New Deal was crippling business initiative. Mowrer was appalled that some of his writer friends were turning to communism out of disgust with the failure of Hoover and Roosevelt to solve the unemployment problem. He could not understand why Americans felt "so sorry for themselves" when, even in distress their living standard remained higher than that of Britain at its best.[37]

Mowrer returned again in 1936 from his *Daily News* post in Paris, after a brief visit to the Spanish Civil War. Although, as he later wrote, he felt for the first time that he understood "the full impact of the New Deal and the clash of emotions it was causing," he found himself unable to take sides in the American presidential election. He thought Roosevelt and his advisors were bent on creating "a legal revolution" and drastic social change. He was troubled by the New Deal's appeal to the masses in whose wisdom he had little confidence. In his memoirs, Mowrer recalled that both he and Paul had feared "an alliance of the plebs and the king against the barons." He conceded that the Republicans could not disavow responsibility for the Depression, but noted that Roosevelt still had failed to decrease the unemployment rate. Despite Mowrer's belief in equal rights for all, he was troubled by Roosevelt's appeal to ethnic minorities and seriously doubted "the viability of a permanently pluralistic society." Perhaps his experiences under two dictatorships and the priority which he accorded individual rights blocked Mowrer from acknowledging the

New Deal as a constructive influence on the American scene. When in 1939 he at last had an interview with the president, Mowrer, by then an ardent advocate of American support for resistance to totalitarianism, found the experience "disillusioning."[38]

As might be expected, the correspondents' views of America varied in perceptiveness as well as in ideological slant. Interesting as the opinions were, they did not show an unusual degree of originality. The opinions they expressed on political developments reflected a range of views from right to left broadly similar to those of their fellow countrymen. None of their ideas differed greatly from what critics at home had been saying. At first glance this may seem surprising because their experience and success as observers of other societies might appear to have prepared them well for commenting on their own. There were, however, important differences in the occasions and circumstances of their observations that may help to explain the character of their comments.

Few of the correspondents spent nearly as much time in the United States during these two decades as they did overseas. This was particularly true in the 1920s, although even in the thirties when trips home were more common they seldom stayed or travelled in the United States for more than a few weeks at a time. And those who returned more or less permanently in the thirties, such as Swing, Seldes, and Stowe, spent much of their time thinking and writing on international topics. Swing and Seldes were unusual in the opportunities they had to write and think at some length on American topics. For the rest, their responses were impressionistic, based on scattered reading, quick observation, and casual conversations with whatever friends or acquaintances they happened to encounter. With the exception of Seldes, Swing, and Edgar Mowrer, none seemed to proceed from a carefully thought-out position regarding the institutions and forces underlying and giving direction to American life.

AMERICA AND THE WORLD

There was, of course, a major exception to the lack of structuring theories or perspectives just referred to. Most of the correspondents, after assessing the European political and economic scene, had concluded that the United States must overcome its reluctance to involve itself actively in international cooperative efforts for peace and stability. For many, the conclusion had been reached quite early in the twenties; but after 1936 it became a virtual consensus among them, differences having chiefly to do with the timing, character, and direction of American involvement called for. Vincent Sheean was not alone when, after the fall of France in 1940, he "wanted to help my own countrymen realize the urgency and the danger" surrounding them.[39]

The basis for agreement that the United States must assume a more active role lay more in the reporters' recognition of Europe's weaknesses and of American power than in any thoughtful appraisal of the nation's ability and inclination to support a carefully calculated policy of collective security. Nevertheless, this argument in its various forms constituted the chief message concerning America's role and status in world affairs that the correspondents attempted to convey to their fellow countrymen. And as the decade of the 1930s approached its climactic end they urged it ever more openly, fervently, and unreservedly.

Perhaps the earliest, and certainly the most determined, of the American journalists in his conviction that the United States had a role to play was Clarence Streit, since 1929 the *New York Times*'s representative at the League of Nations. Disillusioned with the Versailles settlement, Streit had taken little interest in the League of Nations before assuming this post. A passionate idealist, he shared with many others a sharp disappointment at America's failure to join the league and at the league's inability to offer an alternative to traditional, "illusory, fantastic, exploded and explosive" balance-of-power politics. Closer observation confirmed his view that the league, for all the idealism that had entered into its creation, was a failed instrument. Streit argued, as did others, that modern technology had created a world in which political and economic interdependence demanded cooperation among peoples and nations to preserve peace and order. The league's shortcomings demonstrated for him the need for an international organization that could not be manipulated by the victorious Allies for their own selfish ends.

Streit soon began to consider alternative forms of world government that might be less prone to manipulation by powerful national interests. His search gained greater urgency as the League of Nations failed either to deal successfully with Japanese, Italian, and German aggression or to provide a framework within which legitimate claims for the adjustment of national borders and conflicting interests could be peacefully resolved. By 1933 he had evolved an outline for a union of democratic nations, including the United States, which he began to circulate. As international conditions deteriorated, Streit became increasingly convinced that only drastic measures along the lines of his proposal offered a way out of the impasse into which world politics had fallen.

In 1938 Streit wrote the *Times*'s managing editor, Edwin L. James, requesting permission to return home to discuss a book he had prepared. Streit hoped that the *Times* might endorse his proposals. James had himself taken an active interest in strengthening the league during his European years, but he informed Streit that the newspaper could not actively support him. James had offered to assist Streit in finding a publisher but whatever help he contributed was insufficient, since a few months later Streit was considering organizing his own publishing operation to get his ideas into print. Before the year's end he received James's reluctant permission to return home to lecture on his ideas at Swarthmore College.

Streit's Swarthmore lectures became the skeleton of the proposal which he was able to publish under the title, *Union Now*, as the international crisis intensified in 1939. His scheme envisioned a "federal union" of the North Atlantic democracies which he compared to the government established by the American Constitution in its accountability directly to the people rather than to the national governments involved. The attractive power of such a democratic union, he argued, was such that people living under authoritarian regimes would be so drawn to it that they eventually might overthrow their governments in order to join. Participation of the United States in such a federation of democracies was essential, he believed. Peace was a world, not simply a European, problem; American efforts to evade involvement reflected merely "wishful thinking."[40] Recognizing that Americans were not yet ready to commit themselves, Streit was determined to do all he could to bring them around. He gave up his newspaper career to concentrate on promoting his plan of federation, which seemed to prosper as the onset of war focused attention on the issue.

After the fall of France, Streit tried to adapt his plan to changing circumstances by proposing the creation of an Anglo-American federation; but the spread of hostilities diverted public interest to more pressing matters. The return of peace in 1945 once again aroused widespread discussion of issues related to world order and government, and Streit's movement recaptured public attention. Within a few years, however, it fell victim to the psychology of the cold war, as did many other efforts to build international cooperation. Streit himself continued the struggle, testifying before Congress and publicizing his plan in every possible way.[41]

Well into the 1980s he was still determinedly at it, honored by all but with little hope of further gains for the foreseeable future. Striet's transition from journalism to advocacy, like that of Seldes, marked a direction in which a growing number of correspondents were moving as the world crisis swirled around them.

Few could match Streit's record of unreserved dedication, but others also drew upon their fund of experience to urge that Americans face up to the changes threatening traditional policies and relationships. The collapse of Europe, to the journalists' way of thinking, demanded new American initiatives while the failure of the United States to readjust its policies called for extraordinary efforts to alert its citizens to the urgent need for change. Throughout the thirties Leland Stowe crisscrossed the United States on his annual lecture tours, exposing his audiences to the outlook of an experienced Europe-watcher and attempting to sensitize them to the meaning of Europe's crisis for their own country. A list of the titles of some of these lectures suffices to indicate their thrust: "Europe and America in 1934," "The Shift of Responsibility to America" (1934), "An Era of Acute Nationalism" (1934), "The Battle Against What People Do Not Want to Believe" (1934), "Can World Peace Machinery Be Effective?" (1934), "French Democracy's Fight For Survival" (1936), "The Americas and Europe's Armageddon" (1938–39), "What Europe Taught Me About America" (1938–39).[42]

From 1936 to 1939 Dorothy Thompson also took advantage of her many opportunities as a columnist and popular speaker to argue forcefully that Americans must face up to the dangers confronting them. Nazism could not be appeased, she held, it could only be confronted. Distressed that a "large part of our population still apparently cherish the illusion that North America is not quite on this planet," Thompson insisted that "our two oceans connect us with the rest of the world; they do not separate us." She termed the neutrality bills under consideration in 1937 "the greatest Pontius Pilate act in history" because of their denial of the fact and the evil of international aggression. "America is a world power," she insisted. "There is only one way we can be assured of peace, and that is to use the immense power and position of this country to see that no world war occurs, to act like a great nation, instead of behaving as though we are in the position of Denmark." She presented a post-Munich "Obituary for Europe": ". . . with this goes the last vestige of law in Europe, the last shred of prestige of either Great Britain or France, the last hope of settling anything by negotiation, compromise, treaty and law, or by anything whatsoever except sheer brute force.... The United States this morning is isolated." Peace without virtue was not true peace, rather it was the beginning of a world-threatening crisis. By early 1939 Thompson was telling her readers, "There is already an undeclared world war, and we are already in it." Again and again she returned to the theme of America's involvement with others: "...this country is of all countries in the world the most susceptible to what happens outside its own borders."[43]

Carroll Binder also concluded that the time had come for knowledgeable journalists to state their views openly. He felt that America and perhaps all democracies had a tendency to oversimplify difficult problems and a disinclination to face unpleasant realities. Americans should understand how they appeared to others—prone to offer gratuitous advice but unwilling to accept responsibility. America's isolationism was deeply unrealistic; and although Binder still hoped that the nation could remain neutral, he argued, despite his Quaker background, that the time might well come when it would be in the nation's interest to fight. In any event, he told audiences, neutrality legislation was unwise. Contrary to the "Pied Pipers of illusory 'anti-war' proposals," it was not wise to tie the president's hands with neutrality legislation.[44]

Raymond Swing had similarly concluded by 1939 that he was justified in openly assuming an activist position, despite the fact that he had become an established and influential radio newsman. After a trip to Czechoslovakia, he accepted a position as board chairman of the Council For Democracy, sponsored by Henry Luce, which advocated support for the European democracies. In February 1939 he contributed an introduction to a symposium titled "Calling America" in *Survey Graphic*, in which he argued that a world war more serious than the last might be expected within "a year or two." Democracy and minority rights were seriously imperilled in America as well as Europe, he urged. Neutrality could no longer protect America against the new forms of propaganda and infiltration that had arisen. Democracy could protect itself against the totalitarian ideologies that threatened it only by the power of "a still stronger idea properly understood and clearly discernable to the rest of the world." In such an ideological contest, the defense of minority rights and equal opportunities was more important than ever.[45]

Swing's plea was followed by others from John T. Whitaker and Edgar Mowrer, contributors to the same symposium. Whitaker argued that dictatorships had shown how majorities, as well as minorities, could be suppressed through a combination of coercion and "bread and circuses." Mowrer used the threat to hold that democracy, in times of severe crisis, might be justified in calling for "the outlawry of certain organized opinions." Advocates of tyranny need not be allowed freedom "to plot the overthrow of society in our midst," he insisted. "A doctrine that denies liberty should find no room for public utterance in a free society." Some might think his argument extreme, Mowrer conceded, but "politically the limits of tolerance [were]...coming dangerously close."[46]

At the time few Americans would probably have accepted the argument that democracy must limit its own operations in order to survive. But, in his sense of the degree to which the approaching confrontation would engulf the democracies and the authoritarian nations alike, Mowrer was closer to reality than he seemed. Within two years his view had won the support of government officials and others at the highest levels. Not only as advocates but also as prophets of what the future held in store for America, the correspondents had been well prepared by their years overseas.

The question of how successful they were in alerting their audience to the perils it faced can probably never be fully answered. Later, Paul Mowrer quite accurately argued that in the decade before Pearl Harbor it was the newspapers "more than anyone else, either in or out of the government, who, through their correspondents abroad, accurately informed the American people on what was going on in the world" and of the dangers ahead. And Carroll Binder held that through the efforts of American journalists any interested American could have learned all he needed to know to comprehend the shape and sources of the threat to peace. But even Binder acknowledged that whether the public actually read what was presented it was another matter.[47] Certainly none could deny that Adolf Hitler, in the end, was the master persuader in this regard as in others. Sensitively and accurately as the correspondents may have measured the European scene, they themselves conceded their frustration in swaying their readers' attitudes at least until Hitler had converted their warnings into openly menacing realities. They anticipated and helped to point a direction for changing public opinion more than they were able to lead it.

The truth seems to have been that even with the perspective and experience they had gained abroad, the correspondents were both too close to and too far from the United States to view it either impartially or profoundly. From the perspective of Europe they hardly could have avoided thinking warmly of America in the 1930s. And their increasingly cordial reception at home can only have heightened their regard for it. They managed to pinpoint some of the nation's peculiarities with an especially sharp eye, but, with few exceptions, they were hardly prepared to be severely critical. They acknowledged its blemishes but probably accepted them more readily for having already confronted less attractive alternatives overseas.

10

Editorial

■ In 1940 Eugene Lyons, editor of *The American Mercury* and a former United Press correspondent in Russia, termed the foreign correspondent's career "a dead end." Few newsmen who had served overseas for any length of time were still doing so, Lyons noted. "The rest are editing magazines, writing columns, lecturing to women's clubs and Rotary luncheons, writing novels, doing scenarios, acting as public relations counsel, raising cabbages, or editing books by foreign correspondents."[1] Lyons acknowledged a few outstanding exceptions to his rule: Edgar Ansel Mowrer, recently driven from a third European capital, Paris; the indefatigable Leland Stowe, who signed on with the *Chicago Daily News* for a second distinguished career as a war reporter when he was denied a wartime overseas assignment by the *New York Herald Tribune* on the grounds that he was too old for such demanding activity; and H. R. Knickerbocker, his outstanding reportorial skills unfortunately sapped by his craving for alcohol.

Had he wished, Lyons might have added still other occupations that were, or were soon to be, filled by former foreign correspondents. Radio news had already claimed Raymond Swing and William L. Shirer; indeed, Lyons himself referred to what he termed "an epidemic fondness for radio microphones" among members of the group. And, as the United States drew closer to full military engagement, the government would call upon still others to fill a variety of diplomatic, intelligence, and propaganda posts. Edmond Taylor, Wallace Duell, and John T. Whitaker were employed by the Office of Strategic Services, wartime predecessor of the Central Intelligence Agency, as were Andrew Berding and Peter Dewey, who had served the Associated Press in Rome and the *Chicago Daily News* in Paris, respectively. Vincent Sheean served with the Army Air Force Intelligence and found a former colleague, the *Chicago Tribune*'s Jay Allen, in the Psychological Warfare Section of the U.S. Army in Casablanca. The wartime staff of the Office of War Information included Frederick Kuhn, Percy Winner, Edgar Mowrer, and Joseph Barnes, as well as Wallace Carroll, who served for a period as deputy director.[2] The truth seemed to be that, however "dead" the future might appear for experienced foreign correspondents in their own field, the outbreak of hostilities had heightened appreciation elsewhere of the skills and knowledge they could bring to the nation's service. Never before had their prestige and influence stood so high.

Yet in another sense, Lyons's pronouncement was correct. Having achieved a level of expertise and recognition their predecessors would have deemed inconceivable, these correspondents had reached the limits of possibility as far as their own field was concerned. A few, among them Edwin L. James, Wythe Williams, Paul Mowrer, and Carroll Binder, had already traded the reporter's notepad for an editor's desk. From that vantage point Mowrer and Binder, for reasons already noted, may have had less scope than they had hoped to enjoy for improving the treatment of international news. In James's case, the rise in the stature of the *New York Times* as a journal of international affairs coincides roughly with his assumption of editorial duties in the early 1930s. In view of James's notoriously relaxed editorial approach, however, it is by no means clear that he can be credited with the paper's success.[3]

There were other examples of the pattern that Lyons observed. Dorothy Thompson continued her newspaper column throughout the war years. Having triumphantly achieved the independence to which he aspired with the publication of *Inside Europe*, John Gunther managed to sustain it with a popular series of volumes on Asia, Latin America, Africa, and even the United States. William L. Shirer later digested the piles of evidence produced for the postwar Nuremberg trials to write *The Rise and Fall of the Third Reich* (1960), a massive history of the German saga he had covered earlier. In so doing he, like Thompson and Gunther, withdrew from the ranks of working correspondents. For the others, however, the future—despite the immediate opportunities presented by the war—

must have looked discouraging. Their exodus to higher paying, more responsible positions in government and elsewhere testified to their own judgment concerning opportunities in international journalism.

Lyons attributed the correspondents' dilemma to two conditions, each endemic to the field. The first grew from the institutional constraints of their status as employees subject to the control, direction, inclinations, and ideas of remote editors over whom they exercised only limited and intermittent influence. However able, intelligent, perceptive, diligent, and well connected a correspondent might be, or become, he remained after all a "hired hand." He could attain neither wealth nor independence, however hard he tried; he could not free himself from subordination to others who by the nature of their responsibilities were likely to be less knowledgeable than he about subjects he deemed vital. Such constraints, aggravating the correspondent's long-standing problems over salaries, expenses, and editorial policy, had embittered relations with home offices. The model of professionalism which had emerged in the course of these disputes had represented in large part an effort to cope with the correspondents' subordinate position. The ultimate inadequacy of the professional ideal, however, lay in its inability to redress the status and power balance that was inherent in the structure of journalism.

The second obstacle to fulfillment noted by Lyons lay in what he termed the "rapid obsolescence" experienced by correspondents. An able, aggressive newsman, whatever his background and training for international reporting, could with a few years of diligent effort acquire virtually all the connections and insights needed to perform his duties. Beyond that, he could do little that would significantly increase either his usefulness or his income and status. To complicate matters further, the greater his success the greater was the likelihood that he would find himself associating with leaders in other fields—government, business, and cultural life—whose power, income, or prestige were significantly greater than his own. Such unequal relationships on more than one occasion had proved an invitation to bitterness, drunkenness, or indebtedness, if not all three, for frustrated correspondents who could hardly be blamed for resenting a system that held them in a position of permanent subordination. It is little wonder that morale sometimes sagged or that their complaints of ill treatment and lack of appreciation by home offices occasionally struck a rather sophomoric tone.

A final source of frustration and disappointment not acknowledged by Lyons arose from the correspondents' recognition that the great majority of their readers, until quite late in the thirties, failed to share their interest in or understanding of international affairs. Lacking evidence that their efforts were appreciated by the ultimate consumer and the encouragement that such appreciation entailed, there was little to sustain them but a gradually diminishing pleasure in the life they led and in the traditional newsman's competitive pursuit of story "breaks." The sense of futility that dogged their efforts did not begin to wane until the problems to which they had been calling attention for a decade or more became obvious at last.

Against this substantial list of disappointments and frustrations, how can we assess their careers and contributions? Not as failures in any personal sense, because they can hardly be held responsible for the institutional structure of journalism or for the self-centeredness of American public opinion, both of which they worked valiantly and with limited success to alter. And, whatever their disappointments, their efforts had substantially enhanced the quality of American journalism.

First among their accomplishments must unquestionably be counted the creation of a system of international reporting that has seldom since been equalled in quality. From the limited, uneven, gossip-laden reporting of the nineteenth century, foreign correspondence emerged by the middle of the twentieth as a solid, sensitive, and comprehensive public service. Grounded as foreign correspondence was in the vast technological changes that tied the nations of the world into an increasingly tight knot of interdependent—if inharmonious—interests while simultaneously building a complex and rapidly responsive international communications network, this international news system was nevertheless ultimately the handiwork of the men and women who had labored on its behalf. It had been far from an entirely smooth and satisfactory development, of course. In addition to the problems already mentioned, there had been a parallel rise in manipulative techniques to control, censor, distort, or otherwise confuse the public's access to accurate information. Ironically, the correspondents' very accomplishments may have encouraged some of these efforts to obstruct their work.

Sometime in the 1930s or early 1940s, according to one scholar, international news reporting reached "the high-water mark of its development," with more newspapers and readers than it has enjoyed at any other time in history.[4] It was none too soon. The Second World War made greater demands on American journalism than the field had ever faced before. It also accelerated the growth of more intimate, difficult relations between the press and government, including the United States government. Still, the foreign correspondence system entered the war at the peak of its preparation and effectiveness. That its experience, know-how, and understanding of world affairs were so well developed accounts for the government's rush to enlist the correspondents' expertise on its own behalf.

In the light of these accomplishments a second question arises, as it did for the correspondents themselves. Granting their abilities, ingenuity, and achievement, what can be said of their influence in informing their readers about the international events, issues, and prospects that were so powerfully to affect their lives? On this crucial matter, a clear answer is not possible. Even a full accounting of the number of lines of international news printed and the number of newspapers sold, were it feasible to produce, would not permit a final conclusion about the influence they exerted. What readers read, and what they thought of it, remain questions about which we can do little more than speculate.

Beyond the evidence of their growing acceptance and popularity as writers and lecturers, there is little firm ground for evaluating their influence. Probably Carroll Binder's judgment was not far from accurate when he wrote in the early 1940s that the American press was as complete and reliable a source of information on world affairs as any available. It had greater resources and more independence of government influence than even the British press. American diplomats were little, if any, better informed—and some far less so—than were many foreign correspondents. Yet Binder had to concede that the American public did not necessarily read or understand all that was presented to it; he could only argue that for those interested the necessary information had been made available.[5]

Some have held that the foreign correspondents played a crucial role in persuading the American people to abandon neutrality and isolation and to support assistance to the hard-pressed western European democracies.[6] But the evidence for such an argument is circumstantial at best. Some correspondents were certainly early advocates of American resistance to the totalitarian threat, and a number participated actively in organizations pressing for involvement by the United States. That they helped and that they supplied a valuable source of initiative, background information, and perspective is beyond question. But, without minimizing their contribution, they themselves would probably have been the first to concede that the chief objects of their fear and concern, Adolf Hitler and his allies, did the most to arouse Americans from the dream of isolation.

Finally, it is important to see the lives and work of the foreign correspondents in a still broader perspective, as one element—and a hitherto unappreciated one—in the growth of a more cosmopolitan American outlook on world affairs. That this evolutionary cosmopolitanism remains far from fully matured even today is obvious; but that it has grown from fairly rudimentary and limited beginnings at the turn of the century is equally significant.

The correspondents reflected in their own lives and thinking, in fact, both the general widening of Americans' international horizons and their ultimate ambivalence. For some journalists, the very choice of international careers had reflected a sense of the incompleteness and limitations of American life and culture. Their upbringing and education had awakened in them interests and values they found unsatisfied at home and for which other Americans as well as they themselves had long looked across the Atlantic. The United States by the early twentieth century was beginning to produce a more broadly educated middle class than ever before. Yet many members of this class, especially the more intellectually or esthetically inclined, still felt little assurance that the society which had created them knew what to make of them, how to use them, or, indeed, was much interested in the problem.

For most of the journalists who, regardless of the motives that took them to Europe, remained there for any length of time, the experience of living outside the United States brought satisfactions and opportunities which, they were convinced, would have been denied them at home. Europe, thus, reinforced their sense of America's provincialism. Yet it also opened their eyes to relationships between American developments and those occurring elsewhere which demonstrated the fundamental interdependence of nations and peoples under the conditions of modern life. The resistance they encountered in communicating this sense of interrelatedness only strengthened them in the conviction that they were citizens of a larger community than the United States alone, with a responsibility to point their fellow Americans toward a larger image of the nation and its place in the world.

Still, from the beginning they had found aspects of Europe, notably its time-worn national and ethnic antipathies, cramped and confining in light of American openness and possibility. As new ideologies and economic pressures enflamed the Continent's historic tensions, they came to see the United States in a more favorable light as a repository of freedom, opportunity, and resilience: a hesitant, but necessary counterweight to the Old World's traditionalism and revolutionary authoritarianism. As the path of international politics turned toward war, most correspondents looked homeward with increasing enthusiasm. They were less inclined than formerly to look critically upon the United States. And when at last the nation took its stand against Germany and Japan they readily placed themselves at its service. Initially, it had been America that had awakened their cosmopolitanism; now ironically it was Europe that ended by stirring their latent Americanism. For all their vaunted rebellion and "radicalism," most had been at heart conservative: children of the new middle class, skeptical at the outset, but in the end hesitant to abandon many of the value patterns in which they had been raised.

Their writings and their example directly attracted members of succeeding generations to the correspondent's career that they had helped to create. For still a larger audience they presented a new model, highly visible, of the twentieth-century American as world citizen. Sensitive to the inevitably increasing involvement of the United States in international affairs, open and receptive to the distinctive values and institutions of other peoples, they nonetheless retained their fundamentally American optimism and commitment. In thus combining an American outlook with a warm appreciation of alternative sources of value, they offered a nation on the brink of unprecedented world power an example of constructive, concerned, realistic cosmopolitanism. The influence exerted by their example may be impossible to measure, but its significance was heightened by the whirlpool of events that inexorably drew the United States toward a new international status and role.

There was, however, a less fortunate side to the correspondents' new identification with American causes. Service to their country in time of crisis may have seemed a logical extension of earlier efforts to arouse the United States against totalitarianism. Yet, in identifying themselves so closely and unequivocally with a cause and a government, however admirable, they risked losing the independent posture essential to the professional ideal they had so long hoped to establish. Even for those who remained outside the government, wartime pressures and patriotism inevitably—as in the past—increased the difficulty of maintaining a critical and objective posture. World War II thus proved both a fulfillment and a threat to American foreign correspondence. It offered a stage and a story worthy of journalism's finest talents and experience. Yet it presented a new danger in the form of a government more benign, but nonetheless extremely powerful and persuasive and no less determined to manage its relations with the press and the public than those the young correspondents had confronted earlier in Europe.

The erstwhile correspondents' reactions to these new pressures and temptations varied almost as much as had their earlier approaches to journalism. At one extreme was Edgar Ansel Mowrer, whose underlying conservatism was heightened by the war and who became an ardent participant in anti-Communist causes in the 1950s.[7] At the opposite end of the political spectrum was that inveterate outsider, George Seldes, whose unrelenting critique of journalism, capitalism, and America's imperialistic tendencies through his independent newsletter, *in fact*, earned him unjustified criticism as a "Communist sympathizer" during the same years.[8] Between the extremes, however, there remained an observable tendency in American journalism to soft-pedal its criticism of American foreign policy, at least until the Vietnam era.

After World War II, still more powerful and pervasive forces brought pressures on the press that it found virtually impossible to resist entirely. The ideological twistings, turnings, and conformities exacted by the cold war tended to distort journalism's commitment to independence as a matter of the highest priority. Governments of all political persuasions recognized and practiced to an extreme the latest forms of opinion manipulation, backed by power and resources hardly imagined earlier. The emergence of the press as the "fourth branch of government" embodied both the new recognition of its ability to influence opinion and the danger it faced of cooptation by more powerful political and economic interests. Furthermore, postwar "consumer culture," exemplified and institutionalized through the new medium of information and entertainment, television, altered the character of news itself. The precise character and consequences of these changes remains a subject of continuing debate, but their influence must in some measure account for observable changes in print journalism: reduced and less regular coverage in all but the major world centers and a further heightening of the already existing tendency to feature sensational, colorful stories at the expense of serious background description and analysis.

There remain, of course, some notable resisters of the general tendency. A few newspapers, such as the *New York Times*, the *Wall Street Journal*, and the *Christian Science Monitor*, have in many respects improved the quality of their international coverage. *Time* and *Newsweek*, on occasion, mobilize substantial resources for comprehensive coverage of major stories. With the support of such powerful publishers, correspondents such as Seymour Hersch, David Halberstam, Strobe Talbott, and others maintained a high standard of reporting and interpretation. In the tradition of George Seldes, committed journalists such as I. F. Stone have shown that determination and intelligence can still challenge entrenched authority. And minority opinion journals keep the tradition of lively, independent reporting alive. Yet journalism's seemingly endless struggles against ever greater odds, battling pressures to bias, truncate, or sensationalize the news, and its successes, even when backed with impressive resources, have been exceptions to the general rule.

Contrasted with such developments, the difficulties and dangers of the twenties and thirties seem in retrospect relatively simple and straightforward. Reporters had been challenged to do their best and, despite troublesome problems, had risen to the occasion. The freedom and opportunity offered had been extraordinary and had been seized upon by a group of young Americans conscious that a new, richer, but more interdependent and complicated world culture was emerging. Caught up in the toils of change themselves, they had tried to alert others to some of its dimensions. Their efforts, far from completely successful, nevertheless earned the admiration of those who understood them at the time; these remain worthy of appreciation as the future they in some measure anticipated has become reality.

Notes

Preface

1. Bernard Weisberger, *The American Newspaperman* (Chicago: Univ. of Chicago Press, 1961), 122–27; Michael Schudson, *Discovering the News: A Social History of American Newspapers* (New York: Basic Books, Harper Torchbook edition, 1978), 88–120.

2. Victor Rosewater, *History of Cooperative Newsgathering in the United States* (New York: D. Appleton, 1930), 330–32; Melville E. Stone, *Fifty Years a Journalist* (Garden City, N.Y.: Doubleday, Page, 1921), 243ff. For a summary of early American foreign correspondence, see Robert W. Desmond, *The Press and World Affairs* (New York: D. Appleton-Century, 1937), 10–32, 39–50, and Desmond, *Windows on the World: The Information Process in a Changing Society*, 1900–1920 (Iowa City: Univ. of Iowa Press, 1980), 107–43, as well as John Hohenberg, *Foreign Correspondence: The Great Reporters and Their Times* (New York: Columbia Univ. Press, 1964). See also Joseph J. Mathews, *George W. Smalley: Forty Years a Foreign Correspondent* (Chapel Hill: Univ. of North Carolina Press, 1973), 1–36, 48–98; Don C. Seitz, *The James Gordon Bennetts, Father and Son: Proprietors of the New York Herald* (Indianapolis: Bobbs-Merrill, 1928), 220, 276, 351–54, 361; Weisberger, *The American Newspaperman*, 101–2; Schudson, *Discovering the News*, 50–60, 65.

3. Exceptions are James D. Startt, *Journalism's Unofficial Ambassador: A Biography of Edward Price Bell*, 1869–1943 (Athens: Ohio Univ. Press, 1974); Benedict Karl Zobrist, "Edward Price Bell and the Development of the Foreign Service of the *Chicago Daily News*" (Ph.D. diss., Northwestern University, 1953); Jerome E. Edwards, *The Foreign Policy of Col. McCormick's Tribune, 1929–1941* (Reno: Univ. of Nevada Press, 1971). See also Robert W. Desmond, *Crisis and Conflict: World News Reporting Between Two Wars, 1920–1940* (Iowa City: Univ. of Iowa Press, 1982).

1. Beginnings

1. American exports of gold, silver, and machinery more than doubled in value between 1890 and 1910, from $910,000,000 to $1,919,000,000. Imports were similarly affected, rising from $823,000,000 to $1,645,000,000. U.S. Department of Commerce, Bureau of the Census, *Historical Statistics of the United States, 1795–1945* (Washington, D.C.: U.S. Government Printing Office, 1949), 244. The numbers and interests of American businessmen in Europe were sufficient to support the formation of American chambers of commerce in France (1894), Germany (1903), Italy (1915), and the United Kingdom (1916). Tourist data from U.S. Department of Commerce, Bureau of the Census, *Historical Statistics of the Untied States from Colonial Times to 1976,* Part 1 (Washington, D.C.: U. S. Government Printing Office, 1976), 402. Overseas residents were estimated in ibid., 9. James A. Field, Jr., *Americans and the Mediterranean World* (Princeton, N.J.: Princeton Univ. Press, 1969), and Lilian S. Rosenberg, *Spreading the American Dream: American Economic and Cultural Expansion, 1890–1945* (New York: Hill and Wang, 1982), offer comprehensive interpretations of American overseas expansion in the nineteenth and twentieth centuries.

2. Schudson, *Discovering the News,* 69–70; Gerald Langford, *The Richard Harding Davis Years: A Biography of Mother and Son* (New York: Holt, Rinehart and Winston, 1961). On Davis as a model for later correspondents, see Linton Wells, *Blood on the Moon* (Boston: Houghton Mifflin, 1937), 10; Herbert L. Matthews, *World in Revolution: A Newspaperman's Memoir* (New York: Scribner's, 1972), 3; Paul Scott Mowrer, *The House of Europe* (Boston: Houghton Mifflin, 1945), 247.

3. Stone, *Fifty Years a Journalist,* 243–48.

4. Charles H. Dennis, *Victor Lawson: His Time and His Work* (Chicago: Univ. of Chicago Press, 1935), 260–64; "History of *Chicago Daily News* Foreign Service," *Chicago Daily News,* 8 May 1971.

5. Weisberger, *The American Newspaperman,* 143–45, 150; W. A. Swanberg, *Citizen Hearst: A Biography of William Randolph Hearst* (New York: Scribner's, 1961), 101ff., 116–49; Swanberg, *Pulitzer* (New York: Scribner's, 1967), 222–39, 246–53; Seitz, *The James Gordon Bennetts,* 61–62, 120–21, 158, 203, 361, 376; Meyer Berger, *The Story of the New York Times, 1851–1951* (New York: Simon and Schuster, 1951), 101–7, 129–30, 133–34, 208; Elmer Davis, *History of the New York Times* (New York: The New York Times, 1921), 275, 280.

6. Larzer Ziff, *The American 1890s: Life and Times of a Lost Generation* (New York: Viking Press, 1966), 146–49; Schudson, *Discovering the News,* 69–71.

7. Ernest Earnest, *Expatriates and Patriots: American Artists, Scholars and Writers in Europe* (Durham, N.C.: Duke Univ. Press, 1961), 271–73, stresses the midwestern elements in the literary exodus. On missionaries see Valentin H. Rabe, "Evangelistic Logistics," and Clifton J. Phillips, "The Student Volunteer Movement," in John K. Fairbank, ed., *The Missionary Enterprise in China and America* (Cambridge: Harvard Univ. Press, 1974), 74–76, 98.

8. Edward Price Bell, "Seventy Years Deep," 78–79, 112, unpublished autobiography in the Edward Price Bell Papers, Newberry Library, Chicago, Illinois.

9. Ibid., 132, 168–69, 216, 223–25, 330; Startt, *Journalism's Unofficial Ambassador,* 6–14. Subsequently, Bell described the impact of the railroad, mails, telephone, and newspapers on the remote Raccoon Valley. The Franco-Prussian War of 1870 "was nothing" in

the minds of valley residents, he wrote, whereas the Russo-Japanese War thirty-five years later presented an "absorbing drama, fertile of opinion and of feeling." Bell, "On American Graft," undated clipping from the *London Daily Mail*, in "Works: Newspaper Articles, 1896–1931," Bell Papers.

10. Frederic Wile, *News Is Where You Find It: Forty Years' Reporting at Home and Abroad* (Indianapolis: Bobbs-Merrill, 1939), 1–38.

11. Webb Miller, *I Found No Peace: The Journal of a Foreign Correspondent* (New York: Simon and Schuster, 1936), ix–x, 1–21.

12. P. S. Mowrer, *House of Europe*, 1–26; review of Mowrer's *Balkanized Europe* (New York: E.P. Dutton, 1921), *Hyde Park* (Chicago) *Weekly,* November 4, 1926; P. S. Mowrer, "Biographical Articles and Notices," Paul Scott Mowrer Papers, Newberry Library, Chicago, Illinois. Another midwesterner, Hans von Kaltenborn grew up in Merrill, Wisconsin, where his family read and spoke the father's native German. Hans was educated at the German Academy in nearby Milwaukee. Yet Kaltenborn later remembered his youthful reading of *Tom Sawyer* as the source of his desire for adventure. He trained for journalism with the help of a correspondence course paid for by his father and was already a reporter for the *Merrill News* at the outbreak of the Spanish-American War. H. V. Kaltenborn, *Fifty Fabulous Years, 1900–1950: A Personal Review* (New York: G. P. Putnam's Sons, 1951), 3–5; "The Reminiscences of H. V. Kaltenborn," Columbia University Oral History Research Office, Radio Unit, typescript, 3–11.

13. Raymond Swing, *"Good Evening!" A Professinal Memoir* (New York: Harcourt, Brace and World, 1964), 4–30.

14. Malcolm Cowley, *Exile's Return: A Literary Odyssey of the 1920s* (New York: Viking Press Compass Edition, 1969), 71–73.

15. Edgar Ansel Mowrer, *Triumph and Turmoil: A Personal History of Our Time* (New York: Weybright and Talley, 1968), 3–10, 26–47.

16. Louis Lochner, *Always the Unexpected: A Book of Reminiscences* (New York: Macmillan, 1956), 6–16.

17. William H. Stoneman, "Autobiography," ms., Box 1, William H. Stoneman Papers, University of Michigan.

18. Albion Ross, *Journey of an American* (Indianapolis: Bobbs-Merrill, 1957), 11.

19. "John Gunther," *Current Biography: Who's News and Why, 1940* (New York: H. W. Wilson, 1941), 356–58; John Gunther, "Autobiography in Brief," ms., n.d., 89–90, in John Gunther Papers, University of Chicago; Mrs. John Gunther, interview with author, New York City, 9 January 1979.

20. William L. Shirer, *Twentieth Century Journey, The Start: 1904–1930,* vol. 1 of *A Memoir of a Life and Times* (New York: Simon and Schuster, 1976), 14–16, 191–97.

21. Edmond Taylor, *Awakening from History* (Boston: Gambit, 1969), 7–24.

22. Marian K. Sanders, *Dorothy Thompson: A Legend in Her Time* (New York: Avon Books, 1974), 1–21; Mr. and Mrs. Leland Stowe, interviews with author, Ann Arbor, Michigan, 1 December 1975 and 17 August 1977; Negley Farson, *The Way of a Transgressor* (New York: The Literary Guild of America, 1936), 1–21; George Seldes, *Tell the Truth and Run: My 44 Year Fight for a Free Press* (New York: Greenberg, 1953), xi–xix.

23. Lochner, *Always the Unexpected*, 3, 6, 18–38.

24. Louis Lochner, "Internationalism Among Universities," *University of Wisconsin Alumnus,* n.d. [1913?], in Louis Lochner Papers, Wisconsin State Historical Society, Madi-

son. H. V. Kaltenborn, about the same time, helped to found the Cosmopolitan Club for international students at Harvard. "Reminiscences of H. V. Kaltenborn."

25. P. S. Mowrer, *House of Europe*, 91–110.

26. E. A. Mowrer, *Triumph and Turmoil*, 11–12, 18–25; E. A. Mowrer to Nell Mowrer (his mother), undated letters written from the University of Michigan, in E. A. Mowrer Papers, Library of Congress, Washington, D.C.

27. Bell, "Seventy Years Deep," 216–27; Richard Rovere, "Inside," *The New Yorker*, 23 August 1947, 33; Mrs. John Gunther, interview with author, New York City, 9 January 1979; John T. Whitaker, *And Fear Came* (New York: MacMillan, 1936), 43–46.

28. Vincent Sheean, *Personal History* (New York: The Literary Guild of America, 1935), 1–24. Plano, however, did offer Sheean exposure to its small, cultured German elite. See Vincent Sheean, *This House Against This House* (New York: Random House, 1946), 50–51.

29. Wile, *News*, 20; Stoneman, "Autobiography."

30. Edgar Snow, *Journey to the Beginning* (New York: Random House, 1958), 3, 11, 28, 30; Ross, *Journey of an American*, 12–13.

31. Clarence Streit, interview with author, Washington, D.C., 25 October 1975; Clarence Streit, *Union Now: A Proposal for a Federation of the Democracies of the North Atlantic*, 15th ed. (New York: Harper and Brothers, 1940), 288–90; "Clarence Streit," *Current Biography... 1950*, 552–54.

32. Bell to Lawson, 15 April 1923, "Outgoing Letters," Bell Papers.

33. Shirer, *Twentieth Century Journey*, 17–22, 83, 165–70, 192–93, 203.

2. Apprenticeship

1. Mathews, *Smalley*, passim; Zobrist, "Edward Price Bell," 41, passim. The *Times* began an overhaul of its European service in 1907, but Wythe Williams later noted that as head of its Paris office in the late 1920s he was the only *Times* bureau chief on the Continent to hold an American passport. Bell to Dennis, 9 May 1907, Bell Papers; Wythe Williams, *Dusk of Empire: The Decline of Europe and the Rise of the United States, as Observed by a Foreign Correspondent in a Quarter Century of Service* (New York: Scribner's, 1937),8.

2. Bell, "Seventy Years Deep," 132–216, 230–45, 312–15, 330–31, passim; Wile, *News*, 31–38; Dennis, *Victor Lawson*, 260–64; Startt, *Journalism's Unofficial Ambassador*, 9–22.

3. Wile, *News*, 26–38, 68–70.

4. Bell, "Seventy Years Deep," 331–36; Lawson to Bell, 13 February 1903, 16 February 1909, 25 February 1909, Bell Papers.

5. Wile, *News*, 76–112, 175.

6. Lawson to Bell, 26 December 1901; Bell to Wile, 8 June 1905; Bell to Dennis, 14 June 1905, Bell Papers.

7. Zobrist, "Edward Price Bell," 43, 47–48, 56, 71–78, 80.

8. Bell to Dennis, 6 August 1901 and 15 June 1905, Bell Papers.

9. Bell to Mrs. Victor W. Lawson, 17 February 1909, 2 March 1909, 21 May 1909, 31 January 1912, Bell Papers; Startt, *Journalism's Unofficial Ambassador*, 36–37; Bell to Dennis, 24 June 1907 and Bell to Mrs. Victor W. Lawson, 21 May 1909, Bell Papers.

10. Bell to E. T. Heyer, 25 June 1901; Bell to Wile, 2 August 1901, Bell Papers.

11. Bell to E. Johnson, 19 July 1910; Bell to E. T. Heyer, 25 June 1901, Bell Papers.

12. Williams, *Dusk of Empire,* 1–8, 10–33, 56ff.; "Wythe Williams," *Current Biography ... 1942,* 824–26.

13. P. S. Mowrer, *House of Europe,* 82–115.

14. Ibid., 129–37; Mowrer to Bell, 31 May 1910, 6 June 1910, Bell Papers.

15. Bell to P. S. Mowrer, 31 May 1910, 6 June 1910, Bell Papers.

16. P. S. Mowrer to Bell, 4 June 1910, 8 June 1910, Bell Papers.

17. P. S. Mowrer to Bell, 27 February 1913, 13 March 1913, Bell Papers; P. S. Mowrer, *House of Europe,* 157–66.

18. Swing, *"Good Evening!"* 1–33.

19. Ibid., 36–37; P. S. Mowrer, *House of Europe,* 209; P. S. Mowrer to Bell, 17 February 1913, 19 February 1913, 19 March 1913, Bell Papers.

20. Swing, *"Good Evening!"* 37–42; P. S. Mowrer, *House of Europe,* 137; Wile, *News,* 187.

21. P. S. Mowrer to Bell, 19 February 1913, Bell Papers.

22. Startt, *Journalism's Unofficial Ambassador,* 30–41; P. S. Mowrer to Bell, 30 June 1916, Bell Papers.

23. Bell, "Seventy Years Deep," 371–72.

24. Swing, *"Good Evening!"* 42; P. S. Mowrer, *House of Europe,* 245.

25. Miller, *I Found No Peace,* 1–38, 54, 126, 172.

26. Edward Gibbons, *Floyd Gibbons, Your Headline Hunter: A Biography* (New York: Exposition Press, 1953), 25–49, 53–79, 91, 111.

27. Seldes, *Tell the Truth,* 1–40.

28. E. A. Mowrer, *Triumph and Turmoil,* 26–48, 52–78, 101–2.

29. P. S. Mowrer, *House of Europe,* 241–55, 262–63, 271, 283; P. S. Mowrer to Bell, 30 June 1916, 3 September 1917, 7 November 1917, 20 November 1917, 4 December 1917, 3 January 1918, 14 January 1918 (two letters), 10 April 1918, 15 June 1918, 13 August 1918, Bell Papers.

30. P. S. Mowrer to Bell, 26 April 1917, 10 May 1917, 11 June 1917, 3 September 1917, Bell Papers.

31. Wythe Williams, *Passed by the Censor: The Experience of an American Newspaperman in France* (New York: E. P. Dutton, 1916), 9–13, 53–59, 73, 94, 120–27, 145; Williams, *Dusk of Empire,* 12.

32. Williams, *Passed by the Censor,* 4–5, 22–24, 154–55, 256–67. See Also Emmet Crozier, *American Reporters on the Western Front, 1914–1918* (New York: Oxford Univ. Press, 1959), 192.

33. Swing, *"Good Evening!"* 47–87, 107–11, 120–22.

34. Bell to Dennis, 12 October 1914, quoted in Zobrist, "Edward Price Bell," 183–85; Lawson to Bell, 20 July 1915, 31 August 1915, Bell Papers.

35. Startt, *Journalism's Unofficial Ambassador,* 47–80.

36. Phillip Knightley, *The First Casualty: From the Crimea to Vietnam, The War Correspondent as Hero, Propagandist, and Myth Maker* (New York: Harcourt Brace Jovanovich, 1975), 79–136. Frederic Wile later wrote: "Modern war, from a foreign correspondent's standpoint, consists principally of two things—censorship and rumors." Wile, *News,* 274.

37. David Darrah, *Hail Caesar!* (Boston: Hale, Cushman and Flint, 1936), 3–12, 14–19.

38. Streit to Edwin L. James of the *New York Times, New York Times* Papers, New York; Clarence Streit, interview with author, Washington, D.C., 28 October 1975.

39. Lochner, *Always the Unexpected,* 45–52, 57–76.

40. Farson, *Way of a Transgressor,* 21, 49–50, passim; "Negley Farson," *Who's Who in America, 1938–39* (Chicago: A. N. Marquis, 1938), 873.

41. Darrah, *Hail Caesar!* 9.

3. Comrades and Rivals

1. Cowley, *Exile's Return,* 3–10, argues that it was a "lost generation" only in certain limited, idiosyncratic respects.

2. Lochner, *Always the Unexpected,* 1, 78–114.

3. "Clarence Streit," *Current Biography... 1950,* 552–54; Clarence Streit, interview with author, Washington, D.C., 28 October 1975; letter from Streit to his family, dated 8 July 1920, copy in my files; Clarence Streit, *Where Iron Is, There Is the Fatherland* (New York: B. W. Huebsch, 1920).

4. Farson, *Way of a Transgressor,* 404–38; "Negley Farson," *Who's Who in America, 1938–39,* 873; Negley Farson, *Sailing Across Europe* (New York: The Century Company, 1926).

5. "John Gunther," *Current Biography... 1941,* 356–58; Mrs. John Gunther, interview with author, New York City, 9 January 1979; Desmond, *Crisis and Conflict,* 320–21.

6. Sheean, *Personal History,* 25–33.

7. "Sigrid Schultz," *Current Biography... 1944,* 601–2; "Sigrid Schultz," *Who's Who in America 1936–37,* 2165; Sigrid Schultz, interview with author, Westport, Connecticut, 8 August 1978; Desmond, *Crisis and Conflict,* 301. For discussion of other women correspondents, see Mary Knight, "Girl Reporter in Paris," in Eugene Lyons, ed., *We Cover the World, by Fifteen Foreign Correspondents* (New York: Harcourt, Brace and Company, 1937), 277–97.

8. Sanders, *Dorothy Thompson,* 19–46.

9. Sanders, *Dorothy Thompson,* 44–82; Dorothy Thompson, "Diaries," 1920, Dorothy Thompson Papers, George Arents Research Library for Special Collections, Syracuse University Library, Syracuse, New York.

10. Leland Stowe, interview with author, Ann Arbor, Michigan, 1 December 1975; Leland Stowe to author, 1 July 1981; Stowe, "Magazine Articles for Various Publications," Box 3, Folder 4, Stowe Papers, Wisconsin State Historical Society, Madison.

11. "Herbert Renfro Knickerbocker," *Current Biography... 1940,* 460; James E. Abbe, "Men of Cablese," *New Outlook* 162 (December 1933): 27–32.

12. Stoneman, "Autobiography."

13. Taylor, *Awakening from History,* 60–75, 92–95.

14. Herbert L. Matthews, *The Education of a Correspondent* (New York: Harcourt, Brace, 1946), 5–7, 13–21; Matthews, *World in Revolution,* 3–41, 56, 62.

15. Whitaker, *And Fear Came,* 43–58, 63–66, 88–90.

16. Shirer, *Twentieth Century Journey,* 34–35, 60, 216–27, 230, 321, 438–41.

17. Startt, *Journalism's Unofficial Ambassador,* 51–54, 60–64, 71–72, 84–95, 219n.

18. P. S. Mowrer, *House of Europe,* 353–71, 390; P. S. Mowrer, *Balkanized Europe;* Sheean, *Personal History,* 87–89. For the Abd el-Krim interview, see *Cincinnati Times-Star* clippings, 22 June 1925 in Mowrer, "Biographical Articles and Notices," P. S. Mowrer Papers. John Bass, another *CDN* correspondent, had collaborated with an economist, Harold G. Moulton, in an earlier analysis of international economic relations, *America and the Balance Sheet of Europe* (New York: Ronald Press, 1921).

19. Startt, *Journalism's Unofficial Ambassador,* 50; P. S. Mowrer, *House of Europe,* 209ff.

20. John Gunther to Helen Hahn, n.d. (1925), Gunther Papers, New York City; Sanders, *Thompson*; Leland Stowe, interview with author, Ann Arbor, Michigan, 17 August 1977. Concerning Paris staff relations, see P. S. Mowrer to Bell, 27 February 1913, 3 March 1913, 9 March 1913, 11 June 1917, 3 September 1917, 7 November 1917, 14 December 1917, 14 January 1918, 14 April 1918, Bell Papers. For Mowrer's reorganization proposal, "Suggestions for Reorganizing the Foreign Service," see P. S. Mowrer to Bell, 6 May 1920, 1 August 1921, P. S. Mowrer File, Bell Papers.

21. Swing, *"Good Evening!"* 129–62, 168–74, 184–85, 193–210.

22. Williams, *Dusk of Empire,* 213–30.

23. E. A. Mowrer, *Triumph and Turmoil,* 74–80, 101–2, 120–44, 150; E. A. Mowrer, *Immortal Italy* (New York: D. Appleton, 1922).

24. Seldes, *Tell the Truth,* 119, 86–138.

25. Seldes, *Tell the Truth,* 151–78, 187–92, 248.

26. Seldes, *Tell the Truth,* 123–26; Gibbons, *Floyd Gibbons,* 128–203.

27. Shirer, *Twentieth Century Journey,* 216; E. P. Bell, undated fragment, Mary Bell File, Bell Papers.

28. Thompson, "Diary," 9 September 1927, Thompson Papers.

29. Wile, *News,* 76, 88–96, 104. Wythe Williams noted the establishment in London in 1912 of the first night club owned by an American, Jack May's Cosmopolitan Artists Club. Williams, *Dusk of Empire,* 18. By June 1906 Bell had already interviewed Selfridge on his plans to settle in London and was advising him to establish a post office and visitors' center at "your shop." Bell to Selfridge, 26 June 1906; Bell to Dennis, 12 February 1909, Bell Papers.

30. Bell to Dennis, 7 June 1911, Bell Papers; Wile, *News,* 116, 151–52, 175, 193, 213. John Gunther, looking back on the thirties in 1962, wrote that most correspondents "travelled frequently, met constantly, caroused, took in each other's washing and, even when fiercely competitive, were devoted friends." Gunther, *A Fragment of Autobiography* (New York: Harper and Brothers, 1962), 6.

31. P. S. Mowrer, *House of Europe,* 142–47, 159–61, 212–17, 245–47; Williams, *Dusk of Empire,* 25–36.

32. Bell to Dennis, 11 June 1901, Bell Papers.

33. E. A. Mowrer, *Triumph and Turmoil,* 76–79, 133; Matthews, *World in Revolution,* 57–58, 100; Bell to Dennis, 11 June 1901, Bell Papers; Taylor, *Awakening from History,* 77; Seldes, *Tell the Truth,* 170–71, 187–89, 194–96.

34. George Seldes, *Lords of the Press* (New York: Julian Messner, 1938), 286–90; Seldes, *You Can't Print That! The Truth Behind the News, 1918–28* (New York: Payson and Clark, 1929), 229–38; Darrah, *Hail Ceasar!* 29–44.

35. Sanders, *Thompson,* 81–89; Seldes, *Tell the Truth,* vii–ix.

36. Correspondence concerning *Ring Round Vienna* is in Box 150, John Gunther Papers, University of Chicago. John Gunther, *The Lost City* (New York: Harper and Row, 1964), 14, 17, 88–90. For Louis Fischer's description of Gunther, see his *Men and Politics: An Autobiography* (New York: Duell, Sloan and Pearce, 1941), 153.

37. Gunther, *Lost City,* 17, 90; Gunther, *A Fragment of Autobiography,* 3–8; Taylor, *Awakening from History,* 92–93. Letters from Vienna to Junious Wood of the *Chicago Tribune,* 31 July 1930, and Webb Miller of the United Press, 24 July 1930, are in a folder titled "Letters, 1930" in the possession of Mrs. John Gunther, New York City.

38. Whitaker, *And Fear Came,* 70, 81.

39. Whitaker, *And Fear Came,* 90–91; George Seldes, *Iron, Blood and Profits: An Exposure of the World-Wide Munitions Racket* (New York: Harper and Brothers, 1934), 346; Taylor, *Awakening from History,* 156–69.

40. Swing, *"Good Evening!"* 151; E. A. Mowrer, *Triumph and Turmoil,* 156–63, 177, 194–99.

41. Ross, *Journey of an American,* 37–39; Abbe, "Men of Cablese"; P. S. Mowrer, "Notes," Box 2, P. S. Mowrer Papers; John Gunther, "London Diary," December 1935, 7, Gunther Papers, New York City.

42. Lochner, *Always the Unexpected,* 153. The Adlon Bar, in particular, and Berlin more generally seem to have offered particularly strong temptations, to judge by the number of journalists whose work suffered from the association. The career of H. R. Knickerbocker was perhaps the most important individual casualty. In a confidential, undated letter Paul Mowrer commented to Edward Price Bell in 1920, "Decker confirms my opinion that the trouble with Berlin is the Adlon Bar." And as early as 1906 Bell had written to C. H. Dennis, "It seems to me that the café is the curse of continental correspondence. Here, the journalists gather and eat and smoke and drink and dream." Bell to Dennis, 15 March 1906, Bell Papers.

43. Lochner, *Always the Unexpected,* 106–8, 138, 167; letters from Lochner to his father, dated 18 November 1925, 11 June 1926, 3 July 1926, 25 November 1926, 18 May 1927, 7 April 1928 in "Correspondence—Additions," Box 47, Lochner Papers.

44. Lochner, *Always the Unexpected,* 174–77; Lochner to his father, 3 January 1925, Lochner Papers.

45. Sheean to Gunther, 28 March 1935, Sheean File, Gunther Papers, New York City; Bell to Dennis, 22 August 1910, Bell Papers.

46. Brown to Dennis, 15 March 1929, Charles H. Dennis Papers, Newberry Library, Chicago, Illinois.

47. Sheean, *Personal History,* 52–53, 81–84.

48. Seldes, *Lords of the Press,* 283–97.

4. Initiation: Europe from Impressions to Analysis

1. Akira Iriye, *Across the Pacific: An Inner History of American-East Asian Relations* (New York: Harcourt, Brace and World, Harbinger edition, 1967), 5–7.

2. George W. Smalley, *Anglo-American Memories* (New York: G. P. Putnam's Sons, 1911); Frederic W. Wile, *The Men Around the Kaiser: Makers of Modern Germany* (Indianapolis: Bobbs-Merrill, 1914); Wile, *The Assault: Germany Before the Outbreak and England in*

Wartime (Indianapolis: Bobbs-Merrill, 1916); Wile, *Explaining the Britishers* (New York: George H. Doran, 1919); Carl Ackerman, *Germany: The Next Republic?* (New York: George H. Doran, 1917).

3. Startt, *Journalism's Unofficial Ambassador,* 16.

4. Bell, "Seventy Years Deep," 222–25, 364–69; Startt, *Journalism's Unofficial Ambassador,* 14, 22–26, 30–40; Bell, undated fragment, Mary Bell File, Bell Papers; Bell to Dennis, 21 April 1901 and 15 March 1906, Bell Papers.

5. Bell to P. S. Mowrer, 6 June 1910; Bell to C. B. Jamison, 11 July 1905, Bell Papers; Bell, "Seventy Years Deep," 373, emphasis in original.

6. Bell to Mary Alice Mills, 18 June 1896, Bell Papers.

7. Wile, *News,* 70, 76, 88–96; Williams, *Dusk of Empire,* 15, 31–33.

8. Bell to Wile, 8 August 1901; 27 January 1902, 20 Februrary 1902, 6 September 1904, 14 October 1904; Bell to Dennis, 18 September 1901, 28 September 1906, Bell Papers; Wile, *News,* 112–18, 128–29, 156, 174, 239.

9. Swing, *"Good Evening!"* 36–42, 47, 52, 107–10, 120–22; Bell to Lawson, 13 January 1914, Bell Papers.

10. P. S. Mowrer, *House of Europe,* 134, 138, 142, 147, 160–61, 209, 213–17; clippings from the *Chicago Daily News* in Scrapbook, "Prewar and Wartime Materials," Box 2, and diary entry, 20 November 1912, P. S. Mowrer Papers; P. S. Mowrer to Bell, 22 July 1912, Bell Papers.

11. P. S. Mowrer, *House of Europe,* 135, 157–58.

12. P. S. Mowrer, *House of Europe,* 135–37, 157–59, 166, 202–4, 219; undated memo, probably 1913, in "Works," P. S. Mowrer Papers; P. S. Mowrer to Bell, 2 December 1912, 17 February 1913, 20 February 1913, Bell Papers. In the latter letter, Mowrer commented incidentally on the importance of status for a journalist by suggesting that the title of "director," rather than mere correspondent, on his card would add to his prestige in Paris. This may also have been a not particularly subtle way of fishing for a promotion.

13. E. A. Mowrer to Nell Mowrer, 10 February 1911, 7 March 1911, E. A. Mowrer Papers.

14. P. S. Mowrer, *House of Europe,* 150; E. A. Mowrer, *Triumph and Turmoil,* 12–17, 25–37.

15. P. S. Mowrer, *House of Europe,* 362–71; Scrapbook on *Balkanized Europe;* "Practical Pan-Islamism," ms. in file "Morocco—Articles On," P. S. Mowrer Papers.

16. P. S. Mowrer, *Balkanized Europe,* 9, 13–15, 31–41, 50–56, 116–22, 135–39. P. S. Mowrer, "The Assimilation of Israel," *Atlantic Monthly* 128 (July 1921): 101–10.

17. Farson, *Sailing Across Europe,* 24, 48–49, 76–77.

18. Farson, *Sailing Across Europe,* 114, 176, 182, 195, 217, 258, 286, passim; Farson, *Way of a Transgressor,* 395–97, 408–51.

19. E. A. Mowrer, *Immortal Italy,* 2–6, 11–13, 17.

20. E. A. Mowrer, *Immortal Italy,* 22, 28–31, 39–46, 49, passim; E. A. Mowrer, *Triumph and Turmoil,* 142–46. Yet Mowrer, war-weary in Rome in June 1917, had written his mother, "...you do not know how good American institutions and all the rest can seem from here—wonderfully free and simple, and not essentially more tainted with commercialism than the rest of the world, in fact, rather less!" E. A. Mowrer to Nell Mowrer, 21 June 1917, E. A. Mowrer Papers.

21. Swing, *"Good Evening!"* 129–30; Lochner to his father, 7 August 1925, Box 47, Lochner Papers.

22. Box 42, clippings from the *Chicago Daily News,* 1928, 1929, 1930; Box 44, File 5, Gunther Papers Addenda, University of Chicago.

23. Stoneman, "Autobiography"; Darrah, *Hail Caesar!* 22; Shirer, *Twentieth Century Journey,* 216–17, 363; Taylor, *Awakening from History,* 32–37, 67–68.

24. Leland Stowe to author, 1 July 1981; Stowe to his sisters, 19 February 1929 (copy in author's possession), Stowe Papers.

25. Ross, *Journey of an American,* 14–16.

26. Edgar Ansel Mowrer, *This American World* (New York: J. H. Sears, 1928), 1–2, 29–30, 94, 125–27, 181, 196, 215–19, 237–40, 266, passim. Mowrer's wife wrote that her husband was receiving invitations to speak on his book at universities and other intellectual centers. Lilian Mowrer to Dorothy Thompson, n.d., series I, Incoming Mail, Thompson Papers.

27. Gibbons, *Floyd Gibbons,* 253.

28. Ben Hecht, *A Child of the Century* (New York: Simon and Schuster, 1954), 267–70, 317–19.

With Hecht's departure, foreign correspondence lost a sharp observer and a vivid phrase-maker. In the midst of the Spartacus movement he had cabled Chicago that the "german bolshevik revolution to date consists ninety percent rumors ten percent bad shooting." His cabled description of the fledgling German republic was even more graphic and explicit: "On eve weimar national assembly germany sounds like political tower babel stop the capital plastered crisscrossed with lithographic shrieks has appearance free forall cubist exhibition stop...between trying to convince world germany starving trying to regain toehold on vanishing colonies trying persuade german workmen germany is socialist state while endeavoring reassure outside world it is not, present ebert scheideman government sound coherant [sic] as a boiler factory." Reporting on an interview with the foreign minister, Hecht wired, "I left historic room conscious of having spoken to affable combination bismarck and hinky dink of south clark street chicago."

Charles Dennis objected strongly to the latter characterization but Hecht was irrepressible. Shortly he wired again that "quibbling idealists and desperate disheartened political jongleurs thriving in and out of seats of government today had comparitively [sic] little to do with the greatness of yesterday's germany." Various "socialization plans...like little wingless doves have been continually despatched from ark of state only to collapse ere theyd [sic] cleared the deck," he later reported. "Berlin Despatches," 12 February 1919, 2 February 1919, 3 February 1919, 5 May 1919, Ben Hecht Papers, Newberry Library, Chicago.

29. Samuel Spevack, "Four Years In Europe Made Me An American," *Saturday Evening Post,* 198 (29 May 1926): 27ff.

30. George Seldes, *Can These Things Be!* (New York: Brewer, Warren, and Putnam, 1931), 12–21ff.; Seldes, *Tell the Truth,* 225–26.

31. P. S. Mowrer, *Balkanized Europe,* 1–6, 26, 43, 56–61, 76–82, 159–68, 265, passim. Mowrer's discussion of European reactions to postwar American relief and reconstruction missions highlights the gap that existed between American and European assumptions. American efforts, he stated, had three broad purposes: humanitarian contributions to relieve suffering; technical assistance demonstrating American methods for restoring the European economy; and psychological efforts aimed at reducing the "war mentality" of suspicion and resentment. He concluded that the first objective had been fulfilled, the second substantially blocked by political obstacles, and the third "least successful" because of failure to appreciate the extent of European suspicions and resentment. Mowrer's report on

postwar nationalism was termed "un ouvrage remarquable" by *Paris Midi,* 5 December 1920. Scrapbook, P. S. Mowrer Papers.

32. E. A. Mowrer, *Immortal Italy,* 306–7, 360–61, 373–78, 382, 395–98.

33. E. A. Mowrer, "The Fascisti and Italy's Economic Recovery," *Forum* 69 (February 1923): 1198–1206; E. A. Mowrer, "The Rule of the Fascisti," *Forum* 69 (March 1923): 1299–1307.

34. Untitled article for the *Chicago Daily News,* 28 July 1923, clipping in Container 62, "Papers," E. A. Mowrer Papers.

35. E. A. Mowrer, "The Rule of the Fascisti," *Forum* 69 (March 1923): 1299–1307; E. A. Mowrer, *Triumph and Turmoil,* 75–78, 101, 133–42; John P. Diggins, *Mussolini and Fascism: The View from America,* (Princeton, N.J.: Princeton Univ. Press, 1974), 14–16, 18, 20–26, 42–46, passim. When Edgar left Italy, Paul wrote to their father that exposure to the more rational politics of the Weimar Republic might complete his younger brother's political education after the heady Italian climate. P. S. Mowrer to his father, 9 January 1924, P. S. Mowrer Papers.

36. Seldes, *Tell the Truth,* 167–200; Seldes, *Can These Things Be!* 150–66; Seldes, *Sawdust Caesar: The Untold History of Mussolini and Fascism* (New York: Harper and Brothers, 1935), 172, 306, 331–32, passim. Under similar circumstances, when he was under government pressure in the Soviet Uniton, the *Tribune*'s publisher had backed Seldes. (Moderwell changed the spelling of his name to Motherwell, apparently between 1927 and 1928.)

37. P. S. Mowrer, "The New Journalism" and "A Reporter's View of Life," undated mss., Box 2, P. S. Mowrer Papers; Swing, *"Good Evening!"* 146; P. S. Mowrer, "The Press and the Public," in *The Educational Role of the Press* (Paris: League of Nations International Institute of Intellectual Cooperation, 1934), xvi–xix, 213–18, copy in P. S. Mowrer Papers. P. S. Mowrer, "The Problem of French Finance," *The New Republic* 25 (16 February 1921): 342–43, pointed out that the French were waking up to the realities of the nation's financial plight. Higher taxes would be needed to reduce debts. The Germans would be expected to begin reparations soon. Too poor to rebuild its devasted areas, France was still militarily strong and now needed to reform its administration and financial procedures.

38. Williams, *Dusk of Empire,* xvi–xix, 213–18.

39. Wythe Williams, "Herriot—The Frenchman of the Minute," *Saturday Evening Post* 197 (6 December 1924): 15ff.; Williams, "The Caillaux Comeback," *SEP* 197 (27 December 1924): 17ff.; Williams, "Overbalance of Power," *SEP* 197 (10 January 1925): 5ff.; Williams, "The Case for France," SEP 198 (24 October 1925): 45ff.; Williams, "Great for Geneva," *SEP* 198 (28 November 1925): 25ff.; Williams, "Does France Intend to Pay?" *SEP* 197 (11 April 1925): 28ff.; Williams, "A Disarmament Periscope," *SEP* 197 (5 May 1925): 41–42.

40. Sheean, *Personal History,* 33, 36–40.

41. Sheean, *Personal History,* 36–37, 53–54, 77–82.

42. Wythe Williams, "Germany Saving Herself," *Saturday Evening Post* 197 (28 February 1925): 5ff.

43. Wythe Williams, "Germany's New Bid For Power," *SEP* 197 (14 February 1925): 3ff.; Williams, "The New Hindenberg Line," *SEP* 198 (6 March 1926): 5ff. One of the most knowledgeable correspondents about German political affairs was Louis Lochner, but his letters reflected little interest in the subject until the Nazis took power in 1933. His wide responsibility for news of all of Germany and most of Central Europe, as

well as the Associated Press's restricted coverage, may have contributed to his reticence; but it remains difficult to account for.

44. E. A. Mowrer, *Triumph and Turmoil,* 155–66.

45. E. A. Mowrer, "Treason and the German Republic," *Nation* 120 (11 March 1925): 259–60; E. A. Mowrer, "How the Dawes Plan Works," *Harper's* 153 (October 1926): 592–99.

46. E. A. Mowrer, "Germany Comes Back," *Harper's* 155 (July 1927): 203–9.

47. E. A. Mowrer, "Germany After Ten Years," *Harper's* 158 (December 1928): 61–69.

48. Ibid.

49. E. A. Mowrer, "Unseating 'Kultur,'" *Survey* 61 (1 February 1929): 589–90ff.

50. E. A. Mowrer, *Sinon, or The Future of Politics* (London: Kegan Paul, Trench and Trubner, 1930), 52.

51. Raymond Gram Swing, "The New Radicalism: What Americans Don't Understand About Europe," *Harper's* 157 (August 1928): 333–38.

5. Between Two Worlds: The Correspondent's Roles

1. Bell to Lawson, 23 October 1922, reporting an offer from Curtis, Bell Papers. Carl Ackerman, head of the *Public Ledger*'s new European service, also approached Edgar Ansel Mowrer. Ackerman to John J. Spurgeon, 19 February 1920, Carl Ackerman Papers, Library of Congress, Washington, D.C. Raymond Swing, another *Daily News* correspondent, was hired by the *Public Ledger* in 1924. Swing, *"Good Evening!"* 149. A summary of developments in American foreign news service organization and personnel for this period appears in Desmond, *Crisis and Conflict,* 225–50, 291–362.

2. Leland Stowe, undated memorandum to Richard Kluger, Jack Schnedler, and others, "How Did Your 1930 Pulitzer Prize Really Happen?" 6–7, Stowe Papers, copy in my files. When Stowe received the Pulitzer Prize for reporting the negotiations that produced the Young Plan dealing with the thorny war debts issue, the *New York Herald Tribune* did not even give him a raise. See also Stowe to Mrs. Odgen Reid, 14 November 1937, Stowe Papers, and Richard Kluger, *The Paper: The Life and Death of the New York Herald Tribune* (New York: Alfred A. Knopf, 1986), 233, passim. On Ralph Barnes, see Maurice Hindus, *Hitler Cannot Conquer Russia* (New York: Doubleday, Doran, 1941), 189–90; Stowe to author, 14 July 1983. See also Desmond, *Crisis and Conflict,* 295–302, 304–14, 317–25, 328–35.

3. Lochner, *Always the Unexpected,* 114–26, 138–41, 174–77; Lochner to his father, 21 July 1925, 4 October 1925, 10 June 1926, 11 June 1926, 30 December 1927, 2 February 1928; Lochner round-robin letter to his family in America, 26 March 1929, Lochner Papers. When Lochner returned home in the late twenties and visited the AP headquarters, he was surprised and delighted to find himself accepted as an equal among fellow employees there.

4. Bell to Dennis, 12 April 1901, 17 April 1901, 11 June 1901, 12 June 1901, 17 June 1901, 24 June 1901, 6 August 1901, 3 September 1901; Bell to Wile, 8 August 1901, 4 September 1901, 27 January 1902, 13 February 1902, 20 February 1902, Bell Papers. Bell reiterated this point in a subsequent letter: "The piracy practiced upon our dispatches by certain Ameican newspapers clearly shows that the pirates value our semi-editorial cables on large topics, political, social, and economic, far above the stories dealing with comparatively unimportant news events." Bell to Dennis, 27 February 1902, Bell Papers.

5. Bell to Dennis, 2 August 1901, Bell Papers. On editorial viewpoint, see Bell to Wile, 14 October 1904, 6 September 1904, Bell Papers.

6. Bell's interpretation of Chicago's expectations are reflected in his advice to the *CDN* representative assigned to St. Petersburg at the time of the 1905 revolution. Bell wrote that he assumed Lawson would want Chicago visitors welcomed there as elsewhere. "I am sending you a copy of 'Who's Who in America' and also a map of Manchuria." Bell would also forward American newspapers and had asked headquarters to send "a copy of the *Chicago Directory,* the *Chicago Blue Book,* and of the *Chicago Daily News Almanac.*" Bell to H. Lamarc, 15 and 28 March 1905. On other tourist bureau work, see Bell to Wile, 20 February 1902; Bell to Dennis, 8 March 1906, 24 June 1907; Bell to Lawson, 5 October 1907; Bell to P. S. Mowrer, 6 June 1910, Bell Papers. In 1922 Bell complained to Dennis that visitors from Chicago were taking advantage of the bureau's hospitality. Some were taking "souvenirs" in a fashion that threatened both the budget and the attractiveness of the offices. They had "walked off with small rugs and anything else not nailed down, even to electric light bulbs. We are now endeavoring," he continued, "while exercising every courtesy, to retain at least the more substantial items of property in our reading and writing rooms." Bell to Dennis, 15 April 1922, Bell Papers. On Lord Northcliffe, see Bell to Dennis, 28 September 1906, 19 October 1906, 1 April 1920, Bell Papers.

7. P. S. Mowrer to Dennis, 21 August 1918, copy in Bell Papers; Mowrer to Bell, 12 April 1920, 15 April 1920, Bell Papers. To support his confidence in the effectiveness of the foreign service, Mowrer reported that the circulation manager of the *Fort Worth* (Texas) *Star Telegram* had stated that in six months since its adoption of the *Daily News*'s foreign service, sales had increased from 55,000 to 65,000. Mowrer to Bell, 31 August 1918, Bell Papers.

8. Bell to Dennis, 1 April 1920, 8 June 1920, 11 May 1920, 28 September 1920, Bell Papers; P. S. Mowrer, "Suggestions for Reorganizing the Foreign Service"; P. S. Mowrer, memorandum, 1 August 1921, copy in P. S. Mowrer File, Bell Papers. Bell wrote Dennis in support of Mowrer's earlier memorandum, reiterating his view that leading correspondents—although not the younger reporters—"should be free to release the results of their own study, and to release their personalities also." The "original idea of our service," he reminded Dennis, had acknowledged "the intellectual side of the news" as an important objective and source of prestige for the service. Bell to Dennis, 11 April 1920, 11 May 1920, Bell Papers.

9. P. S. Mowrer to Bell, 10 August 1921, 28 February 1922, Bell Papers.

10. P. S. Mowrer to Dennis, 10 September 1921, 21 September 1921, 28 April 1923, 1 June 1923, 28 August 1923, 11 September 1923, Dennis Papers.

11. P. S. Mowrer, *House of Europe,* 525. For Bell's comments on Dennis's limited, cost-conscious editorial policy, see Bell to Dennis, 8 March 1922, 12 May 1924; Bell to Mary Bell, 26 March 1924, 23 April 1924; Bell to P. S. Mowrer, 17 May 1924, Bell Papers; Hal O'Flaherty to Dennis, 12 June 1924; Dennis to P. S. Mowrer, 18 September 1923, 12 March 1924, 11 April 1924, 19 April 1924, 23 October 1924, Dennis Papers.

12. Dennis to P. S. Mowrer, 16 May 1924, 29 May 1924, 10 September 1924, 14 November 1924, 24 September 1926, Dennis Papers. Mowrer's reaction may be gauged by his response to a Dennis letter indicating that, if more reports of the "sex scandals of rich Americans" in Paris were wanted, a special correspondent should be assigned since his own duties left him no time for such material. P. S. Mowrer to Dennis 9 February 1923, 9 March 1923, 3 April 1923, 11 September 1923, Dennis Papers.

13. Dennis to E. A. Mowrer, 10 October 1924, 20 and 25 November 1925, 8 September 1926, Dennis Papers.

14. Dennis to E. A. Mowrer, 25 November 1925, 8 September 1926, Dennis Papers; E. A. Mowrer, *Triumph and Turmoil,* 176.

15. C. Binder to Dorothy Binder, 9 August 1927; Binder to Dennis, 24 January 1928; C. H. Dennis to Binder, 25 November 1927, 1 April 1928, Carroll Binder Papers, Newberry Library, Chicago, Illinois.

16. Swing, *"Good Evening!"* 138, 141, 147, 149–52.

17. Seldes, *Tell the Truth,* 114, 118, 123, 128–29, 133, 179–81, 187, 192, 209; Seldes, *Can These Things Be!* 166, 198, 229–38; Seldes, *Lords of the Press,* 53, 283–97. Seldes described a concerted effort by the American press and government to get reporters into Russia, at a time in 1920–21 when outside journalists were banned by means of a secret provision written into an agreement for an American famine relief program. He noted that Marguerite Harrison, a *Baltimore Sun*-Associated Press correspondent arrested by the Russians for spying in 1920, later admitted that she had reported for the American military. After a long anti-Communist career, Donald Day eventually found employment in 1943 with the German Ministry of Propaganda. Marguerite Harrison, *There's Always Tomorrow: The Story of a Chequered Career* (New York: Farrar and Rinehart, 1935).

18. William L. Shirer, interview with author, Lenox, Massachusetts, August 1978; Sigrid Schultz, interview with author, 8 August 1978; Seldes, *You Can't Print That!* 268.

19. Taylor, *Awakening from History,* 104, 150, 159, 162–63.

20. Taylor, *Awakening from History,* 167–68, 205–7, 258–60. William L. Shirer had similar experiences with McCormick. Shirer, *Twentieth Century Journey,* 349.

21. Ackerman to J. J. Spurgeon, 22 February 1920, 17 March 1920, 1 April 1920, Ackerman Papers, Library of Congress.

22. Spurgeon to Ackerman, 23 March 1920, 5 May 1920, 25 May 1920, Ackerman Papers.

23. Ackerman to Cyrus H. K. Curtis, 6 July 1921, Ackerman Papers. In a defensive mood, which may have caused him to exaggerate the virtues of his news service, Ackerman informed Curtis that, "almost without exception," the news prepared by the staffs of the *New York Times, New York World, New York Herald, Chicago Tribune, Chicago American,* Associated Press, and United Press was obtained "from the proof sheets of the [London] *Daily Chronicle,* the *Manchester Guardian,* the *Daily Telegraph, The Observer,* the *Daily Express,* Reuters or the Central News."

Wythe Williams had complained to Ackerman at Spurgeon's order to mail Clarence Streit's copy from Turkey, including the only interview that had been recorded with Kemal Atatürk in a year. Williams wanted to cable this obviously important interview regardless of instructions, but had little confidence its significance would be appreciated in Philadelphia. Streit, meanwhile, protested directly to Ackerman and Spurgeon that the *Public Ledger* was printing letters critical of his reports from Turkey without providing him an opportunity to respond. Williams to Ackerman, 24 March 1921; Streit to J. Spurgeon, 19 June 1921, Ackerman Papers.

24. Walter Lippmann and Charles Merz, "A Test of the News," *The New Republic,* 4 August 1920, 2, 5–7, 16.

25. Ibid., 1, 4.

26. Ibid., 3, 41–42; Lippmann and Merz, "More News for the Times," *The New Republic,* 11 August 1920, 299–301. The *Times Index* shows no reference to this article, nor any re-

sponse to it on the part of the paper. Interestingly, Carl Ackerman, who had been reporting on Russia for the *Times,* was one of the correspondents specifically criticized by Lippmann and Merz. For a more detailed discussion of coverage of the Russian Revolution, see Knightley, *The First Casualty,* 138–70. After working with Lippmann for the *New York World* during the twenties, Merz joined the *Times* in 1930 and became an editor in 1938. Desmond, *Crisis and Conflict,* 350–51.

27. Matthews, *Education of a Correspondent,* 21, 31–32, 67–68, 130.

28. Ibid., 141–42, 186; Matthews, *World in Revolution,* 19–20, 25–26, 29–30, 36–39; Gay Talese, *The Kingdom and the Power* (New York: World Publishing, 1969), 54–58.

29. For other examples, see Taylor, *Awakening from History,* 179ff., 205–7, and Seldes, *Tell the Truth,* 242–55.

30. Bell to Dennis, 27 February 1902, 25 April 1905, 11 July 1905, 4 October 1905; Bell to Wile, 22 January 1906, Bell to Lawson, 26 January 1906, Bell Papers. Bell explained his cropping of Wile's reports by referring to his instructions from Chicago: "When you feel like kicking on the way some of your stories have been turned upside down and inside out lately, I . . . recommend that you kick Mr. Dennis. . . . When I change your matter I cut out words to get room for other places on the map of Europe; I do not play football with your phraseology just for the fun of it." Bell to Wile, 27 January 1902, 13 February 1902; Bell Papers.

31. P. S. Mowrer to Bell, 12 April 1918; P. S. Mowrer to Dennis, 21 August 1918, Bell Papers. At least once during the war Mowrer had felt it necessary to complain to Dennis about pressure to send stories by mail instead of cable. No other foreign services, except the *New York Post* and the United Press, were still doing so, Mowrer stated. Mail reports were now accorded such low priority that they were often not printed, he continued, which affected reporters' morale unfavorably. Mowrer to Dennis, 21 August 1918, copy in Bell Papers.

32. P. S. Mowrer to Dennis, 9 August 1922, 3 April 1923, 22 May 1923, 7 June 1923; Dennis to P. S. Mowrer, 9 June 1923, 11 April 1924, 19 April 1924, Dennis Papers. Lawson had written Bell in 1916 that the foreign service had cost the *Daily News* nearly $150,000 the preceding year. In 1918, with the war at its peak, Lawson noted that the cost had risen to over $200,000 of which more that 25 percent had been offset by payments from fifteen papers now buying the *CDN*'s syndicated service. Lawson to Bell, 2 July 1916, 9 August 1918, Bell Papers.

At a time when his relations with Chicago were at their best—he was about to be appointed chief European correspondent—Mowrer wrote Dennis that he was trying to hold down cable volume. Turning the issue to his own advantage, he continued, "our motto of quality rather than quantity, as contrasted to the mere quantity of the *New York Times,* is one source of our strength." P. S. Mowrer to Dennis, 13 July 1922, Dennis Papers.

33. P. S. Mowrer to Binder, 8 March 1929, 8 May 1930, 11 November 1930, Binder Papers.

34. Bell to Dennis, 26 September 1906. Two years earlier Bell had reported that the Associated Press paid its general manager $10,000 a year, while another AP reporter had been hired away by the *London Standard* at the same salary. Bell to Dennis, 29 November 1904; Bell to Lawson, 1 February 1907, 18 March 1914, 17 April 1914, 20 July 1915, Bell Papers.

35. P. S. Mowrer to Bell, 9 March 1913, 16 July 1915, Bell Papers. Mowrer wrote that he had been able to live comfortably in Chicago on less money.

36. Edgar Mowrer's wartime assignment in Italy may not have been considered a full-time one since the *Daily News* already maintained a regular correspondent in Rome. Edgar was

also apparently receiving funds from the United States Committee on Public Information. P. S. Mowrer to Bell, 16 July 1915; E. A. Mowrer, *Triumph and Turmoil,* 101.

37. E. A. Mowrer to Dennis, 3 April 1924, Dennis Papers.

38. Dennis to P. S. Mowrer, 22 January 1924, Dennis Papers. At this point Mowrer was allotted Fr 1000 per month for entertainment expenses. P. S. Mowrer to Dennis, 16 February 1923, Dennis Papers.

39. E. A. Mowrer to Dennis, 6 October 1924, 12 November 1924, 26 November 1924, 5 December 1924, 18 December 1924, 9 April 1925; Dennis to E. A. Mowrer, 27 January 1917, Dennis Papers.

40. P. S. Mowrer to Lawson, "Report on Measures Taken and Results Accomplished in the European Service from October 1, 1922 to March 1, 1924," 15 March 1924, P. S. Mowrer Papers; P. S. Mowrer to Dennis, 3 April 1923, Dennis Papers; P. S. Mowrer to Binder, 8 May 1929, Binder Papers. Binder had found the Rome accounts in disarray upon his arrival there and had written Mowrer that he was confident he could manage the office for 40,000 lire per month, as opposed to the 50,000 lire per month spent while John Gunther and Negley Farson had held the post. Binder to P. S. Mowrer, 13 February 1928, Binder Papers.

John Gunther was considered extravagant by some of his *Daily News* colleagues, Binder included. Gunther's records covering the years 1926–35, show the following expenses: Rome, 1–26 April 1927: hotel, travel, entertainment, fares, newspapers, etc., $512.89; Geneva, 1–29 September 1931: hotel, meals, postage, fares, railroad ticket to Vienna, $457.13; Vienna, 1–26 January 1935: rent, office help, news service, mail, local fares, $371.86. "Expense Accounts, 1926–35," Box 44, Gunther Papers Addenda, University of Chicago. Binder's records, however, include a statement of foreign news service costs for July 1931 indicating that Gunther's Vienna office expenses for the month totalled $1,624, the highest of all offices and compared with $1,498 spent by Paul Mowrer in Paris. Such variations and discrepancies probably stem from different ways of totalling a variety of kinds of expenses or from special expenses relating to a particular assignment or time period. *"Chicago Daily News* Miscellaneous Reports," Binder Papers.

A summary of foreign news service expenses for the years 1919–43 shows them fluctuating between a high of over $350,000 in 1919, 1927, and 1930 and a pre-Depression low of $219,000 in 1923. After 1930 they fell to a low of $153,000 in 1937 before rising again. *"Chicago Daily News* Miscellaneous Reports," Binder Papers.

For further data and Gunther's view of his situation in Vienna, see his letters to O'Flaherty, 5 January, 3 June, and 5 July 1933, Gunther Papers, New York City. Gunther wrote in 1934 that the pressure for economy would force him to give up his office and work at home, where his wife could do his secretarial work without pay. On another issue, he protested in the same letter the *Daily News*'s insertion of "according to reports received" in his stories. "They obviously weaken our stories dreadfully," he wrote. "They make Vienna seem a very hick town getting news out of bottles floating down the river." Gunther to O'Flaherty, 13 January 1934, Gunther Papers, New York City.

41. Hiram Motherwell and Constantine Brown of the *Chicago Daily News* ran up debts that occasioned unfavorable comment. Wythe Williams was criticized by Edwin L. James, European chief for the *New York Times,* for padding his expenses "beyond all reason." E. L. James to F. T. Birchall, 8 January 1930; James to (?) Bright, 7 January 1930, *New York Times* Archives, New York City.

Carroll Binder advised Paul Mowrer in 1934 that the new publisher of the *Daily News,* Colonel Frank Knox, considered outstanding loans from the paper to both Mowrer and Negley Farson unbusinesslike. Binder to P. S. Mowrer, 14 October 1931. Binder confided to his wife that Farson's finances were in "deplorable shape" in 1934 and that he was trying to "dump them on the paper again." Farson, Binder wrote, was charging the *Daily News* twenty dollars per day for family expenses while staying at the Drake Hotel on a visit to Chicago, "which isn't done!" Some foreign service men hád been "hogs" about expenses, according to Binder. Edgar Mowrer, Farson, and Junius Wood were considered the worst offenders. Binder to Dorothy Binder, 20 and 21 June 1934, Binder Papers.

42. P. S. Mowrer to Bell, 20 February 1913, 24 February 1913, 12 April 1920. Dennis had, in fact, approved the sale of *Daily News* material in England ten years earlier. Bell to Wile, 31 January 1913, Bell Papers. After the war, Mowrer secured and relayed to other correspondents guidelines for the sale of news materials to other papers, the central caveat being, "Not too early, not too cheap." Mowrer memorandum dated 9 June 1923, Dennis Papers.

43. Sheean, *Personal History,* 62–76, describes flagrant but comic efforts by the Spanish government to spy upon him and restrict him.

44. Seldes, *Tell the Truth,* 179, 187–90, 194–98. That the *Chicago Tribune*'s acquiescent attitude toward Mussolini was motivated more by financial than ideological considerations is suggested by the fact that Seldes was permitted to have an Italian anti-Fascist as his assistant. Colonel McCormick made no attempt, however, to protect the assistant from imprisonment and death at the hands of the Fascists when he was discovered after Seldes's departure. Seldes had been sent to Rome to replace Vincent Sheean, who had offended the Vatican by his reporting of doctrinal matters. Ibid., 168. See also Seldes, "The Truth About Fascist Censorship," *Harper's* 155 (November 1927): 732–43.

45. Darrah, *Hail Ceasar!* 19–21, 29–34, 36–44, 61, 73. One of Darrah's American assistants, George Nelson Page, eventually became a naturalized Italian and took a position with the Press and Propaganda Bureau as a consultant on relations with the American press.

46. Binder to P. S. Mowrer, 15 August 1927, 2 November 1927, 20 November 1927, 13 February 1928; Binder to O'Flaherty, 2 November 1927, 3 December 1927, 27 December 1927, 28 November 1928; Binder to Dennis, 24 January 1928, Binder Papers. Before he left Rome, however, Binder was once again paying tipsters, among them a "high Domenican [*sic*] monk," and a "Jesuit who revealed hot dope about the Rotary Club." Binder to O'Flaherty, 27 June 1929, Binder Papers.

As early as 1923, Paul Mowrer relayed a report from Edgar in Rome, who had established ties inside the Vatican, that he had been approached with an offer that the *Daily News* become a direct channel for Vatican propaganda in the United States. P. S. Mowrer to Dennis, 4 April 1923, Dennis Papers.

47. Stoneman, "Autobiography"; Frank Knox to Stoneman, 2 November 1931; Renzo Rendi to Stoneman, n.d., Box 1, Correspondence, Stoneman Papers.

48. Seldes, *You Can't Print That!* 9–15, passim. Several correspondents held that the French government respected the ideal of a free press little more than did authoritarian regimes. See, for example, Constance Drexel, "The Foreign Correspondents," *The New Republic* 37 (30 January 1924): 252–54, and Leland Stowe, "Propaganda Over Europe," *Scribner's* 96 (August 1934): 99–101. Noting that several American journalists had been

awarded the French Legion of Honor, Drexel argued that the principle of impartiality should bar correspondents from accepting decorations from foreign governments.

Seldes also reported that the Soviet government had attempted to win friends in the West by subsidizing the French press. When the Russians abandoned the effort, the French responded with strongly anti-Bolshevik propaganda, including stories planted by the French government and Havas, the national news agency. Many American papers, Seldes held, accepted this material at face value. *You Can't Print That!* 229–30. John Gunther, on the other hand, suggested that the *Chicago Tribune* had cut more news out of Seldes's dispatches than had "Lenin, Bratianu [of Rumania] and Mussolini rolled into one." Gunther, "Funnelling the News," *Harper's* 160 (April 1930): 635–47.

49. E. A. Mowrer, *Triumph and Turmoil,* 213–18; Lochner discussed the Mowrer case in letters to his daughter Betty, 2 July 1933, 12 September 1933, Lochner Papers.

50. Lochner, *Always the Unexpected,* 212–15, 223–27.

51. Ibid.; Lochner to his daughter Betty, 11 December 1932, 28 May 1933, 30 June 1933, 6 August 1933, 12 November 1933, 31 March 1934, 11 June 1935, 13 July 1935, 13 April 1936, 14 September 1936; Lochner to Dewitt MacKenzie, executive assistant of the AP, 11 November 1934; Lochner to Kent Cooper, 18 July 1934, 5 August 1935; Lochner to John Evans, AP, 27 February 1938, Lochner Papers.

52. Stowe, "Propaganda Over Europe." See also George Seldes, "The Poisoned Springs of World News," *Harper's* 169 (November 1934): 719–31, in which he notes that the International Press Conference of 1927 had termed peacetime censorship of world news "the greatest menace to the peace of the world" (719).

53. Dorothy Thompson, "The Great War of Words," *Saturday Evening Post* 207 (1 December 1934): 8ff.

54. Edmond Taylor, *The Strategy of Terror: Europe's Inner Front* (Boston: Houghton Mifflin, (1940), 19, passim. In his autobiography, Taylor notes that he had begun thinking about a study of propaganda in 1937. Taylor, *Awakening from History,* 243.

55. Matthews, *Education of a Correspondent,* 35.

56. Sigrid Schultz, interview with author, 8 August 1978. Carroll Binder wrote Paul Mowrer in 1928 that he thought it best to depart from his predecessor's "arms length" stance toward the Italian government. He was soliciting information on fascism from the government press office in order to win favor for the *Daily News,* and he was considering relaying some of the official propaganda as a cover for other, less acceptable, news. Binder to P. S. Mowrer, 13 February 1928.

57. Wythe Williams, *Secret Sources: The Story Behind Some Famous Scoops* (Chicago: Ziff-Davis, 1943), 14–27, 53, 112, 125, 154, passim.

58. Bell to Dennis, 17 March 1902, 1 July 1905; Bell to Lawson, 20 October 1904; Bell to Dennis, 19 October 1906, Bell Papers. Wythe Williams commented on the value of home visits in *Dusk of Empire,* 14–15. Summaries of weekly news reports in home papers, or copies of the papers themselves, were often requested and sent. Among other things, this allowed correspondents to check on the treatment accorded their stories.

59. Binder to O'Flaherty, 14 January 1928, Binder Papers; Seldes, *Tell the Truth,* 90–91; Darrah, *Hail Ceasar!* 51–52; Seldes, *Freedom of the Press* (Indianapolis: Bobbs-Merrill, 1935), 178; Lochner to Kent Cooper, 18 July 1934, 4 December 1936, Lochner Papers; H. Matthews, *Education of a Correspondent,* 119.

6. Toward Recognition and Professional Status

1. A number of journalists, of whom George Seldes was perhaps the most outspoken, criticized the behavior and responsibility of many of their peers. See also the comments of John Lacy, literary editor of the *Boston Herald,* in an essay on "Journalism," in Harold Stearns, ed., *Civilization in the United States* (New York: Harcourt, Brace, 1922), 35–36.

2. Bell, "Seventy Years Deep"; Bell to Dennis, 11 April 1920, 18 December 1922, 8 March 1923, 20 October 1923, Bell Papers. See also chapter 2.

3. P. S. Mowrer, "Suggestions for Reorganizing the Foreign Service," Bell Papers. Emphasis in original.

4. P. S. Mowrer memorandum, 1 August 1921, copy in P. S. Mowrer File, Bell Papers.

5. P. S. Mowrer to Lawson, "Report on Measures Taken and Results Accomplished," P. S. Mowrer Papers.

6. Walter Lippmann, *Public Opinion* (New York: Harcourt, Brace, 1922), 364–65, 398–410, passim. See also Ronald Steel, *Walter Lippmann and the Twentieth Century* (Boston: Little, Brown, 1980), 171–85.

7. P. S. Mowrer to Dennis, 31 August 1922, Dennis Papers.

8. P. S. Mowrer, "The Press and the Public," 43–48.

9. Ibid. In an unpublished manuscript for a work tentatively titled "The New Journalism" and possibly written in the early twenties, Mowrer had termed journalism, "the newest of the great public professions...still to achieve that definiteness of purpose, that tradition, that code of ethics, that technic, which will fairly place it upon a level...with those other high callings." All these prerequisites, he argued, were "in process of formation" in schools of journalism as well as in the minds of working newspapermen. "The New Journalism," undated ms., "Works," P. S. Mowrer Papers.

10. P. S. Mowrer, "The New Journalism"; see also Thompson, "The Great War of Words," for a brief assertion of the relevance of the professional ideal of impartiality in the face of growing organized governmental pressures.

11. Edwin L. James, head of the *New York Times* Paris bureau in the twenties and of its entire European staff from 1924 to 1931, was another influential spokesman for the idea of journalism's responsibility to serve the public according to professional standards. As managing editor of the *Times* during the thirties when the paper greatly strengthened its international coverage, however, James seems to have taken a less than rigorous stance. Edwin L. James obituary, *New York Times,* 4 December 1951, 1ff.; Talese, *Kingdom and the Power,* 56. For a thoughtful critique of the concepts of professionalism and objectivity in journalism, see Schudson, *Discovering the News,* 121–59.

12. Bell to Dennis, 12 May 1905, 15 September 1906, 30 April 1908; Bell to L. Middleton, 18 June 1908, Bell Papers; Startt, *Journalism's Unofficial Ambassador,* 42–43.

13. Startt, *Journalism's Unofficial Ambassador,* 42–43, 70; Bell to Ambassador George Harvey, 1 April 1922, Bell Papers. Selfridge himself told Bell that he had found few men whose knowledge of the European scene matched that of the former Indiana farm boy.

14. P. S. Mowrer to Bell, 31 January 1918, 18 January 1921, Bell Papers; P. S. Mowrer to Dennis, 17 August 1922, Dennis Papers. On a visit to the United States in 1930, Mowrer met with President Hoover at the White House. The two had been acquainted for nearly a decade since Mowrer had written about the postwar relief programs Hoover had administered in eastern Europe. The president had been upset by what Mowrer had written and his advice

to members of the American delegation to the London Disarmament Conference in 1929. Mowrer later told Leland Stowe that Hoover had remarked, "Yes, I know you American correspondents in Paris simply go over and talk to Briand and then sit down and write whatever he wants you to say." Mowrer had not argued the matter, he reported; "What good would it do to discuss it with a mentality like that?" Stowe, commenting on the story in his journal, observed that the president was obviously "ignorant of American correspondents' sense of responsibililty and their effort at fairplay." Mowrer no doubt agreed. Stowe Journal entry, 7 July 1931, Stowe Papers, copy in my possession.

15. P. S. Mowrer to Dennis, 9 November 1921, 3 November 1922, 3 September 1923; Dennis to P. S. Mowrer, 23 October 1923, Dennis Papers; Mowrer, *House of Europe,* 402–9, 609, 577–78.

16. Swing, *"Good Evening!"* 123–26; P. S. Mowrer to Bell, 11 June 1917, Bell Papers. The *New York Times*'s Edwin L. James was also on intimate terms with a number of European statesmen, notably British Prime Minister David Lloyd George. James obituary, *New York Times,* 4 December 1951. At a less serious level, Vincent Sheean hobnobbed with members of Greek and Rumanian royalty in Rome. Sheean to Gunther, 2 October 1929, Gunther Papers, New York City.

17. E. A. Mowrer to Dennis, 2 April 1924, 5 December 1924, 27 April 1925, Dennis Papers; E. A. Mowrer, *Triumph and Turmoil,* 166, 192, 200.

18. John Gunther, "Notes on Dollfuss and the Austrian Situation for Dorothy," undated memorandum, Box 5, Folder 13; "Research Notes for *Inside Europe,*" Box 6, Gunther Papers, University of Chicago. To cite another example, Walter Lippmann queried Leland Stowe on the state of Anglo-French relations in 1931, offering a lead for Stowe to follow up at the same time that he asked for on-the-spot confirmation of a rumor. Lippmann to Stowe, 25 August 1931, Stowe Papers.

Stowe's coverage of the Young Plan negotiations in 1931 and subsequent economic developments brought him into close association with a number of French and American officials, as well as some representatives of leading American banks. He developed a high regard for their honesty and sincerity, noting in his journal that Americans who were chronically suspicious of big business "might be compelled to revise some of their estimates if they could get to know men like [Nelson] Dean Jay, Parker Gilbert and Owen D. Young." Stowe also noted an exchange with American Ambassador Walter E. Edge in June 1932, in which he relayed his conclusions, based on recent discussions in Geneva, that Europe was facing social and economic upheaval in the face of the Depression. Edge, whom Stowe praised for recognizing the importance of public opinion and being readily accessible to the press, was clearly tapping Stowe's mind for information and perspective. Stowe Journal entry, 10 July 1931; Stowe, "Conversation with Ambassador Edge, 2 June 1931," Stowe Papers.

As early as 1929, Ferdinand Eberstadt of Otis and Company (a participant in the recent Paris Reparations Conference) had written the *New York Herald Tribune* expressing admiration for the "accuracy, completeness and reliability" of the reporting of Stowe and his colleague, Ralph Barnes. Eberhardt to A. S. Draper, 16 November 1929, copy in Box 1, File 1, Stowe Papers.

Stowe wrote an old friend in 1933 that former Premier Edouard Herriot had offered to pay his way to accompany him on a trip to the United States when Stowe had indicated that the *New York Herald Tribune* was unlikely to do so. Herriot's offer was quite innocent and natural, Stowe felt; but the reporter understood that acceptance of such an offer would be misinterpreted by Americans who already suspected foreign correspondents of excessive sympathy for European interests. Stowe to Barney Graves, 12 April 1933, Stowe Papers, copy in my possession.

19. Swing, *"Good Evening!"* 123–26; P. S. Mowrer to Dennis, 17 August 1922, 26 February 1923, Dennis Papers. A letter from Herrick to Mowrer expressed thanks for a "suggested plan"—evidently dealing with the troublesome war debt issue—which Herrick had found "most valuable and informing." Mowrer's ideas had been forwarded to "the Secretary," Herrick wrote, and were "thoroughly appreciated and commended." M. T. Herrick to Mowrer, 18 September 1923, Scrapbook, P. S. Mowrer Papers. An examination of Herrick's papers, however, reveals no evidence of meetings or correspondence with Mowrer. Myron T. Herrick Papers, Western Reserve Historical Society, Cleveland, Ohio.

20. Startt, *Journalism's Unofficial Ambassador,* 74–82, 139–44; Constantine Brown (*Daily News* representative in London) to Dennis, 15 May 1929; Dennis to President Herbert Hoover, 1 July 1929, Dennis Papers. Bell's initial assessment of the value of diplomats as news sources was distinctly unfavorable. In 1912 he had advised Paul Mowrer, who was about to depart for the Balkans, "Ambassadors, so far as newspaper work goes, I regard as about the biggest stiffs in the world. However, I suppose we should use them whenever possible." Bell to P. S. Mowrer, 2 December 1912. And Mowrer's description of the system he evolved for rapid evaluation of a nation's sociopolitical status noted the importance of relying on statistical data and the ideas of middle-level civil servants, instead of accepting the views of top governmental and political leaders. Mowrer, *House of Europe,* 362.

21. Seldes, *Tell the Truth,* 86–90. Two years later, Carl Ackerman, representing the *Philadelphia Public Ledger* in London, again served as a go-between trying to arrange a meeting between British and Irish Republican leaders. Ackerman to W. Williams, 2 May 1921, Container 1, Ackerman Papers.

In 1924 George Seldes had given his views on the Russian Communists and German Socialists to Secreatary of State Charles Evans Hughes and President Coolidge. On returning from Mexico in 1927 Seldes criticized the behavior of American agents there to Secretary of State Kellogg. Seldes, *Tell the Truth,* 220–21.

22. Startt, *Journalism's Unofficial Ambassador,* 89–91. Constantine Brown, Bell's London successor, recalled that President Hoover persuaded Walter Strong to send Bell back to London in 1929 to strengthen Anglo-American relations through his friendship with British Conservative leaders. Brown himself was on better terms with British Labor party leaders. Constantine Brown, *The Coming of the Whirlwind* (Chicago: Henry Regnery, 1964), 204.

23. Gunther, "Funnelling the News," 641. Constantine Brown stated that "our foreign correspondents in all capitals always have been of the utmost importance to ambassadors and ministers," and consequently had access to information they could not use in dispatches. Brown also claimed to have acted as a go-between for the French government and Secretary of State Charles E. Hughes at the time of the Ruhr occupation and also for French Finance Minister Poincaré and Secretary of the Treasury Andrew Mellon on debt matters. Brown thought correspondents gained prestige from being invited to embassy and legation functions where they had an opportunity to meet informally with important figures. Brown to Dennis, 10 January 1927, Dennis Papers.

An extreme example, obviously unusual, may have been that of Louis Fischer, who was described by a leading historian of the Spanish Civil War as the "most influential [Spanish] Republican representative in Paris" for directing "an elaborate organization for the purchase of arms and the diffusion of pro-Republican propaganda." Hugh Thomas, *The Spanish Civil War* (New York: Harper and Brothers, 1961), 435n, 495. See also Fischer, *Men and Politics,* 451–52.

George Seldes thought, however, that contacts between reporters and diplomatic personnel were almost entirely on a personal, rather than official, basis. French, British, and Italian government officials cooperated more openly and as a matter of policy with their national journalists. American correspondents and diplomats, Seldes held, had little in common socially or intellectually. Seldes, *You Can't Print That!* 404–5.

24. P. S. Mowrer to Binder, n.d.; Binder to P. S. Mowrer, 15 August 1927; Binder to Motherwell, 15 August 1927, Binder Papers.

25. P. S. Mowrer to Binder, 5 December 1928, 29 January 1929, 8 March 1929; Binder to P. S. Mowrer, 21 January 1929; Binder to O'Flaherty, 23 November 1927, 27 December 1927, 14 January 1928, 14 November 1928; Dennis to Binder, 25 November 1927, 1 April 1928; Binder to Dennis, 24 January 1928, Binder Papers.

26. Binder to P. S. Mowrer, 21 January 1929, 4 February 1929; Binder to Strong, 7 March 1929, 15 August 1929, Binder Papers.

27. Binder to Strong, 15 August 1929, Binder Papers.

28. Binder to P. S. Mowrer, 23 July 1929, Binder Papers.

29. Binder to Dorothy Binder, 18 July 1929, 8 January 1930, Binder Papers. The rivalry for the London position seems to have created hard feelings between Binder and Gunther. Binder wrote his wife that the Gunthers had "exploited" their baby to bluff Chicago "with the threat that the baby would die if J. doesn't do exactly as *he* pleases." After receiving the London assignment Binder expressed concern that both Gunther and Negley Farson might feel he had "schemed" to snatch the post from them. Binder to Dorthy Binder, 21 May 1930, Binder Papers.

30. Binder to O'Flaherty, 25 August 1930, 18 October 1930; Binder to P. S. Mowrer, 18 September 1930; Binder to Dennis, 29 September 1930, 18 December 1930; Binder to Strong, 1 October 1930, 20 November 1930; Binder to E. A. Mowrer, 9 December 1930, Binder Papers.

31. P. S. Mowrer to Binder, 10 February 1931; P. S. Mowrer to Binder, undated handwritten letter (February 1931); Strong to Binder, 20 December 1928, 16 February 1931; Binder to Strong, 13 March 1931; Binder to F. A. Moore, 16 March 1931; Binder to Dennis, 29 May 1931; P. S. Mowrer to Binder, 13 May 1931, 27 May 1931, 30 May 1931, Binder Papers; P. S. Mowrer, undated cable to Dennis, copy in Binder Papers; P. S. Mowrer to Mrs. Strong, 27 May 1931, copy in Binder Papers; Binder to Royal Munger, 18 May 1931, Binder Papers.

32. Binder to P. S. Mowrer, 30 June 1931, 10 July 1931, 17 July 1931, Binder Papers. As early as 1926, Bell had protested to Strong that Dennis and O'Flaherty were ill-suited to supervise the foreign service. "Dennis is ignorant of foreign nations and O'Flaherty is without the experience, culture, innate resepctability, and cautious judgment essential to great journalism. Dennis is not only ignorant of foreign affairs, but prejudiced, slow, vacillating and weak." Bell to Strong, 20 September 1926, Bell Papers. At about the same time, Bell was attempting to influence Dennis by telling him that Lawson "continually used to be saying to us in the foreign field, 'Be internationally sympathetic.' " Bell to Dennis, 28 August 1926, Bell Papers. Since Bell was clearly putting himself forward to Strong as the obvious candidate for foreign editor, his views were probably quite biased. Bell to Strong, 20 July 1926, Bell Papers.

33. Binder to P. S. Mowrer, 16 August, 1 September, 16 September, 1931, Binder Papers.

34. Binder to P. S. Mowrer, 14 October 1931, 11 January 1933, Binder Papers.

35. Binder to P. S. Mowrer, 24 September 1933; Binder to F. Knox, 20 February 1936, 2 March 1936, Binder Papers.

36. Binder to P. S. Mowrer, 24 September 1933; Binder to Herbert (?), 22 October 1935, Binder Papers.

37. See, for example, Frederick Palmer, *America in France* (New York: Dodd, Mead & Co., 1918); Streit, *Where Iron Is;* Wile, *Explaining the Britishers.*

38. Edgar Ansel Mowrer, *Germany Puts Back the Clock* (New York: William Morrow, 1933); Leland Stowe, *Nazi Means War* (New York: McGraw-Hill, 1934); H. R. Knickerbocker, *The German Crisis* (New York: Farrar and Rinehart, 1932); Knickerbocker, *The Boiling Point: Will War Come in Europe?* (New York: Farrar and Rinehart, 1934).

39. Also in 1936 appeared Miller, *I Found No Peace,* and Whitaker, *And Fear Came.*

40. John Gunther, *Inside Europe* (New York: Harper and Brothers, 1936).

41. Vincent Sheean, *Not Peace But a Sword* (New York: Doubleday, Doran, 1939); Vincent Sheean, *Between the Thunder and the Sun* (New York: Random House, 1943); Sheean to J. Gunther, 8 April 1930, 23 March 1931, Gunther Papers, New York City; Sanders, *Dorothy Thompson,* 201–2, 212. Anne O'Hare McCormick also initiated a regular column for the *New York Times* in 1937. Talese, *The Kingdom and the Power,* 53.

42. Bell to Lawson, 15 April 1923, 16 April 1923, 29 December 1923, Bell Papers; Sheean to Gunther, 29 January 1930, 8 April 1930, Gunther Papers, New York City; Sheean, *Personal History,* 324–31; Binder to F. A. Moore, 16 March 1931, Binder Papers. Sheean's sophistication and cynicism, as well, perhaps, as the fact that at this early date the full potential of the lecture circuit as a medium of public information and education was not recognized either by the speaker or his audiences, led him to discourage Gunther from following his lead. He had earned enough money to settle several debts, he wrote, but the expenses were high too: "It's a cheat all around. Those poor clubs pay fantastic prices to hear me talk for an hour ($150 or $200 each), but I spend almost all of it." Sheean to Gunther, 8 April 1930, Gunther Papers, University of Chicago.

43. Leland Stowe, "Lecture Engagements: January-February 1934"; "Lecture Engagements, Autumn of 1935"; Stowe, brochures for 1934, 1937, 1941, 1946–48 lecture tours, Stowe Papers, copies in my possession.

44. On the history of radio and radio news, see Erik Barnouw, *A History of Broadcasting in the United States,* vol. 1, *A Tower in Babel,* vol. 2, *The Golden Web* (New York: Oxford Univ. Press, 1967, 1969).

45. Swing, *"Good Evening!"* 205. As might be expected, Edward Price Bell was early to appreciate the value of radio as a news and publicity medium. After giving a radio talk in 1927, he wrote to Dennis and Strong suggesting that the *Daily News* sponsor periodic radio talks by its staff members. Bell to Dennis and Strong, 28 October 1927, Bell Papers.

46. Stowe, "Explanatory Note: Regarding Letters of Feb. 6 and Feb. 27, 1933, Concerning his NBC Network Broadcast from Paris on Feb. 5th—Called 'Americans and the Man Next Door' "; Stowe to his parents, 6 February 1933, 27 February 1933, Stowe Papers, copies in my possession. See also Stowe, "Radio Broadcasts," Box 5, Folder 1, Stowe Papers.

47. Alexander Kendrick, *Prime Time: The Life of Edward R. Murrow* (Boston: Little, Brown, 1969), 173–84.

48. Robert W. Jones, *Journalism in the United States* (New York: E. P. Dutton, 1947),

506–9, 512–19. Carroll Binder wrote to President James Bryant Conant of Harvard University in 1936 concerning the newly established Nieman Fellowship Program for journalists, that the field needed "men trained to think clearly about contemporary economic, political and social questions and to convey their thoughts and observations compellingly to readers sorely perplexed as to what it is all about." He further expressed his belief that a liberal education, rather than a school of journalism, offered the best preparation for such responsibilities. Binder to J. B. Conant, 18 February 1936, Binder Papers.

7. Europe in Upheaval: The 1930s

1. Sanders, *Dorothy Thompson,* 194–98, 212–16; Seldes, *Tell the Truth,* 225–27, 261; Swing, *"Good Evening!"* 168–74, 184–85, 193–205; James obituary, *New York Times,* 4 December 1951, 1.

2. P. S. Mowrer, *House of Europe,* 628–29; "Mr. Mowrer Remembers," *Time,* 24 September 1945, 62; P. S. Mowrer, "From a Paris Point of View," *Survey* 61 (1 February 1929): 606–7.

3. Farson, *Way of a Transgressor,* 453–54, 487ff., 506, 509–16, 600–602.

4. George Seldes, "The Twilight of the Dictators," *Scribner's,* 89 (May 1931): 465–76; Seldes, *Can These Things Be!* 32, 47, passim.

5. Lincoln Steffens, *The Autobiography of Lincoln Steffens,* vol. 2 (New York: Harcourt, Brace, 1931), 825–30, 850–53; Robert Allen Skotheim, *Totalitarianism and American Social Thought* (New York: Holt, Rinehart and Winston, 1971), 35; Startt, *Journalism's Unofficial Ambassador,* 162–64; Wythe Williams, "Storm Over Europe," *Saturday Evening Post* 203 (6 June 1931): 44 ff.

6. E. A. Mowrer, *This American World,* 1–2, 28–30, 109–16, 181, 194–99, 261, passim.

7. Text of Stowe broadcast, 5 September 1931, Box 5, Folder 1, "Radio Broadcasts," Stowe Papers.

8. Fischer, *Men and Politics,* 161; Taylor, *Awakening from History,* 98, 105–8, 120–29; G. Seldes, "Is the Cannon Fodder Ripe?," *Scribner's* 89 (February 1931): 115–26; Williams, "Storm Over Europe."

9. Dorothy Thompson, "Something Must Happen—German Youth Demand a Different World," *Saturday Evening Post* 203 (23 May 1931): 18 ff.; Thompson, "Why Call It Post-War?—A Study in Illusions," ibid., 205 (23 July 1932): 6ff.; Thompson, "All The King's Horses," ibid., 205 (6 August 1932): 8ff.

10. John Gunther, "Brighter Days in Austria," *The Nation* 132 (21 January 1932): 65–66; Gunther "Graustark Gets Down to Figures," ibid., 133 (15 July 1931): 59–61; Gunther, "French Gold and the Balkans," ibid., 133 (11 November 1931): 511–13; Gunther, "Danube Blues," ibid., 135 (28 September 1932): 275–77; Gunther, "Hazelnuts for Guns," *Saturday Evening Post* 209 (May 1937): 5–7ff.

11. John Gunther, Green Notebook, Number 1 (1931), 136, Gunther Papers, New York City; Gunther, "Europe's Merry-Go-Round," ms., 1932, in letter files, 1932–35, Gunther Papers, New York City; Gunther, "Cabbages for Kings," *Saturday Evening Post* 205 (22 April 1933): 14–15ff.; Gunther to Frank Knox, 13 November 1933, Gunther Papers, New York City. John Elliott, the *New York Herald Tribune*'s, Berlin correspondent, had written to Leland Stowe in February 1931 in a more encouraging tone. Berlin was dull despite peri-

odic promises of excitement. The Germans, Elliott believed, had "a way of disappointing people—they lead up to a climax and then fall away. In spite of what Hilter said at Leipzig last year, I feel sure there will never be any guillotining in Germany. The Teutons haven't got it in them." Elliott to Stowe, 19 February 1931, Stowe Papers.

12. Lochner to his daughter Betty, 30 April 1933, Box 47, Lochner Papers.

13. Ibid. As early as 1931, after interviewing Hitler, Lochner had reported to Kent Cooper that the succession of the Nazis to power would bring great changes; but it was the danger of more formidable competition from the German Wolff news agency about which he seemed principally concerned. In April 1933 Lochner reported that the new Nazi regime was entrenching itself and that a return of the Hohenzollerns now seemed unlikely. Lochner to K. Cooper, 10 December 1931 and 24 April 1933, Box 3, Lochner Papers.

14. Lochner to his daughter, 28 May 1933, 30 June 1933, Lochner Papers.

15. Lochner to his daughter, 2 July 1933, 6 August 1933, 12 September 1933, 21 September 1933, 12 November 1933, Lochner Papers. His position had been made even more difficult by two successive salary cuts, of 10 percent and 13 percent, coupled with the effects of the devaluation of the American dollar in May. Lochner to his daughter, 30 April 1933, 28 May 1933, Lochner Papers.

16. Lochner to Kent Cooper, 22 October 1933, 26 March 1933, Lochner Papers.

17. Lochner, *Always the Unexpected,* 186; Lochner to his daughter, 6 August 1933, 26 December 1933, 10 February 1934, 27 September 1934, 12 October 1934, Lochner Papers. In a letter to Kent Cooper, carried personally by Prince Louis Ferdinand, Lochner wrote in July 1934, "We are sitting on a smoldering volcano." There were reports of internal tensions in the government, and Hitler was becoming less accessible; but President von Hindenberg was failing and no hope for the amelioration of the regime was in sight. Lochner to K. Cooper, 18 July 1934, Lochner Papers.

18. E. A. Mowrer, *Germany Puts Back the Clock,* 5–8, 14–19.

19. Ibid., 15, 102ff., 120–21, 130, 140, 195–204.

20. Ibid., 12–13, 52, 100, 190, 21–22, 178.

21. Knickerbocker, *German Crisis,* 3–6, 120, 143, 241, 253, passim.

22. Ibid., 6, 191–92, 251–53, passim. The sources of support among German voters for the Nazi movement have remained a lively issue of historical scholarship. See Richard F. Hamilton, *Who Voted for Hitler?* (Princeton, N.J.: Princeton Univ. Press, 1982), and Thomas Childer, *The Nazi Voter: the Social Foundations of Fascism in Germany, 1919–1933* (Chapel Hill: Univ. of North Carolina Press, 1983).

23. Knickerbocker, *The Boiling Point,* ix–xi, 3–5, 15, 29, 45, 51, 59, 66–77, 97–98, 181, passim.

24. Ibid., 189–92, 195, 202–5, 208, 211, 239–42, 244–45, 247–49, 266, passim.

25. Stowe, *Nazi Means War,* vi–vii, 4–6. A British edition, titled *Nazi Germany Means War,* had appeared even earlier (London: Faber and Faber, 1933). Stowe's reports, interestingly, were not published in the *New York Herald Tribune.* Stowe speculated that the reason for this omission was that his story contradicted an enthusiastic report on Nazi Germany by Roy Durstine, of the advertising firm of Batton, Barton, Durstine, and Osborne, who was a friend of the newspaper's publisher. Stowe to his parents, 19 November 1933, Stowe Papers; a copy of an excerpt in my possession.

26. Stowe, *Nazi Means War,* 10, 21–23, 27–32, 38–40, 48–49, 66–69.

27. Ibid., 86–89.

28. Ibid., 89–109, 113–28, passim.

29. Ibid., 132–42.

30. Dorothy Thompson, "Back to Blood and Iron: Germany Goes German Again," *The Saturday Evening Post* 205 (6 May 1933): 3–4ff.

31. Dorothy Thompson and Benjamin Stolberg, "Hitler and the American Jews," *Scribner's* 94 (September 1933); 136–46: Dorothy Thompson, "The German Revolution—Continued Story," *The Saturday Evening Post* 207 (8 September 1934): 10–11ff.; Thompson, "The Great War of Words," 8–9ff.; Thompson "Goodbye to Germany," *Harper's* 170 (December 1934): 43–51.

32. Lochner to K. Cooper, 28 July 1934; Lochner to his daughter, 26 January 1936, 30 April 1936, 4 September 1936, Lochner Papers; Lochner, *Always the Unexpected,* 252, 262, 275, passim.

33. William L. Shirer, *Berlin Diary: The Journal of a Foreign Correspondent, 1934–41* (New York: Alfred A. Knopf, 1941), 29–31, 36, 39–41, 51–58, 63, 72, 77–83, 104–8.

34. Ross, *Journey of an American,* 26–27, 37–38, 45–50, 62–78, 83–85, 88–91, 110–12.

35. Taylor, *Awakening from History,* 129–33, 137–45.

36. Sheean, *Personal History,* 39, 48, 52, 356.

37. Matthews, *Education of a Correspondent,* 18–19; Taylor, *Awakening from History,* 98–100, 105–8, 120, 129.

38. Leland Stowe, "The French Election—and Jean Deaux," *Atlantic Monthly* 157 (May 1936): 623–28. Speaking at Columbia University on a 1935 lecture tour, Stowe predicted an increasing likelihood of war by 1940 "unless continental diplomacy radically changes its course." England and France, despite their increasing fear of Germany remained determined "to maintain the artificial superiority of the status quo"; and no nation seemed prepared to make significant sacrifices for the cause of peace. "Lecture Warnings of European War in 1935," copies of newspaper clippings, Stowe Papers, copy in my possession.

39. E. A. Mowrer, "The France of Léon Blum," *Survey Graphic* 25 (November 1936): 612–15ff.; George Seldes, "A Fascist Uprising in France," *The New Republic* 96 (12 May 1937): 11–12.

40. Raymond Swing, "How Britain Revived," *Harper's* 169 (December 1932): 674–83; Swing, "Bristish Experiments in State Intervention," *Foreign Affairs* 15 (January 1937): 290–300.

41. Negley Farson, "England's Foreign Policy," *The Nation* 141 (13 November 1935): 563–65; John Gunther, "The Rhineland Crisis," ibid., 142 (1 April 1936): 407–8; Gunther, "Britain Returns to Arms," *The Saturday Evening Post* 209 (30 January 1937): 8–9ff. Visiting the Welsh mining country in 1937, Gunther was appalled at conditions which he believed involved human suffering as great as any to be found under communism. John Gunther, "London on Edge," *Atlantic Monthly* 159 (April 1937): 390. Ferdinand Kuhn, describing Britain in 1935 during the Italian sanctions crisis, wrote that the nation's leaders had led the people to believe that "an aggressor could be checked without risk," but then they backed away at the first sign of trouble with Italy. The British did not want to fight over Ethiopia, Kuhn believed, and Prime Minister Baldwin deferred to that opinion even at the price of national "humiliation." Ferdinand Kuhn, "Britain—A Story of Old Age," in *We Saw It Happen,* by Thirteen Correspondents of the *New York Times* (New York: Simon and Schuster, 1938), 170–200. See also Carroll Binder, "Europe, 1937—The Clash of Men and Ideas," in "Works-Articles" File, Binder Papers.

42. Diggins, *Mussolini and Fascism,* 42–53, 55–60, 69–70, passim; Hiram Motherwell,

"Mussolini: Emperor of the Latins?" *Harper's* 159 (June 1929): 34–44; Seldes, *Sawdust Ceasar,* xiv–xv.

43. Seldes, *Iron, Blood and Profits,* 3ff.; Hiram Motherwell, "What Does Mussolini Want?" *Review of Reviews* 93 (March 1936): 56–58ff.; Motherwell, "Mussolini's Dream of Empire," *Review of Reviews* 93 (April 1936): 58–60; Seldes, *Sawdust Ceasar,* 363–64.

44. John Gunther, "Mussolini," *Harper's* 172 (February 1936): 296–308; Herbert L. Matthews, *Two Wars and More to Come* (New York: Carrick and Evans, 1938), 14–15; Matthews, *Education of a Correspondent,* 20–21, 25, 31–32.

45. Matthews, *Education of a Correspondent,* 37; Matthews, *Two Wars,* 33, 117, 18.

46. Miller, *I Found No Peace,* 242–47, 263–71, 280, 299–305.

47. Whitaker, *And Fear Came,* 221–24, 267–68. Whitaker concluded that fascism had come to Germany and Italy because the British, French, and Americans had not believed in democracy enough to support and defend it there (272).

48. Whitaker, *And Fear Came,* 5–7.

49. Seldes, *Iron, Blood and Profits,* 10, 131ff., 346; Sheean, *Personal History,* 56–57, 82; Williams, *Dusk of Empire,* 225–27, 232–38, 244ff.

50. Williams, *Dusk of Empire,* 229; Matthews, *Education of a Correspondent,* 32–33.

51. Whitaker, *And Fear Came,* 70, 79–80, 84–94, 96–105, 121–23, 137, 208, 221–23, 233, 242–44, passim.

52. Taylor, *Awakening from History,* 156–73.

53. Taylor, *Awakening from History,* 156–59, 177–78.

54. Whitaker, *And Fear Came,* 88; Streit, *Union Now,* 299–300; Streit to E. L. James, 2 March 1938, *New York Times* Archives.

8. Spain and Beyond

1. Cf. William L. Shirer, *The Rise and Fall of the Third Reich: A History of Nazi Germany* (New York: Simon and Schuster, 1960), one of the most comprehensive, although its focus, of course, is on German events and perspective; Shirer, *The Nightmare Years, 1930–1940,* vol. 2 of *A Memoir of a Life and the Times* (Boston: Little, Brown, 1984); Sheean, *Not Peace But a Sword;* Thomas, *Spanish Civil War.*

2. See chapter 6, pp. 140–42.

3. Gunther, "Europe's Merry-Go-Round," in letter files, 1932–35, Gunther Papers, New York City; Anonymous, *Not to be Repeated; Merry Go Round of Europe* (New York: R. Long and R. R. Smith, 1932); Desmond, *Crisis and Conflict,* 320–21.

4. Gunther, *Inside Europe,* ix. For sales statistics, see *Publishers Weekly,* 9 May 1936, 27 June 1936, 15 August 1936, 6 January 1937.

5. Gunther, *Inside Europe,* 108, 114–18, 133, 224, 339, passim.

6. Leland Stowe to his parents and sisters, 6 February 1929 (copy in my possession); Leland Stowe, "Soul of Spain Unfolds in Vibrancy of Cafe Life" and "Glimpses of Spain: Sherry is a Great Town," in Box 3, Folder 4, "Magazine Articles from Various Publications," Stowe Papers; John Gunther, "What Alfonso Left Behind," *Harper's* 167 (October 1933): 620–32; Gunther, "Spain—Liberalism in Excelsis," *The New Republic* 74 (1 March 1933): 65–67.

7. Matthews, *Education of a Correspondent,* 67; Matthews, *Two Wars,* 18, 179–80, 185, 192–208.

8. Ibid., 208–9, 220, 233, 240–241, 296, 315–17, passim.

9. Matthews, *Education of a Correspondent,* 83, 121, 130–31, 141–42; Matthews, *World in Revolution,* 12, 15, 17–22, 25–26, 29–39, passim; "Mr. Carney of the *Times,*" letter from Frank Edward Manuel, *The Nation* 143 (19 December 1936): 743; Taylor, *Awakening from History,* 179, 205–7.

10. For the *New York Times,* see Talese, *Kingdom and the Power,* 56–58, and Gabriel Jackson, ed., *The Spanish Civil War* (New York: The New York Times, 1972). The latter is a compilation of *Times* reports on the Spanish conflict with dispatches and articles by several staff members. Jackson makes a claim for overall balance and accuracy in the *Times*'s coverage, but he does note errors and that several of the articles contain biased language or interpretations. See, for example, 11–14, 20, 49, 90, 144, 149, passim. For the positions of various Catholic groups and their influence, see Allen Guttmann, *The Wound in the Heart: America and the Spanish Civil War* (New York: The Free Press of Glencoe, 1962), 33, 106, 116–20, 201–3.

11. Matthews, *World in Revolution,* 23; Matthews, *Education of a Correspondent,* 95, 133.

12. Sheean, *Not Peace But a Sword,* 38–40, 69–70, 87, 91–94, 211–12, 233, 290, 303, 324, 364–65, passim.

13. George Seldes, "General Franco's Death List," *The Nation* 144 (15 May 1937): 555–57; Seldes, "Catholics and Fascists," *The New Republic* 97 (9 November 1938): 6–8; Leland Stowe, "Franco Lies To Win," *The New Republic* 91 (19 May 1937): 40–41; Stowe, "Spain's Shirt-Sleeve Heroes," *The Nation* 146 (23 April 1938): 467–69; Stowe, "The Loyalists Still Can Win," *The New Republic* 96 (31 August 1938): 93–95; Stowe, "Evelyn, the Truck Driver," *Harper's* 178 (February 1939): 278–86. John T. Whitaker, *We Cannot Escape History* (New York: Macmillan, 1943), 54, 95, 104, 120, passim.

14. Leland Stowe to his sisters, 21 November 1937, Stowe Papers, annotated copy in my possession.

15. Carroll Binder, no longer an active correspondent, gave an indication of the new direction taken by an increasing number of journalists in a speech entitled, "Can Europe Keep the Peace?" to the Sinai Temple Lecture Forum (of Chicago?) in February 1937. The idea that the United States could successfully isolate itself from Europe's conflicts was no longer tenable, Binder held. "I have come to realize very deeply that that is a *mistaken feeling* [emphasis Binder's] on the part of my countrymen." Speeches, Miscellany, 1937, Binder Papers. See also Binder, "A Journalist Looks at World News," 8 October 1936, in the same collection; Dorothy Thompson, "Propaganda in the Modern World," *Vital Speeches* 2 (4 November 1935): 66–68; Raymond Swing, "Only One Truth," *Vital Speeches* 4 (15 November 1937): 78–80; Taylor, *Awakening from History* 178–79, 180–207.

16. John Gunther, "Who Killed the German Republic?" *The Nation* 136 (10 May 1933): 526–28; Gunther, "Will Austria Go Fascist?" ibid., 136 (12 April 1933): 393–95.

17. John Gunther, "Revolt Against Hitler," *The Nation* 136 (7 June 1933): 636–37; Gunther, "Danger Still in Austria," ibid., 137 (20 September 1933): 320–22.

18. John Gunther, "The Reichstag Fire Still Burns," *The Nation* 137 (13 December 1933): 674–75; Gunther, "Keeping Hitler Out of Austria," ibid., 138 (14 February 1934): 180-81.

19. John Gunther, "The Slaughter in Austria," *The Nation* 138 (21 March 1934): 328–30;

Gunther, "The Struggle for Power in Austria," ibid., 138 (16 May 1934): 557–59; Gunther, "Dollfuss and the Future of Austria," *Foreign Affairs* 12 (July 1934): 306–18; Gunther, "Hapsburgs Again," ibid., 12 (July 1934): 579–91; Gunther, "Policy By Murder, the Story of the Dollfuss Killing," *Harper's* 169 (November 1934): 651–62.

20. John Gunther, "After the Dollfuss Murder," *The Nation* 139 (22 August 1934): 204–5.

21. John Gunther, "The Balkans Swing to Fascism," ibid., 139 (4 July 1934): 13–14.

22. John Gunther, "Dateline Vienna," *Harper's* 171 (July 1935): 198–208; Alexander Kendrick, *Prime Time: The Life of Edward R. Murrow* (Boston: Little, Brown, 1969), 173–82; Shirer, *Nightmare Years,* 303–4.

23. Leland Stowe, "Farewell, Vienna. (February 16, 1938)," Stowe Papers, copy in my possession.

24. Shirer, *Nightmare Years,* 366–78; Swing, *"Good Evening!"* 200; Swing, *How War Came* (New York: W. W. Norton, 1939), 26–33; John Gunther, "Interim Notes on the Crisis," *The Nation* 143 (1 October 1938): 316.

25. Taylor, *Awakening from History,* 243, 250–52, 258–65, 291.

26. H. R. Knickerbocker, "Soviet-German Alliance," *Review of Reviews* 96 (July 1937): 51.

27. Sheean, *Not Peace But a Sword,* 37–40; Sheean, *Between the Thunder and the Sun,* 77–78, 86.

28. Raymond Swing, "Over Here," *Survey Graphic* 28 (February 1939): 55–57 ff.; E. A. Mowrer, "Minorities of Opinion," ibid., 83–84ff.

9. An Ocean Away: Views of America

1. E. P. Bell, "American Character and English Opinion," n.p., n.d., Letterbook, 1907, Bell Papers.

2. E. P. Bell, "American Character and English Opinion," *Chicago Daily News* clipping, 17 May 1906, in "Works—Magazine Articles," Bell Papers.

3. P. S. Mowrer, *Chicago Daily News* clippings, Scrapbook, "Prewar and Wartime Materials," P. S. Mowrer Papers.

4. Bell, *Chicago Daily News* clipping, 19 April 1919, in "Works—Magazine Articles," Bell Papers.

5. E. A. Mowrer, "Jingo Democracy," ms., "about 1920," Box 61, E. A. Mowrer Papers. I have not found a published version of this paper. E. A. Mowrer, *Triumph and Tragedy,* 150–52.

6. E. A. Mowrer, "Our Imaginary Isolation," *Forum* 75 (February 1926): 186–95.

7. Lincoln Steffens, "How Europe Can Help America," *Century* 106 (August 1923): 528–35; H. V. Kaltenborn, "America's Place in the World: Isolation and Insulation Are Alike Impossible!" *Century* 111 (April 1926): 704–12.

8. R. Swing to Betty Gram Swing, undated letters (March and April 1924), in possession of Sally Swing Shelley, Easton, Conn. [excerpts in my possession]. Quotes from following several paragraphs are from same source.

9. P. S. Mowrer, *Our Foreign Affairs: A Study in the National Interest and the New Diplomacy* (New York: E. P. Dutton, 1924), 8.

10. Ibid., 22, 141, passim.

11. Ibid., 47.

12. Ibid., 63–77, 134–48, 152–58, passim.

13. Hans Morganthau to P. S. Mowrer, 8 January 1952, Box 1, "Biographical and Critical Notes," P. S. Mowrer Papers.

14. E. A. Mowrer, *This American World,* 1–3.

15. Ibid., 4–17.

16. Ibid., 28–31.

17. Ibid., 34–38, 57–59.

18. Ibid., 84–96, 98–100.

19. Ibid., 234, 243, 247–64, passim.

20. Lilian Mowrer to Dorothy Thompson, n.d., series I, Incoming Mail, Thompson Papers.

21. Robert T. Elson, *Time Inc.: The Intimate History of a Publishing Enterprise, 1923–1941* (New York: Atheneum, 1968), 1: 104, 258–61; W. A. Swanberg, *Luce and His Empire* (New York: Scribner's 1972) 76, 78, 125–27, passim.

22. Sheean, *Personal History,* 350–56.

23. Stowe, "Americans and the Man Next Door," in "Radio Broadcasts," Box 5, Folder 1, Stowe Papers.

24. Stowe, "Who Is Killing America's Good Name?" [pub. 1932?], Box 4, Folder 3, "Manuscripts, Miscellany, 1925–35," Stowe Papers. Albion Ross, who had returned from Europe to take a job with the *New York Evening Post,* remembered in his autobiography that early in the Depression "the Every-Man-For-Himself America was still flourishing. There was not much evidence of what you could call human solidarity." Ross, *Journey of an American,* 30.

25. Stowe to Harold F. Graves, 28 July 1933, Stowe Papers.

26. Stowe to his parents, 9 January 1934, and Stowe to his wife, 22 January 1934, Stowe Papers.

27. The American Club of Paris, "Speech Made By Mr. Leland Stowe," 29 March 1934, Stowe Papers.

28. Stowe, "The United States and Another European War," *Le Monde Moderne,* 1 January 1935, copy in Box 3, "Magazine Articles for Various Publications, 1927–38"; "Leland Stowe Lecture Engagements, Jan.-Feb., 1934"; "Lecture Engagements, Autumn of 1935: Leland Stowe"; "Europe and America in 1934" (pretour lecture) in "Outlines of Lectures, 1933–34."

29. Stowe, "Rediscovering America," "What Europe Teaches About America," "The Shift of Responsibility to America," and "The Battle Against What People Do Not Want To Believe," in "Outlines of Lectures, 1933–34," Box 8; "Lecture Notes—Spanish Civil War Series, 1936"; "How Long Can Europe Avoid War?" in "Lecture Notes, 1935–36"; Stowe Papers.

30. Swing, *"Good Evening!"* 172–80; Raymond Swing, "Change in America," *The Fortnightly Review,* o.s., 135 (December 1932): 692–702; Raymond Swing, *Forerunners of American Fascism* (New York: Julian Messner, 1935).

31. John Gunther, "U.S.A. Log," 7 October 1934, ms. in possession of Mrs. John Gunther, New York City.

32. Ibid., 5, 6, 9, and 10 October 1934.

33. Ibid., 6, 9, 10, 12, and 14 October, 18 November 1934.

34. Ibid., 10 October 1934.

35. John Gunther, "Slaughter For Sale," *Harper's* 168 (May 1934): 649–59; Streit, *Where Iron Is.* See also George Seldes, "The New Propaganda for War," *Harper's* 169 (August 1934): 540–54.

36. Seldes, *Tell the Truth,* 209–55.

37. E. A. Mowrer, *Triumph and Tragedy,* 230–37.

38. Ibid., 263–64, 302. Louis Lochner, in the midst of Hitler's Germany, had become convinced that the New Deal was an American parallel. Lochner to Betty Lochner, 7 August 1933, Lochner Papers.

39. Sheean, *Between the Thunder and the Sun,* 183.

40. Streit, *Union Now,* ix–xii, 3–5, 36–38, 299–300, passim; Streit to E. L. James, 2 March, 2 June, 5 July, 15 and 29 December 1938, *New York Times* Archives.

41. Streit, *Union Now With Britain* (New York: Harper and Brothers, 1941); Streit, interview with author, 28 October 1975.

42. Leland Stowe, "Outlines of Lectures, 1933–1950," Folders 6 and 7, Box 8, Stowe Papers.

43. Dorothy Thompson, *Let the Record Speak* (Boston: Houghton Mifflin, 1939), 3, 9, 78, 100, passim.

44. Carroll Binder, "The United States in a War-Minded World," *Annals of the American Academy of Political and Social Science* 192 (July 1937): 42–50, revised copy, dated 17 January 1939, entitled "Omaha Speech," in Binder Papers.

45. Swing, *"Good Evening!"* 214–19; Swing, "Only One Truth"; Swing, "Over Here."

46. Whitaker, "Majorities Under Tyranny"; E. A. Mowrer, "Minorities of Opinion."

47. P. S. Mowrer, "Bungling the News," *Public Opinion Quarterly* 7 (Spring 1943): 116–25, copy in "Works," P. S. Mowrer Papers. Carroll Binder, "The Role of the Foreign Correspondent in Shaping American Foreign Policy," ms. [1941?], "Works, Articles," Binder Papers.

10. Editorial

1. Eugene Lyons, "Foreign Correspondent," in Richard S. Benjamin, ed., *Eyewitness, by Members of the Overseas Press Club* (New York: Alliance Book, 1940), 299–300.

2. R. Harris Smith, *OSS: The Secret History of America's First Central Intelligence Agency* (Berkeley: Univ. of California Press, 1972) 57, 90, 234–35, 337; Allan M. Winkler, *The Politics of Propaganda: The Office of War Information, 1942–45* (New Haven, Conn.: Yale Univ. Press, 1978), 74–75, 90–91, 100–101, 106, 111; Edmond Taylor. *Richer By Asia* (Boston: Houghton Mifflin, 1947); Vincent Sheean obituary, *New York Times,* 17 March 1975, 32; Sheean, *This House Against This House,* 175, 191.

3. Turner Catledge, *My Life and the Times* (New York: Harper and Row, 1971), 167–68; Talese, *The Kingdom and the Power,* 38–39.

4. Morris Eckstein, in a review of Desmond, *Crisis and Conflict,* in *The American Historical Review* 88 (December 1983): 1248–49.

5. Binder, "The Role of the Foreign Correspondent in the Shaping of American Foreign Policy," Binder Papers.

6. See comments of Robert W. Sherwood in *Roosevelt and Hopkins: An Intimate Story*

(New York: Harper and Brothers, 1948), 165, and of Dutch journalist Louis DeJong to Leland Stowe, 1 October 1955, Stowe Papers.

7. See correspondence of Mowrer concerning *Western World,* a journal he edited in the fifties, notably letters to Mowrer from [Bishop] G. Bromley Oxnam, 12 December 1957, and from Adlai Stevenson, 22 September 1953, E. A. Mowrer Papers.

8. Seldes, *Tell the Truth,* 261–69.

Selected Bibliography

Manuscript Collections

This study draws heavily on the unpublished correspondence and papers of several key correspondents, especially for an understanding of the development of the correspondents' functions and relationships to each other and to their home offices. Less frequently, but occasionally, journalists seem to have confided their views on political, economic, and other affairs to their letters. Many of these probably were talked out in the course of formal or informal meetings of colleagues. More may well have been lost because of the seemingly contradictory fact that relatively few correspondents seem to have saved much of their private, as opposed to their published, writings. The demands of an active, peripatetic life and lack of space, facilities, and adequate secretarial help may all have discouraged these professional and inveterate writers from preserving many of their private impressions on paper.

Fortunately there are exceptions, men and women whose correspondence does provide a basis for assessing their understanding of significant national and international developments as well as of their own role. The existence of a few such collections serves as an all-too-vivid reminder of how much more insight and information we should have to draw upon had others followed their example.

A major source, by virtue both of the writer's crucial position in the history of foreign correspondence and of his forthright, informal but pointed style, is the Edward Price Bell Papers at the Newberry Library, Chicago, Illinois. Bell's correspondence both with the Chicago office and with *Daily News* reporters throughout Europe is essential for understanding the evolution of professionally minded foreign correspondence.

Equally voluminous although less important are the Carroll Binder Papers, also at the Newberry Library. Binder's letters from his Rome post cover many aspects of a reporter's routine—and not so routine—assignments. His subsequent correspondence, especially with Paul Mowrer, is unique for its insight into an effort by correspondents to assume greater influence over the making of a newspaper's foreign news and editorial policy. The Charles H. Dennis Papers at the Newberry Library offer the invaluable perspective and responses of an editor, the other essential participant in the reporting process. The Victor Lawson Papers, also at the Newberry Library, are particularly useful for the early years of the century during which the Chicago publisher was evolving and adjusting his conception of what an overseas staff should be and do. Lawson's correspondence with Bell and Dennis is most revealing for the years before World War I.

Another major collection is the Louis Lochner Papers at the Wisconsin State Historical Society, Madison, Wisconsin. The value of this collection lies chiefly in the detailed, newsy, and informal picture it supplies of a newspaperman's social and professional life in Berlin during the crucial 1920s and 1930s, as reported in Lochner's steady flow of letters to members of his family in America. Also at the Wisconsin State Historical Society are the Leland Stowe Papers, a large, lively, and revealing assortment of materials emanating from and helping to explain the career of one of the ablest and most active of the foreign correspondent community.

Other collections, although helpful in part, have for a variety of reasons been less so than I had originally hoped. The John Gunther Papers at the University of Chicago contain manuscripts of all the published and a few of the unpublished works of this most prolific of correspondents. Gunther's private papers, including correspondence, notebooks, diaries, and related papers remain at this writing in the possession of Mrs. John Gunther of New York City, who has graciously permitted me to consult them. The Ben Hecht Papers, at the Newberry Library, Chicago, contain only a few folders relating to his brief career as a foreign correspondent in Germany in 1919.

The Paul Scott Mowrer Papers, at the Newberry Library, Chicago, are those of a key figure in the story I have attempted to decipher. Had they been complete they would no doubt have constituted the central collection relating to the topic. Unfortunately, Mowrer apparently destroyed the papers accumulated during his years in France when he returned to the United States in 1934. The existing collection covers chiefly Mowrer's later, post-newspaper years as a writer and poet. It contains, however, some early diaries and notebooks, correspondence, clippings, and reviews concerning his writings on Europe and his autobiography.

The Edgar Ansel Mower Papers in the Library of Congress Manuscript Division, Washington, D.C., deal almost exclusively with his post–World War II activities as an anti-Communist editor and writer. The Sigrid Schultz Papers at the Wisconsin State Historical Society held a few helpful items. Further papers of Ms. Schultz, in her possession at the time I interviewed her, were not available for examination. The William Stoneman Papers at the Bentley Library of the University of Michigan, Ann Arbor, Michigan, also deal chiefly with post–World War II activities but contain some material on his early assignments in Scandinavia and Italy and a short autobiographical sketch.

The Raymond Swing Papers, at the Library of Congress Manuscripts Division also relate primarily to Swing's career after he left foreign correspondence. Little of use to this project was available there, but Swing's daughter Mrs. Sally Swing Shelley of Easton, Connecticut, kindly permitted me to examine and draw upon correspondence between the journalist and members of his family which remains in her possession as of this writing. The Dorothy Thompson Papers at the George Arents Research Library for Special Collections at Syracuse University include correspondence between Thompson and a number of fellow reporters, much of it written well after their times of active service.

I have not been able to consult in person the George Seldes Papers at the University of Pennsylvania in Philadelphia, but an examination of the collection's register and correspondence with Seldes indicate that it, too, contains little or no material covering his years as an active foreign correspondent.

Newspaper archives, another potentially valuable source, generally have not been well organized and maintained. Aside from clipping files, little material pertinent to this topic was to be found in the archives I consulted, those of *The New York Times, The Chicago Tribune,* and *The Chicago Daily News*. Of these papers, only the *Tribune* had a full-time archivist, in 1975 Harold E. Hutchings, who readily made available copies of clippings concerning that paper's staff members. Herman Kogan of the *Daily News* kindly arranged for me to consult those files. A limited number of papers relating to *Times* personnel were opened to me by Chester M. Lewis, Director of Archives.

Interviews

I was able to interview several of the former correspondents, who responded generously to my questions and added further data and insights of their own. I am particularly grateful to the late Sigrid Schultz, William L. Shirer, Leland Stowe, and the late Clarence Streit. Notes based on these interviews remain in my possession.

Books by Correspondents

A central source for the thinking and experiences of the correspondents is, of course, their own published work. Fortunately, many correspondents were induced by a variety of circumstances to write either descriptive, analytical, or autobiographical works. These circumstances included, at an early stage in their European assignments, a conviction that their experiences and observations were of some general interest and significance and that their regular newspaper work did not offer them full scope to present these. As indicated in the text, the hope of supplementing their regular salaries often offered a more pragmatic inducement to attempt publication. I have listed here the volumes most pertinent to this study.

Abbot, Willis J. *Watching the World Go By.* Boston: Little, Brown, 1933.

Ackerman, Carl. *Germany: The Next Republic?* New York: George H. Doran, 1917.

Baldwin, Hanson W. and Shepard Stone. *We Saw it Happen: The News Behind the News That's Fit to Print, by Thirteen Correspondents of the New York Times.* New York: Simon and Schuster, 1938.

Bass, John, and Harold G. Moulton. *America and the Balance Sheet of Europe.* New York: Ronald Press, 1921.

Benjamin, Richard S., ed. *Eyewitness, by Members of the Overseas Press Club.* New York: Alliance Book, 1940.

______. *The Inside Story, by Members of the Overseas Press Club.* New York: Prentice-Hall, 1940.

Brown, Constantine. *The Coming of the Whirlwind.* Chicago: Henry Regnery, 1964.

Darrah, David H. *Hail Caesar!* Boston: Hale, Cushman and Flint, 1936.

Farson, Negley. *Sailing Across Europe.* New York: The Century Company, 1926.

______. *The Way of a Transgressor.* New York: The Literary Guild of America, 1936.

Fischer, Louis. *Men and Politics: An Autobiography.* New York: Duell, Sloane and Pearce, 1941.

Gunther, John. *A Fragment of Autobiography.* New York: Harper and Brothers, 1962.

______. *Inside Europe.* New York: Harper and Brothers, 1936.

______. *The Lost City.* New York: Harper and Row, 1964.

Hecht, Ben. A Child of the Century. New York: Simon and Schuster, 1954.

Kaltenborn, Hans von. *Fifty Fabulous Years, 1900–1950: A Personal Review.* New York: G. P. Putnam's Sons, 1951.

Knickerbocker, Herbert R. *The Boiling Point: Will War Come in Europe?* New York: Farrar and Rinehart, 1934.

______. *The German Crisis.* New York: Farrar and Rinehart, 1932.

Lochner, Louis. *Always the Unexpected: A Book of Reminiscences.* New York: Macmillan, 1956.

Lyons, Eugene, ed. *We Cover the World,* by Fifteen Foreign Correspondents. New York: Harcourt, Brace, 1937.

McCormick, Anne O'Hare. *The World at Home.* Edited by Marian Turner Sheehan. New York: Alfred A. Knopf, 1956.

Matthews, Herbert L. *Education of a Correspondent.* New York: Harcourt, Brace, 1946.

______. *Eyewitness in Abyssinia.* London: M. Secker and Warburg, 1937.

———. *Two Wars and More to Come.* New York: Carrick and Evans, 1938.

———. *A World in Revolution: A Newspaperman's Memoir.* New York: Scribner's 1972.

Miller, Webb. *I Found No Peace: The Journal of a Foreign Correspondent.* New York: Simon and Schuster, 1936.

Mowrer, Edgar Ansel. *Germany Puts Back the Clock.* New York: William Morrow, 1933.

———. *A Good Time to be Alive.* New York: Duell, Sloane and Pearce, 1959.

———. *Immortal Italy.* New York: D. Appleton, 1922.

———. *Sinon, or The Future of Politics.* London: Kegan Paul, Trench and Trubner, 1930.

———. *This American World.* New York: J. H. Sears, 1928.

———. *Triumph and Turmoil: A Personal History of Our Time.* New York: Weybright and Talley, 1968.

Mowrer, Paul Scott. *Balkanized Europe.* New York: E. P. Dutton, 1921.

———. *The Foreign Relations of the United States.* Chicago: American Library Association, 1927.

———. *The House of Europe.* Boston: Houghton Mifflin, 1945.

———. *Our Foreign Affairs: A Study in the National Interest and the New Diplomacy.* New York: E. P. Dutton, 1924.

Ross, Albion. *Journey of an American.* Indianapolis: Bobbs-Merrill, 1957.

Seldes, George. *Can These Things Be!* New York: Brewer, Warren and Putnam, 1931.

———. *Freedom of the Press.* Indianapolis: Bobbs-Merrill, 1935.

———. *Iron, Blood and Profits: An Exposure of the World-Wide Munitions Racket.* New York: Harper and Brothers, 1934.

———. *Lords of the Press.* New York: Julian Messner, 1938.

———. *Sawdust Caesar: The Untold Story of Mussolini and Fascism.* New York: Harper and Brothers, 1935.

———. *Tell the Truth and Run: My 44 Year Fight for a Free Press.* New York: Greenberg, 1953.

———. *You Can't Print That! The Truth Behind the News, 1918–28.* New York: Payson and Clark, 1929.

Sheean, Vincent. *Between the Thunder and the Sun.* New York: Random House, 1943.

———. *Not Peace But a Sword.* New York: Doubleday, Doran, 1939.

———. *Personal History.* New York: The Literary Guild of America, 1935.

———. *This House Against This House.* New York: Random House, 1946.

Shirer, William L. *Berlin Diary: The Journal of a Foreign Correspondent, 1934–41.* New York: Alfred A. Knopf, 1941.

———. *The Nightmare Years, 1930–1940.* Vol. 2 of *A Memoir of a Life and the Times.* Boston: Little, Brown, 1984.

________. *The Rise and Fall of the Third Reich: A History of Nazi Germany.* New York: Simon and Schuster, 1960.

________. *Twentieth Century Journey: The Start, 1904–1930.* Vol. 1 of *A Memoir of a Life and the Times.* New York: Simon and Schuster, 1976.

Smalley, George W. *Anglo-American Memories.* New York: G. P. Putnam's Sons, 1911.

Steffens, Lincoln. *The Autobiography of Lincoln Steffens.* New York: Harcourt, Brace, 1931.

Stowe, Leland. *Nazi Means War.* New York: McGraw-Hill, 1934.

________. *No Other Road to Freedom.* New York: Alfred A. Knopf, 1941.

Streit, Clarence. *Union Now: A Proposal for a Federation of the Democracies of the North Atlantic.* 15th ed. New York: Harper and Brothers, 1940.

________. *Union Now With Britain.* New York: Harper and Brothers, 1941.

________. *Where Iron Is, There Is the Fatherland.* New York: B. W. Huebsch, 1920.

Swing, Raymond. *Forerunners of American Fascism.* New York: Julian Messner, 1935.

________. *"Good Evening!" A Professional Memoir.* New York: Harcourt, Brace and World, 1964.

________. *How War Came.* New York: W. W. Norton, 1939.

Taylor, Edmond. *Awakening from History.* Boston: Gambit, 1969.

________. *Richer by Asia.* Boston: Houghton Mifflin, 1947.

________. *The Strategy of Terror: Europe's Inner Front.* Boston: Houghton Mifflin, 1940.

Thompson, Dorothy. *Let the Record Speak.* Boston: Houghton Mifflin, 1939.

Wells, Linton. *Blood on the Moon.* Boston: Houghton Mifflin, 1937.

Whitaker, John T. *And Fear Came.* New York: Macmillan, 1936.

________. *We Cannot Escape History.* New York: Macmillan, 1943.

Wile, Frederic. *The Assault: Germany Before the Outbreak and England in Wartime.* Indianapolis: Bobbs-Merrill, 1916.

________. *Explaining the Britishers.* New York: George H. Doran, 1919.

________. *The Men Around the Kaiser: Makers of Modern Germany.* London: H. Heineman, 1913; Indianapolis: Bobbs-Merrill, 1914.

________. *News Is Where You Find It: Forty Years' Reporting at Home and Abroad.* Indianapolis: Bobbs-Merrill, 1939.

Williams, Wythe. *Dusk of Empire: The Decline of Europe and the Rise of the United States, as Observed by a Foreign Correspondent in a Quarter Century of Service.* New York: Scribner's, 1937.

________. *Passed by the Censor: The Experiences of an American Newspaperman in France.* New York: E. P. Dutton, 1916.

________. *Secret Sources: The Story Behind Some Famous Scoops.* Chicago: Ziff-Davis, 1943.

Works on Journalism and the Media

Barnouw, Erik. *A History of Broadcasting in the United States.* Vol. 1, *A Tower in Babel,* and Vol. 2, *The Golden Web.* New York: Oxford Univ. Press, 1966 and 1969.

Berger, Meyer. *The Story of the New York Times, 1851–1951.* New York: Simon and Schuster, 1951.

Catledge, Turner. *My Life and the Times.* New York: Harper and Row, 1971.

Cooper, Kent. *Kent Cooper and the AP: an Autobiography.* New York: Random House, 1951.

Crozier, Emmet. *American Reporters on the Western Front, 1914–1918.* New York: Oxford Univ. Press, 1959.

Davis, Elmer. *History of the New York Times.* New York: The New York Times, 1921.

Dennis, Charles H. *Victor Lawson: His Time and His Work.* Chicago: Univ. of Chicago Press, 1935.

Desmond, Robert W. *Crisis and Conflict: World News Reporting Between Two World Wars, 1920–1940.* Iowa City: Univ. of Iowa Press, 1982.

______. *The Press and World Affairs.* New York: D. Appleton-Century, 1937.

______. *Windows on the World: The Information Process in a Changing Society, 1900–1920.* Iowa City: Univ. of Iowa Press, 1980.

Edwards, Jerome E. *The Foreign Policy of Col. McCormick's Tribune 1929–1941.* Reno: Univ. of Nevada Press, 1971.

Ford, Hugh, ed. *The Left Bank Revisited: Selections from the Paris Tribune.* State College, Penn.: Pennsylvania State Univ. Press, 1972.

Gibbons, Edward. *Floyd Gibbons, Your Headline Hunter: a Biography.* New York: Exposition Press, 1953.

Gramling, Oliver. *AP: The Story of News.* New York: Farrar and Rinehart, 1940.

Hohenberg, John. *Foreign Correspondence: The Great Reporters and Their Times.* New York: Columbia Univ. Press, 1964.

Kendrick, Alexander. *Prime Time: The Life of Edward R. Murrow.* Boston: Little, Brown, 1969.

Kluger, Richard. *The Paper: The Life and Death of the New York Herald Tribune.* New York: Alfred A. Knopf, 1986.

Knightley, Phillip. *The First Casualty: From the Crimea to Vietnam, The War Correspondent as Hero, Propagandist, and Myth Maker.* New York: Harcourt Brace Jovanovich, 1975.

Laney, Al. *Paris Herald: The Incredible Newspaper.* New York: D. Appleton-Century, 1947.

Langford, Gerald. *The Richard Harding Davis Years: A Biography of Mother and Son.* New York: Holt, Rinehart and Winston, 1961.

Lippmann, Walter. *Public Opinion.* New York: Harcourt, Brace, 1922.

Mathews, Joseph J. *George W. Smalley: Forty Years a Foreign Correspondent.* Chapel Hill: Univ. of North Carolina Press, 1973.

Mowrer, Paul Scott. "The Press and the Public." In *The Educational Role of the Press.* Paris: League of Nations International Institute of Intellectual Cooperation, 1934.

Rosewater, Victor. *History of Cooperative Newsgathering in the United States.* New York: D. Appleton, 1930.

Rovere, Richard. "Inside." *The New Yorker,* 23 August 1947.

Sanders, Marion K. *Dorothy Thompson: A Legend in Her Time.* New York: Avon Books, 1974.

Schudson, Michael. *Discovering the News: A Social History of American Newspapers.* New York: Basic Books, Harper Torchbook edition, 1978.

Seitz, Don C. *The James Gordon Bennetts, Father and Son: Proprietors of the New York Herald.* Indianapolis: Bobbs-Merrill, 1928.

Startt, James D. *Journalism's Unofficial Ambassador: A Biography of Edward Price Bell, 1869–1943.* Athens, Ohio: Ohio Univ. Press, 1974.

Steel, Ronald. *Walter Lippmann and the Twentieth Century.* Boston: Little, Brown, 1980.

Stone, Melville E. *Fifty Years a Journalist.* Garden City, N.Y.: Doubleday, Page, 1921.

Swanberg, W. A. *Citizen Hearst: A Biography of William Randolph Hearst.* New York: Scribner's 1961.

———. *Pulitzer.* New York: Scribner's 1967.

Talese, Gay. *The Kindgom and the Power.* New York: World Publishing, 1969.

Weisberger, Bernard. *The American Newspaperman.* Chicago: Univ. of Chicago Press, 1961.

Zobrist, Benedict Karl. "Edward Price Bell and the Development of the Foreign News Service of the *Chicago Daily News.*" Ph. D. diss., Northwestern University, 1953.

General Works

Childer, Thomas. *The Nazi Voter: The Social Foundations of Fascism in Germany, 1919–1923.* Chapel Hill: Univ. of North Carolina Press, 1983.

Cowley, Malcolm. *Exile's Return: A Literary Odyssey of the 1920s.* New York: Viking Press Compass edition, 1956.

Diggins, John P. *Mussolini and Fascism: The View from America.* Princeton, N.J.: Princeton Univ. Press, 1974.

Earnest, Ernest. *Expatriates and Patriots: American Artists, Scholars and Writers in Europe.* Durham, N.C.: Duke Univ. Press, 1961.

Guttmann, Allen. *The Wound in the Heart: America and the Spanish Civil War.* New York: The Free Press of Glencoe, 1962.

Hamilton, Richard F. *Who Voted for Hitler?* Princeton, N.J.: Princeton Univ. Press, 1982.

Hollinger, David. "Ethnic Diversity, Cosmopolitanism and the Emergence of the American Liberal Intelligentsia." *American Quarterly* 27 (May 1975): 133–51.

Jackson, Gabriel. *The Spanish Republic and the Civil War.* Princeton: Princeton Univ. Press, 1965.

———, ed. *The Spanish Civil War.* New York: The New York Times, 1972.

Jones, Howard Mumford. *The Age of Energy: Varieties of American Experience, 1865–1915.* New York: Viking Press, 1971.

Lochner, Louis P. "Internationalism among Universities." Boston: World Peace Foundation Pamphlet Series, Vol. 3, No. 7, Part 2. July 1913.

Ribuffo, Leo. "Fascists, Nazis and American Minds: Perceptions and Preconceptions." *American Quarterly* 26 (October 1974): 417–32.

Skotheim, Robert Allen. *Totalitarianism in American Social Thought.* New York: Holt, Rinehart and Winston, 1971.

Stearns, Harold, ed. *Civilization in the United States.* New York: Harcourt, Brace, 1922.

Taylor, A. J. P. *The Origins of the Second World War.* New York: Atheneum, 1961.

Thomas, Hugh. *The Spanish Civil War.* New York: Harper and Brothers, 1961.

Ziff, Larzer. *The American 1890s: Life and Times of a Lost Generation.* New York: Viking Press, 1966.

Newspaper and Journal Articles

Articles by and about the journalists and their work are too numerous to list separately here. They are, in any case, classified and located more appropriately according to subject matter in the notes following the text.

Index

Morrell Heald is Samuel B. and Virginia C. Knight Professor of Humanities at Case Western Reserve University. His publications include *The Social Responsibilities of Business: Company and Community* and *Culture and Diplomacy: The American Experience.*